AAX-0748
VC-Lib

P9-CDJ-269

STRESS MANAGEMENT FOR LAW ENFORCEMENT OFFICERS

WAYNE ANDERSON

DAVID SWENSON

DANIEL CLAY

WITHDRAWN

PRENTICE HALL
Englewood Cliffs, New Jersey 07632

Library of Congress Cataloging-in-Publication Data

Anderson, Wayne,
    Stress management for law enforcement officers / Wayne Anderson,
David Swenson, Daniel Clay.
        p.   cm.
    Includes bibliographical references and index.
    ISBN 0-13-146945-2
    1. Police—United States—Job stress.   2. Police—United States—Psychology.
3. Stress management—United States.   I. Swenson, David.   II. Clay, Daniel.   III. Title.
HV7936.J63A53   1995
363.2'2'019—dc20
                                                                                                94-36883
                                                                                                CIP

Editorial/production supervision,
    interior design, and electronic composition: *Barbara Marttine*
Cover design and cover illustration: *Merle Krumper*
Acquisitions editor: *Robin Baliszewski*
Editorial assistant: *Rosemary Florio*
Director of Production: *Bruce Johnson*
Managing editor: *Mary Carnis*
Manufacturing buyer: *Ed O'Dougherty*

©1995 by Prentice Hall, Inc.
A Simon & Schuster Company
Englewood Cliffs, New Jersey 07632

All rights reserved. No part of this book may
reproduced, in any form or by any means,
without permission in writing from the publisher.

Printed in the United States of America

10 9 8 7 6 5 4 3 2 1

ISBN   0-13-146945-2

Prentice-Hall International (UK) Limited, *London*
Prentice-Hall of Australia Pty. Limited, *Sydney*
Prentice-Hall Canada Inc., *Toronto*
Prentice-Hall Hispanoamericana, S.A., *Mexico*
Prentice-Hall of India Private Limited, *New Delhi*
Prentice-Hall of Japan, Inc., *Tokyo*
Simon & Schuster Asia Pte. Ltd., *Singapore*
Editora Prentice-Hall do Brasil, Ltda., *Rio de Janeiro*

Contents

Section II Specific Stress Factors in Law Enforcement

Section III Controlling Stress

Acknowledgments

Without considerable help from law enforcement officers, a book of this nature could not be written. The authors would like to extend their appreciation to the officers and administration of The Columbia, Missouri: Duluth, Minnesota; East Lansing, Michigan; and Superior, Wisconsin police departments and the Missouri State Highway Patrol. Some officers were particularly cooperative in helping us understand the stresses involved in law enforcement and we would like to give special recognition to:

Deputy Chief Carroll Highbarger, Detectives Michael Himmell, Susan Stoltz, Susan Wooderson, and officers Skip McQuire, Fontela Ford, and Zim Schwartz from the Columbia, Missouri, Police Department.

Brian Horn, Patricia Nowak, East Lansing, Michigan, Police Department, Chief Scott Lyons, and officers Tim Hansen, Peggy Price Johnson, Donetta Wykstrom, Bob Brasel, Duluth, Minnesota Police Department.

Lieutenant Terry Moore, Captain Charles Jackson, and Troopers Chris Ricks, Randy Becker, Ken Pesout from the Missouri State Highway Patrol.

Benn Johnston, San Bernardo Sheriff's Department; Doyle Barker, Chief, Superior, Wisconsin Police Department; Joan McNamara, Los Angeles Police Department; Ed Lemon, St. Paul, Police Department; Mike Lyman, Columbia College Law Enforcement Program, Pat Patterson, Retired from law enforcement in Alaska, and Michael Tate, Probation Officer, Minnesota Department of Corrections.

Daniel Clay would like to thank the officers from Roseau County, Minnesota, United States Border Patrol, Minnesota Highway Patrol and Minnesota Department of Natural Resources Conservation Officers for sharing their personal experiences during long conversations with him while he was a police officer.

We would like to express our appreciation to the following reviewers for their insightful suggestions of ways to improve this text: Lois A. Wims, Ph.D., Salve Regina University; Thomas C. Mijares, Ph.D., Southwest Texas University; Thomas F. Adams, Rancho Santiago College; Donald J. Melisi, Middlesex Community College; Richard R. Becker, Sam Houston State University; John Sloan, Ph.D., University of Alabama at Birmingham.

Wayne Anderson, David Swenson, Daniel Clay

1

❖

Sources of Stress

Two bomb technicians set up a rigging that uses a rope for the remote removal of a suspect device. (Photo from files of the Missouri State Highway Patrol)

Persons in many occupations may argue that they face more physical danger than police officers. Construction workers, miners, stunt pilot,s and demolition workers are all exposed to potential death and physical injury more consistently than law enforcement personnel. However, few occupations encounter the same variety of stressors, amply reported in the research literature. Stressors, the reader will recall, are the first elements or stimuli in stress conditions, and police officers face them in abundance. The possibility of physical danger is only one of many. (Bartol, 1983, p. 69)

❖ OBJECTIVES

1. To provide an overview of the book's contents.
2. To underscore the fact that healthy people seek stress.
3. To introduce the reader to the wide range of stressors a law-enforcement officer is exposed to on the job.
4. To emphasize how knowledge of the nature of stresses can prepare officers to deal more adequately with these stresses.

❖ INTRODUCTION

Stress can be defined as any event that requires us to adjust in some manner—physiological reaction, thinking, feeling, or behaving. As such, it is not possible (nor desirable) to try to totally avoid stress. It is an inevitable part of dealing with the changes that confront us in life.

In thinking about stress, we prefer the approach of Hans Selye (1974), a major researcher who concluded that any demand made on a person that requires some response is stress. This can be pleasant or unpleasant—when it becomes unpleasant, he would label it *distress*.

Selye believed that healthy individuals need stress and that inactivity for any period of time is highly negative or distressing for most people. His general concept of what is stress includes experiences that give joy, fulfillment, and self-expression. The law-enforcement personnel we work with have a higher than average need for activity, and we would label them *stress seekers*. The fact that law enforcement can be a dirty, dangerous job is exactly why many officers like what they are doing. Stress becomes a problem only when there is so much of it that it becomes distress.

It is the authors' conviction that, if law-enforcement officers know what aspects of their job are likely to cause stress, they are much better prepared to deal with those situations when they become distressful. This book approaches the management of stress in a number of ways.

1. *Stress is a normal reaction to a demanding situation.* If an officer knows that disturbed sleep and loss of appetite are part of a normal reaction to life-threatening situations, such as a shooting incident, he or she is less likely to become additionally worried about those symptoms or imagine that an emotional breakdown is being experienced.
2. *Stress prepares the officer to react.* An officer who knows what a defensive attorney is likely to do in the courtroom to make him or her look bad to the jury can be mentally prepared to use techniques that minimize the effect of the defensive attorney's attack.

3. *We teach officers ways to avoid stress situations.* For example, stress will be less for officers if programs can be developed that bring the public into a cooperative rather than an adversary role.

4. *We teach techniques to cope with stress.* When all else fails, and it will in many cases, the officer needs to know a variety of techniques to lower the tension level in his or her life. This book presents techniques that law-enforcement personnel have found most helpful in preventing the harmful side effects of stress.

❖ SOURCES OF STRESS

People enter criminal justice for a variety of reasons. Among the most often cited in employment interviews are helping people, job security, working outdoors, decision making, variety, and challenge. In the field, many officers acknowledge an additional interest that has led them into the profession: they have a high need for excitement and want a certain amount of risk in their life (e.g. Meagher and Yentes, 1986). Unless applicants in criminal justice have been raised in families where close friends or relatives work in the field, it is likely that they are reacting to career stereotypes rather than practical reality. Although applicants may be aware of many of the tasks, they are less aware of the specific strains and consequences of the work to which an officer must become adjusted.

Too often the main source of information that most applicants have about law enforcement comes from movies and TV shows in which police work is high-speed chases and shoot-outs, and the hero always catches the criminal using standard procedure and receives community praise. We regularly hear officers complain about how unrealistic these presentations are. The reality is very different. There are often long periods of relative inactivity and boredom punctuated by emergencies and chaos. The criminal is not always caught and, if caught, is not always convicted—the danger to the officer is not likely to be the high-speed chase but an angry spouse in a domestic dispute.

In many cases, what gives officers indigestion and raises their blood pressure are such factors as inadequate support from administration, lack of public backing, and having to deal with the sudden death of children.

No matter how hardy or tough people think they are when they join a law-enforcement agency, the pain and suffering they are exposed to, the administrative hassles they have to put up with, and the hostility of some of the people they are trying to protect will eventually have negative mental and physical effects unless effective stress-coping strategies are learned and practiced. Stress-management techniques must become as much standard issue as any other piece of life-saving equipment.

Dealing with traumatized victims of crimes, severely injured persons, and dead bodies frequently causes officers to turn off their feelings as a way of controlling their own painful emotional reactions. Later, we will discuss how turning off emotional reactions can lead to problems both on and off the job.

❖ TWENTY YEARS ON THE JOB

Because law-enforcement work is so important to society and the discretionary powers that officers are given are so enormous, much care is taken in screening candidates for training. The testing candidates for law enforcement go through is intended to ensure that they are in both excellent physical and mental condition. When an officer is commissioned, he or she is healthier, more intelligent, and in better mental health then the average person.

Despite the good condition they are in at the beginning of their careers, it is notable that after 20 years on the job officers show a higher rate of stress-related illnesses, both physical and psychological, than the general public. Studies show that police have more heart attacks, heart disease, and diabetes (Violanti, Vena, and Marshall, 1986) than many other work groups.

Anson and Bloom (1988) found that police officers and prison guards scored significantly higher on scales measuring chronic occupational stress than probation officers, fire fighters, and emergency medical technicians. There is also an increased risk of death from cancer of the colon and liver (Violanti, Vena, and Marshall, 1986). This last risk is probably confounded by high alcohol consumption among officers as a stress-management technique.

In the mental health area, law-enforcement officers have higher rates of suicide, alcoholism, and divorce than the general public (Burke, 1989; Heiman, 1975; Terry, 1981). A study by Beutler, Nussbaum, and Meredith (1988) found that within 4 years of starting in law enforcement, officers were at risk for using alcohol as a preferred coping method for dealing with the stress of work. One point we will be making throughout this book is that it isn't necessary for officers to have so many stress-related problems. We believe that, while law enforcement is by its nature stressful, steps can be taken to lessen its negative impact.

In the chapters that follow we will introduce and discuss alternative ways of dealing with stress, and show law-enforcement personnel how stress can be prevented from causing the negative effects found in the studies that have just been cited.

For a program of stress management in law enforcement to be successful, it is not enough just for individual officers to become aware of and develop methods for dealing with the stresses of the job. At some point, supervisors and administrators in law-enforcement departments need to recognize that the stresses we will be talking about are a serious problem and interfere with the effectiveness with which departments can carry out their mission. To run an effective law-enforcement agency, administrators need to be concerned about the morale and psychological welfare of their officers.

We have noted a healthy trend around the country for administrators to be more aware of the negative effects of working in law enforcement. The trend can be seen in *The Police Chief* journal, which in recent years has had more articles discussing both the need and procedures for setting up training programs to help officers deal with the variety of physical and mental hazards that they face on the job. For example, there is now more emphasis than in the past on setting up exercise programs for officers. These programs are seen not only as ways to ensure good physical condition of the officers, but also as ways of building stress tolerance. In keeping with this development, some departments now insist on regular tests of officers' physical condition, much like the military.

❖ MENTAL PREPARATION

Besides keeping physically fit, one way of dealing with stress on the job is to be mentally prepared for the situations that produce stress and for the emotional reactions that can follow. Unexpected events are more stressful than those for which the officer is prepared. In medicine it has now been discovered that surgery patients who understand the operation they are to undergo and the amount of pain to be expected need less pain killer after the operation and heal faster. We believe that the same general principle holds in law enforcement. An officer who knows the possible dangers that exist in a situation can anticipate the various things that are likely to happen. If the officer has thought about how he or she will respond and has consequently worked out strategies for handling potentially dangerous situations, the negative impact will likely be less.

After a dangerous or tense situation, most officers have some physical and emotional reactions based on the excitement, fear, or anger that they felt during the event. If the officer knows ahead of time that a normal consequence of some events are nightmares or a startle response, experiencing these events will be less disturbing because they are expected.

Law-enforcement officers already receive considerable training on how to handle themselves physically in dangerous situations. They take target practice and learn physical defense and emergency medical techniques. We are suggesting there needs to be more emphasis on the emotional consequences of what is happening to police officers, because they also need to be prepared to deal with the mental hazards of the job.

Just as an officer has training in how to disarm a suspect, he or she also needs training in dealing with the emotional impact of situations that most officers must face at one time or another. Being called to a scene where an individual is threatening suicide is an example of a crisis with which most officers have to deal at one time or another. In training, the officers could practice talking a suicidal person out of jumping or pulling the trigger. The training could then follow with a session on how the officer might deal with the emotions aroused when the person cannot be prevented from killing himself or herself. Because of this kind of mental preparation, when the officer is then faced with an actual suicide scene, it will be less stressful.

❖ OVERVIEW

In the remainder of this chapter we present an overview of the sources of stress for which law-enforcement officers need to be mentally and physically prepared. These factors will then be discussed in more detail in individual chapters. In each chapter we will give specific suggestions for lessening the impact of, and coping more effectively with stress.

The stresses reviewed here include dealing with discretionary power, death, injury, personal failure, dangerous situations, officer misconduct, poor supervision, disturbances, the court system, criticism from the media and public, special job assignments such as undercover work, and changes in work conditions. We also preview our chapters on special problems of minorities and women in law enforcement and the stressors unique to rural policing.

❖ DISCRETIONARY POWER

One attraction of law enforcement is the discretionary power the officer has to enforce or not enforce a particular law. There are a large number of local, state, and federal laws, and if all of them were enforced to the maximum, the court system would be even more overwhelmed than it is at present. Most officers, after a few years on the job, become street wise in finding laws to cover situations. If they wish to, most officers can find some law to apply to almost any circumstance.

This discretionary power is also a stress factor. Having to make constant decisions about how to deal with other peoples' actions, to question or not question, to arrest or not to arrest, can at times be a burden, especially since the public at large and the court system in particular will be second guessing the officer's decision.

❖ DEATH

The average citizen only rarely encounters a dead body. There are individuals in their forties who have never seen a dead person, even in a hospital or at a funeral. These deaths are clean and sanitized compared to the street and home deaths that law-enforcement officers must deal with regularly. When an officer encounters a death, all of the senses and a wide range of emotions are likely to be involved.

There are at least six different kinds of situations in which officers encounter death: shootings in which the officer or a partner is involved, mutilating accidents, the deaths of children, suicides, murder, nonmutilating accidents, and natural deaths. Also, delivering death messages to survivors in any of these cases can be extremely stressful for the officer assigned the duty.

Police shootings.   Police officer-involved deaths are usually shootings where the officer kills someone, or is wounded, but they also include situations where an officer's partner is killed. Even when the officer is involved in a justified shooting of a perpetrator, he or she is likely to have strong negative reactions, which can include vivid flashbacks of the event, sleeplessness, and irritability. We will discuss these reactions and some ways of dealing with them under post-shooting stress reactions.

Mutilating accidents.   Most frequently, mutilating accidents that officers encounter involve automobile accidents or, in more rural areas, accidents involving farm machinery. While accidents of this sort can become almost routine, occasionally one will be particularly ghastly, and it will leave the officer shaken. Disastrous accidents involving airplane crashes, multiple auto fatalities, and multiple shooting victims are particularly stressful. In these cases and others, such as the Hyatt Regency collapse in Kansas City in which many people died, the officers who were involved in the rescue and clean-up operation often had posttraumatic stress reactions, and many of them resigned their commissions within the next year.

We have also found that, when an accident victim dies while the officer is with them but is helpless to save the individual's life, the officer may be left with a feeling of guilt that continues to haunt him or her.

Suicides.   The most stress-creating suicide is one in which another officer takes his or her life. We have seen some particularly strong stress reactions on those rare occasions when an officer has committed suicide in the presence of other officers. Even when the officer does not have a personal relationship with the victim, the suicide of a fellow officer has an impact on him or her.

There will be differing degrees of intensity of the reaction, depending on who the victim is and the state of the body. If the officer is present when the suicide takes place, the amount of stress will depend on the relationship established with the suicidal person and the expectation the officer has that he or she should have been able to prevent the death. On occasion the officer may feel relief that a person has committed suicide, such as when hostages are being held by the suicidal person. Going to the scene of a completed suicide and facing the distressed family members who have just found the body of their loved one is another aspect that can cause distress.

Murder.   Stress comes in at a number of points when the officer is confronted with a murder. First, there is the body to deal with. This can vary from the corpse looking like someone sleeping to a mutilated body with 27 stab wounds and a battered face. Young officers report that even when faced with a disfigured body, some old timer will be likely to talk about the case he handled that was even more ghastly. Second, there is the stress of questioning witnesses, knowing that some of them may be suspects. Finally, the officer may be the one who has to tell the relatives that a family member has died.

Natural deaths.   After several experiences with natural deaths, officers find them the least difficult to handle, even if the officer may be present when the individual dies from a heart attack or stroke. The most distress caused by natural deaths is likely to occur when the officer has to take a body out of a room where it has been lying undiscovered for days and is decomposing. Officers report that the offensive odor of decaying human flesh can hang in their memory indefinitely, turning their stomachs just thinking about it.

The officer's contact with death moves him or her into a world apart from ordinary citizens. Even when the death is not particularly traumatic, the officer's personality is likely to be changed. The experience doesn't enrich them, it just changes them. Some officers may become harder, colder, and less compassionate. Others may become more compassionate and sensitive, philosophical, and more committed to their profession. In some cases the primary emotion may be anger. The reaction depends not only on the kind of death the officer has to deal with, but also on the personality and philosophy of life of the officer involved.

❖ INJURY

Here we are speaking of physical injuries to the officers themselves or to other officers as a source of stress. Officers give the highest stress rating to incidents involving shooting, but auto and other accidents also fall into this category (Sewell, 1981). For example, an officer we know tore up his knee while stopping a bar fight, an injury that kept him out of work for two months. Even more stressful to this officer than the injury were his medical bills, which were only partly paid for by his insurance.

❖ PERSONAL FAILURE

Just short of getting wounded in a gun fight as a way of making an officer miserable are indications that he or she is not succeeding at the job (Sewell, 1981). Being dismissed from the force or suspended is especially hard to deal with. Other events in this category include failure on a promotion examination or when the individual feels that an incompetent officer has been promoted over him or her. This fear of personal failure or a bad evaluation as a source of stress is always present due to constant scrutiny by the public, which can lead to complaints that interfere with an officer's advancement.

Promotions are slow in most departments, and there are a limited number of upper-level positions. Because there are so few openings, those who work hard for promotion and are passed over may become bitter or resigned to being stuck in their present slot indefinitely. In either case the officer is likely to be less than enthusiastic about his or her duties. In many cases the officer cannot take another job because of the time already invested toward retirement. Others who are willing to give up retirement benefits may find that alternative employment does not pay as much as their present job (Burke, 1989).

❖ DANGEROUS SITUATIONS

The excitement of danger and a chance to do the valuable job of protecting the public from criminals are good reasons for becoming a law-enforcement officer. Pursuit of an armed suspect, a barricaded hostage taker, riot control, a felony in progress, or participation in a narcotics raid are all adventures that many officers face. Most officers expect these things to happen as part of the job, and they are all situations that most officers not only take part in, but are also the kind of risk taking that they look forward to.

When an officer is involved in a chase, his or her adrenaline will be pumping, senses will be operating at top efficiency, and many officers feel this excitement as a peak experience. It may take hours for the officer's nerves to settle down after the event is over, and it will usually leave the officer with a good story or two to tell around the station. Some officers become adrenaline-high junkies, seeking out danger and taking unnecessary chances to get it. Like fighter pilots, they push the edge of the envelope to see what they can get away with.

On the other hand, people can get seriously injured or killed in these situations, and if the officer doesn't have a death wish, like Mel Gibson did in *Lethal Weapon*, then he or she is going to be frightened. Being normal, the officer may find that the situation that caused the fear replays itself in the following weeks when the officer experiences cues that remind him or her of the incident. The replay will often bring back the emotions connected with the original circumstance and a repeat of the fear felt at the time.

❖ OFFICER MISCONDUCT

Personal corruption, accepting of a bribe, brutality, and drug and alcohol abuse all create stress in the individual who experiences them. But the distress is not only felt by the offender, observing corruption or police brutality, or associating with someone who abuses drug or alcohol, creates stress in nonoffending officers because of the negative emotions aroused. Officers identify so strongly with each other that when one officer breaks the rules the others often feel guilty by association.

Law-enforcement personnel feel a stronger identification with other officers than employees in other lines of work. When another officer does something wrong and draws attention to his or her misconduct, it becomes stressful even to those officers who are not engaging in misconduct. Because of their strong feelings about public reactions to misconduct, police often close ranks behind someone who has offended, and attempt to deal with the problem within the department.

The criminal indictment of a law-enforcement officer and the negative news coverage that results may make officers defensive and irritable when anybody questions their integrity. Despite officers' negative reactions to corruption in others, they don't like to be assigned to take charge of an investigation of another officer. It takes a different kind of law-enforcement officer to conduct an internal investigation without having a feeling of disloyalty to the profession.

❖ SUPERVISION

Some people reach their level of incompetence early in their careers. That is, they were perfectly good employees at one level, but promotion requires them to perform beyond what they are capable of. One of these people promoted above their level to perform well may end up as a supervisor. On the other hand, the conflict an officer has with a supervisor may not have anything to do with the supervisor's competence, but instead with conflicts between two differenct personalities.

Whatever the reason, incompetence on the part of the supervisor or personality clashes with a supervisor are among those stresses that most officers don't anticipate. It will be a constant source of irritation when an officer works under a supervisor knowing that evaluations are going to be in the hands of someone the officer sees as incompetent, or who he or she dislikes.

Even when a supervisor is liked and his or her style of management is approved of, just readjusting to the new ways this supervisor wants things done can increase the amount of stress an officer feels on the job.

❖ HANDLING DISTURBANCES

Here are some of the reoccurring tasks of the officer on the street: taking a mentally ill paranoid person to the hospital, breaking up a bar fight, arresting a suspect in a mugging, handling a domestic disturbance when the wife has obviously been beaten but refuses to press charges. These are difficult but routine duties. Most officers learn to cope well with these situations and take them in stride. But these daily hassles do add up and take away some of an officer's ability to manage other stressors that they need to deal with.

Then there are the lesser run-ins officers have with citizens: verbal abuse from a women who has been stopped for running a red light, dealing with a drunk who insists it's the officer's job to take him home, interrogating a suspect in a burglary. In small doses these characters all help to make an officer's work meaningful and interesting. Dealing with too many of these borderline characters in a short period of time, however, can make the officer's distress level go up. One sign that the stress has gotten too high is when the officer finds it harder to report to duty. Or the officer may find his or her intake of alcohol goes up, or he or she gets edgy and strikes a prisoner or a suspect who has mouthed off or pushed the limits in some other way.

❖ THE COURT SYSTEM

There are two sources of stress in the court system: (1) the officer's personal involvement, such as testifying on the stand, which can make him or her anxious and (2) the frustration the officer may feel with the system because it is unfair or because the officer feels no control over its decisions. An officer's first appearances in court are likely to cause some degree of anxiety. Probable-cause hearings, trials, and especially cross-examination may be stressful. Many officers, however, adjust rapidly, and after a few courtroom appearances for minor crimes, they are ready to appear on the stand to testify on more serious offenses.

When an officer testifies, it may seem to him or her that there has been good preparation for the case and with the right evidence and a solid confession. Attention has been paid to all the legal possibilities—only to see the prosecutor make an unfair plea bargain which puts the perpetrator back on the streets. Or the officer appeared at the trial, the accused has been found guilty, but due to a procedural error he is released. The officer may be a witness and the defense attorney may harass him in court, trying to make the officer look ignorant and prejudiced. A confession may even be thrown out due to a technicality.

It may all be in a day's work, and mentally the officer can talk himself into thinking, "Oh well, maybe next time." Or "It's my job to arrest them and make a case, it's the prosecutor's job to convict them. It's not my fault the guy's back on the street." Many officers, however, will believe that the legal system is failing not only them but the public as well. They may feel that they are in the position of the man who digs perfectly square 6- by 6-foot holes in the ground and then fills them in again, a total waste of time and energy.

❖ OUTSIDE CRITICISM, THE MEDIA, AND PUBLIC OPINION

The headline reads, "Officer slays teenager." The story fails to mention that the youth was armed and got off the first shot. The press viewing with alarm an officer's actions, or second guessing what should have been done, can weigh heavily on that individual. Reporters do not always realize that decisions need to be made in the heat of action and that later, when all information about the incident is available, a particular decision may not have been the best possible one.

The new school of investigative reporting by people in the media emphasizes making public servants look bad, whether they are law-enforcement personnel or politicians. As a result of press bias, some departments give as little information as possible to reporters.

Criticism of an officer's actions can also come from political officials who take an interest in the case for its publicity value, or because one of their important supporters has been accused of illegal acts. Damaging criticism in some cases can also come from citizens who have unreasonable complaints.

❖ SPECIAL JOB ASSIGNMENTS

An officer has drawn the attention of the assistant chief, who gives him a special assignment: public relations, crime prevention, or the hostage negotiation team. It could also be decoy duty, a stakeout, or maybe even an undercover assignment. The undercover assignment will be especially stressful if the officer has to remain under for any length of time. Officers who come back from a long undercover assignment may find it difficult to fit themselves back into regular law-enforcement duties. We will discuss at some length the stresses of undercover work and the negative consequences it has for the officer involved.

❖ CHANGE IN WORK CONDITIONS

One of the most frequent stresses in police work is shift change. This is especially detrimental to performance when it happens every 2 weeks, since many people take 4 or 5 days to readjust the chemistry of their bodies to the new schedule. Other changes that add stress to an officer's system are promotion, reassignment to another unit, assignment of a new partner, new or unfamiliar equipment, a new area, or any new responsibility. Because of the universality of shift work in law enforcement, we will devote Chapter 5 to its consequences and to possible ways of managing the resulting stress.

Negative Experiences

Some infrequent events such as a police strike, job-related illness, and annual evaluations can all require adjustments that place demands on a person's system. Other stresses are the result of the requirement for officers to always be on call for emergencies. For example, an officer may be at home relaxing after a hard week and get a call to a assist with crowd control at a large fire because the officers on duty are already busy with other calls.

❖ UNIQUE STRESSORS OF MINORITIES AND WOMEN

For women officers, especially, a sexual advance by another officer is stressful, and for any officer sexual advances by others can be upsetting depending on the ethical beliefs of the officer. Women and blacks may also feel stressed because they are sometimes not respected by citizens or other officers.

❖ POSITIVE EXPERIENCES

In Chapter 2, when we discuss Holmes's theory of stress, we will see that even positive experiences, added to everything else going on, can push a person over his or her zone of stability. According to that point of view, awards, a letter of recognition, or successful clearance of a case can still be the straw that breaks the camel's back. On the other hand, many officers find that handling a difficult assignment or facing a dangerous situation adds to their competence and feelings of self-esteem. Knowing that what you are doing is worthwhile, even if stressful, builds your zone of stability.

❖ EUSTRESS—THE "GOOD" STRESS

To this point, it sounds as if people in their right mind would never enter criminal justice due to the risks of critical incidents and stress effects. There are, however, very persuasive positive effects of stress that couteract the downside. Selye (1974) coined the term *eustress* to describe these positive consequences of personal strain.

If you consider those personal qualities that you most value in yourself, they are most likely ones that you did not easily develop, but that were earned in the most challenging situations. That is the principle underlying eustress: Stressful situations require us to become more resourceful and creative. Sometimes they require us to forego our exaggerated sense of self-sufficiency and reach out to family, friends, peers, and other supports to develop a heightened sense of community. At other times we appreciate our inner strength by surviving what at first seems intolerable or, as the Marines say, "what doesn't kill me makes me stronger."

Stress requires you to put aside minor concerns and decide what is really important. What are the principles that give meaning and direction to your life? What exactly is it that drives you in this profession? Who can you really count on, who cares for you, when the chips are down? The answers to these questions in times of need enable officers to grow personally more than is possible in nearly any other profession. As psychologists who regularly work with officers in many criminal justice specialties, we have had conversations in which we profoundly admire the resiliency and resourcefulness of officers. That is one reason we have chosen to work closely with people in the criminal justice system and to write this book.

SUMMARY

Law-enforcement work exposes officers to unusual circumstances and places demands on them that are not faced by most other occupations. The officer has to deal with death, injury, brutality, and the mentally ill. All these are situations that are seldom dealt with by the regular citizen. Despite the fact that these things may be stressful, most officers find that their work is interesting and stimulating because they are called on to deal with out of the ordinary situations. If there are too many demands, they can cause distress. To prevent burnout, the officer must be mentally prepared for a variety of situations and trained to practice stress-management techniques.

QUESTIONS

1. Given all the negative stressors discussed in this chapter, why would anyone want to be a law-enforcement officer?
2. What positive stressors do you expect to experience in law enforcement?
3. Which of the possible stressors had you already considered, and which were new to you?
4. This early in the course, what kind of stress-management techniques are you most likely to use?
5. What are likely to be the most stressful situations for you at this point in your career? Least stressful? Why?
6. What kind of problems are you presently best equipped to handle? Least equipped? Why?
7. Are these sources of stress different from, or similar to, the sources found in other vocations?

REFERENCES

Anson, R. H., and M.E. Bloom (1988). Police stress in an occupational context. *Journal of Police Science and Administration 16*, 229–235.

Bartol, C. R. (1983). *Psychology and American Law*. Belmont, CA: Wadsworth Publishing Co.

Beutler, L.E., P. D. Nussbaum, and K. E. Meredith (1988). Changing personality patterns of police officers. *Professional Psychology: Research and Practice 19*, 503–507.

Burke, R. J. (1989). Career stages, satisfaction, and well-being among police officers. *Psychological Reports 65*, 3–12.

Heiman, M. F. (1975). Police suicide. *Journal of Police Science and Administration 3*, 267–271.

Meagher, M. S., and N. A. Yentes (1986). Choosing a career in policing: A comparison of male and female perceptions. *Journal of Police Science and Administration 14*, 320–327.

Selye, H. (1974). *Stress without Distress*. Philadelphia: J. B. Lippincott Company.

Sewell, J. D. (1981). Police stress, *FBI Law Enforcement Bulletin*, April, p. 9.

Terry, W. C. (1981). Police stress: The empirical evidence. *Journal of Police Science and Administration 9*, 61–74.

Violanti, J., J. E. Vena and J. R. Marshall (1986). Disease risk and mortality among police officers: New evidence and contributing factors. *Journal of Police Science and Administration 14*, 17–23.

2

❖

Zone of Stability:
How Much Stress Is Too Much?

A 14-year-old boy is attended by rescue workers after being hit by a car while riding his moped. An officer gathers information to make a report on the incident. (Photo from the *Columbia Missourian* files)

Stress is the spice of life. (Hans Selye)

❖ OBJECTIVES

1. To explain the individual's need for a range of stress.
2. To introduce the concept of zone of stability.

3. To examine the pathological effects of both boredom and too much stimulation.

4. To show the various factors that control the range of stress that an officer can handle effectively.

5. To give some suggestions for building the ability to cope with stress.

❖ INTRODUCTION

In this chapter we explore some of the characteristics individuals have that influence how much excitement and change (stress) they can have in their lives and still enjoy what they are doing. We will discuss the bad effects of boredom and underscore how the lack of stimulation increases a person's feelings of distress. A person's goal should be to find the optimum level of stress that he or she needs to feel alive and challenged, but not distressed. Living well is a balancing act in which we sometimes misjudge what we can handle and end up being uncomfortable. Successfully handling stress increases a person's competence to handle even more stress well.

We will present a checklist to measure how the amount of stress a person is experiencing is affecting him or her. At the end of the chapter we will introduce ways that coping skills can be increased to handle stressful situations, an idea that will be developed more fully in later chapters.

❖ ZONE OF STABILITY

Excitement and adventure—healthy people seek it out and often pay to bring it into their lives. Boredom pushes people into a search for action. People vary in what turns them on: fast cars, night clubs, hang gliding, horror movies. Even people with a low need for physical action lie on the couch watching second-hand thrills on TV.

We need excitement or stimulation in our lives, but too much or too little and there are problems. The range of stimulation (excitement, arousal) from the least to the most the individual can handle without signs of distress is what we call that person's *zone of stability*. When a person is functioning within his or her zone of stability, in terms of the number of stresses that he or she must deal with, the individual will feel comfortable and will be enjoying life. When the amount of excitement is above or below the person's zone of stability, he or she will be uncomfortable and will show a range of symptoms indicative of distress.

Although most discussions of stress focus on the upper end, where there is too much stimulation or excitement, we have become aware in our work that lack of stimulation or boredom is also very stressful for most people. With rare exceptions, individuals thrive on having variety and challenge in their lives. If children are not stimulated by being handled and talked to, they will fail to develop normally. Studies on rats, which are killed after an experiment and their brains examined, show that lack of a stimulating environment results in a failure of the brain to develop normally (Levine, 1960). In human adults who work in boring jobs, intelligence goes down and they may develop physical symptoms.

To be comfortable, people need to have a certain amount of excitement, some considerably more than others. The stress researcher Zuckerman (1976) believes that there is a group of people who see activities such as car racing, which most people find dangerous, as exciting rather than stressful. He calls this group Type T, or thrill seekers.

Brown (1981), in his work with police officers, concluded that they were not danger lovers, but neither did they seek security. Individuals who choose to become officers could not stand the idea of sitting at a desk shuffling papers or working on an assembly line. Although law enforcement has many dull moments, there is always the possibility that something exciting will happen. The officer never knows when a robbery or burglary will take place. As one New York City officer put it, "around that next corner something could happen that could make my whole day exciting."

On the other hand, although all officers by the nature of the work have some degree of risk taking in their makeup, they do differ on the degree of "sensation seeking." Officers who do not want to be physically endangered can opt for a safer, inside job and feel vicarious risk and thrill through their peers on the street. In larger agencies for example, they may get an assignment in training, record keeping, or taking police photographs. Officers who like more action can go into undercover work or act as decoys.

An experienced court bailiff worked part-time as a game warden, not as much for the extra money as for the experience reported:

> I love the outdoors, fishing and hunting, and it really gripes me to see people abuse it. I like the chance to put my wits against poachers who have spent thousands putting together a system to cheat the public. I suppose it's almost like a strategy game—trying to think like they do; anticipating what they will do next. Setting the stage and just waiting for them to fall into it. All the sitting in the rain and snow and mud is just background noise to being able to do something that counts, and outwit those guys.

❖ THE NEED FOR STIMULATION AND RISK

The problem most active people have to face is finding their optimum level of stress, that is, the level at which they feel they are operating at their best. For law-enforcement officers, this level may be quite high. For everyone, however, there is some level when there is more pressure and change than the individual has the physical and mental resources to deal with—at that point stress will have become distress. When the pressure builds high enough, we expect the person to begin to have physical, mental, and emotional problems. For examples of some of the symptoms of stress that indicate that a person is beyond the limits of their zone of stability, see the list of stress exhaustion symptoms in Table 2-1.

When a person shows a number of these symptoms it is a sign that he or she is functioning outside of his or her zone of stability and needs to do one of

TABLE 2-1   STRESS EXHAUSTION SYMPTOMS

Check the symptoms of stress exhaustion you've noticed lately in yourself

Physical	Emotional	Spiritual
__appetite change	__anxiety	__emptiness
__headaches	__frustration	__loss of meaning
__tension	__the blues	__doubt
__fatigue	__mood swings	__unforgiving
__insomnia	__bad temper	__martyrdom
__weight change	__nightmares	__looking for magic
__colds	__crying spells	__loss of direction
__muscle aches	__irritability	__needing to prove
__digestive upsets	__"no one cares"	__self
__pounding heart	__depression	__cynicism
__accident prone	__nervous laugh	__apathy
__teeth grinding	__worrying	
__rash	__easily discouraged	
__restlessness	__little joy	
__foot tapping		
__finger drumming		
__increased alcohol, drug, tobacco use		

Mental	Relational
__forgetfulness	__isolation
__dull senses	__intolerance
__poor concentration	__resentment
__low productivity	__loneliness
__negative attitude	__lashing out
__confusion	__hiding
__lethargy	__clamming up
__whirling mind	__lowered sex drive
__no new ideas	__nagging
__boredom	__distrust
__spacing out	__fewer contacts with friends
__negative self-talk	__lack of intimacy
	__using people

Reprinted with permission from *Structural Exercises in Stress Management*, Volume 1, Nancy Loving Tubesing and Donald A. Tubesing, Editors. (c.) 1983 Whole Person Press, PO Box 3151, Duluth MN 55803, (218) 728-6807.

three things: (1) change or modify the situation, (2) get out of the situation or (3) find some methods of relieving the stress. Of course, there is one more thing the person can do, which is to do nothing, in which case he or she can expect the symptoms to become worse over time. In Chapter 3, we will discuss some of the long-term physical problems that result from living in a constantly stress filled environment.

The screening for recruit positions in law enforcement done by most departments is intended to choose candidates who have a wide zone of stability. Experience over the years has shown that only men and women who can deal with both the extremes of boredom and fast-changing pressure are going to make good officers.

In our conversations with police, we find that most of them complain about the periods when nothing is happening and really look forward to calls that bring them into action. The excitement of the job makes the boring parts worthwhile. The possibility of doing a wide variety of exciting things is one of the leading reasons they give for choosing policing as a career and they prefer to work in departments that give them an opportunity to have adventures. Officers who continue to like their work report to us that what they do is important, often misunderstood by others, but important.

Even with the care taken in choosing recruits with these strengths, there are still marked limits to what can be expected from law-enforcement personnel. Despite what members of the public seem to think, putting on a uniform does not make the wearer immune to having nightmares after a plane crash where the officer has to pick up pieces of human bodies.

We will discuss what makes up too much stimulation shortly but at this point we want to go back and look at the effects that too little activity or an unchanging environment that is unbearably dull can have.

❖ BOREDOM AND LACK OF STIMULATION

It has been recognized for some years that nonstimulating environments prevent children from developing their aptitudes and intelligence. A classic study was done by Wheeler (1942) on East Tennessee mountain children, which found that (1) their IQs went down over time due to lack of intellectual stimulation, and (2) as stimulation increased in the community, the younger children's IQs were higher than their older brothers and sisters.

In the early 1960s the pathology of boredom received a considerable amount of attention in research on sensory deprivation. During the Korean War the Chinese used isolation and sensory deprivation to prepare American prisoners of war for brainwashing (e.g., Brownfield, 1965; Vernon, 1963).

The standard treatment involved weeks of isolation in a bare room with either no stimulation or only negative stimulation, such as hunger. As a result, the POWs in their eagerness for stimulation, were often willing to listen to and believe, temporarily at least, the political ideas the communists were attempting to force on on them.

Later in the United States, studies were run to see what the limits of boredom might be. Psychologists were interested in finding out what symptoms individuals developed in totally nonstimulating situations. The big question was at what point would a person's mind become disorganized. Volunteers were put in empty rooms with nothing to read or listen to. Sometimes they were blindfolded and a white noise (such as a droning fan or soft static to cover other sounds) was placed in the background. In other experiments they were placed in tanks of water at body temperature with no sight or sound available to them. The more complete the lack of sight, sound, and touch, the sooner the individual became disorganized, started to see things that were not there, and felt the pain of isolation. Normal, healthy people sometimes had waking hallucinations during the experiments that were created by the brain in order to produce the minimum required stimulation (e.g., Brownfield, 1965; Vernon, 1963).

Other studies of workers on their jobs found that any environment that was low in stimulation had negative effects on people. It was established that only people with certain mental abilities could work on an assembly line for any period of time without having marked symptoms. Three types of people could stand the assembly-line work: those who were mentally dull, those who found ways to turn off their minds or trance out at work, and those who could fantasize while working.

The rest of the workers were not only uncomfortable with the boredom of the assembly line, as shown by high absenteeism, but there was another negative side. Some of this group would find ways to make the job more stimulating by fouling up the work. For example, they would put nuts in the frame of a car to cause difficulty in locating rattle. People who have spent a long time working on assembly lines have a greater falling off in mental ability than people who work at more stimulating jobs. Dull, routine tasks are bad for the mental health of most relatively intelligent people.

One major motivation for what humans do may be based on our need for stimulation, that is, a need to break the boredom. Zuckerman's (1976) sensation seekers are at the high end of the need for stimulation, but we believe that even normal people seek out stimulation when the situation becomes too boring. One motivation behind the criminal behavior of street gangs may be their need for excitement and adventure. In gang warfare, besides the need for group membership, we are seeing a need for risk and challenge. These are the same motivations that under the right conditions lead to heroes and noted adventurers.

So what do Columbus, Jesse James, and Chuck Yeager have in common? Explorers and air-force pilots share with delinquents and criminals the need for a high level of excitement and risk in their lives. They are all sensation seekers.

Even relatively normal people like amusement parks, with their breathtaking rides and horror movies that make them recoil in fear. The stimulation they give to the person helps banish boredom. Our point here is that for most people boredom is uncomfortable, and they go seeking to find or create some kind of excitement, even if it involves danger.

Law-enforcement officers expect, and some even look forward to being exposed to physical danger. When a captain called off a nighttime search for a perpetrator who had shot at an officer because, "it's dangerous, someone might get hurt," it became a running joke in the squad. Who else was supposed to go after armed culprits? Someone from the National Guard who worked in a drugstore during the week? Their courage had been called into question and the slight was not easily forgiven. After all, they were the cops and danger was their business. Implying that an officer is a coward is not something that is done lightly around a police department.

❖ MEASURING LIFE'S STRESS

On the other side of the zone of stability from boredom are the pressures from too much excitement or stimulation in one's life. Holmes and Rahe (1967) developed a scale they called the "social readjustment rating scale." This scale allots points to the kinds of changes in a person's life, and the total of these points is an indication of how close that person is to exceeding his or her stress limits and to showing the kind of symptoms listed in Table 2-1.

Holmes and Rahe developed this scale after they observed that, when patients had a number of recent changes in their lives, they were more likely to come down with colds or the flu. Further research showed that people with a large number of changes in their lives were also more likely to have accidents or show psychological symptoms. This scale is given in Table 2-2. When people were asked what was the most stressful thing they had to adjust to, most said it was the death of a mate. Therefore, when they were developing the scale, Holmes and Rahe arbitrarily assigned 100 points for the death of a mate and had judges rank other events using this as their point of reference.

EXERCISE 1

At this point, we suggest that the reader go over the symptoms in Table 2-1 and then total up the stress points given in Table 2-2. This should give a rough idea of where you stand in relation to your zone of stability.

The authors' experience is that the number of points that should be assigned to a stressor will vary somewhat from individual to individual. For example, we have had clients in therapy who showed little stress reaction to a divorce, whereas other clients found their whole world falling apart. Although the number of points assigned to a life change is relative to who is making the judgment, Holmes and Rahe's scale does provide a rough guide as to how many recent changes in his or her life a person has had to adjust to.

TABLE 2-2   THE SOCIAL READJUSTMENT RATING SCALE

Life Event	Mean Value
1. Death of spouse	100
2. Divorce	73
3. Marital separation from mate	65
4. Detention in jail or other institution	63
5. Death of a close family member	63
6. Major personal injury or illness	53
7. Marriage	50
8. Being fired at work	47
9. Marital reconciliation with mate	45
10. Retirement from work	45
11. Major change in the health or behavior of a family member	44
12. Pregnancy	40
13. Sexual difficulties	39
14. Gaining a new family member (e.g., through birth, adoption, oldster moving in)	39
15. Major business readjustment (e.g., merger, reorganization, bankruptcy)	39
16. Major change in financial state (e.g., a lot worse off or a lot better off than usual)	38
17. Death of a close friend	37
18. Changing to a different line of work	36
19. Major change in the number of arguments with spouse (e.g.,) either a lot more or a lot less than usual regarding childrearing, personal habits, etc.)	35
20. Taking out a mortgage or loan for a major purchase (e.g., for a home or business)	31
21. Foreclosure on a mortgage or loan	30
22. Major change in responsibilities at work (e.g., promotion, demotion, lateral transfer)	29
23. Son or daughter leaving home (e.g., marriage or attending college)	29
24. Trouble with in-laws	29
25. Outstanding personal achievement	28
26. Wife beginning or ceasing work outside the home	26
27. Beginning or ceasing formal schooling	26
28. Major change in living conditions (e.g., building a new home, remodeling, deterioration of home or neighborhood)	25
29. Revision of personal habits (e.g., dress, manners, associations)	24
30. Trouble with the boss	23
31. Major change in working hours or conditions	20
32. Change in residence	20
33. Changing to a new school	20
34. Major change in usual type and/or amount of recreation	19
35. Major change in church activities (e.g., a lot more or a lot less than usual)	19
36. Major change in social activities (e.g., clubs, dancing, movies, visiting)	18
37. Taking out a mortgage or loan for a lesser purchase (e.g., for a car, TV, or freezer)	17

continued

TABLE 2-2 *continued*

Life Event	Mean Value
38. Major change in sleeping habits (a lot more or a lot less sleep or change in part of day when asleep)	16
39. Major change in number of family get-togethers (e.g., a lot more or a lot less than usual)	15
40. Major change in eating habits (a lot more or a lot less food intake, or very different meal hours or surroundings)	15
41. Vacation	13
42. Christmas	12
43. Minor violations of the law (e.g. traffic tickets, jaywalking, disturbing the peace)	11

T. H. Homes and R. H. Rahe, "The Social Readjustment Rating Scale," Pergamon Press Ltd. Oxford, England. *Journal of Psychosomatic Research 11*, 213–218, 1967.

Holmes felt that most people reached a critical level of stress at 300 points, where there is about an 80% chance of developing some kind of stress-related symptom in the next year.

Athough 300 points is a general guide, in our experience it takes considerably fewer changes in their lives for some individuals to be pushed into the range where they show symptoms. On the other hand, some people's stress tolerance is truly impressive. One of the authors who has worked with the U.S. Air Force in Europe has seen fighter pilots with over 400 accumulated points who were relatively symptom free and able to carry out their flight duties at a high level. Another one of the authors worked with a woman military police officer who had an average of 600 points over a 4-year period. She had been particularly hardy in resisting the strains of changed relationships, specialization, crisis events, and relocation. She finally decided to take care of the minor stress symptoms that were gradually becoming major ones. Everyone is different in what they can tolerate.

On the Holmes–Rahe scale, even good events, such as the birth of a child or marriage, put a strain on the individual's system, and Holmes believes that if too many positive changes occur the person can develop the same symptoms that they would from negative events like a divorce or loss of a job.

In one case an administrator of a criminal justice program consulted one of the authors regarding stress-related symptoms. He was puzzled why both he and his wife (not in the field) should be experiencing discomfort when all seemed to be going well. He had recently received a promotion, started a new program for tracking probationees, bought some land for a dreamhouse, published a training manual, and started raising spaniels (which was a lifelong ambition). His wife had become pregnant with a second child they had been long awaiting, had sold a new line of clothing designs, and was excitedly planning for their new house. The problem— not too much negative stress, but too much positive stress! Remember, stress is anything that requires you to change; to adjust how you think, feel, and behave. Too much of even a good thing can often produce serious symptoms of stress.

Some writers on stress (e.g., Thoits, 1983) disagree with Holmes and Rahe's idea that positive events also lead to stress symptoms. There is some evidence that positive changes may even lead to a greater capacity to cope with other problems (Kanner et al., 1991).

The police stress scale that we will be referring to in this book attends mostly to negative events in an officer's job. Positive events, such as a promotion, are assigned only a limited number of stress points. Table 2-3 gives the 25 highest-rated stress items for police work. There are no positive items in these 25 top stress items, all of which are negative experiences.

Athough most theories hold that it is the accumulation of a number of stressful events that finally leads to stress symptoms, in law enforcement it is possible for one event to push someone into a full-blown stress disorder. A shoot-out in which an officer is wounded and kills the perpetrator has the potential of driving the officer beyond the zone of stability and into a posttraumatic stress reaction with its accompanying nightmares, crying spells, and panic attacks. Contrary to what many people think these reactions to a major stress have nothing to do with the officer's virility. Because of the potential for these events to cause problems, we discuss them at length in Chapter 8.

TABLE 2-3   25 MOST STRESSFUL LAW-ENFORCEMENT CRITICAL LIFE EVENTS

1.	Violent death of a partner in the line of duty
2.	Dismissal
3.	Taking a life in the line of duty
4.	Shooting someone in the line of duty
5.	Suicide of an officer who is a close friend
6.	Violent death of another officer in the line of duty
7.	Murder committed by a police officer
8.	Duty-related violent injury (shooting)
9.	Violent job-related injury to another officer
10.	Suspension
11.	Passed over for promotion
12.	Pursuit of an armed suspect
13.	Answering a call to a scene involving violent nonaccidental death of a child
14.	Assignment away from family for a long period of time
15.	Personal involvement in a shooting incident
16.	Reduction in pay
17.	Observing an act of police corruption
18.	Accepting a bribe
19.	Participating in an act of police corruption
20.	Hostage situation resulting from aborted criminal action
21.	Response to a scene involving the accidental death of a child
22.	Promotion of inexperienced or incompetent officer over you
23.	Internal affairs investigation against self
24.	Barricaded suspect
25.	Hostage situation resulting from domestic disturbance

Source: James D. Sewell, "Police Stress," *FBI Law Enforcement Bulletin,* April 1981, p. 9

In their work, law-enforcement officers often come in contact with citizens who have a very low tolerance for stress, people who show major symptoms under circumstances that the officer would not pay much attention to. These people will be a threat to others around them because they may explode under pressures that are hardly apparent to others. Some explosive murderers studied by the first author were sent into a murderous rage by a slighting remark, a car cutting in front of theirs on the street, somebody bumping against them in a bar, and the like.

In 23% of the cases studied by the FBI of officers killed in action, the perpetrator was a dependent personality type (Uniform Crime Reports, 1992). These were otherwise calm and agreeable individuals who were sitting on an emotional volcano. Their zone of stability had been cut to the point where it took only a minor confrontation to set them into a murderous frenzy.

❖ INFLUENCES ON THE SIZE OF THE ZONE OF STABILITY

What influences the range of stress tolerance that a person is likely to have? The foundation on which the zone of stability is built is the individual's genetic makeup. Some interesting studies have been done on identical twins raised apart that provide evidence that psychophysiological responses to stress are inherited (Bouchard, et al. 1990).

Temperament traits are ways of reacting to situations; they appear early in childhood and stay with the person the rest of his or her life. Some temperamental characteristics that are heavily influenced by genes are proneness to anger, shyness, empathy, and activity level. Studies on identical twins raised apart show that even what fears a person has are based to some extent on inherited family traits. Tendencies to develop hypertension also show a genetic influence. A person's zone of stability then depends partly on the genetic structure their parents passed on to them.

Given equal innate strengths, however, we can point to at least five factors that influence how resistant a person is going to be to stresses in their life:

1. Childhood experiences
2. Changes in life over last 1 to 2 years
3. Ongoing irritations or problems
4. Inner critic or irrational beliefs
5. Stigmas

Childhood traumas. Several studies have been done on the influence of early childhood experiences on adult adjustment. One of the most complete studies was the Midtown Manhattan Study (Srole, et al., 1962); everyone in the selected area of Manhattan was given a complete psychiatric interview, which included an investigation of a large number of childhood experiences and an analysis of present functioning. The symptoms the psychiatrists looked for included physical conditions such as hypertension and skin rashes and psychological problems such as nervousness and alcoholism.

The childhood experiences that were found to relate to later adjustment were (1) parents' poor physical health, (2) parents' poor mental health, (3) childhood economic deprivation, (4) childhood poor physical health, (5) childhood broken homes, (6) parents' character negatively perceived, (7) parents' quarrels, (8) disagreements with parents, and (9) physical abuse and/or sexual abuse. Each item could earn more than 1 point; for example, 2 points were given for mother's poor mental health and another 2 if the father also had poor mental health.

The larger score, the more likely that an individual would show symptoms of emotional problems or have problems getting along with others. The effect of the points was additive, that is, a person who had a score of 7 would have more signs of maladjustment than a person who has 3. In terms of the zone of stability, a large number of negative events in childhood narrows and lowers the range within which the person can function comfortably. Suspects who come from deprived backgrounds where they were exposed to the childhood experiences listed previously become frustrated easily, and often explode into physical violence with no justification. Officers who work with them become aware that there is no rheostat to their anger, it's off or it's on. On the other hand, a person from a background where these childhood experiences did not happen is more likely to put up with frustration and control anger even under very stressful conditions.

Changes in life are cumulative.   We have already discussed the Holmes–Rahe theory that the number of changes in a person's life influences how much additional stress they can handle. A few changes such as a promotion or buying a new house, and the individual will probably continue to feel comfortable. Add a divorce and a change in social life, and the individual will lose some of his or her flexibility and have a smaller zone of stability. Holmes believes that the stress caused by a change is adjusted to over time. This suggests that if individuals can distribute the changes in their life (i.e., not try to do too many things during a short period of time) they are less likely to accumulate a critical number of stress experiences.

Table 2-3, which lists what police officers rate as most stressful, makes it clear that some police assignments use up more of an officer's zone of stability than others. There are high-intensity assignments, such as undercover work, not listed in Table 2-3 that have the potential for exceeding an officer's tolerance in less than a year.

Present or ongoing irritations.   Ongoing problems, none of which are major in and of themselves, cut down on an officer's ability to handle other stresses. Examples of these are poor relationship with spouse, chronic medical condition such as an allergy, debts, ill or fading parents, equipment that keeps breaking down, or difficulty with a supervisor.

Although these problems by themselves are irritating, it is in combination with the other factors that we have mentioned that they cause trouble. If the zone of stability is already overloaded, a small irritant can sometimes cause an inappropriate response. Some hassles, such as poor relationship with a spouse, the officer can do something about by taking steps to change them. Others, such as an unpleasant in-law, need to be avoided, and still others, such as a critical supervisor, the officer will have to develop stress relievers for (e.g., exercise program or hobby).

Inner critic.   Normal individuals have an internal voice that evaluates what they do and makes comments on the adequacy of the person's actions. This voice is called by various names: conscience, superego, or top dog, for example. Most individuals selected for police work have a relatively friendly inner voice that is accepting of how they do things. Many people, however, have a critical, carping inner voice that is always pointing out how inadequate they are. Regardless of how well others think they do, these individuals' own sense of perfection nags at them, leaving them feeling incompetent. Individuals who view everything they do as negative will have a smaller zone of stability and correspondingly less stress tolerance.

The psychologist Albert Ellis (1987) believes that most psychological problems come about because of the irrational beliefs that people have. When events do not happen the way the person feels they should, the inner critic overwhelms them with guilt and feelings of inadequacy and inferiority.

Some of these irrational beliefs that narrow a person's zone of stability are as follows:

1. The idea that it is a dire necessity for an adult to be loved or approved for everything he or she does by every significant person in his or her community.
2. The idea that one should be thoroughly competent, adequate, and achieving in all possible respects if one is to consider oneself worthwhile.
3. The idea that there is an invariably right, precise, and perfect solution to human problems and that it is catastrophic if this perfect solution is not found.
4. The idea that it is awful and catastrophic when things are not the way we would like for them to be.

Here are some ways of using the inner voice to increase the zone of stability:

1. Learn to talk back to one's inner critic and point out how the constant carping isn't doing anybody any good.
2. Learn to be less concerned about what other people in general think.
3. Use one's self-talk to provide encouragment and support instead of criticism.

In the authors' experience, many law-enforcement officers are already very good at these three psychological skills.

Being accepted by others is important to most people. But prejudice exists, and it is hard for an individual to feel good about himself or herself if others view him or her negatively. Is there something about a person that others automatically respond to with dislike? Many individuals that law-enforcement officers come in contact with are stigmatized in some way: mental illness, prison record, working as a prostitute, and the like. Most of these groups expect negative reactions from people as soon as the stigma becomes known.

Unfortunately, among some groups in the community, law-enforcement officers are a stigmatized minority. In their minds the sight of a uniform brings forth thoughts of "stupid cop" or "brutal cop." In some areas of law enforcement the prejudice stigmatizing the individual exists among members of the department. An officer who is a member of a minority group, or a woman in such situations may become cautious and defensive because the individual doesn't know how he or she is going to be treated. Or they may assume that they are going to be put down or their abilities dismissed before other people get to know them.

❖ BUILDING THE OFFICER'S ABILITY TO COPE

What kind of things strengthen an officer's ability to handle stress and build his or her zone of stability? In this chapter we introduce some ideas that will be more fully developed in later chapters as we discuss the different varieties of stress that law enforcement personnel face. At this time we are mostly concerned with illustrating the factors that contribute to a good zone of stability, our point being that officers can build up and increase their ability to cope with stress.

Support system. Law-enforcement officers have a ready-made support system consisting of other officers, but the system doesn't always work well. Officers understand the problems of and have a special feeling for, other members of the squad in a way that citizens or even spouses do not easily understand.

On the other hand, officers feel a need to protect their image as "real men" and have to be careful about how they complain or talk about their emotional responses to events around other officers. To admit to a strong emotional reaction to an accident they have just handled or that they were afraid during a violent confrontation may get an officer labeled at best as a "wimp."

When we talk about postshooting reactions, we will see that officers offering support sometimes respond in a way that is opposite to what the officer involved in the shooting needs at that time. That is, the officer giving support may make a statement like, "Good job, killer, that dirtbag deserved it." An officer after even a clean shoot may be feeling badly about what happened and a statement like this only makes him or her feel worse.

Coping skills. The experienced officer on the job has developed wisdom, and part of the wisdom is the ability to handle situations in the most efficient way. The old hand may not always do the job by the book but will use methods that have been found to work for him or her. While an officer's formal academy training is supposed to give him or her basic coping skills, many of the best coping skills will be learned from other officers in the field and from what is learned from experiences on the street.

One coping skill everyone could probably learn to use better is the ability to talk oneself through a tough situation with positive self-talk. "I can handle this. I just need to keep my cool. They are scared as I am. I can't let them see how nervous I am."

Certain stress situations lend themselves to this kind of self-talk, and we will give examples of how to use this technique when we discuss stresses in law enforcement.

SUMMARY

Officers function within a zone of stability. Too little stimulation, and they go looking for excitement. Too much stimulation, and they begin showing symptoms of distress and may avoid their responsibilities. Childhood traumas, too many changes in a short period of time, ongoing irritations, too much self-criticism, and stigmas can all lower the amount of stress a person can handle before starting to show symptoms. A good support system and the development of coping skills can increase an officer's zone of stability.

CASE PROBLEMS

At this time we would like you to practice some internal self-talk to get in the habit of protecting yourself in situations that could lead to stress if you don't cool down your own emotions. We believe that mentally preparing yourself for different stressful eventualities is one way of controlling stress in your life.

Case 1. You have made a slight mistake on an arrest report and your sergeant or supervisor discovers it. He is letting you know in an overly harsh manner that you should not have been so careless.

A. What do you say to yourself to keep your cool? Be specific as to the statements you will make.

B. When you have your reactions under control, what can you say to him to indicate that, although you made a mistake, there is no need for him to react to this strongly? Again, be specific as to what you would say.

Case 2. You have recently joined a new bowling team and several of the new team members are starting to give you a hard time about being a "cop." The jokes become stronger as they kid you about rescueing cats all day and giving out parking tickets.

A. What do you say to yourself to contain your emotions? Again, be specific as to what words you would use to yourself in your mind.

B. When you have yourself under control, what words would you use to tell your team members that you do not appreciate their kidding?

REFERENCES

Brown, M. K. (1981). *Working the Street: Police Discretion and the Dilemmas of Reform*. New York: Russell Sage Foundation.

Bouchard, T. J., D. T. Lykken, M. McGue, and N. L. Segal, (1990). Sources of human psychological differences: The Minnesota Study of Twins Reared Apart. *Science 250*, 223–228.

Brownfield, C. A. (1965). *Isolation: Clinical and Experimental Approaches*. New York: Random House.

Ellis, A., and W. Dryden, (1987). *The Practice of Rational-Emotive Therapy*. New York: Springer-Verlag.

Holmes, T. H., and R.H. Rahe, (1967). The social readjustment rating scale. *Journal of Psychosomatic Research 11*, 213–218.

Kanner, A. D., S. S. Feldman, D. A. Weinberger, and M. E. Ford, (1991). Uplifts, hassles, and adaptational outcomes in early adolescents. In A. Monat and R. S. Lazarus (eds.), *Stress and Coping*, 3rd ed. New York: Columbia University Press.

Levine, S. (1960). Stimulation in infancy. *Scientific American 202*, May, 80–86.

Sewell J. D. (1981). Police stress, *FBI Law Enforcement Bulletin*, April, p. 9.

Srole, L., T. S. Langner, S. T. Michael, M. K. Opler, and T. A. C. Rennie, (1962). *Mental Health in the Metropolis: The Midtown Manhattan Study*. New York: Blakiston Division, McGraw-Hill Book Co.

Thoits, P. A. (1983). Dimensions of life events that influence psychological distress: An evaluation and synthesis of the literature. In H. B. Kaplan (ed.), *Psychosocial Stress: Trends in Theory and Research* (pp. 33–103). New York: Academic Press, Inc.

Tyler, L. E. (1965). *The Psychology of Human Differences*. New York: Appleton-Century-Crofts.

Uniform Crime Reports Section (1992). *Killed in the Line of Duty: A Study of Selected Felonious Killings of Law Enforcement Officers*. Washington D.C.: Federal Bureau of Investigation, U.S. Department of Justice.

Vernon, J. A. (1963). *Inside the Black Room*. New York: Clarkson N. Potter, Inc.

Wheeler, L. R. (1942). A comparative study of the intelligence of East Tennessee mountain children. *Journal of Educational Psychology 33*, 321–334.

Whole Person Press (1983). Stress exhaustion symptoms. *Structured Exercises in Stress Management*, Volume 1. Duluth, MN: Whole Person Press.

Zuckerman, M. (1976). Sensation seeking and anxiety, traits and states, as determinants of behavior in novel situations. In I. G. Sarason and C. D. Spielberger (eds.), *Stress and Anxiety*, Vol. 3, pp. 141–170. New York: John Wiley & Sons, Inc.

3

❖

The Physiology of Stress

STAR team members escort a convicted murderer from a motel after his escape plan ended up in a 6-hour standoff. (Photo from the *Columbia Missourian* files)

❖ OBJECTIVES

1. To describe the body's response to stress.
2. To identify primary symptoms of stress reaction.
3. To understand how relaxation techniques interrupt the stress response.
4. To know the effects of nutrition and prolonged stress on stress physiology.

❖ INTRODUCTION

At first glance, understanding the physiology of stress may sound like a purely academic task with little relevance to the practice of law enforcement. However, awareness of the changes that occur in your body as a result of a stressful situation is the foundation of most stress-management programs. There are several reasons why this information is important:

1. You need to be able to identify the early warning signs of stress symptoms in yourself, other officers, and victims. These physical symptoms can produce psychological effects such as alterations in judgment, attention, concentration, and mood that are directly related to how well you can carry out law-enforcement functions.
2. When you understand and accept the changes in your body as normal signs of mobilization for stress, they are less apt to add to your distress.
3. Awareness of stress symptoms enables you to monitor the severity and progression of symptoms in yourself and others.
4. Most stress-management techniques are designed to reduce stress symptoms, and you will know what to observe as indications of improvement.

❖ MIND AND BODY: IMAGINATION BECOMES REALITY

Mind and body are so closely interwoven that the body cannot tell whether stress is real or imagined. Whether you anticipate an event, experience it directly, or simply recall it, your body reacts to prepare for it. This is most often experienced when watching an exciting movie or participating in a training exercise: You logically know it is not real, but then you feel your heart and breathing rate increase, muscles tense, and adrenaline flush into your system.

This preparation for action has been called the *fight–flight reaction* (Cannon, 1932) and refers to the basic survival function of defending or escaping. Hemingway referred to this reaction as "the honorable art of getting the hell out of there."

The way our bodies function can be a double-edged sword: on the one hand preparing us for action and, on the other, not knowing when to turn off to let us recover. A part of our central nervous system is the *autonomic* or "automatic" *nervous system* (ANS). This part enables our bodies to function without having to consciously think about making them work. For example, without our awareness or concentration, the heart beats, respiration occurs, digestion progresses, and a myriad of essential physiological processes continue uninterrupted by thought.

The ANS is subdivided into the *sympathetic* (active) and *parasympathetic* (passive) nervous branches that are responsible for the functions of mobilizing or relaxing the body. Most of the time, these are in gentle rhythmic interplay in which we move through periods of activation and relaxation. Under stressful conditions, however, we may become mired in prolonged activation of the fight–flight response.

In the early stages of arousal, the vegetative or relaxing processes in the body that are controlled by the parasympathetic branch begin to shut down. They are replaced by the action functions of the sympathetic branch of the autonomic nervous system. Digestion slows and the sphincters (round muscles in the stomach, bowel, and bladder) tighten since no food will be digested under emergency conditions. The heart rate and blood pressure increase so that blood can carry oxygen faster to the large muscles that are beginning to tighten for action. The pupils dilate to take in more light to see better. Hearing and smell become acute. The clotting capacity of the blood increases to prevent potential blood loss in case of injury, and the hands and feet become cold (hence having "cold feet") as blood moves from the extremities.

CASE EXAMPLE

Patrol Officer Angela Montoya is moving into position with other officers for a drug bust at a known dealer's house. As she positions herself to the side of the back door, she becomes acutely aware of the confining tightness of her Second Chance body armor. She smells the fragrance of lilacs in the distance and kitty litter closer by. There was the chirp of a nearby hidden cricket. As she tells her partner that she is ready, she feels the dryness of her mouth and throat and how slightly hoarse her voice sounds. In the interminable seconds before entering, she flips through the scenarios and procedures she has studied and practiced. Catching herself thinking, and not sensing, she focuses intensely on the texture of the flaking door paint and the feeling of the checkering of her pistol grip.

In the rush of entering, she smartly cracks her knee on the point of a heavy oak table but only hears the sound of the table moving and feels nothing. Caught up in the rapid moments of strategically moving through the house, she loses all sense of clock time; sometimes things seem to move in slow motion, at other times she can barely recall the blur of moving down a darkened hallway. At the turn of each corner she anticipates an armed perpetrator, perhaps hidden or holding a hostage, and focuses on the recognition cues for immediate action.

As they arrive at the top of the stairs on the second floor, she notices the strong need to urinate, but suppresses the urge and the inappropriate thought of looking for a bathroom. The pistol grip feels damp in her cool hands, and she notices the tension in her grip.

As they move down a hallway, the lead officer is thrown back as a closet door explodes open into him and a huge man tries to bolt past. She begins to see him moving in slow motion and spots several openings for a take down. She feels an extraordinary rush of energy as she agilely sidesteps the man, tripping him, and follows him to the ground, feeling for the angle of his wrist for a hold. Though twice her size, she feels a surge of power and forces his arm behind him and twists his wrist firmly as his back bucks in pain. Other officers rush to further subdue him and remove a knife from his other hand, which she had not seen.

Two other suspects are captured as they attempt to leave through an upper-story bedroom window. The all-clear signal is given and Angela feels herself sigh and breathe deeply, not recognizing that she had been holding her breath for an interminably long time. While the muscles of her arms and back relax, she notices the still loud pounding of her heart and the feeling of her toes throbbing from the pulse. She feels giddy and wonders if anyone sees her steady herself by touching the wall on the way down the hall and stairs.

Driving back to the station, Angela feels exhilarated. The seatbelt feels awkward and constraining, and she wants to move while she talks. Her voice is fast and loud, but so is her partner's and it does not matter right now. She and her partner relive each instant as if they were replaying the decisive moments of a football game. She notices some tension remaining in her upper back and moving into her neck, and wonders whether she will have a tension headache before the night is over.

Back at the station the replays continue for the next hour, as other officers add to the unfolding story. Angela has showered and changed, but notices that she is still perspiring. Slightly limping, she also has noticed a large, painful bruise starting to spread on her knee and wonders where she got it. Looking in the mirror, she holds out her fingers and notices the tips still trembling. She makes fists trying to regain steadiness, but they continue shaking.

Going to her car, Angela scans the parking lot. Even though it is a police lot, she cannot yet reduce her vigilance. Driving home, she anticipates other drivers more than usual. She missed dinner and wonders why she does not feel hungry yet. She feels high and wonders how long it will take her to get to sleep. She notices the tension in her back moving more into her neck and the beginnings of a headache. She thinks of where the aspirin is located and a good book she has put off reading.

The book is interesting, but Angela finds images of the bust intruding into her concentration. Before falling asleep two hours later after much restlessness, she has replayed the scenario repeatedly in her mind. She thinks of the knife she had not spotted and what might have happened. Each time, her heart beats faster, adrenalin pumps through her body, and her muscles tighten again just as they did in the situation. For two of the next three nights she has a recurrent dream in which the scenario is replayed in various ways. It fades over the next week and does not return. Angela is over this stress reaction and prepares for the next inevitable one.

The function of the stress reaction is to prepare an officer for action. Within certain boundaries, this has strong survival value. If the arousal did not occur, the vigilance, strength, and disregard of pain so necessary for coping with violence would not be available. In contrast, overreaction of the stress response may produce unwanted side effects such as excessive anxiety or panic attack.

A further complication in the stress response is that the body cannot tell the difference between negative and positive stressors; the body reacts to both the same way. For example, when you finally make a solid arrest on a particularly elusive case, receive a commendation or promotion, win a marksmanship competition, or experience any other positive event, your body interprets the change in the same way it would a negative event. This makes a stress reaction particularly unexpected and confusing to officers who believe that they should be experiencing stress symptoms only after negative circumstances. All changes require you to adjust your physiology, feelings, thoughts, and behaviors in some way. Table 3-1 lists the major signs and symptoms of stress.

The Yerkes–Dodson Law (Yerkes and Dodson, 1908) was one of the first formulations about the relationship between the level of stress and its effects. Their research concluded that very low or very high levels of stress were both debilitating, while moderate levels of stress enhanced alertness, motivation, and performance. The Canadian stress researcher, Hans Selye (1976), concurred much later, emphasizing that the purpose of stress management was not to eliminate stress, but to control it so that an optimal level of arousal is present.

Selye (1976) also described three stages of reaction called the *general adaptation syndrome* (GAS). It refers to a collection of physiological signs (syndrome) as the generalized arousal of the body helps adapt to the stressor.

TABLE 3-1   SIGNS AND SYMPTOMS OF STRESS

Activation of the sympathetic nervous system produces the following:

Heart rate increase
Blood pressure increase
Large muscle groups tense
Adrenaline rush
Increased blood sugar
Hypervigilance
Pupils dilate
Increased hearing acuity
Increased blood clotting
Increased metabolism
Blood flow increases to heart, lungs, and large muscles
Perspiration, especially to palms
Digestive secretions slow
Dry mouth due to saliva decrease
Bowel activity decreases
Extremities become cool
Sphincters tighten
More white blood cells enter the bloodstream
Cholesterol remains in the blood longer
Dilation of the lung passages and increased respiration

Stage 1: Alarm

The alarm or acute stage of the GAS often comes as a shock to the body as the stressful situation initially affects the person. Normal functioning is lowered as the person begins to orient to the source of stress and mobilize a response. This stage is often observed in victims of crime or accidents who seem dazed, confused, and disoriented. To them, the situation may seem unreal or dreamlike. Thinking is often slow and labored, and coordination is poor. They may not notice that they have been injured or feel the pain. Usually, this period is fairly brief, often only seconds, but under conditions of severe shock it can last for hours or, rarely, days. If the defensive reactions that are mobilized by this stage are successful, the body can return to normal and the alarm is over.

Stage 2: Resistance

If the stress continues, during the resistance or recovery stage remarkable resources are mobilized for a full-scale emergency. The senses, strength, and alertness are all enhanced and prepared to be used in the fight–flight response. Officers in foot pursuit of a suspect often experience this stage, when they use speed and strength they did not think possible. There are occasional reports of officers exhibiting exceptional feats of strength in this stage such as tearing doors off a car on fire to extract a passenger. This high level of optimal functioning cannot be maintained for long periods of time, although a high level of general arousal may persist for weeks or even months.

Stage 3: Exhaustion

If the officer does not take time out to recover from the stress, eventually all the adaptive resources will be used, resulting in exhaustion, collapse, or even serious physical or emotional illness. In some cases when the fight–flight system has been overused, it rebounds and activates the relaxation response. This accounts for incidents of accidental urinating, soiling, or sleeping when the stressful nature of the situation should be eliciting just the opposite response.

In moderate cases of exhaustion, most people experience fatigue and may eventually collapse. During this final stage, attention and concentration are poor, reasoning and judgment are slow and perhaps illogical, and moods become unsteady.

It becomes clear that, without recognizing stress and taking corrective action, an officer may eventually become incapacitated, experience serious health consequences, or become a risk to others due to diminished alertness, judgment, and skill. The following example of the effects of stress on an officer points up the fact that an assignment as a dispatcher, which is sometimes seen as "light duty," is anything but light.

CASE EXAMPLE

Officer Wotczak had been recently hired and assigned dispatch duty partly because of his prior medical rescue background. The crises of the Saturday night shift had been routinely handled until about 1:00 A.M. when an auto accident was reported. The incident involved an infant in the back seat who was severely injured. Wotczak's background had prepared him to take action—not to sit in a location remote from the accident and talk to officers at the other end.

He began to think of all the potential problems and complications, how he might have to communicate all these to the attending officers, their limited medical experience, and the probable death of an infant. He began stuttering. At first there was stuttering at the beginning of words, then repeated and confused pronunciations—finally silence. He froze with self-consciousness, feeling overwhelmed with so many options and so little control and being unable to act himself. After several sessions of counseling, he was able to resume active duty, but was not again assigned to dispatch.

It is important to recognize that not all stressors are necessarily traumatic. Many events are to be expected in the normal course of development in life. Holmes and Rahe (1967) devised an inventory of stressful life events in the general population that vary widely in severity of the stressor. We have introduced this scale in Chapter 2, and the reader should review the scale at this time. The scale rates death of a spouse as the most stressful, incurring 100 points, while minor violations of the law (e.g., parking tickets) are assigned only 11 points. Some of these life changes occur when graduating from school, changing employment, or moving to shift work. A total score of more than 300 points suggests about an 80% chance of developing symptoms of stress reaction within the year, while 150 to 300 points reflect a 50% chance, and less than 150 points only a 30% chance. The scale, however, does not take into account one's style, stress-management skills, or social support system, all of which may modify the results. In the experience of one of the authors (Swenson), a particularly resilient military policewoman experienced from 600 to 1400 points annually over a 6-year period before she finally succumbed to stress.

Other researchers (Kanner et al., 1981) argue that daily hassles may exact an even more subtle and insidious toll on health. Hassles refer to everyday irritations, frustrations and pressures, which can include misplacing car keys, spilling coffee, breaking a pencil lead, broken shoelaces, and constant interruptions. This conception of stress recognizes the cumulative nature of minor stressors that can result in stronger stress effects on health than major life changes might have.

❖ NUTRITION AND STRESS PHYSIOLOGY

Most people are more careful about what they put in the gas tanks of their cars than what they eat. While nutritional research is often inconsistent and still incomplete regarding what is considered the perfect diet, some general observations can be made that might increase your stress resistance.

Under stress, most people tend to lose their appetites and eat less, eat irregularly, and eat poorer quality of food. This means a significant decrease from the typical 1800 calories for men and 1400 calories required for women to maintain normal activity, let alone during a stressful period. In addition, vitamins B and C are depleted by stress (as well as air pollution such as from traffic exhaust). Combining this with the fewer digestive enzymes and decreased absorption of nutrients, it is remarkable that the body can function at all during high stress because of energy depletion.

After 24 hours of sustained stress, the blood sugar reserves become reduced to produce mild hypoglycemia (low blood sugar), resulting in depressed and fatigued feelings. There is reduced blood pressure and flow to the kidneys, which results in sodium retention, which contributes to high blood pressure. The urine that is passed contains zinc as a trace element, which is why the taste of food diminishes during stress and wound healing is slower. Iron is excreted, which can decrease hemoglobin, increase fatigue, and make you look pale and become more susceptible to infections. Magnesium is also passed, which affects the utilization of carbohydrates, again lowering energy reserves.

While this sounds grim, there are several things that you can do to bolster your stressed nutritional system. Many people resort to artificial means to regain temporary functioning. They take caffeine or over-the-counter stimulants to remain alert, take large doses of vitamins to replace depleted resources, or gulp down messy concoctions of condensed liquid vitamins or "power" bars. Unfortunately, these measures seldom work, or work for long, and can further strain the system. For example, caffeine can increase irritability and interfere with sleep; vitamins A and D are fat soluble and can be stored in the body to toxic levels; high doses of vitamins C and B have been shown to be related to kidney problems and nerve damage; and condensed "food" seldom provides the proper balance or texture required by a healthy body.

The recommendations are plain and simple. Here are the *do's* and *don'ts* to follow during a stressful period:

DO'S:

1. Drink plenty of water during stressful periods. Normally, drink a quart per day, but a half-gallon per day during stress.
2. Eat a balanced diet of fresh foods including fruits, vegetables, and grains.
3. Maintain an exercise program to help maintain your appetite and encourage the body to store and metabolize calcium and protein.

DON'TS:

1. Decrease your artificial sugar intake since it provides no nutrition and can use up energy reserves to digest it.

2. Decrease salt intake since it may add to the already high blood pressure.
3. Limit or stop alcohol consumption during stressful periods since it is an empty calorie nutritionally and interferes with sleep and judgment.
4. Limit caffeine (including tea, coffee, chocolate, some soft drinks, and some medications like headache and PMS remedies.)

❖ LONG-TERM STRESS EFFECTS

When stress is experienced beyond the person's ability to cope, the level of emotional tension may become somaticized or expressed through physical symptoms. Although the term *psychosomatic* has come to mean imagined illness in layperson's terms, it technically refers to the transformation of emotional stress into physical illness.

Vulcano, Barnes, and Breen (1984) conducted a study of 571 Canadian police officers in which they found an incidence of psychosomatic symptoms higher than for the general population. The symptoms included nervous stomach and stomachaches, constipation, ulcers, colitis, indigestion, diarrhea, headaches, high blood pressure, and asthma. A high incidence of psychosomatic symptoms was also shown by Reiser and Geiger (1984) in their study of officer's posttraumatic reactions to shootings.

There is a story about a frog that fell into a pot of cool water that was set on a fire. The water was cool at first so the frog was not startled to jump out. As the water began to heat up gradually, the frog continued to adapt to the increasingly warmer water so that the difference was barely noticeable. The story goes that the water continued to heat up as the frog continued to adjust—until the frog was finally cooked!

When the human body is aroused for very long periods of time, it also tends to adjust to more permanent conditions. The idea of *homeostasis*, or balance in the body is similar to a thermostat that gets set higher due to persistently cold weather. The higher temperature becomes the new standard, and it automatically turns on when the temperature, or in this case a stress-activated nervous system, drops below its new set point.

Recalling Selye's GAS, the body's resources tend to "burnout" after long periods of stress exposure. Under repeated exposure to intense stress, the demands on certain organs begins to produce physical changes in them: the adrenal glands, which produce adrenalin, become swollen; thymus and lymph nodes, which promote immune resistance, become smaller; certain types of white blood cells decrease; and the stomach lining becomes inflamed. Although the psychological reasons for certain organ systems to be chosen as the outlet for stress symptoms or illness have been long disputed, the concept is an important one.

As an analogy, consider the systems of the body to be a chain of connections. Each link of the chain represents a different organ system of the body that is connected to the heavy weight of a stressor. When the weight is picked up for a short distance and then dropped, we metaphorically have *frequency* of stress; when it is hoisted to a height and dropped, we have *intensity* of stress; and when we hold it up for a prolonged period, we have *duration* of stress. Under any of these conditions, it is likely that a weakness in some link in the chain will become evident. Perhaps this will be due to a constitutional weakness in the makeup of the chain; perhaps the strain aggravates a weakness caused by previous misuse; perhaps it is just chance. But a weakness develops in some link, some system, and the symptoms produced become apparent.

The body has a remarkable degree of strength and resilience in its systems. To say that stress can burn out a system sounds ludicrous after hearing some of its capacities. For example, the heart, which is the size of a fist and weighs less than a pound, circulates blood through about 60,000 miles of blood vessels in the human body in less than a minute. About 2,000 gallons of blood are pumped per day and about 55 million gallons in a lifetime!

Yet, despite it resources, the heart has its limits. For every pound of extra fat, another 2,300 feet of extra vessels are needed. The effort needed to push blood the extra distance makes the heart work harder and increases blood pressure. With every decade over age 30, the heart's ability to pump decreases 6 to 8 percent, blood pressure increases 5 to 6 percent, and blood vessels lose some of their elasticity. Even transient stress increases serum cholesterol, which eventually lays down deposits in the arteries thereby increasing blood pressure and the potential for blocking even more. In one study of 7,000 males (Tucker, Cole, and Friedman, 1987), the level of serum cholesterol was found to be more related to the perception of problems rather than the presence or nature of the problems themselves. It appears that "what we think, is what we get."

The connections between work stress, high blood pressure, and coronary heart disease (CHD) are well established: The more times a day blood pressure becomes elevated, the more it tends to stay there and become the new set point. Chronic high blood pressure affects over 35 million Americans, but frequently goes undetected (25%) because it does not present symptoms until late in its development. The incidence is higher among Afro-American women (39.8%) and Afro-Americank males (28.3%) than whites (about 20%).

Normal blood pressure is about 120/80. The first number (120) represents the systolic pressure in the arteries as the pulse of blood surges through with the heartbeat. The second number (80) is the diastolic and is probably more important, since it reflects the residual tension after the pulse. When the dual pressures exceed 140/90, or the borderline range, the condition is said to be *hypertensive*. The long-term effects of chronic hypertension include increased risk of stroke, atherosclerosis (fatty deposits building up on the arterial walls), arteriosclerosis (hardening of the arteries), kidney disease and damage, broken blood vessels in the eyes, and heart attack. Advances in antihypertensive medical therapy have been very successful and early diagnosis and treatment are important. Behavioral methods of self-regulation (e.g., meditation, yoga, biofeedback, and relaxation techniques) have been helpful but must be adopted into a regular daily routine.

❖ HEADACHES

Headaches are probably one of the most common forms of physical complaint. Some studies indicate that as much as 90% of the general population suffers from them (Falletta, 1986), and over 25 million people suffer from recurrent headaches (Veninga and Spradley, 1981). Most are stress related and can be caused by muscle tension or increased blood flow. Muscle tension headaches are usually experienced in the temples, forehead, or back of the head and neck. When the muscles contract, the blood supply to the surrounding muscles is squeezed and the tissues do not get sufficient oxygen. As a result, they release pain-inducing chemicals that send the pain message to the brain.

These contraction headaches are most often due to emotional stress involving muscular tension (e.g., frowning, sustained readiness for action), maintained poor posture (e.g., over a steering wheel or desk), or eye strain. Some of the techniques for preventing or reducing headache pain are summarized in the accompanying box on Coping with Tension Headaches.

Blood-flow or migraine-type headaches are somewhat different. The arteries of the brain look like the detailed branching of a tree and are actually called the vascular tree. As noted in the discussion on blood pressure, there is a residual tension in the blood vessels. When a person is under stress, the vessels are constricted in order to move blood faster to the areas that need it. Correspondingly, most people do not experience vascular headaches while under stress.

It is when the stress is relieved, for example, when taking a vacation, getting off shift, or completing a demanding case, that the blood vessels begin to

TABLE 3-2   COPING WITH TENSION HEADACHES

Do neck and head rolls to the sides, up, and down several times during the day to stretch contracted neck muscles.

Start and stay with a regular exercise program that can help release residual tension.

Learn effective techniques for relaxation and keeping a low level of arousal: yoga, meditation, progressive relaxation, biofeedback, and self-hypnosis are examples.

Choose chairs, head rests, pillows, and other furniture that assist with proper support and posture.

Take brief and frequent stretch breaks from your work station or patrol car.

Be aware of your stress level so that you can keep it under control by using effective techniques.

TABLE 3-3   POSSIBLE ALLERGENIC FOODS

Meats and fish: liver, pickled herring, dried sausage, aged beef, hot dogs, bacon, smoked ham, salami, anchovies

Dairy products: aged or strong cheeses, sour cream

Beverages: beer, wine (especially red wines), coffee (excessive amounts), brandy, champagne

Other foods: chocolate, nuts, ripe bananas, citrus fruits, fava beans, olives, raisins, Chinese foods (due to MSG additives), steak and seasoned sauces, peanut butter, heavily salted foods

relax. In fact, they relax too much; they rebound in parasympathetic response and become engorged with blood as they dilate. The throbbing, pounding headache of vascular headache sufferers comes from the pulse surging through the enlarged cranial vessels.

There can be additional triggers to headaches, especially vascular headaches. Diet may influence the onset of some headaches (see Table 3-3) for some people who may have very sensitive or allergic systems. Environmental substances such as smoke or volatile fumes (e.g., paint, gas, chemical odors), too much or too little sleep, or emotional stress can cause vascular headaches.

❖ MUSCULAR RESPONSE

When muscles become tense for prolonged periods of time, they tend to remain contracted. This "bracing" (Brown, 1977) for action can eventually become a bodily expression of one's attitude of defensiveness or readiness to react to threat. It can also be the result of competitive, angry, or apprehensive feelings. While at first this may sound like a reasonable way to stay prepared, tight muscles actually interfere with rapid response. The continuing tension can also produce tension headaches, muscle stiffness and aching, cramps, fatigue, and backache (Holmes and Holmes, 1970).

Muscular tension can also occur in the temporomandibular joint where the lower jaw hinges to the upper jaw. This complex joint composed of several muscles and ligaments can develop problems—temporomandibular joint syndrome (TMJ). Although it can develop due to malocclusion of the teeth, nail biting, pipe smoking, blow to the head, and gum chewing, it most often develops due to clenching or grinding the teeth due to stress. The range of TMJ symptoms can include ringing in the ears, dizziness, earaches, migraine headaches, facial pain, and popping or clicking sounds when the mouth opens and closes. Estimates of TMJ vary from 28% to 86% in the general population, depending on the severity of symptoms (Henig, 1988).

❖ THE IMMUNE RESPONSE

One of the most complicated and sophisticated systems in the body is the immune system. Its function is to reduce the body's susceptibility to infection and disease. When invasion by a foreign substance occurs, a series of defensive actions occurs in which the invader is identified, antibodies are produced, and inflammation occurs where the battle occurs. T-lymphocytes or T-cells are produced by the thymus gland and fight bacterial and viral infections, as well as cancer cells and fungi.

Although the immune system was thought to be relatively independent of the rest of the body, recent evidence shows that, like the rest of the body, it is sensitive to regulation by the brain (Ader, 1983; Locke, 1982). Even daily mood has been found to be related to fluctuations of immune system indicators (Stone et al., 1987). The hypothalamus and pituitary glands in the brain produce substances that affect the adrenal glands, which in turn produce hormones that stimulate the immune system. Unfortunately, the adrenals also produce some hormones (especially cortisol, related to cortisone) that tend to suppress T-cells. Consequently, over a stressful period, resistance to infections and diseases decreases and the person may have increased susceptibility to colds and flu. There is also evidence that prolonged stress impairs the production of natural killer cells that destroy cancer cells (Shavit et al., 1984).

When special antibodies combat the invading antigens in the body, the rupture of two types of blood cells results in the production of toxic substances into the bloodstream. Histamine is one of these products and is commonly recognized as the swelling reaction that occurs around poison ivy infection. Stress can also induce the release of histamine that may produce an allergic response evident in hives, hay fever, breathing congestion, and even asthma.

❖ THE STRESS SYMPTOM CHECKLIST

The checklist given in Table 3-4 is not intended to be inclusive of all stress symptoms, nor should it substitute for a thorough and professional assessment of reaction to stress. However, an occasional check of your stress symptoms can alert you to potential concerns that may require attention. Many of these symptoms are broadly experienced by the general population at some time. Other symptoms may be indicators of serious conditions and should be immediately checked (e.g., blurred vision or chest pains). Consider these symptoms an early warning system that not all is well with the body in its reaction to stress. You need to attend to these symptoms and the stressful conditions that are producing them.

❖ HOW STRESS-MANAGEMENT TECHNIQUES WORK

Hundreds of techniques have been used by people in various jobs across different cultures that have had some success in reducing the symptoms of stress. Unfortunately, no one technique seems to work for everyone. Nonetheless, these

TABLE 3-4   STRESS SYMPTOMS CHECKLIST

Trouble getting to sleep or staying asleep	Constipation
Nightmares	Nausea, upset stomach
Feeling anxious and tense	Vomiting
Pulling or twisting hair	Appetite increase or decrease
Sweating (when not exercising)	Weight loss/ or gain
Blurred vision	Increase in use of alcohol or medications
Skin rash	Upper respiratory colds
Irregular menstruation	Shortness of breath
Restlessness	Difficulty breathing
Itching	Memory blanks
Biting nails	Rush of ideas
Shaking or trembling	Day dreaming
Chest pains	Confusion
Impatience	Poor concentration
Irritability	Indecisive
Thoughts of hurting others	Worrying
Feeling inferior to others	Persistent instrusive thoughts
Feeling unattractive	Feeling impending danger
Feeling lonely	Desire to escape or hide
Decreased interest in social activities	Feel tight bands around head or body
Blaming self	Sense of choking or tightness in throat
Oversleeping	Numbness in parts of the body
Awakening too early in morning	Muscular weakness in part of the body
Grinding teeth	Decreased sex interest
Tightness in jaw	Feeling guilt, shame, or embarrassment
Tension headaches	Thoughts of death or suicide
Muscular stiffness and aches	Fatigue, lack of energy
Nervous tics and mannerisms	Apathy
Cold hands or feet	Lack of pleasure in things
High blood pressure	Feeling depressed
Racing heart or palpitations	Crying spells
Dizziness or light headedness	Feel trapped
Diarrhea	Future looks hopeless

techniques have certain aspects in common that interfere with the stress response.

The primary way in which stress-management techniques work is to turn off the sympathetic nervous response and activate the parasympathetic or relaxation response. This allows the activation systems to take a rest and the body to recover its energy through regular appetite, digestion, sleep, and rest. Attention is also redirected from the stressor to some less problematic focus. Finally, use of a technique permits the person to feel a sense of control over reactions, time, and tasks that may not have been possible during the stressful situation.

Most people have unfortunately become experts at scanning their inner or external environment looking for cues that trigger a stress response. For example, we experience impatience as we drive behind very slow drivers, watch clocks in anticipation of something, and notice muscle tension as anxiety increases. The problem is that this kind of expertise in noticing things that make us tense has not allowed equal time to attend to cues that tell us to relax. We have become very skilled at unconsciously getting tense, and are relatively inexperienced and unskilled in learning how to release the tension in the body and chatter in the head.

As an effective stress-management technique is practiced and becomes adopted into your life-style as a beneficial habit, you lower your threshold of awareness to stress. That is, you become more aware of it, rather than less aware. However, rather than suffering longer from prolonged awareness and exposure, the awareness leads to automatically turning on the relaxation response. Even after an intense stress (e.g., domestic violence, high-speed chase, or shooting), it is possible to rapidly regain control over your stress physiology.

Biathletes provide an excellent example of self-regulated stress. They must race on cross-country skis for several miles and then compete in marksmanship at several designated sites during the race. This kind of activity requires intense physical exertion followed by equally intense quieting response and concentration. Biathletes accomplish this most often by using a combination of biofeedback-facilitated relaxation and meditation or self-hypnosis to develop skill in self-regulation. As a result, they arrive at the shooting site and immediately slow the heart, respiration, and muscle tension to where they can aim and shoot between the slower heart beats!

The specific instructions for practicing relaxation and mind-quieting techniques will be described in detail in Chapter 17.

SUMMARY

This chapter has described your early warning system—your body's reaction to stress. You may experience and display stress symptoms through your physiology, expression of feelings, cognition, and behavior. These reactions may be subtle and minor or serious and potentially debilitating. Stress progresses through several stages, but can be reduced or redirected by applying appropriate stress-management techniques. These techniques work by interrupting the arousal of the sympathetic nervous system and activating the relaxing influence of the parasympathetic nervous system. A well-balanced diet can provide needed energy to help resist stress, whereas inadequate nutrition can weaken resistance and even add to the stress reaction. Prolonged stress has been linked to a variety of chronic or life-style diseases, such as high blood pressure and coronary heart disease.

QUESTIONS

1. Think of a time when you were intensely stressed. What were the signs and symptoms you noticed in yourself?

2. Did you have secondary reactions to your primary symptoms? For example, did you feel worried or anxious if you felt stomach or chest pains? What other secondary reactions have you experienced?

3. Make a list of your meals for the last few days, including snacks. If you were under stress, what would the effects of this diet be on your already stressed system?

4. Freeze! Right now as you are reading this! Quickly scan your body for tensions, imbalances in posture, and unnecessary bracing. Now, readjust your posture and relax as much as possible while still remaining upright and alert. Experiment with this at other times during your normal workday.

REFERENCES

Ader, R. (1983). Developmental psychoneuroimmunology. *Developmental Psycholobiology* 16, 251–267.

Akerstedt, T., and L. Torsvall (1985). Napping in shift work. *Sleep 8(2)*, 105–109.

Brown, B. B. (1977). *Stress and the Art of Biofeedback.* New York: Harper & Row, p. 28.

Cannon, W. B. (1932). *The Wisdom of the Body.* New York: W. W. Norton.

Falletta, B. A. (1986). *Headaches.* Springhouse, PA: Springhouse.

Henig, R. M. (February 9, 1988). The jaw out of joint. *Washington Post,* Health, p. 16.

Holmes, T. H., and R. H. Rahe (1967). The social readjustment rating scale. *Journal of Psychosomatic Research, 11,* 213–218.

Holmes, T. S., and T. H. Holmes (1970). Short-term intrusions into life-style routine. *Journal of Psychosomatic Medicine, 14,* 121–132.

Kanner, A. D., J. C. Coyne, C. Schaefer, and R. S. Lazarus (1981). Comparison of two modes of stress measurement: Daily hassles and uplifts versus major life change events. *Journal of Behavioral Medicine, 4,* 3.

Locke, S. E. (1982). Stress, adaptation, and immunity: Studies in humans. *General Hospital Psychiatry 4,* 49–58.

Reiser, M., and S. P. Geiger (1984) Police officer as victim. *Professional Psychology: Research and Practice, 15(3),* 315–323.

Rosa, R. R., M. J. Colligan, and P. Lewis (1989). Extended workdays: Effects of 8-hour and 12-hour rotating shift schedules on performance, subjective alertness, sleep patterns, and psychosocial variables. *Work and Stress, 3(1),* pp. 21–32.

Selye, H. (1976). *The Stress of Life.* New York: McGraw-Hill.

Shavit, Y., J. W. Lewis, G. W. Terman, R. P. Gale, and J. C. Liebeskind (1984). Opiate peptides mediate the suppressive effect on natural killer cell cytotoxicity. *Science 223*, 188–190.

Stone, A. A., D. S. Cox, H. Valdinarsdottir, L. Jandorf and J. M. Neale (1987). Evidence that secretory IgA antibody is associated with daily mood. *Journal of Personality and Social Psychology 52*, 988–993.

Tepas, D. I., and R. P. Mahan (1989). The many meanings of sleep. *Work and Stress 3(1)*, 93–102.

Tucker, L. A., G. E. Cole, and G. M. Freeman (1987). Stress and serum cholesterol: A study of 7000 adult males. *Health Values 11*, 34–39.

Veninga, R. L., and J. P. Spradley (1981). *Work stress connection*. Boston: Little, Brown.

Vulcano, B. A., G. E. Barnes, and L. J. Breen (1984). The prevalence of psychosomatic disorders among a sample of police officers. *Social Psychiatry 19(4)*, 181–186.

Yerkes, R. L., and J. D. Dodson (1908). The relation of strength of stimulus to rapidity of habit formation. *Journal of Comparative and Neurological Psychology 18*, 459–482.

4

❖

Conflicting Demands
of Law Enforcement

Officer patrols a jogging trail following a recent daylight slaying on the trail.
(Photo from the files of the *Columbia Missourian*)

❖ OBJECTIVES

1. To discuss the conflicting demands placed on law-enforcement officers.
2. To illustrate how these demands place special stresses on officers.
3. To show how these demands change or modify the personalities of law enforcement personnel.

❖ INTRODUCTION

Law-enforcement work is unique in that it often calls on the officer to behave in two conflicting ways within a short period of time. To do a good job demands two personalities for the price of one. The behavior of an officer toward a citizen when that officer is engaged in routine public service work or while helping someone who has a medical emergency can be expected to differ markedly from the same officer's behavior while engaged in contact with someone who has just committed a crime.

For example, at 10:30 P.M. Officer McIntire receives a call from a motorist who is locked out of her car. When he arrives, he finds a very embarrassed lady, who apologizes for the inconvenience. By both his body language and the tone of his voice, McIntire conveys that he is helpful and friendly.

After he gets back in his car, he receives a call from a halfway house for young felons to quiet a disturbance. When he arrives, he is greeted with name calling and insults by one of the residents, who appears to be drunk. Several other men are standing back, but seem to be egging him on. At this point McIntire makes eye contact with the man making the disturbance, moves just outside what he thinks will be the man's critical attack distance, places his hands on his hips and in a command voice asks him, "What seems to be the problem here?" By his body posture and tone of voice he conveys to the man that he will do whatever is necessary to bring him back into line.

The major proportion of most officers' time is spent doing a variety of community services, and only about 30% of the work is directly related to law breaking, requiring that the officer use the full role of authority the law provides. For example, Scott (1981) analyzed over 26,000 calls for police services from 24 police departments. In descending order of frequency, the calls were for: citizen wants information 21%, nonviolent crimes 17%, assistance 12%, public nuisances 11%, traffic problems 9%, citizen wants to give information 8%, interpersonal conflict 7%, suspicious circumstances 5%, medical assistance 3%, dependent persons 3%, internal operations 2%, and violent crimes 2%.

An early source of stress for young officers may come from the fact that they joined the department because they wanted to support law and order, only to find that they are expected to provide less glamorous human services. Instead of arresting and helping to convict felons, they spend most of their time in such tasks as locating and rescuing pets, unlocking cars, delivering messages, and leading parades, all the while acting in a considerate, friendly manner.

❖ POLICE PERSONALITY CHARACTERISTICS

To do both crime control and investigation and the public service roles required by law-enforcement work calls for an unusual combination of personality characteristics. Based on our observations of law-enforcement officers, our experience in law enforcement, and a review of the literature we have identified five personality characteristics or traits that we believe to be necessary for the successful performance of the wide variety of duties a law-enforcement officer is expected to carry out. These personality characteristics are (1) emotional restraint, (2) emotional expressiveness, (3) group cohesiveness, (4) independent style, and (5) realistic orientation (Kunce and Anderson, 1988).

Emotional restraint.   The professional police officer must be able to control anger when confronting an offender to make certain he does not go into a rage when verbally abused (Eldefonson, 1973; Gibson, 1982; Hogan, 1971; Levy, 1967). This does not mean that officers do not on occasion meet a situation where their controls break down, as in the Rodney King episode in Los Angeles. But this is not a routine reaction, and most officers most of the time keep their emotions under control, even when confronted with cursing, spitting, fighting, or assorted other insults.

For example, Officer Lewis gets called to a domestic disturbance about two in the morning. As he approaches the house, he can see through the window the man of the house beating his wife. Entering the house, officer Lewis identifies himself as a police officer and orders the man to stop. The man tells him to get the hell out of his house—he can take care of his own wife. The man keeps striking the woman. Officer Lewis feels a strong sense of concern for the woman, especially as she resembles his own wife. A rage rises up in Lewis, and he pulls the man off the woman and shoves him against the wall. The man then kicks Lewis and screams obscenities at him.

Officer Lewis's first impulse is to thump the hell out of the man with his stick and drag him off to jail. At the same time, and in conflict with that impulse, he also feels that his first attempt should be to talk to the man, to try to calm him and see if the situation has any remedy. In some states, of course, there is a built-in remedy in the laws that mandate arrest for domestic violence.

Emotional expressiveness.   Experienced officers usually learn that there is magic in the use of words. If they don't already have a bit of the "gift of gab," they soon learn it as a way of avoiding physical confrontation, settling anxious people down, and dealing with accident victims. An important aspect of work in law enforcement is the ability to talk to people and to be enthusiastic (Muir, 1977; Gibson, 1982).

For example, Sergeant Briscow is called to a fight outside of the Silver Bullet, a bar known for brawls. When he approaches, he sees two men arguing loudly and swinging at each other. Briscow learns that one of the men was just notified by his wife that she wanted a divorce. Furious, he jumped in his Ford pickup and came down to the bar to pick a fight with someone. Sergeant

Briscow takes the man aside and in a slow, calming voice tells him he has a right to be angry. Keeping his own breathing slow and controlled, he continues to talk to the man, calming him down and getting him to discuss his options about the divorce. He also reduces the anger by accepting it as a normal response under the circumstances.

Group cohesiveness. The police officer must be able to depend on fellow officers and to follow group norms (Adlam, 1982; Gibson, 1982). A law-enforcement officer is very much a part of a team, and later we will see how anything bad that happens to one officer creates stress in other officers. One of the biggest shots of adrenaline an officer is likely to get is in response to the call, "Officer down."

For example, Patrolman Olson is called to back up another officer who called for assistance at a local park. He arrives to find Officer Tangell arguing with a motorcyclist whom he intends to a arrest for DWI. Two other motorcyclists stand to the side looking on. Noticing his backup has arrived, Tangell moves to handcuff the man. The biker strikes at Tangell's face, there is a burst of blood from his nose, and he drops to the ground. Olson rushes at the biker, throws his shoulder into his stomach, and knocks him to the ground. He begins cuffing the biker when Olson notices the other two bikers surrounding him and moving in. Officer Olson talks the other bikers down while Tangell gets off the ground and regains control of the situation.

When Officer Tangell became temporarily disabled, Olson felt a responsibility for his safety. This immediately caused him to go into action without much consideration for his own welfare. His main commitment was to help a fellow officer. Although in some places the officer involved would have drawn his weapon, in Olson's community to draw your weapon too early is considered by fellow officers a "chickenshit" response.

Independent style. In addition to working well with a team, by the nature of police work the officer should have the ability to be persistent and self-sufficient in carrying out tasks independently (Beutler and O'Leary, 1980; Lawrence, 1984). It is not uncommon for an officer to be called on to take command in a crisis situation.

For example, Officer McKenzie is the first to arrive at the scene of an accident. She observes two vehicles severely mangled and notices a man who appears to be in a daze walking around. She checks both vehicles and finds a man unconscious and bleeding from a head wound in one car and a young girl severely injured in the other. She returns to her car to call for help and notices that cars are beginning to stop and watch the scene, causing another traffic hazard. The man walking around suddenly begins to scream angrily that nobody is helping his injured daughter in the second car. Officer McKenzie is expected to attend to the injured, keep the traffic moving and the crowd under control, and calm down the angry father. Besides being able to take independent action, she needs to have the qualities in the next category, realistic orientation.

Realistic orientation. A logical, practical, and organized style of thinking is important for decision-making skills, as opposed to a creative or impulsive style (Gettinger, 1981; Males, 1983; Pugh, 1986). For example, Detective Schultz comes to the scene of a murder where a man has been shot and killed. He first looks over the room carefully checking for evidence before he touches anything. He records all items that might be evidence in his notes and has pictures taken. There is a bullet lodged in the door sill, which he carefully removes. After finger printing the deceased, he begins to canvas the area for witnesses. His procedures are logical and orderly. They have been developed so that he will not miss any possible evidence, and he is careful not to jump to conclusions without checking out all the possibilities.

❖ CONTRADICTORY REQUIREMENTS OF POLICE WORK

These five characteristics that are seen as important to success in law enforcement pose a set of contradictions or paradoxes in terms of opposite qualities. To do his or her job, the police officer's personality needs to contain contrasting, apparently opposite characteristics.

Emotionally restrained–expressive. The officers should be emotionally restrained while being emotionally expressive. "Don't let them make you blink, convey the idea you've seen it all. You got to be cool." Contrasted with "Smile and be friendly to that little old lady, or show the children that cops are the good guys."

Empathic–firm. Officers must be empathic, yet authoritatively firm. It is expected that police will be able to tune into the feelings of victims and be supportive. At the same time, it is expected that an officer can take control at an accident scene or head off a physical confrontation by the force of his personality.

Group dependent–independent. Officers should be group dependent, but also independent. For example, they should support the team, but be willing to risk disapproval by exerting independent behavior (Beutler and O'Leary, 1980). This duality will be important when police corruption or mistreatment of prisoners is involved. Officers who have to make a choice between being connected with illegal acts as part of the group and standing up for their own moral values can be stressed by the pressure involved.

Boredom–excitement tolerance. Law-enforcement officers must tolerate considerable boredom, but be able to react quickly to crisis. Much of the work is routine and there is very little danger; on the other hand, getting careless can be fatal. An officer might spend 5 hours cruising with no action or calls and be lulled into mild stupor, and then receive a call to a domestic disturbance in which a weapon is involved and every one of his or her senses has to be operating at its peak within seconds.

Work hard–accept failure. An officer must be willing to work very hard to clear cases, but is not supposed to get upset when the courts release offenders.

For example, while on a routine patrol, Officer Cray observes a vehicle being driven recklessly. The vehicle flees when Officer Cray activates his lights and siren. After a chase exceeding 100 miles per hour, the vehicle becomes stuck in mud. Cray chases the suspect down on foot and wrestles him in the mud and puts the cuffs on him. When the suspect is placed in the patrol car, he forces himself to vomit in the back seat and then proceeds to kick the rear window out. Two months later the judge drops felony charges and gives the perpetrator probation. When the perpetrator leaves the courtroom, he looks directly at Officer Cray with a smile and winks.

Patient–stubborn. An officer must have the ability to not give up easily and be patient, but not be stubborn. For example, during an interrogation an officer is expected to be patient and persistent when questioning the suspect while being careful not to engage in any activity that could be labeled harassment.

Suspicious–tolerant. Even the realistic orientation that officers are expected to have can present a paradox because officers tend to change with experience. Most officers become more suspicious of other people's motivations as they deal with the deviousness of citizens. At the same time, after seeing the bad side of humanity, many officers become more tolerant of people's behavior (Adlam, 1982).

Another way of looking at the conflicts of being an officer is given by Muir in his book *Police: Streetcorner Politicians*. Table 4-1 provides a summary of Muir's thinking.

❖ JOB HASSLES

Besides the stress that results from the conflicting demands placed on law enforcement officers, there are also hassles and annoyances happening day to day on the job. Police officers are exposed to dangers that place a burden on their adrenalin systems, and these stresses may have long-term consequences both for their physical health and for changes that take place in their personalities. At this point we present an overview of these hassles, which we explore in more depth later in the chapters in Section II.

TABLE 4-1   INCOMPATIBILITY OF MORAL INJUNCTIONS

On The One Hand	On The Other Hand
Stick to your responsibility.	At one time you are crimefighter, psychiatrist, social worker, minister, doctor—and you're the only one around.
Don't cover a job alone.	Handle your own load; that is, avoid making unnecessary calls to other officers for help.
Deter the incidence of crime.	Don't jack up a neighborhood.
Don't get involved.	You gotta have empathy.
Don't turn an officer into Internal Affairs.	Don't do anything illegal or wrong.
Be firm: don't lose face.	The first thing is, you're nice.
Don't break the law to enforce the law.	Use your discretion.

Source: William K. Muir, *Police: Streetcorner Politicians*. Chicago: University of Chicago Press, 1977, p. 192.

Fear and danger.   Whether police officers admit or talk about it, the day-to-day job of working in law enforcement contains dangerous elements. Weapons are readily available in the community, and the officer approaches many situations in which they might be available. For example, a silent alarm has gone off in a dark building, the officer is approaching a suspicious automobile, or the officer has a call to a domestic disturbance. In any one of these situations, there is the potential for violence. This can and should provoke a defensive fear reaction—fear of serious injury, fear of disability, fear of death. Although the frequency with which serious injury occurs is actually less frequent than it is in other dangerous professions, the unexpectedness of such incidents creates an environment that is emotionally hazardous. As discussed in Chapter 3, the strain of preparing the system for danger time after time has negative effects on the body and the mental health of the officer.

People pain.   The street is full of people suffering and agonized, both physically and mentally. For many officers on the streets, brutality, pain, and death will become normal, usual, and eventually almost routine. No matter how police officers may come to adjust to these conditions, their presence wears away at one's spirit and takes a toll on the officer.

The startle.   Law enforcement has often been characterized as containing much boredom. Depending on the type of city, shift, beat, time of year, and other conditions, periods of boredom do exist. Yet, at almost anytime, a quick response to a particular condition is required, and such a response is jolting to one's physical and mental state. Almost anything can happen anytime, and the unexpectedness of events is very much part of the job.

Consequences of actions.   Law enforcement is a serious business. It is demanding both physically and mentally. Things done well or by the book should pose no problem to the officer. Still, the laws they are asked to enforce are not always supported by the public. In many situations, and frequently in those appearing to be benign or routine, consequences can be severe for even an accidental and unintended mistake. Citizen complaints, disciplinary actions, and civil litigation occur with frequency, sometimes to the point of creating timid behavior among police officers. Sometimes a fear, almost always a concern, the police officer continually must be aware of his actions, their appropriateness, and the possible adverse consequences.

Orders are orders.   In line with the preceding problem is one pointed out by Bouza (1990): officers must carry out orders that may conflict with their values or, if they have no stand on the question, they may be asked to support one policy one time and a different policy a short time later. One day they must arrest abortionists, and the next they are to protect them and arrest those who are interfering with abortion. The officer must enforce laws, not question them, at the same time that he or she must act independently and have considerable discretionary power to arrest or not arrest.

Hostile–friendly.   Brown (1981) suggests another factor that arouses tension in officers and contributes to their change in attitude. In going about their job of protecting people, law-enforcement officers often encounter ambivalence and hostility, rather than appreciation for what they are doing. This rejection of the value of what the officers offer forces them back on each other for support and removes them further from the public that they are commissioned to protect.

This dependence on each other for support in the face of what they see as a hostile, fickle, public creates a bond of solidarity among officers. A part of the police mystique is the wholehearted way in which officers back up and support another officer when needed. Brown feels this bond permits fallible men to perform an arduous and difficult task.

❖ THE EFFECTS OF THESE FACTORS ON OFFICER PERSONALITY

While we may seem to be overemphasizing our point, we believe that work in law enforcement is different from work in other fields. There is more on-the-job excitement, and the officer is brought into contact with the weird, the morbid, the grotesque, and the unusual. Officers encounter aspects of human behavior that other people will likely never see, people who are actively suicidal, people hallucinating, severely injured victims of assault, dead bodies, and the aftermath of disasters. On the job they will have experiences and adventures that will not even make sense to their nonpolice friends. All these experiences bring about the growth of coping skills that allows them to continue to function in this stress-filled environment.

How do police officers handle the dualities and stresses of the job that we have been discussing here? Interviews with officers who have been on the job for years indicate that there are four ways that the pressures of police work affect them (see, e.g., Adlam, 1982; Anderson and Bauer, 1987; Pugh, 1986).

A small minority of officers deny that the work experiences have any effect on them. They feel that they are the same persons now both on and off the job as they were when they started.

A small minority of law enforcement officers feel that they have developed an *on-duty* personality, which they put on when they put on the uniform. This personality is different from their leisure and/or natural personality, and they feel in effect that they are two different people.

The largest group of officers recognize they have been affected by their work experiences and its demands, but have interwoven these new elements into a *core* personality both off and on duty. They are basically the same persons they were, but have some new ways of acting and doing things that they see as different from the way they were.

A small minority go one step further and feel they have been strongly affected by their experiences, and have developed a new personality that extends into off duty life. These individuals are living their role of police officers both on an off duty. In effect, they have a new script by which they run their lives.

What are these major personality changes that these officers are talking about when they say that working in law enforcement has changed them?

1. A law-enforcement officer is in a position of authority; as a result, her or his level of self-confidence and assertiveness gradually increases.

2. There is an emotional hardening or development of a protective shell that insulates them from the disturbing incidents that all officers face from time to time.

3. Because of the element of danger in the job, officers become especially attuned to signs indicating potential violence or law breaking, and they become more suspicious and distrustful.

4. Seeing the worst side of people, law-enforcement officers lose their naiveté and become more cynical. This also makes them more suspicious and distrustful.

5. They then become either more intolerant, bigoted, and punitive or more broad-minded and compassionate. They are not likely to remain middle of the road in their attitudes.

6. Most control of people is done by talking to them. As law-enforcement offices improve their communication skills, they become more manipulative and play mind games with people to see how they will react. Control can become very important to an officer both off and on duty.

SUMMARY

How officers will deal with the stresses of police work depends on the interaction of three major factors, which we have discussed in these first three chapters. First, there is the officers' basic zone of stability or the strengths of personality that he or she brings to the job. Second are the coping skills he or she has learned or developed to deal with the stresses faced.

Finally, there are the stresses themselves. A stressor that at one time may cause little reaction can, under other circumstances, create major problems for the officer. After a relatively quiet week, a domestic disturbance call with a hostile husband may be treated with humor and the man eased out of his negative mood.

On another occasion after a hard week, a bitch of a day with a reprimand from a supervisor, the officer may consciously push the husband into striking him, resulting in a physical confrontation and an arrest for assaulting an officer.

The chapters in Section II will take up specific types of stressors and ways that officers might prepare themselves for stress, or better manage stress after it occurs.

QUESTIONS

1. What do you see as good childhood experiences for someone who is going to make a career of law enforcement?
2. Most police recruits are low in anxiety and hostility. How does that help them adjust to the dualities of the job?
3. As you read the chapter, what was your personal reaction to the fact that you have to act like two different people?

REFERENCES

Adlam, K. R. (1982). The police personality: Psychological consequences of being a police officer. *Journal of Police Science and Administration 10*, 344–349.

Anderson, W., and B. Bauer (1987). Law enforcement officers: The consequences of exposure to violence. *Journal of Counseling an Development 65*, 381–384.

Beutler, L. E., and D. O'Leary (1980). Psychological screening of police candidates. *Police Chief*, August, 38–40.

Bouza, A. V. (1990). *The Police Mystique*. New York: Plenum Press.

Brown, M. K. (1981). *Working The Street: Police Discretion and The Dilemmas of Reform*. New York: Russell Sage Foundation. p. 115

Burbeck, E., and A. Furnham (1985). Police officer selection: A critical review of the literature. *Journal of Police Science and Administration 13*, 58–69.

Eldefonson, E., ed. (1973). *Readings in Criminal Justice*. New York: Collier-Macmillan.

Furcon, J. E., and E. G. Froemel (1973). The relationship of selected psychological tests to measures of police officer job performance in the state of Illinois. Chicago: University of Chicago, Industrial Relations Center. Cited in G. S. Matyuas (1980), *Police Selection and Performance*. Ph.D. Dissertation, University of Missouri—Columbia.

Gettinger, S. (1981). Psychological testing of recruits can screen out the real turkeys. *Police Chief*, March, 29–40.

Gibson, J. (1982). Square pegs in square holes. *Police Review 90*, 1702–1707.

Hogan, R. (1971). Personality characteristics of highly rated policemen. *Personnel Psychology 24*, 679–686.

Kunce, J. T., and W. P. Anderson (1988). Assessment of nonpathological personality styles of policemen. *Journal of Clinical Psychology 44*, 115–122.

Lawrence, R. A. (1984). Police stress and personality factors: A conceptual model. *Journal of Criminal Justice 12*, 247–263.

Levy, R. J. (1967). Predicting police failures. *Journal of Criminal Law, Criminology, and Police Science 58*, 265–276.

Males, S. (1983). *Police management on division and subdivision*. Police Research Services Unit, Internal Publication, p. 168. cited in Burbeck and Furnham (1985).

Muir, W. K. (1977). *Police: Street Corner Politicians*. Chicago: University of Chicago Press.

Pugh, G. M. (1986). The good police officer: Qualities, roles, and concepts. *Journal of Police Science and Administration, 14*, 1–5.

Scott, E. J. (1981). *Calls for Service: Citizen Demand and Initial Police Response*. Washington, DC: U.S. Government Printing Office.

5

Shift Work

Police officer checks the shotgun in her squad car at the beginning of her night shift. (Photo from the *Columbia Missourian* files)

❖ OBJECTIVES

1. To identify the physiological, psychological, and social consequences of shift work.
2. To explore administrative interventions to reduce adverse shift-work effects.
3. To recommend techniques that officers can use to cope more effectively with the stresses of shift work.

❖ INTRODUCTION

It is estimated that about 25% of all workers in the United States have nontraditional schedules (Dunham, 1977), with some manufacturing areas as high as 43% (Owen, 1976). Public service and crisis intervention especially require around-the-clock availability. However, the physiological, psychological, and social requirements imposed by shift work can become additional stressors to police officers, a fact cited in nearly all the literature reviewing law-enforcement stress.

In 1978, the National Institute of Occupational Safety and Health issued a warning that shift work and rotating shifts posed a significant health risk to workers (Colligan et al., 1978). Studies with animals show a range from 5% to 20% shorter life-span associated with weekly time schedule changes (Moore-Ede and Richardson, 1985).

About 20% of shift workers in general, including police officers, resign due to their inability to successfully adapt to rotating shift work (Brusgard, 1975). Some physicians even advise shift-stressed workers to find new jobs during traditional work hours (Frese and Okandek, 1984). For those unable to adjust, but who remain on the job until they reach their breaking point, ill health may persist long after shift work is discontinued.

There are other complications. Horstman (1978) found a positive correlation between the number of nights worked and reported complaints of brutality by officers. A higher incidence of police accidents, as well as civilian accidents, is reported during night shift (O'Neil, 1986). There is also a higher incidence of serious illness and disability among officers on rotating shifts (Tasto and Colligan, 1978; Jacobi, 1975).

❖ THE PHYSIOLOGY OF SHIFT WORK

Like most organisms, humans have a biological clock that regulates periods of activity and inactivity. These 24-hour cycles are called *circadian rhythms*, meaning "about a day." Exposure to light and darkness helps establish physiological cycles, even in blind individuals (Hollwich and Dieckhues, 1971).

The particular organ that appears responsible for this regulation is the suprachiasmatic nuclei, a small cluster of nerve tissue located just above and connected to the point where the optic nerves cross in the brain. Stimulated by nerve impulses resulting from exposure to light and dark, this photosensitive nerve center sets and resets the biological clock. Nearly all the physiological systems of the body participate to some degree in this rhythm: there are variations in blood chemistry, glandular activity, digestion, brain waves, and level of arousal.

Jet lag has many of the same effects as shift work. Lag can occur when crossing three or more time zones, with the result that a person's circadian rhythm is no longer in agreement with periods of light and darkness. Symptoms of jet lag include sleep problems, irritability, loss of appetite, fatigue, and poor memory, which can last for days. Subtle indicators of circadian rhythm, such as temperature, show that it can take up to 5 weeks to readjust regardless of sex or age, although some studies suggest that people over age 40 require somewhat longer (Klein et al., 1972; Klein et al., 1970).

Most shift-work schedules involve 4 to 7 days on and 2 to 4 days off. If the officer strictly adheres to the same sleeping hours both on and off shift week, the body can usually adjust to a new sleep pattern in about a month. Unfortunately, most of the world, including friends and families as well as shopping and recreation, primarily hold to a daytime schedule. Furthermore, night-shift routines affect dating opportunities, marriage and child-care patterns, and eating routines. Inevitably, the night-shift officer will cut sleep short in order to take advantage of daytime activities during off-duty daytime hours. This throws the body's sleep adjustment processes into disorder, and the readjustment period must start all over.

Consider Officer Barry's description of what shift work was like as a new patrol officer:

> The first night I was pretty excited to get started on the new job. There was so much to learn, so many places we checked, people to talk to, that I couldn't have gotten tired. I guess that began to wear off after the third night. I had heard that shift work would be tough but I had no idea. I'd been cheating a bit by staying up during the day and it just caught up with me. I remember feeling spacey, I just couldn't focus, couldn't remember names, places, or things I'd just read. Later, I began to feel jittery and jumpy. Walking around in the fresh air and checking building security helped, but I felt I was going to jump out of my skin when we sat in the patrol car for long. Even when we stopped for dinner, which was really breakfast, I didn't feel like eating, and the coffee just made my stomach worse. I even spilled a cup on myself in the car later, just out of clumsiness. By the end of the night I was beginning to wonder whether I'd made the right decision to hire on. My partner seemed kind of amused with my problem, but he gave me some good advice about adjusting to shift work. I guess it worked cause I'm still here. I don't think I've ever completely adjusted to night shift, but it's not really bad anymore.

❖ NAPPING

Appearing in the battlefield at all times of day and night, Generals MacArthur and Eisenhower had reputations for never requiring sleep. In fact, they had learned to take full advantage of the effectiveness of napping when the opportunity arose. Between 30% and 50% of rotating shift workers in industry confidentially report falling asleep on the job at least once a week —on all shift periods.

The characterization of some people as "night owls" and "day larks" is not folklore. Tepas and Mahan (1989) designed a study in which 2,340 industrial workers were grouped according to whether they worked days or nights and preferred days or nights. The findings indicated that those who worked nights but preferred days had a more difficult time going to sleep and had a greater number of workday naps than did other groups. Those who preferred and worked nights were found to tolerate night work quite well. In another study, Akerstedt and Torsvall (1985) found that, although night-shift workers napped, this discontinued when they were transferred to day work.

When day workers rotate to night shift, sleep averages about 5.5 hours, in contrast to the typical 7 or 8 hours required for adequate sleep (Colligan et al., 1978). Workers on night shift eventually build up a sleep deficit that affects performance. Pitts (1988) studied physicians on night shift and found that individuals with a sleep debt of 3 or more hours showed decreased efficiency in reasoning. Such deficits can result in unintentional brief periods of dozing, or even "micro-sleep" in which the individual may slip in and out of sleep only seconds in duration.

❖ SHIFT SCHEDULES

Shifts generally follow one of two schedules: Three 8-hour shifts (day shift starting at 7 A.M. swing shift at 3 P.M.; and graveyard shift at 11 P.M.) or two 12-hour shifts (starting 7 A.M., and 7 P.M.). Some schedules are fixed and officers are permanently assigned to a shift period; others provide rotation through each shift in an attempt to fairly distribute the inconvenience. A few departments recognize that some individuals prefer days or nights and create a modified permanent shift schedule that includes both permanent and rotation options.

Even when shifts occur during the day, there can be some hardship when nonstandard work periods are set. Many departments have experimented with 12-hour work schedules over a 3- to 4-day period, followed by days off. In one study (Rosa, Colligan, and Lewis, 1989), 8- and 12-hour shift day workers were compared with each other. After a 7-month adaptation period, workers who had the longer days showed decreases in performance and alertness, reductions in sleep, and complaints of disruptions in other personal activities. However, reports of decreased stress from other sources were probably due to the shortened workweek.

Rotating shifts have been instituted in many departments to make shift patterns more equitable. In these cases, an officer may work a particular shift for a period, anywhere from 2 weeks to 3 months, and then move to another shift period. Shifts are usually rotated counterclockwise, although in one department (Freden, Olsson, and Orth-Gomer, 1984) a clockwise rotation was tried. As a result the officers reported increased feelings of well-being, diminished fatigue, and improved sleep.

❖ SLEEP

Adequate sleep is one of the most important requirements for resistance to stress, emotional health, and effective work performance. There are several stages of sleep, each providing different resources for recovery from the day. The deeper stages of sleep (stages 3 and 4 as measured by brainwaves) are necessary for recuperation from physical fatigue. Stage 5 is called rapid eye movement (REM) sleep, after the movement of the eyes that can be seen under the closed lids as a person dreams. It is during stage 5 that individuals recover from mental fatigue. This stage, however, is the one most disrupted by shift work. It is possible for an officer to get "nearly" enough sleep and feel physically refreshed, but still remain mentally fatigued.

Over 60% of night workers have some degree of sleep disturbances, compared with only 11% of day workers. One study (Webb, 1975) noted that as high as 83% of night workers felt "most tired" on the night shift, compared with only 4% of day shifters similarly complaining. Generally, day and evening sleep durations are 2 hours less than night sleep, quality of sleep is poorer, and getting to sleep and staying asleep are difficult. In addition, appetite decreases, and diarrhea and digestive disorders are reported. Some people are more sensitive to various medications taken in the early morning hours.

❖ SOCIAL EFFECTS

The night work force is largely disregarded by general society in planning schedules for recreation, shopping, family activities, school, banking, and other business. With the exception of some restaurants, groceries, and night clubs, most of the rest of the world functions according to a day schedule. This poses special problems to the shift worker, especially on a fixed night schedule. Even on rotating schedules, most officers find it difficult to do anything other than eat and sleep between duties, and reserve other activities for days off. Leisure activities are restricted, there is less participation in voluntary organizations, and less need fulfillment is reported (Frost and Jamal, 1979).

The difficulties of shift stress add to the potential problems of not spending sufficient time with a spouse and family during their day hours. In a study conducted by the Police Foundation, 30% of police divorces were found to be related to stress in the profession, mostly resulting from shift work (Baxter, 1978). Reduced sexual interest as well as mismatch of spouse's energy and alertness levels can result from shift work. Rotating shift schedules especially require the officer and family to regularly carry schedule books and calendars in order to plan ahead so that changing work schedules will not interfere with family activities.

It is difficult for the shift-working parent to attend school functions, birthday parties, sporting events, and daytime family outings when children are most active. Children also find it difficult to understand why a parent must sleep during the day and why they cannot have loud friends over or must play quietly. They may also attempt to manipulate one parent against the other or have trouble understanding why "house rules" are different when the shift parent is home. Parenting requires very close coordination and caring negotiation of roles and rules. Consider agreeing that the parent in charge is the authority, and do not give permission unless you are the one there to supervise the children.

Single officers on fixed night shift frequently find their social life constricted. Meeting people where one lives or at social occasions becomes difficult since they keep different hours. The people met during night-shift hours are often not the kinds of people with whom the officer would like to maintain a close personal relationship. In order to socialize, the officer must compromise daytime sleep, which then requires body-clock readjustment.

Lieutenant Sheila Borman described the effect of shift work on her family life:

> It's difficult being a woman officer anyway, but when you're not around when your husband is home and the kids are growing up, it's really a problem. There weren't many women officers when I started in the department, and a husband just isn't going to join a social or support group made up of police wives! I didn't want to put any strain on our marriage, so I didn't spend much time with other officers after shift or during "choir practice," so I felt even more isolated sometimes. The hardest part was not being there sometimes for the kids when they had a school play or other special event.
>
> They knew I couldn't be there and why, and I accepted it, but I think I always felt guilty. Being an officer is very important to me, I wouldn't change my mind, but I still feel like I missed something with my family.
>
> When I was on rotating shifts we all had to keep little pocket calendars so that every activity could be scheduled ahead. Sometimes it seemed crazy to have to dig through that little book just to see when I could take them to the library or to the park. I misplaced it one time and felt like I'd lost a family heirloom. When I finally got off shift, I didn't have much time or energy to do anything else but eat, sleep, and take care of essentials. I usually waited for my days off to do anything special with my family. That's tough to explain to young kids—even husbands. But we eventually got used to it—most of it.

Officers generally accept shift work as a given requirement for the job and one to which they must adjust. Neither the department nor the officer has control over the periods of inactivity punctuated by urgent response, limited resources, job overload, court duties, or need to intervene at all hours. There are, however, several aspects of shift stress that are within the scope of administrative and personal control.

❖ ADMINISTRATIVE CONSIDERATIONS

1. *Forward rotations.* Clockwise or forward rotations in shift work (e.g., day to afternoon to night) appear to be less stressful on officers than backward rotations (night to evening to day). A reversal of shift by the Philadelphia Police Department resulted in a 40% decrease in patrol car accidents per million miles driven and a 25% decrease in reports of sleeping while on shift work ("Sweetdreams," *Personnel*, February 1990, p. 7).

2. *Permanent schedules.* Fixed work schedules are easier for people to eventually adjust to. In a study of nurses and industrial workers, Jamal (1981) found that fixed-schedule workers were better off than rotating-schedule workers in their emotional adjustment, job satisfaction, and social participation. There was less absenteeism and tardiness, higher satisfaction with the job, a stronger sense of social participation, and indicators of better emotional health than for officers who worked rotating shifts.

3. *Faster rotations.* If shift rotation must occur, administration should be sensitive to the concerns of officers who feel trapped in an incompatible shift. This may be partly remediated by having faster rotations through shifts so that there are fewer eating and sleep difficulties (Williamson and Sanderson, 1986; Knauth and Kiesswetter, 1987). Based on this proposal, an officer should not be on a shift for more than 4 or 5 days in a row. Czeisler et al. (1981) reported that such a schedule resulted in a fourfold decrease in sleep problems, twofold decrease in daytime fatigue, 40% decrease in auto accidents compared with the previous 2 years, 29% increase in alertness, and fivefold increase in satisfaction with work schedules.

4. *Preferences and proportional staffing.* When shifts can be staffed, at least in part, by selection of individuals who prefer days or nights, there is easier adjustment and higher satisfaction. About 61% prefer permanent day work, 27% prefer permanent nights, and 12% prefer rotating shift work (de la Mare and Walker, 1968). In a typical city, the least service calls are received between midnight and 8 A.M. (22%); 33% occur between 8 A.M. and 4 P.M.; and 45% between 4 P.M. and midnight. This service pattern enables administrators to use proportional staffing to distribute officers according to need and shift preference. A brief questionnaire has been developed to identify morning and evening personnel; it is used to select and place officers in their optimal shift (Smith et al., 1988).

   Rural law-enforcement agencies and small municipal departments are often unable to select according to preference of night or day shift. Most often in a department with five officers, all of them prefer a day schedule. This problem is compounded when the chief insists on straight days. This makes proportional staffing almost impossible with such few officers.

5. *Orientation and training.* Provide orientation and training to new or inexperienced shift-work personnel. Acknowledge the potentially serious impact of shift work and the need to take preventive action and develop effective coping skills. Use more experienced officers to share information on techniques that work. Support officers in their attempts to make the workplace environment more stimulating by modifying lighting and decor and using music, exercise equipment, temperature regulation, and access to healthy snacks. The families of officers should also receive orientation on the effects of shift work and encouragement to openly discuss ways in which they can deal constructively with disruption of family activities and routines.

❖ PERSONAL COPING STRATEGIES

1. *Nutritional coping.* Most officers wait until they start work on the new shift to begin adjusting to it. For those who are contending with adjusting to new job duties, safety procedures, and work relationships, this is the worst time to add circadian adjustment. To help in making the initial adjustment to the first days of shift work, there is advice from jet lag research at the Argonne Nationale Laboratory (Ehret and Scanlon, 1983). For 4 days prior to starting the new shift, practice the "feast–fast–feast–fast" eating pattern. This involves alternating a high-protein breakfast and high-carbohydrate dinner with light meals of fruit, salads, juice, and light soups on alternate days. The last fast period is started on the day of the first shift. Coffee can be drunk only between 3:00 and 5:00 P.M. in this regimen.

   While coffee is almost standard issue to night-shift workers, avoid more than four cups during the shift, and avoid caffeine in any form (e.g., caffeinated soft drinks, tea, chocolate, or aspirin) 5 hours before a sleep period. Tobacco in all forms should also be avoided since nicotine acts as a stimulant. Although some officers take alcohol or sleeping aids (e.g., Nytol, Sominex, Sleep-Eze) to help get to sleep, these drugs interfere with the depth and quality of sleep and are not recommended. Too often a well-intentioned officer can become dependent on these over-the-counter medications or use stimulants to counteract the listlessness and sleepiness they cause and become caught in a stimulant–depressant cycle.

   Many night-shift officers complain that their weight gain is due to a primary diet of poor-quality fast food and snacks. Night-shift workers often eat when they are bored or tired. Soda, chips, and candy should be avoided. Eat three regular meals per day of good-quality food that corresponds to breakfast, lunch, and dinner. Munching on healthy and crunchy fruits, vegetables, and nuts (low salt) can also supplement a regular diet, and the crunchiness can help alertness. Light to moderate amounts of high-protein foods may help maintain alertness, while high carbohydrates may produce the opposite effect (Fernstrom and Wertman, 1971).

2. *Light stimulation.* If you are on desk duty, make your environment colorful, bright, and well lit to stimulate and maintain adjustment of your body clock. If you are on patrol in a dimly lit car, be sure to make frequent runs through lit areas. You can also make frequent stops in brightly lit locations such as hospitals, truck stops, all-night restaurants, and parking lots.

In northern climates and during winter, cold weather requires extensive clothing, and there is limited exposure to sunlight even during daytime. Some people can experience moodiness and even serious depression as a result of limited contact with light. During days off and periods where you should be exposing yourself to sunlight to reset your biological clock, spend plenty of time in the sun or in front of bright, broad-spectrum artificial lighting.

Melatonin is a hormonal substance naturally produced by the pineal gland in the brain in response to the normal daily changes in exposure to natural lighting. The substance helps regulate the circadian cycle by facilitating sleep, and there are current trials in using this substance in a medication form to reduce jet-lag symptoms. It may be possible in the future to take a pill at the beginning and end of a shift cycle that will help shift workers adjust their circadian rhythm to the schedule change.

3. *Psychological techniques.* On a four-night shift, talk yourself through it. A difficult time can be made far less problematic when you can place it in a meaningful perspective and see the end of it.

"Night 1 is only the first night, no problem."
"Night 2 is halfway through, I can do it."
"Night 3, only one more to go."
"Night 4, made it. Tomorrow's off!"

Meditation is popularly known as a relaxation method, but it can also be used to reduce the stress of shift work. Practiced for 20 minutes to a half-hour daily, it can reduce high blood pressure, asthma, high cholesterol, sleep disturbances, irritability, and muscle jumpiness (Penn and Bootzin, 1990). It also enables the officer to learn how to detach from or turn off intrusive and disturbing thoughts of stressful events. Many people report requiring less sleep and being able to enter sleep faster as a result of meditation.

4. *Use your cycles.* People are most alert when body temperature is rising. Once adjusted to shift work, monitor temperature with a thermometer to identify alertness cycles. When possible, do complex tasks that require complicated thinking and judgment when temperature is rising; save routine tasks and paperwork when temperature is lowering. Either monitoring your hourly temperature or just keeping track of your hourly energy level can be used to identify these alertness cycles. If you must work during your low periods, experiment with different ways to keep alert, such as exercise, cold water on your face, cold air from an open window, acupressure, interesting conversation, singing, and so on.

Once on a fixed-shift schedule, try to maintain the sleep schedule even on days off whenever possible. Breaking the schedule for even one day of shopping or recreation will mean that some degree of shift readjustment will be reexperienced when returning to work.

5. *Physical activity.* Exercise can be used to increase energy and alertness, balance appetite, maintain fitness, and facilitate sleep. Exercise early in the day to help feel more alert if attending a meeting or court. Cardiovascular exercise is usually recommended in which you perform a rhythmic activity (e.g., running, biking, cross-country skiing, swimming, or stair climbing) for about 30 minutes, at least three times a week, at your target heart rate. Brief moderate-level exercise in the workplace can also provide stimulation that offsets the effects of sedentary desk work and sleep deprivation. Stair climbing (or stepping exercise equipment), stationary bike riding, t'ai chi (martial arts "shadow boxing"), yoga stretching, isometrics, or calisthenics increase oxygenation of the body, increase respiration, open capillaries in muscle, and increase velocity of nerve impulses. Be cautious of prolonged or high-exertion exercise that can actually increase fatigue.

6. *Break napping.* Try napping for a minimum of 10 minutes during breaks and mealtimes. Anything less than 10 minutes and your body treats it as being awake; longer than 30 minutes can interfere with night sleep and leave you feeling tired. If you know you will miss a lot of sleep (e.g., during natural disaster response or surveillance), take a 2-hour nap beforehand to help you to stay alert.

7. *Sound stimulation.* Moderate levels of sound stimulation (e.g., traffic noise, talking, singing, and music) can be used to sustain arousal and partially counteract the effects of sleep loss. The positive effects of sound stimulation are most beneficial near the end of the shift when arousal deficits are at their highest. While sound should not be so high as to mask attention to important cues, a background level of music may be desirable. Music played randomly with varied rhythm, tempo, and instrumentation is more important than constant music with certain melody or words in affecting alertness.

8. *Sleep effectively.* Clearly and consistently structure your sleep schedule and environment. On the drive home in the early daylight hours, wear sunglasses to decrease the biological clock setting and stimulating effect of sunlight. Sleep immediately after a night shift, rather than before it. Intermittent loud noises interfere with adequate sleep, even when the person is not awakened, and noise is more disruptive when attempting to sleep during atypical schedules.

Make the room dark and quiet by hanging blinds and heavy curtains. Some officers who build new homes or additions intentionally add a few more inches of insulation to walls, use thermopane windows, or locate the bedroom in a remote area of the house, knowing the need for extra quiet.

Disconnect or put silencers or light alarms on doorbells and phones. Fans or air conditioners, white sound generators (low-level "whooshing" sound that masks other noises), and ear plugs can also help reduce disturbance.

Encourage family members to avoid using noisy appliances during sleep periods. Use your bedroom only for sleeping and intimacy so that it does not become associated with other activities that distract from rest. Keep sleep time protected and free from intrusion or unexpected activities such as relatives dropping in and ball games outside the bedroom window. Other people expect you to respect their sleeping hours—you can expect the same.

Officers will occasionally be required or volunteer for extended duty due to emergencies, surveillance, or undercover assignments. If you have to go without sleep, working 2 hours more on 3 consecutive days is less stressful than a full loss of 6 hours sleep at one time. However, even if you lose several days of sleep, this "sleep debt" can be almost entirely recovered by extended sleeping in 1 day.

9. *Develop new friendships*. Cultivate family friendships with other shift-working families. This helps develop a feeling of constancy in relationships and provides a social group for sharing activities. It also affords the spouse of the shift officer with a support system of individuals who understand the unique stresses of shift work.

S U M M A R Y

Physiological, psychological, and social costs are imposed on people who have to work nontraditional hours. The stress of shift work is such that some people have to resign their job and go back to working days. Administration can take a number of actions that will lower the problems caused by shift work; among them are forward rotations, permanent schedules, and staffing by officer preference. In addition, officers can use such personal coping strategies as special diet patterns, more light stimulation, increased exercise, napping, and sound stimulation.

Q U E S T I O N S

1. What symptoms have you observed in yourself or others related to extended working hours or shift work?

2. In what ways could the structure of shift work be redesigned so that stressful effects would be lessened?

3. Of the personal coping techniques listed in this chapter, which would you be more likely to use? Which would you want to learn more about?

REFERENCES

Akerstedt, T., and L. Torsvall. (1985). Napping in shift work. *Sleep, 8(2)*, 105–109.

Baxter, D. (1978). Coping with police stress. *Trooper 3 (4)*, pp. 68, 69, 71, 73.

Bocklet, R. (1988). New York City Program a Success: "Steady" Duty Tours Get Enthusiastic Response, *Law and Order*, February, p. 54.

Brusgard, A. (1975). Shift work as an occupational health problem. *Studia Laboris et Salutis (Stockholm) 4*, 9–14.

Colligan, M. J., D. T. Tasto, E. W. Skjei, and S. J. Pelly (1978). *NIOSH Technical Report: Health Consequences of Shift Work*. Washington, DC: U.S. Department of Health, Education and Welfare, National Institute for Occupational Safety and Health.

Czeisler, C. A., M. C. Moore-Ede, and E. D. Weitzman (July 1981). *Sleep–wake, Endocrine and Temperature Rhythms in Man during Temporal Isolation. The Twenty-four Hour Workday*: Proceedings of a symposium on variations in work–sleep schedules. Washington, DC: National Institute for Occupational Safety and Health.

de la Mare, G., and J. Walker (1968). Factors influencing the choice of shift rotation. *Occupational Psychology, 42(1)*, 1–21.

Dunham, R. B. (1977). Shiftwork: A review and theoretical analysis. *Academy of Management Review 2*, 626–634.

Ehret, C., and L. Scanlon (1983). *Overcoming jet lag*. New York: Berkely.

Fernstrom, J. D., and R. J. Wirtman (1971). Brain serotonin content: Increase following ingestion of carbohydrate diet. *Science, 174*, 1023–1025.

Freden, K., I. L. Olsson, K. Orth-Gomer, T. Akerstedt. (1984). The effect of changing police shift rotation from counterclockwise to clockwise on sleep, stomach troubles and cardiovascular risk factors. [*Stress forsknings rapporter*, Jun. No. 1 9 p29.]

Frese, M., and K. Okandek (1984). Reasons to leave shiftwork and psychological and psychosomatic complaints of former shiftworkers. *Journal of Applied Psychology, 69*, pp. 509–514.

Frost, P. J., and M. Jamal (1979). Shift work, attitudes, and reported behaviors: Some associations between individual characteristics and hours of work and leisure. *Journal of Applied Psychology 64*, 77–81.

Hollwich, F., and B. Dieckhues. (1977). Endocrine system and blindness. In J. Carpentier 2nd P. Cazamian, *Night Work: Its effects on the health and welfare of the worker*. Geneva: International Labor Office.

Horstman, P. Consequences of sequential night work. Unpublished paper, 1978.

Jacobi, J. H. (1975). Redoing police stress: A psychiatrist's view. In *Job Stress and the Police Office: Identifying Stress Reduction Techniques*. Proceedings of Symposium, Cincinnati, OH, May 8–9. Washington DC: US Government Printing Office.

Jamal, M. (1981). Shift work related to job attitudes, social participation, and withdrawal behavior: A study of nurses and industrial workers. *Personnel Psychology 34*, 535–548.

Klein, K. E., H. Bruner, H. Holtmann, H. Rehme, J. Stolze, W. D. Steinhoff, and H. M.

Wegmann (1970). Circadian rhythms of pilot's efficiency and effects of multiple time zone travel. *Aerospace medicine 41*, 125.

Klein, K. E., H. M. Wegman, and B. J. Hunt (1972). Desynchronization of body temperature and performance circadian rhythms as a result of outgoing and homegoing transmeridian flights. *Aerospace Medicine 43*, 125.

Knauth, P., and E. Kiesswetter (1987). A change from weekly to quicker shift rotations: A field study of discontinuous three-shift workers. *Ergonomics 30*, 1311–1321.

Moore-Ede, M. C., and G. S. Richardson (1985). Medical implication of shift work. *Annual Review of Medicine*.

O'Neil, P. S. (1986). Shift work. In J. T. Reese and H. A. Goldstein (eds.), *Psychological services for law enforcement*. Washington, DC: U. S. Government Printing Office, pp. 471–475.

Owen, J. J. (1976). The economics of shift work and absenteeism. In P. G. Rentos and R. D. Shepard (eds.), *Shift Work and Health*. Washington, DC: U. S. Government Printing Office.

Penn, P. E., and R. R. Bootzin (1990). Behavioral techniques for enhancing alertness and performance in shift work. *Work and Stress 4(3)*, 213–226.

Pitts, J. (1988). Hours of work and fatigue in doctors. Editorial, *Journal of the Royal College of General Practitioners*, p. 2.

Ritter, A. (1990). Sweet Dreams. *Personnel, 67*, (2), 7.

Smith, C., C. Reilly, and K. Midhiff (1988). Psychometric evaluation of circadian rhythm questionnaires with suggestions for improvement. Paper presented at annual meeting of the American Psychological Association, Atlanta, Georgia.

Stratton, J. (1978). Police stress: An overview. *Police Chief 45(4)*, (April), 58–62.

Swenson, D. X. (1991). Psychological evaluation of police officers: A program report. Unpublished document.

Tasto, D., and M. Colligan (1978). *Health Consequences of Shift Work*. Department of Health, Education, and Welfare (NIOSH) publication 78-154. Washington, DC: U.S. Government Printing Office.

Tepas, D. I., and R. P. Mahan (1989). The many meanings of sleep. Special issue: Stress and sustained performance. *Work and Stress 3(1)*, 93–102.

Violanti, J. M., and J. E. Vena (1986). Disease risk and mortality among police officers: New evidence and contributing factors. *Journal of Police Science and Administration 14(1)*, 17–23.

Webb, W. W. (1975). *Sleep: The Gentle Tyrant*. Englewood Cliffs, NJ: Prentice Hall.

Williamson, A. M., and J. W. Sanderson (1986). Changing the speed of shift rotation: A field study. *Ergonomics 29*, 1085–1089.

6

❖

Hazards and Danger: The Adrenaline Rush

A group of highway patrol and local police officers separate protestors from demonstrators at a KKK rally. (Photo from the Missouri State Highway Patrol)

Cops either possess or develop, as a result of role assignment (a not to be underrated force), the courage to risk physical harm. They learn how to cope with moments of sheer terror that create urges in the rest of us to flee for our lives. Cops are physically brave and live with the absolute certainty that this is the prime value of their existence. Coward is such a powerful epithet that, even in a professional accustomed to the rawest language, it is a word used very sparingly. (Bouza, 1990, p. 71)

❖ OBJECTIVES

1. To discuss the stress produced by physical danger.
2. To examine the effects on the body of those stresses.
3. To suggest some ways an officer can modify the effects of danger.

❖ INTRODUCTION

Physical dangers are those situations in which the officer is exposed to hazards that can cause injury or death. This would include such situations as pursuit of an armed suspect, entering a dark warehouse to answer an alarm, or going into a domestic dispute where violence is occurring.

Here we are examining the emotional effects of physical danger, which we see as different in some ways from officers' exposure to other people's pain and suffering. For example, it is an emotionally twisting experience for almost all officers at the scene of an automobile accident to take a dead baby out of the arms of an injured mother who is still conscious. We will deal with emotionally stressful events and their effects in Chapter 7.

Law-enforcement officers' reactions to danger represent one of the dualities of police work. On the one hand, fear is a frequent part of the job and officers will complain about the dangers they have to face; on the other hand, their complaining is a cover for their love of action and search for adventure that made police work appealing to them (e.g., Scharf and Binder, 1983; Bouza, 1990; Brown, 1981). The danger makes the job challenging and adds to the importance of what they do.

Officers may deny their fear, but always in the background, as they go about their duties, is that knowledge that there is the possibility of serious injury or death. Jermier (1982) reports that, on the average, patrol officers working urban areas get one call coded as dangerous per day. This is both a positive and negative part of the job. It is positive because it makes the job exciting and meaningful. It is also positive because it gives policing status and prestige with the public, who recognize the risks that officers run. It is negative because the constant attention to possible hazards on the job leads to mental strain, chronic hyper-alertness, and eventually cumulative fatigue.

The research of Jermier et al. (1987) supports the two points just given: (1) the more dangerous the work assignments, the more meaning and significance street officers see in what they are doing, and (2) the more dangerous the officers' assignments, the more likely the officers are to suffer from emotional exhaustion.

❖ LAW ENFORCEMENT A RISKY JOB: TRUE OR FALSE?

In many jobs there are more risks of physical injury than there are in police work. While police injury rates (days lost from work) are twice as high as average occupations, lumber jacks, truck drivers, garbage collectors, and trade contractors have rates two to five times as great as police (National Safety Council, 1981). However, as discussed in Chapter 3, the perception of constant danger produces more long-term negative side effects in law-enforcement officers than it does in other occupations where there is in reality more danger of physical injury or death.

Part of the reason for these negative side effects is that the officer is more aware of potential danger than the individuals in most other dangerous occupations because there are more situations that could become violent. Police officers know injury and death may result at any time because another human being can intentionally decide to hurt them.

This sense of jeopardy from fellow humans is a different feeling than working with a piece of machinery where a mechanical failure could seriously injure the worker. The officer is physically more stressed by police work because there is an increased sense of danger due to the unpredictability of human violence. Most of the time the violence doesn't happen, but when it does, the body had better be prepared for a fight or flight reaction if the officer is going to survive.

This physical preparation for action will occur more frequently for someone answering hazardous calls than for someone walking down a street loading garbage on a truck. As we discussed in Chapter 3, when there is the possibility that a situation could be dangerous, the body will react with increased heart rate, higher blood pressure, the flow of adrenaline, greater alertness, and muscle tension. This rise in tension is added to any other tensions the officer may be having as a result of poor supervision, erratically scheduled court dates, or citizen complaints.

❖ PERSONAL SPACE

Experienced officers know at a gut level what other people are totally unaware of; humans and animals have a need to keep a certain critical distance between themselves and others. For a normal adult American that space is about 18 inches, and more if the person approaching them is a stranger. When someone comes close to the personal space barrier, the person or animal will feel a need to move away or retreat. Many of us feel this at parties when someone gets into our face and we keep backing up until they have us pinned against the wall. This is our *flight distance.* If an animal or person comes within the *retreat distance* and the human or animal can't retreat, then the animal or human will feel a need to attack. In this second case, the person's critical *attack distance* has been violated.

People vary rather widely in the distances that they feel comfortable with having others approach them. An experienced officer knows that assault-prone individuals begin to feel threatened much sooner and at a greater distance from their bodies than does a normal citizen. The first author (Anderson) has run groups for assault-prone offenders on parole. One test we use is to have the offender report when he begins to feel nervous at the approach of another person. We have found that some of these assaultive offenders become acutely uncomfortable when the other person gets as close as 4 feet. One group member, who was notorious for fighting with police officers, had a critical distance of 6 feet. He took pride in the fact that it often took four officers to subdue him. We know officers who use their knowledge of critical distances to get obnoxious individuals to attack them so that they can arrest them for assaulting an officer. Good interrogators know when to move into a suspect's critical fight and flight distances to make him nervous and more likely to confess.

❖ EXPECTING THE UNEXPECTED

THE CASE OF THE GENTLE DRACULA

At three o'clock on a Friday afternoon, Scott Welch and his partner, George McDare, patrol officers in a large urban area, are called to take Henry, a 35-year-old mental patient, back to the VA hospital.

When he hears the nature of the assignment, Scott's heartbeat increases and he becomes more alert. Because a mental patient is involved, the thought that the situation could be dangerous goes through his mind. When the officers arrive at the house, the patient's 60-year-old mother meets them at the door and explains that her son (Henry) has not taken his medication for the last month and for the last three weeks he has been living in their unfinished basement.

She tells the officers that Henry has refused to let anyone come down into the basement and has been insisting she bring him blood sausage to eat. She says he has been sleeping during the day, but sneaks around the house at night. She reports he has, on occasion, gone out at night and comes back into the house just before sunrise. When asked, she informs the officers that Henry has no weapons available to him and that he is not dangerous.

When Scott knocks at the door leading down into the basement and asks if he can come in, Henry tells him to stay out. Scott has not been reassured by the mother's belief that her son is harmless and thinks, "Oh shit, these guys can hurt you." His blood pressure goes up a notch and his heart rate is now 100 beats per minute. His muscles are tense and ready for action. He decides to call for a backup team.

When the officers enter the darkened basement, they find a skinny man with long stringy hair sitting in a homemade coffin. He is dressed in black trousers and black T-shirt and has a large black bath towel tied as a cloak around his neck. Henry looks so weird that Scott's first impulse is to laugh, but he reminds himself that crazies do unexpected things. When he asks Henry to come with them, he refuses to leave the basement, saying that he will die if they take him into the sunlight.

One of the other officers helps Henry out of the coffin and takes him by the arm to lead him up the stairs. Henry kicks the officer's feet out from under him and begins flailing with his arms in all directions. While Henry is slender, in his frenzy he is unbelievably strong and it takes all four officers to subdue him.

The situation is made more difficult for the officers by the mother, who gets in their way trying to protect her son. She is screaming, "Don't hurt him, don't hurt him. He's all I've got." The officers finally cuff both the patient's hands and feet and carry him screaming from the house to Scott's car, where he wails all the way to psychiatric hospital. There the staff place him in restraints and tranquilizes him with drugs.

Later in the day, Scott feels pain in his thigh where he was evidently kicked but didn't notice it at the time. His heart continues to beat fast for some time afterward, and he feels slightly light-headed and high. Colors seem unusually bright and he is aware of the differences in the skin texture of people's faces. Their faces stand out so distinctly it is almost hard to look directly at them. Scott is having an adrenaline high.

Comments on the Case of the Gentle Dracula. The four officers involved in bringing Henry to the hospital now have a story to tell back at the station that others will find hard to top, but their adventure also illustrates the unpredictability of the job. A police officer is never sure what to expect on a call. As many officers have told us, "Just when you think you have seen it all, something you've never heard of before happens."

Scott's alertness based on a moderate level of fear in dealing with a mental patient was appropriate. The fear gave him better reaction time and greater strength. But it also left him with excess tension and used up some of his zone of stability. Excitement provided by a call of this nature is stimulating, but too many calls to handle hazardous situations can cause negative physical consequences to build.

Because this case history revolves around a mental hospital patient, it also illustrates another hazard of being a police officer. Officers come in contact not only with criminals and angry citizens, but with the most unpredictable of humans, the psychotic. Most people fear someone who is acting crazy because crazy people are unpredictable. Not knowing what to expect means that the officer must be especially alert to danger cues in order to be able to react quickly.

Ex-cons tell us that in a prison setting those prisoners who get a reputation for being crazy are left alone by even the toughest inmates because of the danger an unpredictable person presents. As one con said, "When I saw him sittin' there stuffin meatloaf down his shirt, I knew he weren't nobody to fuck with."

Because some mental patients are dangerous, when one needs to be transported to a psychiatric facility, it becomes a law-enforcement officer's job to see that he or she gets there. Sales (1991) found that, when the police are called to take a mentally ill person to a mental health facility, the patient is likely to be severely disturbed. Often the police are called when the person is homicidal or suicidal; that is, when they're dangerous, they become the police's responsibility. Half of the time these patients require restraints and a quarter of them need tranquilizing medication when they get to the emergency room. All the while the officer is expected to treat the patient with humanity and care.

In Chapter 4 we discussed the paradoxes or dualities involved in being a police officer. Another paradox exists around the idea of danger; that is, police officers see their jobs as being both safe and unsafe. Officers recognize that there are actually few on-the-job injuries; on the other hand, they recognize that they are constantly entering situations where there is a very real possibility of getting hurt. The assault rate against officers in police departments runs at the rate of from 16 per 100 officers in small city departments to 19 per 100 in departments from cities with over 25,000 population. (Cullen et al., 1983)

This leads to a second paradox: sensitivity to possible danger is both positive and negative. It is positive because the officer stays alert to potential risks. Carelessness can lead to injury and even death. In simulated situations where the officer was required to make judgments about whether or not to draw a weapon and then to shoot or not shoot at a possible assailant, those officers who drew their weapon early and shot at an appropriate time would have been killed in one case out of three. Those who waited and were not alerted to the danger until later would have been killed in two cases out of three. (Dwyer et al., 1990)

On the other hand, if someone is constantly aware of danger and the body stays in a constant state of preparation for action, there will be heightened work stress. Besides developing the physical symptoms we discussed in Chapter 3, the officer may experience additional depression. (Cullen, 1983)

THE CASE OF THE SAFE DOMESTIC DISPUTE

A routine call can be dangerous because the officer answering it sees it as routine. But even usually safe situations will on occasion turn dangerous. Routine traffic stops and minor calls to aide a citizen can end up in a felony arrest with a high chance of someone being injured. For example, a week following the Gentle Dracula case, Scott Welch is called to a domestic disturbance. The couple, the Sturms, are well known to Scott from previous calls and he expects to encounter the usual script. George Sturm will have come in drunk, Emma Sturm will have been nagging him about his drinking, and when he told her to lay off she just screamed louder. He then threw her against the wall and started hitting her with his fists. Hearing her screams, the neighbors called the police.

On previous occasions, Scott has managed to talk them into settling their argument, and when he has asked Emma if she wanted to press charge, she has refused. He expects the same thing will happen this time.

Scott is in a one-man car. When he arrives at the house, he waits for his backup and they go in together. Emma's face is bruised and she is crying. Tonight, instead of being contrite, George is different. He tells Scott, "You sons of bitches got no right interfering with a man chastising a wife who's got a sharp tongue. Now get the hell out of my place."

Scott says, "Let's just you and me go in the kitchen and talk about this."

At this point, George swings at Scott who sidesteps and reaches for his cuffs. Emma grabs an ashtray off the table and throws it at Scott's head. It misses. But before his partner Mike can respond, she throws herself on Scott's back, one arm around his neck, the other scratching at his face. George hits Scott, screaming, "Leave my wife alone, you son of a bitch." On the way to the station, both are screaming about police brutality.

Comments on the Case of the Safe Domestic Dispute. Was the Sturms' attack on the officers totally unexpected? Probably not. Unpredictable? Probably. Calls to control a family disturbance were rated by police as having a higher degree of physical danger present than other calls. Unless lulled into inattention by previous contacts with the family, officers going into a family fight usually go in alert and vigilant (Baumann et.al., 1987). They know from experience that many of the injuries that officers suffer come from intervening in a domestic fight.

Then there are the other calls that come on a regular basis: the response to a silent alarm, felony-in-progress call, officer needs assistance call, barricaded suspect. All these situations could lead to possible physical injury, and the average patrol officer in a large city can expect to be sent into one of these potentially dangerous situations on average of once a day. This doesn't mean a call coded "hazardous" will turn out to be violent, but it does mean an officer's alertness to that possibility will be high, and as a result the fight and flight physical reactions will occur.

❖ LISTENING WITH THE THIRD EAR

Because danger and the potential for violence come from other people and cannot be predicted with any assurance, officers develop a high degree of skill in reading their surroundings. Details such as what people are carrying or their way of moving or even missing elements in the environment can ring a bell of caution in a well-trained officer. Watch two officers talking on the street. They don't watch each other, they are constantly checking the street, watching the people to pick up anything out of the ordinary.

Patterns of behavior become clear to an officer working a particular area. The officer begins to be able to infer things about a person by gestures, dress, manner of walking, or other behavior. Although we have known some defense attorneys who objected to profiling because it may select out for attention certain minorities, it is almost impossible by the very nature of the work for officers not to develop in their minds a picture or profile of who is most likely to be dangerous or who is most likely to be doing something that is illegal.

The profile comes about in a number of ways and will differ from officer to officer. One problem of training someone to profile who the potential offenders are is that those officers who do it well cannot always explain to someone else what they are responding to. Some officers say their "gut" tells them. In psychology, we would get a little fancier and talk about someone's good clinical judgment.

Some of the ways the profile is built are as follows:

1. The officers know the territory and are acutely conscious of anyone or any thing that is out of place.
2. Other officers and trainers have pointed out things that need to be watched for.
3. A high level of alertness in dangerous situations gives the officer greater sensitivity to clues that indicate that something is wrong with a person or situation.
4. An officer's unconscious puts patterns together and rings bells of danger when the pattern is wrong in some way.
5. Those officers who have previously been in dangerous situations often respond to cues in new situations that remind them of the danger.
6. Some officers just learn to expect the worst of everybody.

A state highway patrol officer makes a large number of busts for possession of drugs when he stops cars on a major highway for minor infractions. He doesn't do this by random stops, but by knowing the characteristics of people who are likely to be driving drugs across the country.

If law-enforcement officers had to give full attention to everything going on and all the people around them, they would be exhausted. Instead they use cues for identifying certain kinds of people as dangerous or certain situations as perilous. In our first example, Scott knew there was potential danger when he was told Henry was to be taken back to a psychiatric hospital. The clue may be a particular kind of haircut, an unusual kind of outfit, or an attempt made to hide something quickly when an officer comes on the scene. The clues by themselves may not cause alarm. However, combinations of clues very often raise the suspicion level. Thus, the police officer, as an occupational necessity, becomes a suspicious person.

The citizen may be perfectly honest and attending to his or her own business but be in a place where the officer feels something is out of place. The most frequent citizen complaint comes from African Americans who are questioned for being in an area where the officer expects to see only whites. Or it may be that the citizen's dress is inappropriate to the scene and officer stops him to ask some questions.

This suspiciousness can lead to difficulty for the officer. A Washington University professor was stopped and interrogated by Frontenac, Missouri, police while he was waiting for his wife and children outside a shopping center. He believed it was because he is African American. He later received an apology from the mayor of Frontenac.

The stopping of a citizen to question him or her is provoking and intrusive to almost everybody. Instead of seeing it as the officer doing his or her job of maintaining the peace, the person sees a suspicious officer who is interfering with the citizen's rights. He or she may even interpret the officer's behavior as hostile. We now have an angry citizen, which may make the officer's work more difficult either now or at a later date when he or she might need to rely on citizen cooperation in a situation where order must be maintained.

There can be danger because people are intimidated by police officers. One of the authors (Anderson) was running a program to train officers as peer counselors and asked the officers in training not to wear their uniforms or guns to the training sessions. To test the officers' skills in peer counseling, at the end of the training program they had to counsel an officer who was in uniform. Afterward the trainees said, "Hey, these guys are intimidating: it takes a while to get used to talking to someone in uniform when you're not."

Being intimidated, the citizen is not at his or her best, and if she or he reads suspiciousness and/or hostility into the situation, the officer can forget about getting cooperation. A St. Charles County, Missouri, sheriff's deputy grappled with a burglary suspect while a crowd of onlookers did nothing, refusing to even flag down one of the several police cars that were cruising the area in search of the deputy.

Being faced with an uncooperative citizen makes an officer even more suspicious, which will lead to more antagonism on both sides (for example, see Wilson, 1968). It should not be surprising under the circumstances that some officers feel, "Why should I break my back to protect someone who wouldn't give me the time of day?" The officer sees himself as doing a dangerous job to protect a person and cannot even expect help from him or her when the chips are down.

The citizen, on the other hand, prefers to see the police officer as an automaton, because once the police officer's humanity is recognized, the citizen necessarily becomes implicated in the police officer's work, which is, after all, sometimes dirty and dangerous. What the police officer typically fails to realize is the extent he or she becomes tainted by the character of the work performed. The effect of citizen attitude toward law-enforcement officers will be more fully discussed in Chapter 10.

❖ TAKING CARE OF YOURSELF

What can an officer do to take care of himself or herself?

1. You can mentally prepare yourself through mental role play to deal with problem situations and can practice seeing yourself handle them effectively. You need to know the scripts of what can happen. Situations where officers

often have worked out scripts ahead of time as to possible interventions are dealing with a possible suicidal jumper, family violence, talking to a barricaded subject, and handing a belligerent drunk.

2. Find ways to come down off the adrenaline high besides other high-risk activities such as alcohol. In Chapter 17, we give a series of things an officer can do to lower the tension after a critical event. Because each technique affects each individual differently, officers need to try a variety of techniques until they find the ones that work best for them.

3. Find comrades who share your attitudes and whom you can talk to about what happened. Particularly, seek officers who are willing to admit that they also get scared when dealing with high-action situations. Some departments have trained some officers to debrief individuals who have been in high-risk situations.

4. Reframe what is happening. Tell yourself, "I need the sweating palms and fast heart rate, my reflexes are better, my blood will clot faster, I can think more clearly. Afterward tell yourself, it's over now, I don't need the tension, it has served its purpose.

5. After a high-tension day, you may need to work off the tension; exercise, sex, or a massage all help to relieve the tension by using the muscles in a way your body has prepared you to.

THE CASE OF TERRY

We will close this chapter with a case to illustrate how complicated a dangerous situation can become for the officer involved. Even what appears at first to be a routine call of a drunk driver in a minor accident can turn into a dangerous situation with negative emotional consequences for the officer involved.

The officer involved in this case was Terry Moore, a highway patrol officer, who was about to get off duty at 1:00 A.M. He received a call to check a car in a ditch on a side road. As he drove up to the scene, he saw that the older-model Chevy Caprice had the rear bumper on the far side of the ditch and the front bumper on the side near the road. With the bumpers holding it up, the car was hanging several feet above the center of the ditch.

Terry made a careful approach and saw no activity in the car. The doors were locked and Terry flashed his light into the car and saw what appeared to be a person lying on the front seat with his head on the driver's side. Knocking on the window failed to arouse the person. The front driver's side window was down 6 inches, just enough space for Terry to get his left arm in and reach down to unlock the door. At this point he switched his flashlight into his right hand.

As Terry opened the door the man sat up, hands shoulder high and palms open. As if in recognition, the stranger said, "Oh, it's you. Glad to see you." Terry identified himself as a state trooper and asked the motorist what the problem was. The motorist then started his right hand moving toward the inside of his leather jacket. While the man could have been reaching for his wallet, Terry's alert system went off and he felt a charge of adrenalin shoot through his body.

Everything went into slow motion and details became very sharp. He was aware that the man was wearing a cheap leather jacket with cracks in it. There was a bulge on the right side. Terry swore at himself for being caught with his flashlight in his right hand.

As the man's hand was moving toward the inside of his jacket, Terry's left hand was moving to stop it. The man's hand reappeared holding a small pistol. Every detail of the gun stood out in Terry's eyes. With the light of the flashlight bouncing off it, the barrel appeared to be the size of a cannon. Terry said, "If there was a gnat on the sight, I would have been aware of it, the details were so sharp."

As the cylinder of the revolver began to turn, Terry's left hand finally reached the gun. He grasped the revolver around the cylinder and squeezed hard, preventing the cylinder from moving around under the firing pin. He then dropped his flashlight in the car seat and used his right hand to push the barrel down away from himself, hoping to break it lose from the man's grasp.

The man screamed, "You're breaking my finger you son of a bitch." Terry remembers saying, "Who cares," and continued to twist. The man finally released the gun.

After handcuffing the man and placing him in the patrol car, Terry started back to the County Sheriff's Office where the man could be jailed. On the trip the man said, "I know you all have a job to do, and I respect you for doing it, but I'll kill everyone of you mother-fuckers if I get a chance."

The thought flashed into Terry's mind, "I should have shot him."

Routine? Yes, yet Terry was left with some problems. First he now felt vulnerable in a way he didn't before. The man he arrested could have killed him. Second, he found he has homicidal thoughts he didn't know he was capable of. Third, he felt stupid for having his flashlight in his right hand so he couldn't get at his pistol. If he had had his pistol in his hand, he would have shot the man. Fourth, he feels guilty for not killing the man even after he took the pistol away, because now the man may kill an officer at a later date. Then Terry would be a contributing factor. Fifth, he feels he cannot discuss his thoughts and feelings about this with anyone else because he will lose his credibility as an officer who knows what he is doing.

The fear of talking about it is so strong that he will not discuss the situation with anyone for 11 years, despite the fact he can remember every detail of what happened as if it were only a week ago.

SUMMARY

Because of what officers do, danger and the resultant fear are a regular occurrence. Individuals attracted to law enforcement have a higher need to take risks than people in most other occupations. Officers who lose their alertness are in hazard, yet too much alertness to what is going on around them takes a physical and emotional toll. Officers can alleviate some of this stress by (1) mental rehearsal, (2) using relaxation techniques, (3) using other officers to debrief with after a dangerous assignment, and (4) working off tension by exercise.

EXERCISE

In a city where officers patrol in one-man cars, you are called as backup into the projects where a group of African Americans has surrounded a patrol car in which an officer is holding a suspect in a drug deal. As you pull up, you are also surrounded and they begin to rock your car.

1. What are your feelings?
2. What actions will you take?
3. What will you do after the incident to settle yourself down?

REFERENCES

Baumann, D. J., D. F. Schultz, C. Brown, R. Paredes, et al. (1987). Citizen participation in police crisis intervention activities. *American Journal of Commuity Psychology 15*, 459–471.

Bouza, A. V. (1990). *The Police Mystique: An Insider's Look at Cops, Crime, and the Criminal Justice System*. New York: Plenum Press.

Brown, M. K. (1981). *Working the Street: Police Discretion and Dilemmas of Reform*. New York: Russell Sage Foundation.

Cullen, F. T., B. G. Link, L. F. Travis, III, and T. Lemming (1983). Paradox in policing: A note on perceptions of danger. *Journal of Police Science and Administration 11*, 457–462.

Dwyer, W. O., A. C. Graesser, P. L. Hopkinson, and M. B. Lupfer (1990). Application of script theory to police officers' use of deadly force. *Journal of Police Science and Administration 17*, 295–301.

Jermier, J. M. (1982). Ecological hazards and organizational behavior: A study of dangerous urban space–time zones. *Human Organization 41*, 198–207.

Jermier, J. M., J. Gaines, and N. J. McIntosh (1989). Reactions to physically dangerous work: A conceptual and empirical analysis. *Journal of Organizational Behavior 10*, 15–33.

National Safety Council (1981). *Accident Facts*. Chicago: The Council.

Sales, G. N. (1991). A comparison of referrals by police and other sources to a psychiatric emergency service. *Hospital and Community Psychiatry 42*, 950–952.

Scharf, P., and A. Binder (1983). *The Badge and the Bullet: Police Use of Deadly Force*. New York: Praeger.

Wilson, J. Q. (1968). *Varieties of Police Behavior*. Cambridge, MA: Harvard University Press.

7

❖

Dealing with Death
and Severe Injury

A four-car accident on a rural route killed two drivers and injured a county deputy after a high-speed chase. (Photo from the *Columbia Missourian*)

❖ OBJECTIVES

1. To examine the different situations where officers encounter death.
2. To mentally prepare the officers for the reactions they are likely to have to dead bodies and the severely injured.
3. To suggest techniques that are useful in helping officers to deal with the anxiety aroused by these situations.

Individuals do not enter law enforcement mentally or emotionally prepared to deal with the dead, dying, or seriously injured. They must learn how to cope with the normal anxiety this is caused by dealing with (1) dead bodies, (2) persons who have been severely injured, and (3) persons who have just been through a traumatic event such as an auto accident or a rape.

Not to be affected by other people's pain requires an adjustment period for officers. It takes experience and time for most officers to learn to deal with their own feelings about death. In addition, to be effective in law enforcement, officers need to develop ways of protecting themselves against the powerful emotional responses that they will be exposed to in others in these life and death situations.

The degree of disturbance felt in working with dead bodies and people in pain varies from officer to officer and for the same officer over time. A supervisor in a crimes against persons section of a police department told us, "If an officer has a problem with dealing with death, he won't last. He won't make it. It's one thing to deal with the body, but then to check it for manner of death, photograph it, and follow that body up and deal with the autopsy adds another stage to dealing with it that can really get to some officers."

Officers learn to deal with the dead in a variety of ways and go through various stages of acceptance. With one exception, officers we interviewed had a clear memory of the first dead body they dealt with. A typical example follows:

> My first death was when I was on street patrol and it was a suicide. I was very young. It sticks in my mind because it was very difficult to walk up to observe the body. He had apparently been dead for several hours. But then I found that I went ahead and proceeded to take care of things and get reports written. I just worked the case and got through it. I sort of surprised myself. I didn't have any special reactions to it afterward. Partly because I didn't have to deal with the family.

One experienced officer who had seen many dead bodies, mostly as a result of car accidents, reported,

> Most police officers get to the point where they see people almost as cattle. You wipe out the emotion side of the scene of the accident and they're just objects. This object and this object and you get their names and write them down. Usually it doesn't bother you. If you didn't do it that way, you'd lose your cool and start wanting to beat drunks senseless. Your whole psyche would be all tied up and you'd never be able to leave your work. One area where most police officers continue to have trouble is where there are kids involved.

Many officers do handle the stress of dealing with the dead by withdrawing their feelings from the scene and rejecting any emotional involvement. The comparison of people to cattle is an example of one way in which an officer can depersonalize the situation.

If officers cannot find some way of protecting themselves from other people's pain, they are likely to become depressed from working with death. This can lead to the officer deciding to leave law enforcement because he or she is too uncomfortable with the assigned duties. It is possible that the officer does not recognize that emotional burnout is the reason he or she is leaving, only that he or she has lost enthusiasm for the work.

Most officers go through stages in developing their tolerance for death and severe injuries. Different officers will be at different stages, with some stuck at a certain stage that allows them to be comfortable, but that outsiders may see as a poor way of handling stress. For example, members of a number of professions use black humor as a technique for controlling their anxieties about doing the things required by their job. Surgeons, undertakers, and police all have a reputation for jokes about death that outsiders label as "sick humor." On the other hand, if the humor lowers the tension level and allows the individual to carry out his or her assignments, who is to label it as "sick?"

At some point even officers who are well conditioned to death are traumatized by a death they have to deal with. In talking with officers we find that four situations are especially stressful:

1. Making a death report to next of kin.
2. Receiving a call to an incident involving a death that has special personal meaning, such as that of a friend.
3. Dealing with the death of another officer.
4. Dealing with a major catastrophe, where there are many dead, such as a plane crash.

We will discuss each of these problem situations in some depth.

❖ DEATH REPORT TO NEXT OF KIN

Officers find death notification a difficult assignment, especially if the report is to parents of the accidental death of a child. Based on the tactics used by U.S. marshals in delivering death notifications, there are three identifiable stages in communicating bad news (McClenahen and Lofland, 1976): Preparation, delivery, and support.

Stage 1: Preparation. The function of this stage is to create a self-protecting sense of social distance for the officer. While inexperienced officers are often highly concerned about the response of the recipient, more experienced officers are concerned about the effect on themselves and whether they can contain the emotional reaction of the recipient. Officers may remind themselves that the recipient is a stranger and different in background in some distinctive way (e.g., race, education, socioeconomic level, or appearance), or that they will not have to provide follow-up support once the family or minister is notified. They may replay past death notifications and rehearse wordings aloud as they drive to the destination. Feelings of avoidance are strong at this point and the officer may rely on "regulations" and "routine" duty to mentally justify the discomfort. There may be some truth to the buffering of social class distancing for the officer. For example, there is some evidence that middle-class patients in hospitals are not usually told they are dying, whereas lower-class patients who are in general hospitals tend to be informed in often insensitive and even abrasive manners (Sudnow, 1967).

Stage 2: Delivery.   Experienced officers often provide a "presaging" or gradual lead up to the actual confirming information of a death. This is often done with the hope that the facts will "speak for themselves" and relieve the sender from the ominous task. Many officers report that the formality of the setting, presence of uniforms and badges, and use of titles provides further official buffering so that it is not as personalized. The actual delivery of information usually only takes seconds.

Stage 3: Support.   The reaction of the recipient can range from silent shock, to hysteria, to aggression (e.g., "kill the messenger"). This is often the worst part for the messenger, who often makes a shift in attitude from an impersonal and official informer to providing more personal support. Sometimes the facts may be manipulated by calibrating details or possibilities in the situation: "It was over very quickly and there was no suffering." "Your wife is gone but your daughter is still fighting and needs your help." Some of these tactics are based on the idea that it could always have been worse or that there is still more to do and the recipient should try to keep composure. More gruesome details are often intentionally left out to avoid further distressing the recipient, or they might be mentioned to emphasize that it was "better" that the victim died. It is during this last stage when recipients are most likely to decompensate, and the officer is left to drive home with high discomfort.

The following report from Susan Wooderson, a officer with 18 years in the department, is representative of the reactions of officers to death notification duty.

> The first time I ran into a situation that bothered me for a long time was when Carroll Highbarger and I had to deliver a death message to a woman who was married to a car salesman. They had just had a new baby, 6 weeks old, just built a new home. Her husband was 26 at the time. He went to work in the morning, didn't

return, and they reported him missing. We found he had taken a couple of juveniles out to show a car, which they decided to steal and then to kill him because they wanted to hear someone plead for his life. One held him, he pleaded for his life, told them he had a new baby and the other then shot him with a shotgun. It was probably the worst case I'd worked.

When we got out to the home to tell his wife he had been murdered, his parents were there and her sister and the baby. As we walked up to the house I remember seeing some initials in the concrete, his plus hers. It was absolutely horrible because we had to tell her what happened.

Everyone just totally fell apart. After 10 minutes of trying to get everybody settled down, someone contacted a minister who was going to come and stay with the family. After another 10 minutes, Highbarger and I left or we would have been down on the floor with the family. I started to actually feel some of what they were feeling. And that was the most horrible feeling I had ever had in my life. All I wanted to do was to get away from it. Having to deliver that death notice bothered me for an awfully long time.

I knew the juveniles who had done it. They were two juveniles who I wouldn't have thought could do this kind of thing. There was no need to murder him. It was such a senseless act. They could have stolen the car without murdering the man. It was just crazy.

I found myself thinking about it a lot. How could God let something like this happen? Most murders I've worked, it's people who get in fights with each other, or someone that gets drunk and kills himself on the highway, or people get in a knife fight at a bar. But here was someone who was just so totally innocent, and had just gone to work to provide for his family and had his whole life ahead of him.

He was close to my age at the time. I would just end up thinking a lot about it. I was living alone at the time and I would be nervous in the house. Hear noises and be superparanoid that someone was going to come in. Hyperalert.

When I worked homicide, I always felt sorry for the victim's family. Cases don't bother me very much. I feel I've gotten stronger. You have to continue with an investigation and not let yourself get too wrapped up in feelings. I still don't like to deliver the death notice. I'd rather get the evidence off the body, attend the autopsy, anything rather than have to deliver the news to the family because their emotions are contagious.

Suggestions. Looney and Winsor (1982) give 16 recommendations for preparing for and delivering death notifications. These suggestions do not make the assignment easy but do help lower the stress that the officer is likely to feel. Despite the strong effect this incident had on Officer Wooderson, her story illustrates many of the important things listed next, that an officer needs to do to lower the negative impact of carrying out this assignment.

1. She had positive identification of the victim before delivering the message.
2. She had as much information as possible about the what, when, where, and how of the death.

3. She carried no personal items of the victim with her.

4. She got inside the residence before she delivered the message.

5. She did not go alone but had another officer with her. In some cases, taking a minister or chaplain will be helpful. (One of the reviewers of this book added at this point, "In my experience as a Detroit Police Officer for over 20 years, I found the presence of a chaplain to be invaluable. The department chaplain is not at the scene to preach or convert, but to facilitate the situation by making notifications to the rest of the family, neighbors, friends, and the church of the deceased. It was not unusual for a family member to contact me several weeks later thanking the department for considering their needs by sending a chaplain."

6. She gave a direct statement so that there was no doubt as to what happened.

7. When the family broke down emotionally, she did her best to console them and arrangements were made for the family minister to come in.

8. The two officers spent time with the family. They did not just come in, give the message, turn around, and walk out.

Besides keeping these recommendations in mind, the officer needs to be prepared for a variety of reactions from the person being notified of the death. The person may become hysterical, physically violent, deny the news, faint, or go into shock. The range of possibilities makes the backup officer a real necessity.

❖ UNEXPECTED IMPACT OF DEATH

If the dying or dead person is a friend or relative or has some connection with the officer, there can be long-term consequences even for an officer who is used to death. State Highway Patrol Trooper Chris Ricks had been around bodies in his father's mortuary, and he is the one officer we met who doesn't remember the first body he dealt with as an officer.

He did have a strong emotional reaction to one death call he dealt with early in his career, which did cause him problems and which he did not talk about with anyone for 13 years.

TROOPER CHRIS RICKS, STORY

It was Christmas night, December 25, 1978. I was on interstate 70, just coming up the ramp to go south on 47, when they called me and said there was a 1050J2, which is a serious accident, in Warrenton, maybe half a mile south of where I was. I remember when I got there, there were very few people around.

There's a slight curve as you come north on 47 in the middle of the business section. Three young boys were driving northbound at a very high rate of speed and slid into the southbound lane and hit a station wagon head on, which had a family in it, a mother, father, and two boys. One of the witnesses said she had seen the whole thing in slow motion. The two cars hit going up almost like a triangle, and then floating back down and separating.

When I got there, there was still the odor that you can smell after an accident, the fuel, the burned tires, the stuff that hits the ground. The dead silence is the amazing thing when you get to scene of a bad accident before the ambulances have arrived. I came around the back of the station wagon and a friend from church, Jim, was trapped behind the wheel. He was very coherent and asked me how his kids were.

I walked over to the other car and all three of the boys in it looked dead. No motion, so I didn't check them for pulses or anything. Both fronts of the cars were totally demolished. Then the first fire truck arrived on the scene, first ambulance, other officers and suddenly the place became crowded.

I crawled into the back of the station wagon and got to his wife who was O.K. She was injured but she wasn't critical. And there was a little boy on the floor there. She asked about her husband. I said, he's fine.

When I got out, they were hooking up the equipment to take the steering wheel off his chest. He asked me about his other son. This was first time I realized a second boy was involved. The little boy, who had been apparently asleep on the front seat, was thrown up under the dash. He wasn't hurt very bad at all. Jim was very concerned about this kid. We got the kid out and I called for a second and a third ambulance.

I went back and was talking to Jim and told him both boys appeared to be OK and his wife was fine. He was very thankful for that. The haunting part is him talking to us, his concern for his children, how they were doing. I don't know if he realized how hurt he was or not. He never indicated that he was in any pain whatsoever.

We worked on getting his wife Shirley out the back of the wagon because the doors were too damaged to open. We got the boys from the other car in one ambulance and the mother and her two sons in another. Jim told them to go, he'd be with them in just a few minutes in the third ambulance.

At that time they pulled the steering wheel off his chest. Jim said, "Oooh," and his eyes rolled to the top of his head and he went just like that. His whole body from chest on down was just mutilated from the impact. As soon as they took the pressure off the bottom of his chest, I guess the blood just drained out of his system. And nobody at the scene, nobody, was prepared for that. Nobody was thinking that he was the one that would die. Maybe a couple of broken legs, but we never thought we had a fatality with him.

The boys in the other car were so drunk that their injuries were very minor. The boy who was driving the other car had a father and a mother who were very respected in the town. They lived two houses from the home of the individual the boys had killed. And it was a small town where everybody knew everybody else. The whole town had to deal with the son of one guy being so drunk and wiped out that on Christmas he hits another family and kills the father.

One way of understanding Trooper Ricks, responses is to look at them from a framework provided by Horowitz (1976) which involves a sequence of outcry, denial, intrusion, working through, and completion.

Outcry is the initial response of the officer, which can be horror, shock, or anger. In Trooper Ricks' case there was considerable anger and frustration.

For me the worst was the anger part of it. To continue the story, the kid got off of it. We had a prosecutor who was worthless. A drunk came in about two months later and he said he saw that car come into the highway and it couldn't have been going more than 20 to 25 miles an hour. And in spite of the fact that there were four or five witnesses who said otherwise, the prosecutor dropped all the charges, including the charges of intoxication. The community went into a complete uproar. In fact, the prosecutor resigned shortly thereafter.

I think if I drove up to an accident and my wife or my children had been injured and some drunk was standing there, I think I'd kill him. It would be my first instinct. I hated that kid in that accident in Warrenton. Literally, his attitude was, "What the hell, I don't care. You can't convict me of anything." I still have some pretty strong feelings of anger about that kid.

A second stage Horowitz points out is *denial*. The officer tries to ward off the pain of the experience by repression or denial. Officer Ricks continues his story:

I don't think it ever bothered me as far as my ability to work, but it did create problems for me at the church. The people there didn't know I was the one who worked the accident because when we work an accident we're pretty transparent. I quit going to Sunday school because I had to sit in the same class with Shirley. And I had to admit I did not want to deal with her pain. She called a lot to ask me questions about the case. And every time the kid would come to the neighborhood and squeal his tires or drive fast she would call and be in tears. I got to the point I just hated to have her call. It was because I wanted that out of my mind. I wanted it to be part of the past.

When these methods don't work, the officer will have *intrusive thoughts*. He will reexperience the event and have nightmares or repetitive thoughts about the incident.

When I was getting the peer counseling (13 years after the event), it was obvious that the peer counselor had understood what I was talking about because he had faced that kind of thing himself. You start second guessing yourself and going over and over the event in your head. You have all those guilt reactions. I kept thinking, what if I had been there a couple of seconds earlier. Had we realized this guy was that damaged below, was there something we could have done? Maybe there was nothing we could have done at that date, but later with better equipment we might have been able to take the door off and put something below him. You still ask yourself those questions.

The whole incident was one where I didn't have nightmares like other guys report, but for 14 years I kept getting a clear picture of coming up that ramp and getting that call.

For years Trooper Ricks had problems with this particular accident, but eventually received some peer counseling from another trooper who had been trained to deal with posttraumatic stress reactions. The reader will note that, although this involved only a couple of hours of contact, it made a significant difference in how Ricks *worked through* the incident and reached a sense of *completion*.

I had never talked about this case until I went to the peer counseling. I didn't want people to know. You know people expect police officers to be totally in control, unaffected by what happens to them. I think there was a lot of anger left over after what happened at the trial. A lot of helplessness. Like most cases, if you wipe them out of your mind and don't talk about it, it's in the past and you don't have to worry about it any longer. I don't think I ever talked to anybody about that case until the peer counseling.

Talking about it made it a lot better because I got off my chest a lot of things that had been bothering me. One problem that all of us face is that we don't articulate our fears because that makes us weak. But if we don't articulate our fears we never face them and they just live back there haunting us. By talking about it I found there really was nothing to fear. The case really didn't bother me after I talked about it.

I realized we had done what we could do. The rescue team worked well. Of the seven people in the vehicles, six of them had fewer injuries because of the expertise of the rescue team. So in a lot of ways I felt a little foolish that I had never talked about it.

We make a mistake by never asking an officer who has worked a bad accident how he's feeling. I remember Davis worked the scene of the fatal accident of his wife and nobody ever talked about it. When that football player from MU was killed, his dad was working that night. Fortunately, another officer got there first. I saw him a lot later and mentioned how sorry I was about his son, and for the next two hours he talked, he cried. He was still sleeping in his son's room. That was his son, but still, over the years you work accidents for people you know. It just builds up over the years.

❖ DEATH OF ANOTHER OFFICER

Because of the strong identification officers have with one another, they react strongly to the death of another officer for any reason, auto accident, heart attack on duty, or other. The death carries a special impact when it is the result of a shooting at which all aspects may not have been handled well. In Chapter 8 we will discuss how officers react when they are involved in a shooting; here we will be discussing how officers react to the death of another officer.

THE ILL-ADVISED ORDER

State troopers received a call for assistance, on August 15, at approximately 11:30 A.M., advising that a man armed with a rifle had killed one man and shot and wounded a couple near a small rural community. Local officers responding found a white male, approximately 30 to 37, barricaded along the river. The responding officers called for additional backup and assistance with the barricaded suspect. Whenever the suspect, who could not be identified, saw a police uniform, he would fire at the uniform.

Members of a special emergency response team of the state troopers responded by helicopter at approximately 12:15 P.M. The team was accompanied by the detachment commander, Captain Jim Ingols. Prior to the departure from the detachment headquarters of the team, the lieutenant in charge of the team had instructed the men that a landing along the river, above and below the suspect, would be made. This would allow for effective containment and apprehension of the suspect at his present location.

While en route to the incident, Captain Ingols, who was not a member of the team, ordered the pilot to overfly the gunman's position prior to the deployment of the team. Ingols wanted up to the minute information on the location of the gunman. Helicopter flight time was approximately 1 hour and 45 minutes. The helicopter pilot was a noncommissioned civilian employee of the department.

As the helicopter overflew the gunman's position, the gunman fired two rounds at the helicopter. One round hit the helicopter fuselage without causing significant damage. The other round hit Trooper Mark Hatfield in the head. Hatfield was sitting inboard of Captain Ingols, who was next to the door. Death was instantaneous.

At the time of the shooting, the range was approximately 50 yards. The helicopter made an immediate landing and the team deployed. After attempting to get the gunman to surrender, the officers returned his fire and killed the man. The gunman was later identified as a ex-psychiatric patient with a long history of psychiatric hospitalizations.

There are likely to be a number of different emotional reactions among the members of the response team who were present at the scene. Other troopers who were not present will also have feelings about the event. These emotions may range from grief to an increased sense of vulnerability to hazards and anger toward the captain for bringing the victim into the line of fire.

Lehman, et al., (1986) in their study of what survivors find helpful, provide some guidance as to what would be helpful for the officers involved in the preceding situation.

1. Providing an opportunity to discuss the death with someone who has suffered a similar experience. This could be done through peer counseling (which we discuss at length in Chapter 18) or by the use of groups of survivors who can discuss their feelings about the event.

2. The authors recommend complimenting the deceased. Police funerals with their words of praise for the dead officer and an opportunity for the department to show its support can be a healing aid.

3. If the officers can be provided an opportunity, perhaps after the funeral, to share memories of the deceased, this can be a good way of providing support for all those concerned with the death.

4. If any officer continues to have a sense of vulnerability, individual counseling with a professional should be provided. The authors believe that such services, by a professional who understands the work that law-enforcement professionals do, should be provided by all law-enforcement agencies.

❖ MAJOR CATASTROPHE

Although rare, major catastrophes play havoc with the psychological defenses of the officers involved who have to deal with the broken remains. In Table 7-1 we list single and ongoing events that can cause posttraumatic stress reactions. Five of the single events that can result in multiple deaths, often with dismemberment, are natural disasters (e.g., earthquake), terrorist attack, technological accident (e.g., escape of poison gas), transportation accident (train or plane), and building collapse.

Frederick (1986, p. 345), in his report on police response to major disasters notes, "Police who worked long hours removing dead bodies from the charred wreckage of a Pacific Southwest Airlines crash a few years ago in the area of San Diego, California, developed marked symptoms of 'burnout' or posttraumatic stress disorder. Similarly, the author has observed that crisis workers in a variety

TABLE 7-1   CAUSES OF PTSD

Single Events
1. Automobile accident
2. Rape
3. Natural disaster: tornado, hurricane, earthquake, flood
4. Shooting incident
5. Terrorism
6. Captivity
7. Technological accidents
8. Victim of crime, mugging, assault
9. Transportation accident: plane crash, train wreck
10. Murder of a family member
11. Building collapse

Ongoing Events
1. Combat
2. Holocaust
3. Torture victims
4. Incest victims
5. Spousal battering
6. Prisoners of war

of catastrophic events both of natural and human-induced type experienced problems of the same type."

Many officers had prolonged stress reactions to the PSA plane crash and filed disability claims and/or left the field of law enforcement. In contrast, officers involved in the McDonald's massacre in San Ysidro, California, had many fewer problems and no disability claims due to stress have been filed (Mantell, 1986). This indicates that skillful incident-specific treatment is required if the reactions are to be dealt with effectively.

Mantell (1986) feels that the officers who answered the call to the shooting in the McDonald's restaurant in the San Ysidro area of San Diego in July 1984 were the forgotten victims. It was the largest single-day mass murder executed by a single gunman in this country's history. Twenty-two children, their parents, and others were killed. Two hundred officers were involved in the cleanup. Some typical reactions of officers and their spouses to the event are given in Table 7-2.

In examining officers' adjustment to what they experienced, Mantell (1986, p. 358) says,

> First, those officers who actively explored the reality issues and searched for information about the tragedy after it was over, fared better. Caplan (1974) noted this as one of his positive patterns of coping with crises. Those who actively sought help from others also did better. They gave free expression to their feelings. They constructed manageable and workable plans for dealing with their reactions to the

TABLE 7-2   SYMPTOMS FOLLOWING THE SAN YSIDRO MURDERS

"I feel guilty, I should have done more."

"My mind wanders, have difficulty concentrating and remembering."

"Since that happening, I get nerves every time I go to a restaurant or where a lot of people gather."

"A couple of nights I would wake up as if having a bad dream. After waking up, I could not remember the dream."

"Can't sleep; hands shaking; a "what if" feeling; loss of memory; a feeling of helplessness; headaches; a feeling I didn't do enough."

"Uncomfortable at work; stripped of police image/confidentiality; absent-minded, at times day dreaming; crying at moments; running away/leave police work; guilt!"

"Short attention span at work, and also nervous or hyper. Worried about my husband's well-being a lot. I cry easier at dumb things, and am worried especially that my husband won't get over this, and we will lose our home and job security."

"Sympathy for families; anger toward gunman; depression."

"Demoralized and humiliated through work situation."

"At first, when the initial call came down, I thought of how terrible a thing it was that had occurred. The professional side of me took over."

Source: Mantell, 1986, p. 359 in *Psychological Services for Law Enforcement*. Washington, D.C.: U.S. Government Printing Office.

event, such as proper pacing and attitude. They also had a basic trust in themselves and were optimistic about the future."

On the other hand, Mantell found that officers who had trouble regaining their former adjustment showed more avoidance—the "What, me worry?" syndrome. They denied that they were having negative feelings about the event and were more prone to refuse assistance. The officers who had adjustment problems were more pessimistic about the future.

Crisis counseling in the street at the McDonald's site was initiated immediately. Reassurance, normalizing, educating, and basic support were the most common therapeutic interventions. As much as possible, all contacts in the field were done away from the action, alone. A positive, consistent, honest and nonjudgmental attitude was most effective. The officers were helped to maintain and in some cases regain control by encouraging them to express their anger—in words—and to understand how normal those feelings were.

Meetings at line-ups for several days following the event were instituted. Again, educating the officers as to what symptoms they could expect and how to deal with their families, reactions were also primary interventions.

SUMMARY

To come in contact with dead bodies or the severely injured is rare for most people, but routine for many law-enforcement officers. Calls that are likely to trouble officers are (1) delivering death notices, (2) the death of a friend, (3) death of another officer, and (4) handling the results of a major catastrophe. Several ways of helping officers to cope are discussed, among them (1) educating officers as to normal responses, (2) discussion of feelings with someone who has had similar experiences, and (3) group discussions with other officers involved in the incident.

EXERCISE

The case that follows raises a number of questions about the possible responses officers can have to death. In this case we take the death of a fellow officer. We ask the reader to look at this case from two points of view: (1) How would you react or what would be your feelings if you had been one of the survivors? (2) Given what we have discussed in this chapter, what kind of help would you provide for the officers who were involved in this case?

OFFICER MAGEE

During the early morning hours, approximately 3:20 A.M. of September 3, a convenience store operator reported being robbed at gunpoint. The suspect was described by the victim as a white male, approximately 180 pounds, 30 to 35 years of age, brown hair, brown eyes, wearing blue jeans and a gray sweatshirt. The gunman had escaped in a two-tone brown, older-model, Chevrolet sedan with a broken left-rear taillight assembly. The gunman was last seen driving eastbound into a residential neighborhood.

At approximately 3:22 A.M., Officer Karen Miller reported that she was following the suspect vehicle just east of the convenience store, and she requested backup. With backup on the way, Officer Miller reported that the suspect vehicle had suddenly stopped in the traffic lane of the residential street.

Officer Miller stopped her vehicle approximately 20 yards behind the suspect's vehicle. As she stopped her vehicle, the suspect began to exit his vehicle. Miller opened her door and ordered the suspect to remain in his vehicle. The suspect continued toward the rear of his vehicle and drew a handgun and fired a round toward Miller. Miller exited her car and moved to the rear of her vehicle and returned fire with a single round. She reported that she was under fire from the suspect. The suspect continued to fire toward Miller. She moved back to a position behind parked cars, away from the suspect, and fired two more rounds. The suspect then entered Miller's patrol car and continued driving eastbound. Miller reported the theft of her vehicle and remained with the suspect's vehicle.

Additional responding officers observed the suspect in Officer Miller's vehicle within one block of the engagement with Miller. Upon seeing the officers responding to assist Miller, the suspect abandoned the patrol vehicle and fled on foot into the residential area. Officers Laughrey and James began pursuit of the suspect on foot into the residential area, losing sight of him in an area of heavy foliage (large evergreens).

Two on-duty K-9 officers had responded and two off-duty K-9 officers were called to the scene. At approximately 3:35 A.M., the general area had been secured and a search began with the on-duty K-9 officers under the command of Lieutenant J. Knapp. Knapp had instructed the two K-9 officers, paired with two other officers, to begin a search of the area where the suspect was last seen.

Officer B. Evans with his partner King, along with Officer W. Knight, began clearing the northern segment of the area. On the southern segment, Officer K. Williamson with his partner Rex, along with Officer J. Magee, began their search. Rex had alerted to movement ahead of the team in the foliage. Officer Magee was slightly ahead of Williamson and Rex. As Magee was moving along a large evergreen, in advance of the K-9 team, a shot was fired from within the branches of the evergreen, striking Magee. The projectile entered Magee's upper chest, just above the protective vest, at the base of the neck. The shooting was witnessed by four officers. Rex immediately attacked the suspect and an arrest was made. Paramedics, who had been called to stand by, immediately responded to Magee. Magee's injury was reported at 3:52 A.M. Magee was pronounced DOA.

QUESTIONS

1. How is Officer Miller likely to feel about her actions in this incident?
2. How are the other officers present likely to feel about the actions of Officer Miller?
3. How will the officer with Magee at the time of the shooting be affected?
4. What reaction are other officers in the department likely to have to Miller's actions, Williamson's actions, and Lieutenant Knapp's decisions?
5. How are Williamson and Knapp likely to feel after this incident?
6. What kind of support or help would you give each officer involved in this incident to ensure his or her adjustment?

REFERENCES

Caplan, G. (1974). *Support Systems and Community Mental Health: Lectures on Concept Development.* New York: Behavioral Publishers.

Frederick, C. J. (1986). Post-traumatic stress responses to victims of violent crime: Information for law enforcement officials. In James T. Reese and Harvey A. Goldstein (eds.), *Psychological Services for Law Enforcement.* Washington, DC: U.S. Government Printing Office.

Horowitz, M. J. (1976). *Stress Response Syndromes.* New York: Jason Aronson.

Lehman, D. R., J. H. Ellard, and C. B. Wortman (1986). Social support for the bereaved: Recipients' and providers' perspectives on what is helpful. *Journal of Consulting and Clinical Psychology 54,* 438–446.

Looney, H., and J. L. Winsor (1982). Death notification: Some recommendations. *The Police Chief,* March, 30–31.

Mantell, M. R. (1986). San Ysidro: When the badge turns blue. In James T. Reese and Harvey A. Goldstein (eds.), *Psychological Services for Law Enforcement.* Washington, DC: U.S. Government Printing Office.

McClenahen, L., and J. Lofland (1976). Bearing bad news: Tactics of the deputy U.S. Marshall. *Sociology of Work and Occupations 3(3),* 251–272.

Sudnow, D. (1967). *Passing on.* Englewood Cliffs, NJ: Prentice Hall.

8

❖

Postshooting Trauma

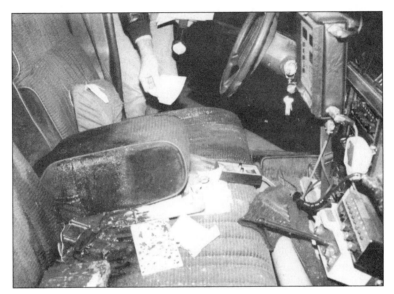

The front seat of a patrol car in which the officer was shot and killed. (Photo from the Missouri State Highway Patrol)

❖ OBJECTIVES

1. To show that officers, reactions to shootings aren't like those portrayed in movies or on TV.
2. To demystify responses to near death experiences and show the range of normal responses to shooting incidents.
3. To discuss factors that modify how officers are affected by a shooting incident.
4. To illustrate by the use of case histories how this information is applied in real-life situations.

❖ INTRODUCTION

In Chapter 7 we discussed how dealing with the dead and severely injured can cause strong stress reactions, some of which haunt the officer for years. Since the Viet Nam war, long-term negative reactions to a critical incident has been referred to as a posttraumatic stress reaction. In this chapter, we will concentrate on shooting incidents, since they are among the most traumatic events that can happen to law-enforcement officers.

The emotional reactions to an involvement in a shooting incident are very similar to those caused by any life-threatening event, whether it be an automobile accident or an earthquake. In Chapter 7 we made it clear that posttraumatic stress disorders (PTSD) follow not only the officer's personal exposure to extreme danger, but also from dealing with dead bodies or seriously injured people. In the case of a shooting, the officer is dealing with both extreme danger to self and the death or serious injury of someone else.

Do all officers have posttraumatic stress reactions after a shooting incident? Solomon (1988) estimates that about one-third of the officers have a mild reaction, one-third have a moderate reaction, and one-third have a severe reaction to being involved in a shooting incident in which someone is killed. How strongly an officer reacts to an exchange of gunfire where someone is injured or killed depends on a number of variables. First, of course, is where the officer stands in relation to his or her zone of stability. How strong was it to start with and how damaged has it been by other recent events?

Even if the officer has a solid zone of stability and good mental preparation for an armed confrontation, other factors will influence whether there will be mild, moderate, or severe emotional reactions. The major factors are as follows:

1. Degree of threat to the officer's life, which includes wounds to the officer
2. Amount of warning the officer has before the shooting starts; if the action occurs suddenly, the officer's sense of control of the situation may be minimal
3. How long the danger persists
4. Amount of conflict the officer has about the situation, that is, the security the officer feels in his judgment to shoot
5. Related to factor 4 is the difference in reactions between officers involved in a "clean" shooting and those involved in a morally or legally questionable shooting
6. Who is the deceased, with age and gender of the dead person being important
7. Administration support for the officer's actions?
8. How the media treats the situations; do they report the facts, support the officer, or roast him or her?

TABLE 8-1   FACTORS THAT INFLUENCE AN OFFICER'S
REACTIONS TO A SHOOTING

1. Mental preparation for the confrontation
2. Recent events influencing the officer's sense of vulnerabilty
3. Amount of control the officer has over the situation
4. Degree of personal threat to the officer
5. The duration of the event
6. Degree to which the officer feels the shooting is justified
7. Support from other officers
8. Support from administration and the community
9. Age and sex of the deceased

To illustrate what can normally be expected in the way of emotional reactions to a shooting incident, we will discuss the reactions of several officers to actual shooting incidents in which the offender was killed. In reading these cases keep in mind the influences on an officer's reactions, given in Table 8-1. In the first case, Trooper Becker, the officer, was also wounded after an intense exchange of gunfire.

THE CASE OF OFFICER BECKER

It was approximately 6:30 in the evening. I was on routine patrol. Troop C hit the tone alert and put out a description of a vehicle that had two occupants who were wanted in connection with a burglary two counties south of where I was located. The subjects had stolen arms and ammunition and were to be considered armed and dangerous. Approximately 2 minutes after the broadcast, a vehicle and occupants fitting the description passed my location.

I began following the vehicle keeping a respectful distance. I was in a fully marked patrol car and my closest backup officer was Trooper Dale Springs, 15 to 20 miles north of me. I stayed behind the vehicle waiting for Trooper Springs to arrive so we could make the stop together.

The subjects in the vehicle were aware of my presence. They exited onto a state blacktop road. The driver was looking around like he was lost, and the further we went out onto the black top the slower their speed got. I had the uneasy feeling something was about to happen.

As I followed them, I had picked up my shotgun. This was prior to our being issued the magazine extension, and we only carried four shells in the magazine and left the chamber empty. I chambered a round of "00" buck. As we continued out Highway DD, we approached a hill crest, and two young sisters, I believe their ages were 13 and 16, were walking down the shoulder of the road in front of us. As I crested the hill the suspects stopped their vehicle and both doors flew open; instinctively I slowed my vehicle and threw the door open. The passenger jumped out and began firing at me with a revolver. Later, I found out it was a .38 Smith and Wesson.

I exited my car, with it still in gear, at the same time the driver exited his car and fired a shot at me from a revolver, which was also discovered later to be a .38 Smith and Wesson. The driver was approximately 30 feet away from me with no obstructions or cover between us. The two girls walking down the road were over his right shoulder and, therefore, I held my fire because I had "00" buck and undoubtedly the girls would have been injured. At this time, he crisscrossed from the driver's side to the passenger's side, where his accomplice stood still firing at me. Both vehicles were still in gear.

The reader should notice Trooper Becker's memory for details and that he is processing many factors at once. Under the stress of extreme danger, some officers find that everything seems to be happening in slow motion. For others, time speeds up and everything happens very quickly. The awareness of sensations also differs from officer to officer; sounds can seem louder or diminished; visually, some officers see a great amount of detail, but others may have tunnel vision. This means that afterward in the debriefing interview the officer's report on what happened may contain distortions; for example, the officer may misjudge how long the event took or may miscount the number of shots fired. If the officer gets tunnel vision, he may not be able to describe background features since his attention was focused totally on the face, hands, or weapon of the perpetrator.

Without standing up from behind my car, I just held my shotgun up over my head and fired a shot in desperation at the driver as he was crisscrossing. Needless to say, I didn't hit anything. At this time both of the subjects advanced toward my car, at which time I'm at the left rear wheel. The driver went to my right rear wheel with just the car's width between us. The passenger was near the right front wheel. The three of us are bobbing up and down trying to keep visual observation of where the others were.

All the time the driver, who was on the other side of the trunk from me, was yelling at me, and cursing me, telling me to throw my weapon down.

Knowing this much about the incident, we can predict this officer is going to have at least a moderately severe reaction to this event since there are two armed men within feet of him. The perpetrators have every intention of killing Trooper Becker, and he is definitely not in control of the situation.

At this time, I did think I was going to be killed. I didn't think I had any chances of survival. I was anticipating their rushing around the car, and I felt that one of them would undoubtedly inflict a wound on me. In an act of desperation, I told the driver, "OK, I give up." I stood partially up, hoping that he would stand up. I didn't want to give up my weapon because it was in the back of my mind if I surrendered they would lie me down in the road ditch and kill me anyway. I kept my shotgun below the trunk deck where they couldn't see it. As I stood partially up, I raised my shotgun just above the trunk and fired one round through the back glass, hoping the glass or metal or just anything would knock him down. At this point, my car began to accelerate and left the roadway, and the three of us were fully exposed facing each other.

The driver began running backward to my left. The accomplice began running to my right. Both of them were still firing at me as they were running. I swung at the driver who was back-pedaling to my left. At this point, my car went off into the road ditch and stopped at a wire fence. The driver, seeking cover, made a mad dash for it. I was shooting from the hip, trying to lead him. I fired the third round out of my shot gun and missed him. All in one motion, I swung on his accomplice, who was running to my right, and fired my fourth and final shot at him. I hit him and saw him go down the ditch embankment where I could no longer see him.

By this time, the driver had taken a position behind my patrol car's left rear fender. He fired and struck me in my right thigh. Not realizing I'd emptied my shot gun, I swung on him and pulled the trigger, and the firing pin landed on an empty chamber. At this time he got down on all fours and scampered to the front of my car, where I couldn't see him.

I went for cover behind a small tree in the ditch and began to shoot from a prone position with my revolver.

Although the situation was seemingly hopeless, the officer kept processing what was happening. He was not taking unnecessary risks, but trying different things to break the deadlock. With one culprit seemingly out of the way, the odds are more even. The fact that Trooper Becker is wounded will increase the chances for a more severe posttraumatic stress reaction.

We continued to exchange shots till my backup arrived, and the subject behind my car gave up. We discovered his accomplice had sustained a fatal wound in the back of his neck. I couldn't see him, but his partner could, and he gave up since the odds were now two against him.

The bullet had gone in my thigh on one side and left an exit wound. There were no major arteries or bones struck. I was hospitalized for a couple of days and was out of work, recuperating for approximately 2 weeks. The driver was convicted of first-degree assault and given a life sentence for shooting me. He also got a few years for the burglary he pulled. Each of them were about 21 years of age and had about 10 felony convictions. They had escaped from an honor-system prison in New Hampshire and had committed burglaries in Florida, Tennessee, and Missouri.

The fact that these were convicted criminals who had serious intentions of killing Trooper Becker helped alleviate any guilt he might have had in connection with killing another person. His reactions over the next few days were among those we would expect in this situation and are normal for a mentally healthy individual.

That night, after I had given all the basic information to the investigating officers, I couldn't sleep. I recall the nurse coming on two occasions and giving me something to try to help me sleep. I had plenty of time to think and spent the time second-guessing myself. Was there something different I might have done?

There had been a lot of lead put in the air during the shoot-out, so my main concern was for those two girls walking down the road. They miraculously escaped any harm whatsoever.

After the first couple of days, I went from a feeling of being fearful and scared of the unknown to a feeling of anger at the two suspects. To think that somebody would try to take my life and deprive me of seeing my kids grow up and spending time with my family. Just the fact they tried to kill me made me extremely, extremely angry and bitter toward these subjects.

I was not proud that I had taken a human life. But I thought there might be something wrong with me because I had no feeling of remorse. I wasn't elated or happy, but I was so bitter toward what had happened that I had no remorse for it.

Long-term effects vary from person to person, but there are some consistencies across officers. These symptoms may show within a few days or take months to develop. They may last a short period of time or go on for years. The most frequent symptoms are the following:

1. Flashbacks to the incident that are very vivid and often in slow motion. Minimal cues that remind the officer of the incident may bring them on.
2. Sleep disturbances, which include problems in going to sleep, waking at odd times, or not getting back to sleep.
3. Nightmares. Although a form of sleep disturbance, their frequency and persistence makes them primary among the symptoms.

Less frequent symptoms are the following:

4. Depression, which may include crying spells in an individual who does not ordinarily cry.
5. Helplessness and fearfulness. The sense of invulnerability is damaged and the officer becomes overly cautious and suspicious.
6. Emotional withdrawal from fellow officers and/or family.
7. Hostility toward the department and the system, particularly if the officer believes that the event has been mishandled.
8. Appetite changes, usually loss of appetite, but it can be increased appetite in some cases.

Again, Trooper Becker is a good example of some of these symptoms.

It was a long time, maybe 2 or 3 years, before I could get over this hatred for the two who tried to kill me. With the passage of time, I finally got a handle on it.

It's like one these old cliches about a wreck always happens to the other guy. This had driven home the point that it can happen to me. It can happen to any of us at any time. I've tried to be more careful, more cautious, out there.

As far as job-wise, I feel very fortunate the good Lord spared me. I've learned to appreciate life a little more. I try to spend good quality time with my wife and kids. It just reinforced the fact we can be taken any time.

There was a period for a long time, maybe 5 years, I had reoccurring nightmares. It was always the same scenario. Different places and different faces. I had dreams of having multiple adversaries in shooting incidents where I would shoot, shoot, and shoot and they would never fall. They would keep advancing toward me. These nightmares have diminished through the years. I still have them occasionally, I'd say once every 6 months. I guess something like this stays in your subconscious. I think I've been able to relate better to some of my subordinates and some of the guys I work with over the years.

How can a department best ensure that an officer's emotional reactions to a shooting incident will be kept to a minimum? Based on the literature and our interviews with officers involved in shootings, we have nine suggestions for anyone who is in a position to help law-enforcement officers deal with their reactions.

1. The officers need to be reminded of what reactions they can expect. Going over the symptoms we presented earlier with the officer can be reassuring to someone who is having a strong emotional reaction to a shooting incident.
2. Avoid any suggestion or accusation of wrongdoing during the debriefing interview. Some officers complained they were treated as if they were guilty of a crime. The officers should be briefed on the nature of the investigation procedures so that they can appreciate the necessity for administration getting all the facts about the incident. Procedures, such as depositions and court proceedings, should be reexplained and any special procedures that the department requires gone over. This would include such items as the requirement to see a counselor within 24 hours of the shooting, to ride with another officer for a day or two following an incident, or to surrender a firearm during the investigation.

TABLE 8-2   TALKING WITH A FELLOW OFFICER ABOUT HIS OR HER INVOLVEMENT IN A SHOOTING

1. Be an active listener; let the officer talk if he or she wants to. Don't be overactive.
2. If you've had a similar experience, it sometimes helps to share it, but don't make it appear that your situation was worse than his or hers.
3. Be aware that it is normal to have a stress reaction to a shooting and that the officer will probably be feeling vulnerable and a bit unsteady.
4. Don't assume the officer is proud of the shooting. Hold back on congratulations.
5. Don't second-guess the officer's motivation or what he or she should have done.
6. Be supportive. Ask if there is anything you can do. This may include discussing the situation with the officer's family or going home with the officer and not leaving him alone immediately after the traumatic incident. This is particularly important in today's world, when a higher percentage of officers are single or divorced and living alone.

3. Connected with the debriefing interview is weapon removal. Officers are disturbed at having their weapon taken away from them, particularly if it is done in a public situation. They feel it casts a shadow of guilt over them. As one officer said,

> I hope that taking a member's weapon away from him for ballistics and other purposes would be done out of view of fellow officers and the public. I think if the public or other officers see someone who's just been involved in a shooting incident standing around with an empty holster with his supervisor in custody of that weapon, it automatically reflects or puts a false feeling into the public's mind that this officer has done something wrong.

In addition, to the officer the firearm has become an extension of the body for self-protection. Most officers feel extremely vulnerable "surrendering" their firearm after a life-threatening event. What most police officers do not realize is that weapon removal must be done immediately in order to maintain an unchallenged chain of evidence. This procedure must be followed irrespective of the weapon's type or ownership. Some departments, of course, handle this by giving the officer another weapon to carry.

Another officer said,

> After my incident, I was thinking, "Gosh was there something I could have done differently? Was there something I did wrong?" You have all these questions racing through your mind and I think we do the officer involved an injustice if we take his weapons away from him the wrong way. It just adds to his confusion and the feeling that maybe he did do something wrong.

4. The department must be aware of the officer's family. While not all family members have a strong reaction to the officer's involvement in a shooting, most do. It is recommended that someone accompany the officer home and explain to them what has happened. Additionally, the department psychologist, counselor, or chaplain should visit the family to continue the debriefing process.

Statements from several officers giving their reactions after an incident illustrate the need here.

> I think that counseling should also be made available at the option of the members' spouses. At the time this happened, although I had been a police officer 3 years and a trooper 2 years, police life was strange to my wife, but when something like this goes down, they're at a loss. They don't know what to expect. They're confused. They're scared. I think someone should sit down with the member's wife and explain to her what has happened and what is going to happen, what she can expect: the depositions, the court proceedings, possible residual effects it might have on her husband. They need to be given an opportunity if they so desire. There should be some kind of peer counseling offered to them.

My wife experienced just as much trauma as I have, only on a different scale. She was fearful. Neither of us knew, given that both of the individuals involved in the shooting were from out of state, anything about their history or their family background. We didn't know if they might have family members or friends who would try to retaliate against me.

5. People need to be cautious of what they say to an officer afterward. Other officers unintentionally often say the wrong thing. The inappropriateness of some statements will be obvious to most people, such as "Good shooting, killer." The perceived offense in other statements is more subtle. In making the comment, the officer may be wondering how he or she would have reacted and say something that the officer involved in the shooting sees as second-guessing his or her decisions. For example, "Well if it would have been me, I would have known they were dangerous, and I would have called for a backup before I approached their car." The officer involved in the shooting is very likely to see this as questioning his or her judgment.

Some 4 years after my shooting, another officer reported to me that he was talking to some officers and they thought I had set the guy up. If that information was floating around for 4 years, it irritates me, and it just shocked me for someone to come up 4 years later and tell me there's rumors floating around I had set the guy up.

The following comment from an officer involved in a shooting is representative of what they see as happening. "People didn't know how to react. Later, some people would come up and congratulate you. But people don't know how to react to you. They don't know if they should say something, should they ask you about something, or should they act as if it just didn't happen?"

6. Support from other officers. On the other hand, what other officers say can be very helpful in dealing with the emotional responses the involved officer may be experiencing.

I got great moral support. I got cards. I got letters. I got telephone calls from members of the patrol all over the state, from surrounding departments, from people I didn't know. This reassurance was, I believe, the biggest factor helping me get through the situation.

7. Most officers involved in shootings need counseling and professional debriefing after an event. While most officers interviewed received no professional counseling after the event, all felt it would have been helpful. Here is a representative statement:

I didn't seek any psychological counseling at the time because I was afraid of how it would have made me look weak and unable to cope. I think the general orders we have now that has mandatory counseling for anybody that has gone through a traumatic incident is one of the best policies that this organization has ever come out with.

They also believe that an opportunity to talk with someone who has been through a similar event would have been helpful. One officer who had been in a shooting where he killed the subject had an opportunity to talk with another officer following that officer's involvement in a similar situation.

> It really helped Sam for me to talk with him afterward and it gave me some pointers. The only mistake I made with Sam was that after the situation was over he made mention of the fact that he wished somebody had gone home to his house with him that night. Because everything was fine at the scene, I'd let him keep his gun for the time being so that he didn't stand out like a sore thumb, but after all was said and done, he went home alone that night and it was then that stuff started to hit him. If I had to do it over again, now I would go home with him and just let him talk, because your adrenaline's going and you need some way to vent your energy, somebody to go for a walk with, or do something that's physical exertion to burn up some of that energy. So it helped me a great deal, just that one situation I went through, in knowing how to handle Sam's shooting situation.

8. The officer needs some time off after any major incident to get resettled and beyond the adrenaline high. This could be 1 to 3 days, but more than that is probably not required, except in unusual circumstances.

> I finished my report that night because I had to leave for a State Troopers Association meeting the next day. The next day I drove down to the meeting, and my wife had asked if I was all right and could I drive and I said yes. But apparently I wasn't, because my thoughts were on the shooting and not on what I was doing, so I ran four stop signs on the way down. I just wasn't paying attention.

9. The officer involved may need to be mentally prepared for negative media coverage. This is particularly true in some areas, where headlines may make the officer look like a murderer of children if he kills a teenager in a shootout. If the deceased is a member of a minority group, some newspapers may imply that racial prejudice was involved. Officers sometimes feel that the story carried in the media has little relationship to the actual event as it happened. If the shooting is a high-visibility incident, an attempt should be made to protect the officer from intrusive media reporters.

❖ OFFICER VICTIMS

Which officers are most unlikely to survive a shoot-out with an offender? Some light is cast on the subject by the FBI report *Killed in the Line of Duty* (1992). The FBI studied the deaths of 54 law-enforcement officers by 50 offenders. Offenders were interviewed in depth about the incident, and other background information was available on the dead officers. In the incidents studied "39 percent were arrest or crime-in-progress situations; 22 percent traffic pursuits/stops; 13 percent disturbance calls; 11 percent handling/transporting/custody of prisoners; 7 percent investigating suspicious persons/circumstances; and 7 percent other circumstances" [page 4].

Seventy-three percent of the killings occurred on a street, highway, or parking lot, 12% in private dwellings, and 10% in public buildings. The killers were most frequently antisocial and dependent personality types. For this chapter, we are most interested in a behavioral description of the victim officers, which is given in Table 8-3.

The FBI concludes in their report that there were five general areas where officers by better training and use of procedures could lower the hazards of their work.

1. *Procedural errors.* This includes failure to wait for backup or improper use of handcuffs.
2. *Absence of procedures.* How should an officer respond to a drawn weapon? Should the occupants of a stopped vehicle exit the car?
3. *Conflicting procedures.* This is where the established procedures conflict with the officer's safety, for example, having a rule that an officer can draw a weapon only when drawn on first.
4. *Training.* Departments need to consider special training: how to work with mentally disordered, postincident evaluations, staying abreast of new developments in equipment.

TABLE 8-3   BEHAVIORAL DESCRIPTORS OF VICTIM OFFICERS
___

Friendly to everyone

Well-liked by community and department

Tends to use less force than other officers felt they would in similar circumstances

Hard working

Tends to perceive self as more public relations than law enforcement service oriented

Uses force only as last resort; peers claim they would use force at an earlier point in similar circumstances

Doesn't follow all the rules, especially in regard to:
- Arrest
- Confrontation with prisoners
- Traffic stops
- Waiting for backup (when available)

Feels he or she can "read" others and/or situations and will drop guard as a result

Tends to look for the good in others

Laid back and easy going
___

Source: Federal Bureau of Investigation (1992).

5. *Correct procedures*. Even when an officer follows all procedures correctly, there are still incidents that are unpredictable and can result in death or injury for the officer. This does not preclude an attempt to cover these situations in training.

❖ PUTTING IT ALL TOGETHER

We will present one more case as an example of an officer who was mentally prepared and followed appropriate procedures, and, while not perfectly handled by his superiors, much of what we have suggested previously was carried out. As you read the case history of State Trooper Ken Pesout, pay attention to the way in which he processes what happened. When he begins to report his reactions following the shooting, keep in mind the normal symptoms we have been discussing in this chapter.

THE CASE OF TROOPER KEN PESOUT

The day of my shooting I was working radar enforcement. I had stopped a car for speeding on the ramp of northbound 55 onto 270. The driver of the car, a white male dressed in a nice outfit, couldn't produce a driver's license. I brought him back to my car, but when he got in, he immediately said he knew where his driver's license was. He got out and hurried back to his car, while I stayed in mine. He got into his car and slid across the front seat, and I noticed that he reached down under the front seat right toward the middle of the seat, and I knew that when he had gotten out he stated that the license was in his glove compartment.

Having been up to the car, I knew there was no compartment in the bench seat. When I saw him reach down, I thought that he was pulling out some type of weapon. So I immediately got out of my car and walked 6 feet off to the left of my car. He slid back across the seat, and I could see his eyes go across the rear-view mirror checking my position, but he didn't notice that I was out of the car. He apparently still thought I was sitting behind the steering wheel.

He got out of the car with the gun in his right hand, stood up facing forward, raised the gun and pointed it at the steering wheel where I would be sitting. With his peripheral vision, he picked me up and noticed I had gotten out of the car and turned with the gun pointed directly at me.

As he was coming out of the car, I had already taken my gun halfway out of my holster anticipating that something was wrong. The only mistake I made at that point was that I should have taken my gun all the way out. Fortunately, when he pointed the gun at me, I was able to pull my revolver and was lucky that my first shot hit him in the right side of the head. That was enough to keep him from shooting me. I fired a total of four shots all of which struck the subject and he was pronounced dead later on that day.

Immediately afterward, I was kind of high. It was exciting, my adrenaline was going. I immediately called in on the radio notifying the office what had happened and that was all relatively easy and came across pretty clear. Then I administered first aid to the subject and my next thought was to start processing the scene, obtaining the license plate number, VIN number, the color of the car, and everything. I found I was unable to do that. I went up to write down the VIN number off the car and my hands were shaking and I couldn't do that. I couldn't write anything down. So, I just quit until help arrived at the scene.

At that time Corporal Autry arrived, and from that point everything went on pretty smoothly. Lieutenant Duckworth came down and talked with me, took my statement, and told me to go on home. He didn't insist I go to the office and write a report immediately [not many departments would allow this]. He told me to write it whenever I felt like it. Just go on home and relax as much as I could, and that made a big difference.

Afterward, my corporal and sergeant and I drove to my house, and my wife was out raking leaves. I remember this like it was yesterday. They walked up to her and told her I had been involved in a shooting and killed a guy.

Lieutenant Duckworth handled the situation very professionally at the scene. He did have to take my gun away from me, which is standard procedure. We sat in the patrol car together, and he took my statement in a brief way so he could understand what happened and he could contact the media so I wouldn't have to. So, as I said earlier, he told me to go home and not worry about the report, that I could write it tonight or tomorrow morning, whenever I had a chance. Had he demanded that I go the office and write the report immediately, it would have been altogether different. So I'm thankful he was there to handle it the way he did and that was extremely helpful.

I think it opened my eyes, and a lot of peoples' eyes, that it can happen to the highway patrol; it's not just something in St. Louis County or sheriff's deputies. It can happen and it happens quick, and on bright sunny days. The individual I shot had six felony warrants for his arrest, was driving a stolen car, had stolen merchandise in the car, and was speeding. On just your first glance, you would think he was a law-abiding citizen, well dressed. I realize how fast it can happen.

The thing I'm most grateful for is just a year or two prior to this situation the department had gone from bull's-eye targets to silhouette targets, and the training I received in shooting silhouette targets made a big difference. Because, once the situation starts it's all reaction. There's no thinking involved, and whatever you've been trained to do is what you're going to do, and you just don't have time to think or make adjustments to the situation. You just react.

It's made me more cautious throughout the rest of my career. I'd much rather get a complaint from a law-abiding citizen that I pulled my gun out in a traffic stop than to find out later that I needed it. So it makes me more cautious, and I'm not afraid to take my gun out and hold it down along the side of my leg.

For a good year and a half after the shooting, I couldn't sleep at night. I'd go to bed at 10 o'clock, at 2 o'clock I'd roll over and hadn't had an ounce of sleep, and I'd still be wide awake. I'd get up the next morning at 6 o'clock, go to work at 7 o'clock, and just be physically drained. And at that particular time there was no help, no counseling, for those involved in these situations. And it affected the way I worked, mainly due to the lack of sleep.

I experienced other symptoms of wanting to be by myself and not working with other people. So it did have some long-lasting effects for a year and half to 2 years. Now it's been so long that I realize that the main thing that helps is time. You tend to forget certain things about it, and it's easier to talk about as time goes on.

The only thing I dislike now is the red-handled gun [practice in handling simulated traffic stops that involve shooting incidents] training. I've been through a shooting and I definitely don't like the red-handled gun training. It's good, but it just bothers me when we do it. Because when you do it with the red-handled gun, it's a game and on the road it's not. And I don't know if the training is beneficial or not, but it bothers me.

Here are some questions for you to think about in relation to the case we have just been discussing.

1. What was there about this situation that helped keep the officer's reactions relatively mild?
2. What symptoms did the officer show immediately after the shooting?
3. How did the officer in charge of the follow-up investigation ease the situation for the officer involved in the shooting?
4. What long-term consequences were there for the officer involved and how might they have been made less stressful?

SUMMARY

It is normal for officers to have a strong reaction to near death experiences such as being shot at. These reactions are increased if someone is killed. The strength of the reactions will vary depending on such factors as duration of the incident and degree of threat. The most frequent symptoms are flashbacks, sleep problems, and nightmares. Following the incident, the officer involved needs to talk to someone with training in dealing with postshooting trauma. Other officers should be careful what they say about the incident, and administration should handle the investigation in a way so as not to put the officer in bad light.

REFERENCES

American Psychiatric Association (1987). *Diagnostic and Statistical Manual of Mental Disorders* 3rd ed., revised). Washington, DC: American Psychiatric Association.

Federal Bureau of Investigation (1992). *Killed in the Line of Duty (A Study of Selected Felonious Killings of Law Enforcement Officers)*. Washington, DC: U. S. Department of Justice.

Geller, W. A. (1985). 15 Shooting reduction techniques: Controlling the use of deadly force by and against police officers. *The Police Chief*, August, 56–58.

Morrison, J. (1982). Officer killed zone. *The Police Chief*, July, 49–50.

Ochberg, F. M. (1991). Post-traumatic therapy. *Psychotherapy 28*, 5–15.

Solomon, R. M. (1988). Post-shooting trauma. *The Police Chief*, October, 40–44.

Solomon, R. M. (1990). Administrative guidelines for dealing with officers involved in on-duty shooting situations. *The Police Chief*, February, 40.

Stratton, J. G., D. A. Parker, and J. R. Snibbe (1984). Post-traumatic stress: Study of police officers involved in shooting. *Psychological Reports 55*, 127–131.

9

❖

Supervision

Officers in a unit meeting with their sergeant. (Photo courtesy of the Duluth, Minnesota, Police Department)

❖ OBJECTIVES

1. To understand how supervisors contribute to stress in officers.
2. To describe ways supervisors can decrease officers' stress.
3. To identify the major sources of stress for supervisors.

❖ INTRODUCTION

Law-enforcement officers, by the nature of their assigned task, have been given unusual powers. If not properly controlled, these powers can lead to corruption, a fact that has led to considerable concern about supervision and the following of regulations. The resultant supervision, however, places unneeded stress on many officers without solving the underlying problem of the occasional abuse of power. We will examine the effects on officers and on the supervisors who are given the job of enforcing regulations.

❖ REGULATIONS AND THE STREET COP

Flexibility and freedom of action are necessary for the effective performance of their assigned duties by patrol officers. This discretionary power helps the officer respond in the most appropriate way to a particular situation. For example, an officer sees a man going down the street trying the doors on cars. Should the individual be stopped and searched? Or perhaps intervention might wait until the individual opens a door and takes something out of a car? If the person is well dressed, is the officer likely to wait for more evidence of criminal intent before acting?

An officer answers a call to a domestic dispute; both parties have obviously been beaten around the face. The woman appears to have gotten the better of the physical confrontation, and the man is sitting on the sofa crying. The man wants to have her arrested and press charges against her; she wants the officer to "get the hell out" of their house. What does the officer do? It greatly depends not only on the laws pertaining to spousal abuse, but to the couple's reaction to the officer's interventions, assessed degree of risk, previous experience with the couple, and so on. All these factors influence the judgment the officer must make on the scene.

These kind of situations demonstrate how officers are being called on to make complex, high-risk judgments on the spur of the moment in response to a fluid situation. Faith has to be placed in the training and ethics of the officer who is on the scene making that judgment. Rules simply cannot be written to cover all the real-life possibilities that arise in the course of a day on the street.

The development of many different situations and the presence of diverse possibilities in these situations require that officers must be given considerable power and freedom to respond, depending on the officer's reaction to the circumstances that exist at the time.

Officers on a beat or special assignment have more discretion over their work than do employees in almost any other job. Perhaps only farmers and professors have more freedom of choice about how to use their time and less interference in their decisions. As Brown (1981) and Guyot (1991) point out, despite the constant availability of radio contact, patrol officers spend as much as 60% of their time out of the immediate control and sight of their supervisors. Some officers, who work in departments where their supervisors are tied to their desks by paper work, estimate that 80% to 90% of the time they are not directly supervised. With computers now keeping track of and profiling officers' activities, this may change, but we don't feel it will necessarily be for the better. The authors believe that, even if it became possible to monitor all of an officer's decisions as they were made, such complex monitoring would interfere with the officer's ability to carry out effective law enforcement.

According to the view that we are presenting here, the most freedom from close supervision in the law-enforcement department belongs to the officer "on the street"; in contrast, supervisors and administrators generally have less opportunity to make independent decisions.

❖ DISCRETION AND CORRUPTION

Police scandals of past years have demonstrated how a corrupt officer who is inadequately supervised can do considerable harm. In the past there has been a history in many departments of widespread corruption in the form of the acceptance of bribes, covering for thieves, and brutality. This lack of adequate departmental control over the behavior of some of its officers threatened to tarnish the reputation of police officers in general. The public often felt it could not trust anyone connected with the force.

When a department has been permeated with corruption, it is difficult for young officers joining the force to resist the pressure to engage in similar illegal and unethical acts because of the models and group pressures provided by the senior members of the force.

Charges of corruption in the past resulted in police departments becoming highly sensitive to the possibility of reoccurrence. The Knapp Commission Report (1973) states, "The rookie is faced with the situation where it is easier for him to become corrupt than to remain honest." Part of the problem is that satisfactory performance as a law officer, such as making good arrests and keeping peace in the area, can occur while also taking small bribes and being occasionally brutal to prisoners.

This danger of corruption has led to an interesting paradox in thinking about police work that creates considerable tension in departments. Police officers on the street must have considerable freedom of behavior to carry out their duties, *but*, because of the fear of corruption, the department must exercise control over their behavior.

How to control patrol officers' behavior and ensure that they are doing their job and at the same time staying honest is a big question. Thus far we have seen no totally satisfactory solution. What we do see are insufficient attempts to find an answer.

❖ ADMINISTRATION BY REGULATION

Because police departments have quasi-military structures (e.g., military ranks, hierarchical organization, and chain of command), control has been centralized at the top. This belief that effective decisions must be made at the highest levels and passed down is now being strongly questioned in industry (e.g., Deming, 1986; Peters and Waterman, 1982). However, law enforcement lags in incorporating new management concepts into its administrative practices. Several officers, upon reading the preceding statement, commented that we were being much too kind in using the word lags—they felt management was locked into old-fashioned, traditional ways of doing things.

In an attempt to maintain control at the top and minimize independent thinking in a highly centralized organization, detailed regulations and procedures have been created. Under this philosophy of management, all the officer on the street has to do is follow the regulations to the letter. To make sure that these regulations are enforced, there are a multitude of levels of supervision to watch over and control the behavior of the officers on the street. This is enforced by taking disciplinary action against anyone who breaches the rules of conduct.

Fortunately for the effectiveness of law enforcement, officers do not leave their ability to think independently at home. Rather they are intelligent individuals who have found ways to work within the system of regulations. Walking the line laid down by the regulation makers produces unneeded additional tension for officers.

Brown (1981), Sparrow et al. (1990), and Bouza (1990) are among those who believe that the disciplinary style that grows out of this management philosophy is stress producing and destructive of the potential power of individual officers to do good work on the street. Punishing officers for minor infractions may seem like a good idea to some, on the premise that if we can keep them on the straight and narrow on small problems they will behave well on the bigger issues. In reality, an officer can follow every regulation on the books as far as the supervisor can observe while still doing a considerable number of corrupt and immoral things.

❖ SUPERVISORS AND OFFICER STRESS

In a study of police officer stress in England (Sparrow, et al. [1990] p. 140), the aspects of poor supervision that have the greatest adverse effect on the performance and health of all officers were as follows:

1. Unjust criticism or scapegoating
2. Lack of counseling skills

3. Unrealistic expectations
4. Contemptuous attitudes toward patrol officers
5. Insufficient concern for the individual
6. Poor communication
7. Excessive autocracy and lack of consultation

We don't have a similar study done in the United States, but our experience would lead us to believe that the list is representative of the complaints against supervisors in this country.

CASE PROBLEM 1

Your supervisor calls you in about a complaint he has received about you from a citizen. You are strongly criticized and have little chance to state your side of the story. The supervisor closes the interview with a comment about your eligibility for promotion if this occurs again. Consider the following questions:

1. How do you feel in this situation?
2. What would your response be? Would your response likely help or hinder your handling of the situation?
3. How will this encounter likely affect your work?
4. How could your supervisor have handled it differently?

Manolias (1983) in her report *Stress in the Police Service* concludes that the major stressor for police officers is not their work on the street but their feelings of vulnerability to arbitrary punishment by their own commanders. As the situation now exists, in some departments officers have to take a very protective stance about their mistakes to prevent becoming the target of disciplinary action. As one officer put it, "It's guard your ass because someone up there is hunting for an excuse to chew it out."

Brown (1981) investigated officers' reactions to supervision in three police departments in California, including several sections of the Los Angeles Police Department. Seventy-four percent of the street officers felt that their departments let them have enough discretion in making arrests and tactical decisions. Only 22% thought that most supervisors would not let them make their own decisions.

Despite these statistics, which would suggest that most officers had considerable freedom in carrying out their duties, Brown found 48% of the patrol officers said they were often or very often reprimanded for violations of rules. Sixty-one percent of the patrol officers thought supervisors were overly preoccupied with enforcing trivial rules, and 47% thought supervisors acted as if enforcing rules were their only responsibility. This seemed to be more true in the larger than in smaller police departments. The implication is that some officers may become reluctant to act or become worried about the consequences of their actions if they use discretion.

There are signs that the situation is improving. Recent articles in the *Police Chief* (Dietrich, 1989; Varga, 1988) written for supervisors give instructions for improving the performance of the street officer by improving the level and quality of the supervision they receive. Dietrich especially emphasized the need for more rewards and praise for work well done from the immediate supervisors. Officers say that, if three stripers spent less time trying to discipline their way into getting good work from them and gave a few more words of praise, it would result in increased morale.

In an initiative by the police department in Duluth, Minnesota, all supervisors received extensive training in career planning to assist in the development of their officers. The training included communication and counseling techniques, information on developmental stages of careers, individual and bureau goal setting, and how to link daily performance with annual performance evaluations.

In another study by Kirmeyer and Daugherty (1988), the effects of support by superiors on the perceived workload of 60 police radio dispatchers was examined. They concluded that support from the supervisor moderated the effects of high workload stress, reduced perceived tension and anxiety, and facilitated more positive coping behaviors among the officers.

In industry the question has been raised, "Do we need middle line management at all?" Some very successful companies have gotten rid of much of their middle management, bringing the workers on the line into closer contact with top management. The result has been an increase in productivity and profits (e.g., see Peters, 1987).

❖ QUALITY CONTROL AND LAW ENFORCEMENT

Peters and Waterman (1982) in *In Search of Excellence* have set the direction that many companies have followed. They give eight core characteristics of effective organizations, but suggest these should not be end points in themselves. Within 4 years of their study, nearly two-thirds of the highest functioning organizations had slipped from top position. On reexamination of the businesses, they had failed because they had not kept an adequate focus on the *ongoing process of quality control*.

A related industrial innovation that has implications for law-enforcement agencies has been the use of Quality Circles. These were developed by Deming (1986) and originally introduced into Japan in 1950. This was at a time when U.S. industry was self-satisfied with the lead it had obtained during World War

II and saw no need to change what had worked for so long. The Japanese were rebuilding and not subject to the same constraints. Their willingness to consider and implement innovations, in this case the value of employee involvement in decision making, created an outburst of quality products with which we are still trying to catch up.

The basic idea of *quality circles* is that the individual on the line producing the company's product often knows more about how to improve technique, equipment, and performance than do the managers of the company. The employees are formed into groups that are given responsibilities to talk about the product, their work schedules, task assignment, and other decisions that affect their work and work life. This group is given the power to make recommendations that will be carried out by management. In Chapter 20, we suggest that the chief consider how the functioning of the department might be improved if officers on a shift were given permission to frankly discuss changes in how they do their job and were allowed to make recommendations for activities to improve life for the citizens in their district that would be carried out. All this is premised on their having the ear of top administrators.

This involvement in decision making does not come easily for some, whether supervisor or officer. A training officer related one incident:

> One of our older and more traditional officers was called to a neighborhood by the residents who complained of trucks driving through the area, rather than taking the truck route to a warehouse only a few blocks away. The officer patrolled the area and gave several tickets to the violator. When the supervisor suggested that he might take a more creative, independent, and problem-focused approach by asking the drivers or company dispatcher why they did not use the truck route, he was very reluctant. The job was to follow procedures and write tickets! With encouragement, the officer pursued the issue. He was told by drivers that the trucks could not turn the corner easily because of a pole on the end of the corner. The officer was prepared to go back to ticketing, but his supervisor again encouraged him to find out what type of pole it was. Uncertainly, the officer complied and discovered it was a power pole—and again resigned himself that tickets were the solution. Again with encouragement, his supervisor suggested calling the power and light company to determine whether it could be moved. The officer was certain it could not be moved and that the power company would not be able to make such a change. He was stunned when not only did the power company arrive within 30 minutes, but they apologized that they would not be able to change it until the next morning. The supervisor finally encouraged the baffled officer to go to the neighborhood to inform the residents of the change. He returned after having become the "hero" of the neighborhood and received new status and response in his patrols.

Some officers report that it is some of the so-called "little things" that they would like to have input about: when to change to summer uniforms, the material uniforms are made of, kind of body armor to be worn, choice of cars, and the like. On the car issue, one officer said, "After all its my office and I have to spend 8 hours a day in it."

❖ SUPERVISORS: THE MIDDLEMEN IN THE STRESS EQUATION

We have been considering the stress placed on patrol officers by the administration of the department, particularly the stress that many of them feel in dealing with their immediate supervisor. While some supervisors boast that "we don't get ulcers, we give ulcers," their job is one with a number of pressures that in fact lead to many of the same stress symptoms experienced by patrol officers. Both groups identify primary stressors originating not from the nature of the job, but from the organization, its procedures, and policies (Hillgren et al., 1976). We will now examine the stressors inherent in being a supervisor and suggest some ways in which reducing patrol officers' stress will also make the supervisor's job less stressful.

The sergeant is the first supervisor to arrive at the scene after the patrol officer, taking command of most situations. The sergeant is also the officer who picks up rule infractions by officers and takes disciplinary action. Many sergeants see themselves as mediators between upper administration and the patrol officers. Often they feel protective toward the officers under their direction and want to show them support, as well as how to function more effectively on the street. They can pass on suggestions, demonstrate ways of doing the job, and try to deflect unreasonable pressures from above. On the other hand, they must see that the officers produce results that demonstrate they are doing their job as expected.

Protecting the officers under them and still carrying out the directives of the department can be a narrow line for the supervisor to walk. Officers on the street need a great deal of discretionary power if they are to carry out their assigned task of enforcing the law and assisting the public. As a result, they are often secretive about some of their actions and resentful of close supervision. If a sergeant is too concerned about enforcing the regulations, especially those that the officers see as trivial, the supervisor may find that the officers "dummy up" and do not pass on important information.

Or, if for some reason the sergeant cannot develop good working relations with them, the officers will find some way to effectively cut the supervisor out of the communication loop. The sergeant then finds himself or herself making decisions without proper information. Operating blindly could place the supervisor in a position of career endangerment.

Thus, the major pressure on the middle-level manager comes from the squeeze from top and bottom. Top administration wants the rules strictly enforced. The individuals under supervision want some slack and will resist strict enforcement. According to Trojanowicz (1980), other pressures on the middle-level supervisor include the fact that their role is often not well defined and that they have a lot of responsibility but not much authority.

The supervisor is also given two tasks that are sometimes seen as incompatible: (1) they have to be aware of the emotional and personal problems of those under them and give support, and (2) they have to handle grievances against the officers and discipline them. To be a source of personal support, often a paraprofessional counselor, and also an evaluator and disciplinarian places the supervisor in an often untenable dual role. This means that much of the job stress for supervisors is from emotional factors rather than physical danger, but this remains, nonetheless, highly stressful.

For the most part sergeants like their work, and the stress is much like that of other managers. A study by Norvell et al., (1988) found that, when the supervisors felt that they were distressed by the job, they had both an increased number of physical symptoms and indicated greater job dissatisfaction. Conversely, the more satisfaction these police supervisors had with their work, the fewer physical symptoms they reported.

Bouza's (1990) impression, based on a long career as a police department administrator in New York and Minneapolis, is that sergeants are often good rule followers with good test-taking skills. This is supported by personality assessment using the Myers–Briggs Type Indicator (Myers and McCaulley, 1985), who characterize sergeants as strongly preferring facts over possibilities, as stabilizers rather than innovators in organizations, and as attentive to rules, policies, and regulations. Their greatest challenge is to transform themselves from being order takers into effective order givers. Bouza believes that few departments train their personnel for this switch in roles, with the result being low quality or ambivalent supervision.

To manage their own stress better, middle-line supervisors need to have more control over the situations with which they are confronted. One way they can establish more control is by getting the full cooperation of the officers under their direction. Helping the patrol officers to deal with their tensions on the job and to alleviate their stress feeds back into the system as less stress for the supervisor.

Elsewhere in the book we discuss the emotions that officers will likely feel in a variety of situations and give suggestions for dealing with these emotions. It can be immensely reassuring for them to know that their supervisor appreciates what they are experiencing and takes an appropriate action with them.

Dietrich (1989) in article in *The Police Chief* focuses on anger, sorrow, fear and hate. Most officers learn to hide these emotions from the citizens they deal with because they are expected to be calm and in absolute control of themselves. Consequently, they may be hesitant to share these common emotions even with other officers. Not sharing does not mean they do not suffer the consequences of the stress produced by these emotions.

TABLE 9-1   NAMING EMOTIONS

When a supervisor is discussing an officer's feelings with him or her, it may be better to use words other than anger, sorrow, fear, or hate. Since emotions are felt on a continuum from weak to strong, more appropriate terms may be:

Anger: annoyed, irritated, resentful, surly, mean, vindictive, belligerent, furious, enraged

Sorrow: blue, sad, exhausted, discouraged, regretful, grief, miserable, hopeless

Fear: cautious, concerned, worried, afraid, anxious, apprehensive, terror stricken

Hate: dislike, resent, scorn, revulsion, disgust, detest, despise

---

Since they have been on the street, supervisors have experienced anger, grief, fear, and hate. While many of them have learned to accept these emotions and deal with them, some supervisors still have difficulty acknowledging and dealing with the emotions of their officers. We assume that they possess the skills for handling strong feelings, but for some reason do not always use these skills to their advantage. A range of terms describing emotions commonly experienced by officers is given in Table 9-1.

In an ideal system the sergeant would be the role model for younger officers regarding how to handle intense emotions. By his or her own behavior and self-disclosure, the sergeant could show others how these emotions can be effectively handled.

❖ DEALING WITH PATROL OFFICERS' STRESS

The manner in which the supervisor acknowledges and responds to officers' stress creates the norm to which other officers will later react. Stress reactions should be monitored to ensure that officers are fit for duty. If officers are uncomfortable and certainly if they are impaired in some way, the supervisor should refer them to needed resources. This might involve referral for medical checkup or consultation with a counselor or psychologist. By monitoring the stress levels of officers, the supervisor can more easily identify when overall levels are becoming critical. It may become necessary to conduct reviews of division practices or start a support group if too many people are stressed.

We recommend that supervisors consider the following practices for helping patrol officers deal with their stress.

1. *Use your listening skills.* Check out what you are hearing to be sure you are accurately hearing the facts and tuning into the right emotions. Put into your own words what it is you think the officer is saying and feeling. Acknowledge the underlying emotions if they are not being openly

expressed. Good listening results in improvement in the relationship between supervisors and officers. This addresses a major complaint of officers who do not think their supervisors understand or care enough to listen.

2. *Read people; listen to their body language and what is not expressed.* You know that the emotions we are talking about are normal under some conditions. Watch for what the officer does not say or admit to. Some comment from the supervisor may normalize what has happened. For example, a prosecutor has plea bargained away a good case made by an officer who shows no response. Perhaps recognition on the part of the supervisor could be, "It's really frustrating to see a guy like that get away with it, isn't it?"

3. *Be supportive.* This is more than just backing up the patrol officers. It is actively letting the troops know that you want to help and are available both as supervisor and as a person. Such support involves listening and "reading" as noted above, as well as sometimes advocating for them, temporarily reducing workload, recognizing effective coping, and giving them the opportunity to confidentially blow off steam. The officers need to know that the supervisors are there for them to use as a resource and sounding board.

4. *Reward good work.* Too many officers complain that what all supervisors are interested in is chewing them out for making mistakes. They feel that good work goes unnoticed, and no one but another street officer can recognize it. Verbal recognition increases the officer's self-esteem, and the officer is much more likely to continue doing a good job rather than withdrawing and playing it safe by doing very little. Complimenting an officer in the presence of peers can do much to enhance esteem and status.

   One department we are connected with uses a Goodie Board, that is, a bulletin board placed in a prominent spot to display information about awards, citations, and positive letters from members of the community that members of the force have received.

   You might also consider having regular meetings with your personnel to review good work, emphasize the positive, and listen to their concerns. Awards ceremonies to recognize achievements and good work are a good way to help boost morale. Finally, use officers' experiences during training to promote recognition of their expertise by new officers.

5. *Use discipline fairly.* Regulations get breached and your job will be in danger if you do not enforce them. Be sure, however, that the consequences are known in advance and are appropriate, considering all circumstances. Again, a complaint of many officers is that punishment is often too severe for the infraction and that it is like getting struck by lightning: you don't have much control over who it's going to strike and when. For discipline to work, it has to be predictable and appropriate. This means consistent across officers, and consistent across time.

6. *Encourage the development of support groups for critical incident debriefings, as well as managing other work stresses.* These sessions not only clear the air, but tend to counteract the macho image that officers can take anything and not be affected. They learn to give and receive support, express themselves, develop strong team discussions, and increase trust toward the supervisor for supporting such an activity.

7. *Keep officers informed.* Keep open communications with personnel, explain reasons for decisions, and whenever possible solicit input on decisions that will affect them. Don't assume that the informal system will accurately communicate information without rumor or distortion. For example, if the city council takes an action that is going to influence the department, make sure that the patrol officers learn about it through official channels. Keep an open door where they can check out changes in policy, rules, and assignments.

8. *Encourage problem-focused police work in which officers develop initiative and well-reasoned discretion.* Performance statistics are important, but a good problem-solving officer may do more for the community than an officer who brings in high numbers. This recognition of good problem-solving skills will promote creativity, increase officers' self-esteem, and bring about more constructive long-term solutions to community problems.

9. *Reflect on your style and relationships.* As you develop as a supervisor, your values, priorities, and style of relating will likely undergo subtle changes. It is important to periodically reflect on what is important to you, how your job is changing, and what kind of relationships and professionalism you are generating with your officers.

❖ SUPERVISORY ROLE STRESS

Being a supervisor has its own pressures, which can result in stress symptoms. One way of looking at these problems of being a supervisor is through role theory, which says supervisor problems can be described in terms of the following:

1. *Role ambiguity,* or not having a clear idea of what to do
2 *Role conflict,* or conflicting or incompatible demands
3. *Role overload,* or more to do than there is time for

All three role conditions have been found to be related in various occupations to low job satisfaction, job tension, job-related threat to well-being, low self-confidence and self-esteem, somatic symptoms (e.g., high blood pressure and pulse rate), alcohol abuse, high accident rates, absenteeism, and depression (French and Caplan, 1973, 1980; Holt, 1982; McLean, 1979).

Role ambiguity. One variable defined early in occupational stress studies is that of role ambiguity, or "what am I doing here?" This refers to a relative level of uncertainty or lack of clarity about what one is supposed to do on the job. The person on the job needs to know the responsibilities, work objectives, and the extent to which daily expectations from others may change (Kahn et al., 1964). Other sources of ambiguity include unclear evaluation criteria, uncertainty where to begin with a large variety of tasks, and little feedback on adequacy of performance.

Role ambiguity is most likely when administration or operating philosophy changes or is in transition. Under these conditions, supervisors may be hesitant to exercise initiative and control, to take responsibility, or to perform decisively because the boundaries of responsibility are unclear or shifting. The frustration that is experienced by the supervisor may be expressed in nit picking about the minor areas where certainty exists or simply as an expression of frustration taken out on subordinates. This leads finally to poor working conditions, low efficiency, low morale, and if these are not corrected, high turnover of personnel is the result (Moch et al., 1979).

Individual differences are also a factor in how much role ambiguity a person can handle. For example, most officers and supervisors are disciplined, highly organized people who follow the rules and prefer structure. When these people are faced with an ill-defined or ambiguous job, they feel considerable tension. Some job situations have been estimated to have as high as 60% of their workers complaining of stress due to ambiguity (French and Caplan, 1980).

Role conflict occurs when the supervisor is clear on what is required of him or her, but there are incongruent or conflicting demands. For example, a supervisor might want an officer to provide more detail and clearer writing in reports, while also demanding that more reports be done in a shorter period of time. There may be the pressure of having to get along with diverse people or groups ("stuck in the middle"), having differences in opinion between oneself and one's supervisors and subordinates, or having duties that you really do not like or think you should not have to carry out. Role conflict can be particularly strong with women officers, who must contend with balancing pressures at home and work: being a good mother and wife, dealing with mixed expectations from the public, being tough but feminine, and being true to herself while not being trapped into trying to continually prove herself to male officers.

In one national sample of workers, 48% reported that they were sometimes caught between two or more different sets of demands, while 15% noted such conflict as a frequent and even serious problem (Kahn et al., 1964). Generally, the more time spent interacting with other people and groups, the more likely it is that inconsistent and conflicting demands will be experienced. With the awareness that in this position you cannot please everyone, or rather that you will always displease someone, it can be easier to resign yourself to feelings of futility or not caring. Such supervisors turn a deaf ear to officer complaints and expect officers to learn to deal with problems as they have—by not doing anything.

Individual differences also affect perceived role conflict. Introverts, for example, are often more stressed by this type of conflict than are extroverts. French and Caplan (1980) speculate that, because introverts are more independent than extroverts, their independence is threatened by conflict in social situations. In addition, people who are flexible more often blame themselves for conflict, while rigid people tend to externalize blame to others or the situation.

Role overload. A final type of role stress occurs with role overload, in which the supervisor is faced with demands that exceed the resources or time available. Overload can be considered quantitative, in which there is too much to do for a given time period, for example, too many reports to write, contacts to follow up, or phone calls to answer or return. It can also be qualitative, in which the level of expectations or attainment is too high or the job requires skills and knowledge that exceed that of the person, for example, a new computer network with database and communication system given to an officer with no previous experience in computers. This can be especially strong in high-achievement and quality-driven high-tech departments. Ivancevich and Matteson (1980) compare this situation with an overloaded electrical system, in which the lines attempt to carry much more power than their capacity allows. The result is a blown fuse or tripped switch box, thereby preventing damage to the system. Unfortunately, people do not usually have such effective safety devices, and they can become overloaded with tasks that eventually can impair their performance. Some examples of the sources of overload are given in Table 9-2.

Studies of role overload show that it is common, especially in bureaucracies. In a national survey, 44% of working males report job overload. A study of human service workers showed over 50% experiencing insufficient time, given

TABLE 9-2   SOURCES OF OVERLOAD

Qualitative stressors:
  Difficulty of assignments
  Novelty of tasks
  Uncertainty of outcome
  Ambiguity of situation
  Level of knowledge or skill required
  Standards expected or required

Quantitative stressors:
  Too many phone calls
  Long work hours
  High levels of paper work
  Number of follow-ups
  Multiple tasks

their work demands (Pines and Aronson, 1988). Excessive paperwork and red tape were identified as primary sources of overload by 4,500 police officers (Watson and Sterling, 1969). Police officers were found to have among the highest rates, with over 70% complaining that (Kirkham, 1977)

> Society expects too much of its policemen. Not only are they expected to enforce the law, they must also be curbside psychiatrists, marriage counselors, social workers—even ministers and doctors. A good street officer combines in his daily work splinters of each one of these complex professions, and many more.

A way of thinking about all three of these kinds of role stress is to consider them as requiring high responsibility with low control. Officers and supervisors are highly accountable for their work, yet most of the outcomes depend on people and circumstances outside their direct control. Repeated exposure to this frustration has been termed "learned helplessness" (Seligman, 1979) and can eventually result in feelings of futility, demoralization, lowered motivation, and even serious depression. Officers report such feelings when rules and plans are changed frequently, but with little advance notice. They also feel little control when they are transferred to different partners, areas, or work assignments with no preparation or discussion (Kroes, 1976).

Officers in this dilemma often attribute failure to themselves, while seldom recognizing successes and acknowledging their effective performances. They can become bitter, insensitive, and unresponsive to the needs of others and may give up hope that the system can change for the better.

Although no organizations can eliminate these role stressors, there are several things that can be done to minimize their effects.

1. To reduce role ambiguity, work assignments and tasks can be defined more clearly; policies and procedures must be updated.
2. Channels of communication must be open between levels of administration to periodically check on the clarity of expectations.
3. Select officers and supervisors who have a high tolerance for ambiguity.
4. Decreasing role conflict can be facilitated by supervisors making sure that what they expect of officers is consistent and that they are responsive to feedback from officers when they perceive a conflict.
5. Role overload can be reduced by increasing awareness and assertiveness about limits as to what one can accomplish.
6. Role overload can be reduced by screening for good fit between personal capacities and job requirements, upgrading skills of role incumbents, and assigning reasonable tasks to individuals.
7. In general, allowing supervisors and officers feedback and participation in decisions that affect them and providing appreciation for their efforts can do much to reduce stress levels.

EXERCISE

CASE PROBLEM 2
SUPERVISOR

In Michael Brown's book *Working the Street* (1981), he found that 61% of the officers in the departments he studied agreed with the following statement:

In general, field supervisors in this department are more interested in enforcing petty rules about dress, hair length, and whether or not you wear your hat when you get out of the car or whether you are a few minutes late to work than the sort of job patrolmen do.

1. How accurate is this situation for your department? How do you feel about it?
2. What are the consequences of this attitude on morale and performance?
3. As a supervisor, how would you explain your position on rule enforcement to the officers in your section?

SUMMARY

Supervisors are caught in the bind of giving the patrol officers under them enough discretionary power to do the job well, but at the same time monitoring performance to prevent corruption and ensure effective law enforcement.

The sergeant can lower officer stress by (1) recognizing emotional reactions such as anger and fear, (2) taking the officers personal problems outside the job into consideration, and (3) encouraging good problem-solving skills.

To help middle management (sergeants) avoid stress, top administration needs to recognize the problems created by role ambiguity, role conflict, and role overload and to take steps to minimize them.

REFERENCES

Bouza, A. V. (1990). *The Police Mystique: An Insider's Look at Cops, Crime, and the Criminal Justice System.* New York: Plenum Press.

Brown, M. K. (1981). *Working the Street: Police Discretion and the Dilemmas of Reform.* New York: Russell Sage Foundation.

Deming, W. E. (1986). Out of the Crisis. Cambridge, MA: MIT Press.

Dietrich, J. F. (1989). Helping subordinates face stress. *The Police Chief*, November, 44–47.

French, J. R. P., and R. D. Caplan (1973). Organizational stress and individual stress. In A. J. Morrow (ed.), *The Failure of Success.* New York: AMACOM, pp. 30–36.

French, J. R. P., and R. D. Caplan (1980). In J. D. Adams (eds.), *Understanding and Managing Stress: A Book of Readings.* San Diego, CA: University Associates.

Guyot, D. (1991). *Policing as Though People Matter*. Philadelphia: Temple University Press.

Hilgren, J. S., R. Bond, and S. Jones (1976). Primary stressors in police administration and law enforcement. *Journal of Police Science and Administration 4*, 445–449.

Holt, R. R. (1982). Occupational stress. In L. Goldberger and S. Breznitz (eds.), *Handbook of Stress: Theoretical and Clinical Aspects*. New York: Macmillan, pp. 419–444.

Ivancevich, J. M., and M. T. Matteson (1980). *Stress and Work: A Managerial Perspective*. Glenview, IL: Scott Foresman.

Kahn, R. L., D. M. Wolfe, R. P. Quinn, J. D. Snoek, and R. A. Rosenthal (1964). *Organizational Stress: Studies in Role Conflict and Ambiguity*. New York: Wiley.

Kirkham, G. (1977). From professor to patrolman: A fresh perspective on the police. *Journal of Police Science and Administration 2 (2)*, 127–137.

Kirmeyer, S. L., and T. W. Daugherty (1988). Work load, tension, and coping: Moderating effects of supervisor support. *Personnel Psychology 41*, 125–139.

Knapp Commission. (1973). *Report on Police Corruption*. New York: George Braziller.

Kroes, W. (1976). *Society's Victim—The Policeman: An Analysis of Job Stress in Policing*. Springfield, IL: Charles C Thomas.

Manolias, A. (1983). A preliminary study of Stress in the police service. London: Home Office SRDB Human Factors Group, 13 pages.

McLean, A. A. (1979). *Work stress*. Reading, MA: Addison-Wesley.

Moch, M. K., J. Bartunek, and D. J. Brass (1979). Structure, task characteristics, and experienced role stress in organizations employing complex technology. *Organizational Behavior and Human Performance 24*, 258–268.

Myers, I. B., and M. H. McCaulley (1985). *Manual: A guide to the development and use of the Myers–Briggs type indicator*. Palo Alto, CA: Consulting Psychologists Press.

Norvell, N., D. Belles, and H. Hills (1988). Perceived stress levels and physical symptoms in supervisory law enforcement personnel. *Journal of Police Science and Administration 16*, 75–79.

Peters, T. J. (1987). *Thriving on Chaos: Handbook for a Management Revolution*. Harper Perennial.

Peters, T. J., and R. H. Waterman (1982) *In Search of Excellence*. New York: Harper Collins.

Pines, A., and E. Aronson (1988). *Career Burnout: Causes and Cures*. New York: Free Press.

Seligman, M. E. (1979). *Helplessness: On Depression Development and Death*. San Francisco: W. H. Freeman.

Sparrow, M. K., M. H. Moore, and D. M. Kennedy (1990). *Beyond 911: A New Era for Policing*. New York: Basic Books.

Trojanowicz, R. C. (1980). *The Environment of the First-line Police Supervisor*. Englewood cliffs, NJ: Prentice Hall.

Varga, A. J. (1988). Addressing low morale: The employee interview project. *The Police Chief*, December, 22.

Watson, N., and J. Sterling (1969). *Police and Their Opinions*. Gaithersberg, MD: International Association of Chiefs of Police.

10

❖

Dealing with the Public

A police officer explains to a group of day-camp children how to use 911. He and another officer also discussed bicycle safety and vandalism. (Photo from the *Columbia Missourian*)

I'm not against the police; I'm just afraid of them.

—Alfred Hitchcock

❖ OBJECTIVES

1. To appreciate why the public often fails to understand the nature of work in law enforcement.
2. To discuss the tensions that exist between the police and the public.
3. To understand why police are often distressed by the public's behavior.

4. To look at ways to improve communication and lessen the tensions between police and the public.

5. To stress the point that if the public is working cooperatively with law enforcement the job is easier and less hazardous.

❖ INTRODUCTION

People tend to associate socially with others who they are comfortable with. It is often difficult for law-enforcement officers to find civilians to associate with during off work time with whom they can be relaxed. Factors that make it difficult include the following:

1. Citizens see law-enforcement officers as a threat and are therefore uncomfortable around them.
2. Much of what law-enforcement personnel do is misunderstood by the public.
3. Officers feel as though they can't be "normal" citizens when off duty.
4. Jokes that officers laugh at are sometimes seen by citizens as sick or distasteful.

For these and other reasons, it is a common experience for young officers to find that their social life is more comfortable if they make new friends only with people who are connected with law enforcement. Even people who have been friends for years may be put off by the officer's new role. Officers report that the message comes fairly early in their careers that, once they are identified as being a law-enforcement officer, people view them differently and have trouble relaxing around them.

For example, an officer goes to a party and begins to talk about a call to an emergency situation where a death was involved that had a humorous element to it. The officer notices that the listeners laugh at the wrong time, draw back as if repulsed by what the officer has done, or indicate in some other way that they do not understand what the officer is talking about.

Aspects of the job that the officer takes for granted, such as using a choke hold or handcuffing a suspect may be looked at scornfully or suspiciously. It doesn't take most officers very long to see that they cannot talk freely about their day to day activities to people outside the department.

At a deeper level, however, the problem involves different interpretations between the public and law enforcement as to what the assigned task is. Officers tell us that the middle and upper classes see the role of law enforcement as keeping drunks, drug dealers, prostitutes, and other low life off the street and answering their calls for service when they need help with something. At the same time, the middle class prefers that police officers remain relatively inconspicuous.

❖ PUBLIC MISPERCEPTIONS OF THE POLICE OR WHY THE PUBLICDOESN'T UNDERSTAND

We believe that the public in general has unrealistic expectations of law-enforcement officers and that this places additional stress on officers who try to live up to these expectations. We have all seen movies and TV shows during the course of which the police officer hero, played by Clint Eastwood or Mel Gibson, shoots and kills four felons. The hero of the story suffers no negative reactions and feels no need to take time off between shootings.

In other movies there is the classic chase through the streets of San Francisco or New York in which pedestrians are narrowly missed, cars crash madly into one another, and the hero escapes unscratched with no signs of stress.

Most of this action is totally unrealistic. However, much of how people view police is based on movies and TV, which show some very exceptional and unusual events that can happen to law-enforcement officers. The problem is not that these things don't happen but that they are treated in these shows as if they were normal everyday events. All this has about as much relationship to what really goes on in law enforcement as the old movie westerns with Gene Autry had to the real West.

Part of the public's fascination is with the power that officers are given to enforce the law, including the power to kill. The exciting life of a movie cop is particularly attractive to individuals who are caught in routine, dull lives. In their imaginations they identify with the hero who, with his or her uniform, badge, and sidearm, has been removed from a drab daily existence into a world where there is always action, people are brave, and justice triumphs. What people don't see in these presentations is the boredom, the petty annoyances, add the real human responses to danger and death.

Contact with a police officer and his or her visible symbols of power can create a nervous rush in even the most honest citizen. For example, when a uniformed officer walks into a restaurant, the first thing that most people think about is everything that they have done wrong, like driving with expired plates or not paying a parking ticket. The citizen sees a powerful, emotionless, courageous individual who society has handed some of the prerogatives of "the terminator."

This awareness of what a police officer can potentially do may be one reason that the public becomes so upset when they read or hear about police violence. Officers giving vent to rage and beating someone stimulates the fear of citizen's that they too could have their freedom violently taken away by the police. The fact that the offender may have been dangerous or aggressive is lost in the news story.

In countless movies, such as *Lethal Weapon* and *Dirty Harry*, the power of police to kill offenders distorts the image of the real men and women behind the badge. But the existence of this false picture creates a tension in the relationship between police officers and the public. In effect, the officer is likely to feel, "I'm not who you think I am. I'm a fraud, here under false pretenses."

New television documentaries showing live footage of police at work are more accurately depicting the nature of police work. This has helped the public to appreciate some of the hardships and stresses of being a police officer. These programs have the potential to improve the public's relationship with law-enforcement personnel. However, these shows sometimes continue to glamorize the role of police, without fully considering the adverse consequences of the job that are discussed in this book.

On the other hand, all this media exploitation is not without its positive side. Having the public respect the power of the police does increase the officers ability to keep things under control. Bouza (1990) says that it is one reason that police are likely to want to keep the public from knowing how they really operate and is part of the reason that the public often feels that the message of the police is, "We're the professionals, leave crime control to us and stay out of it."

Our conclusion is that the power image helps officers enforce the law, but it also causes a stress on the officer by forcing him or her to live up to these unrealistic expectations. Of course, officers do on occasion use power techniques to control situations by intimidating people with reflective sunglasses, hands on hips stance, and moving in too close to the other person's personal space.

CASE EXAMPLE

An officer is handling a car accident in which a compact car has nosedived at high speed under the rear end of a semitruck. The driver and front-seat passengers are dead, one child in the rear is dead, and one is severely injured. The officer is expected to establish complete control of the scene by:

1. Administering first aid
2. Keeping the crowd under control
3. Keeping the traffic flowing
4. Preserving evidence at the scene

The officer is not allowed to respond with sadness and anger because:

1. People can't see police officers cry.
2. The officer doesn't have time during a crisis to recognize and deal with emotions, so they are stifled.

This pressure on officers to live up to other peoples' expectations of them is not unusual. Among other professions, doctors, lawyers, and professors all take on some of the characteristics that the public they deal with expects them to have.

Some additional insight into what the public expects police to be like comes from the "Survey of Community Attitudes toward Philadelphia Police: Final Report" (1986). Fifty percent of those polled thought the police were rude,

49% thought the police took bribes, and 66% thought the police used unnecessary force. Despite the negative view of police that these statistics would suggest, only 5% said the police were doing a poor job and 70% rated the police department as good or excellent overall.

❖ WHAT THE PUBLIC WANTS FROM POLICE

The services the public wants from police were studied in order to improve community relations. It was found that what concerns citizens is not what police usually assume concerns the public (Sparrow et al., 1990). Members of the community did not place serious crime high on the list of their demands. Instead they wanted the police do something about drunks, rowdy teenagers, abandoned cars, and the like. The authors conclude that people want police help, but they want it on their terms.

This discrepancy between the public definition of what police should be doing and what the police see as their main responsibility is another point of tension between citizens and police that raises the stress level on both sides. This leads to the question, "Should police continue to highlight their main task as crime fighting or should they broaden it to one of raising the quality of life in the communities they serve?"

Much of what police officers do in the way of public service is almost invisible to the majority of the public, partly because it seems to be taken for granted and not talked about, and certainly not shown in movies or on TV. This would include such acts as changing a flat tire, unlocking a car with the keys locked inside, rescuing a cat out of a tree, and helping track down lost items. The bind here is that publicizing this role could lead to more of these calls, which many officers see as taking them away from their main assignment of stopping crime. On the other hand, publicizing this role could raise the level of cooperation from the public serviced and make crime fighting easier because of additional leads and help from citizens.

❖ FEARS OF PUBLIC ABOUT POLICE OFFICERS

We discussed earlier in this book that society has given police considerable latitude in the use of force. If suspects are to be arrested, areas searched, or people stopped and interrogated, the officers must be assured the discretionary power and force to back up carrying out their duties. But running along with the potential use of force are other concepts necessary to law enforcement: reasonable suspicion, probable cause, questionable circumstances, and articulable grounds (Bouza, 1990).

When these latter concepts are used to stop a white middle-class citizen, the response is likely to be, "Why aren't you out capturing real criminals, instead of harassing honest citizens?" In effect, the middle class is saying, "Use your power to enforce the law, but not on us."

Through its laws, society has given the police the responsibility to keep the underclass under control. However, in carrying out their mission, officers are not to make any mistakes about who is in the underclass. When an officer does a street interrogation on a lower-class individual, he or she is doing his or her duty to protect the common welfare. When the officer does it to a middle-class individual, he or she is guilty of harassment. This can result in phone calls to various officials and perhaps a letter that can end up in an officer's file. Sparrow et al. (1990) cite one officer as saying, "When you're an officer in the suburbs, you're a civil servant. When you're an officer in the ghetto, you're god."

❖ THE SPECIAL CASE OF RACISM

Blacks are much more likely to stopped for interrogation than whites, even when driving equally good automobiles. Brown, in his book *Working the Street* (1981), found that in two of the cities he studied blacks were 14 times as likely to be arrested for traffic offenses as whites. They are also likely to be handled

---

TABLE 10-1   NEWSPAPER STORIES

NEW YORK–Scores of people rampage through streets of Washington Heights, angered by fatal shooting of Hispanic by police officer. One man dies in violence and at least 15 are injured as cars are overturned, fires set, and bottles thrown from windows; bands of 50 to 100 people run through streets, shouting "killer cop" and "justice" in Spanish.

LOS ANGELES–Olympic gold medalist Al Joyner files $2 million claim against Los Angeles, alleging that he was stopped, handcuffed, and forced to kneel at gunpoint by police because he was black.

TYLER, TEXAS–Black anger over several cases of perceived injustices by police and courts has broken usual quiet; protests are loudest over fatal shooting of bedridden 84-year old black woman by white police officer in botched drug raid.

---

more roughly. In contacts between a black citizen and a white police officer, there is often the presumption of prejudice.

The police defense of this special attention is that blacks make up 13 percent of the population but 40 percent of the prison population. (Bouza, 1990, p. 93). It is difficult to reconcile the public's demand for fair treatment of all citizens with crime statistics that suggest that a black is more likely to be a crack dealer or be engaged in burglary. Even the statement we have just made in this paragraph about the greater crime rate among blacks is likely to make some people feel that we have been guilty of racism.

The response of the media in Los Angeles to police use of the choke hold is an example of how a demand to protect a group may lead to endangering the group. The choke hold temporarily cuts off the flow of blood to the brain, causing violent suspects to pass out. The Los Angeles police had to stop using the choke hold after the uproar raised because of a remark made by the then Chief Gates that blacks were somehow different from "normal people" in the flow of blood to the brain. The paradox is that violent suspects who might have been controlled by the choke hold may now end up being killed because deadly force has to used instead.

CASE PROBLEM 1

You have stopped a car for expired license plates. The couple inside the car are a black man and a white woman. She loudly accuses you of stopping them because of your racial prejudice.

1. What is the surface problem?
2. What is your goal in talking to the person? What do you want to happen?
3. What alternative actions are there for you? What would be the outcome of each alternative?
4. What is your recommendation as to what should be done in this situation?

❖ HOSTILITY OF POLICE TO THE PUBLIC

So what do cops see? They see families in the middle of an all-out fight, angry and maybe bloodied; drunks swearing and screaming at each other; people hurt and scared; and the bloodied bodies of accident victims. Most people don't invite the police to their parties where they are on their best behavior; instead their actions bring the police to the brawls and emergencies where people's dark side is in full view. It is the cop's job to deal with and try to control the public's worst instincts and evil desires.

How can the public understand someone who has seen the worst side of people and consequently become cynical about human nature? A point that we keep making in this book is that, in dealing with people's pain and the underside

TABLE 10-2 WHAT COPS SEE

CHICAGO–A man was charged with first-degree murder and aggravated criminal sexual assault for an attack on his girlfriend's 7-month-old son.

CHICAGO–A family of four Laotian immigrants' severely decomposed bodies was found in their apartment.

JEFFERSON COUNTY, MISSOURI–Woman arrested for fatally poisoning her 5-month-old son with antifreeze when he was in foster care.

CHICAGO–The former janitor of a Northwest Side elementary school pleaded guilty to molesting seven girls aged 8 to 15, most of them inside the school.

of life, law-enforcement officers bury their emotional reactions and become cynical. Not having seen what cops see, civilians do not understand their attitude.

Because the public sometimes has little understanding of how police officers see their job, it is easy for the police to react with contempt. The public does not agree with the officers' ideas of what is important and how the job has to be done in a real-life situation. As a result, the public gets upset over what appears to be brutality without having any insight into how these things can happen in the heat of the moment. More often, what is labeled brutality is a symptom of an officer who acts out in the only way he or she knows how under the circumstances. Police can easily resent the expectation that they shouldn't give in to their anger no matter how extreme the provocation.

CASE PROBLEM 2

Some fraternity men are creating a disturbance in a bar. When you approach them, there is a derisive comment about your sexual orientation and a suggestion that (males) your wife is promiscuous with your "pig buddies" or (females) what you really need is to get laid.

1. How does this situation make you feel?
2. What is your right to feel this way?
3. Is your response likely to help or hinder your handling of the situation?

Officers need to be on their toes to respond appropriately to individuals from different social classes and ethnic and racial groups partly because they have different attitudes toward the officer in the blue uniform. To middle-class people, the cop is a civil servant and is not there to arrest them for drunkenness or traffic violations. To someone in the lower or underclass, the police officer is a powerful enforcer who can come down on them hard at anytime, so, except in unusual circumstances, respect and fear are the appropriate response. The lower class is also more likely to respond to the officer with physical confrontation or aggressive language. The underclass is not likely to make any formal protests about police behavior.

The middle class is much more prone to lodging protests and writing letters. Sparrow et al. (1990) report that, while there are genuine complaints made against officers, perhaps as many as two-thirds are the result of malice or the desire for revenge or to obstruct a prosecution, get police attention, or advance some political goal. This kind of inappropriate harassment can lead to officers writing the public off as a nuisance and will go even further toward proving that no one besides another officer can really understand the nature of law enforcement.

CASE PROBLEM 3

You have stopped a Lincoln Continental for driving 55 in a 30 mile an hour zone. The driver is an expensively dressed 60-year-old female. As you are trying to tell her why you stopped her, she vehemently denies doing anything wrong. She states the opinion that "Police officers should be out solving serious crime, not harassing innocent citizens!" As you attempt to interrupt she says, "I know some people with power in this town, you'll be sorry you ever started this."

1. What is the surface problem?
2. What is your goal in talking to this woman? What do you expect to happen?
3. What alternative actions are there for you? What would be the outcome of each altternative?
4. What is your recommendation as to what should be done?
5. What if she were black and wearing blue jeans?

Never to be overlooked as a hazard to the mental health of police officers are the special protest groups who are ready to demonstrate, sometimes violently, to prove how much they love humans, fetuses, animals, horned owls, or forests. On the other hand, it may be a group that demonstrates to show how much they hate blacks, Koreans, injustice, or just police and law in general. Many groups of dedicated people with a cause to advance engage in activities that raise the tension level of law-enforcement personnel.

There are groups who will provoke the police in an attempt to get a strong reaction that can be pointed to as an example of police brutality. The members of the group act as an innocent, injured party with statements like, "see how the police overreact."

Police officers often react to this finger pointing by closing ranks and keeping their own council. With the many ways the public can overreact, the police feel they cannot afford to be open or honest about what is going on. Confession of wrongdoing or honest mistakes can lead to lawsuits or prosecution.

TABLE 10-3   ACCUSATIONS
AGAINST POLICE

MOUNT PLEASANT, NY–Acquittal of Swiss
au pair Olivia Riner in arson murder of
infant Kristie Fischer puts focus back on
investigation by local police. Embarrassing
testimony about police missteps in investigation has become discussion of competence of suburban police departments to
handle anything other than routine tasks.

BELLEVILLE, ILLINOIS–The Illinois
Department of Human Rights will conduct
a full investigation into allegations that
Belleville police harassed black motorists
and tried to keep them out of the city.

NEW YORK–Brooklyn police sergeant is
indicted on charges of beating Ann B.
Dodds, community leader who is member
of his precinct's community council, and
assaulting one of her sons.

Police Need for the Public's Cooperation

Although it is clear that there are reasons for the police and the public to dis-
trust one another, it heightens the danger to both groups when there is a lack of
understanding or cooperation. For example, here is an item from the *St. Louis
Post Dispatch*, "A St. Charles County, MO sheriff's deputy grappled with a burglary suspect while a crowd of onlookers did nothing, refusing to even flag down
one of several police cars that were cruising the area in search of the deputy."

This lack of cooperation by citizens, however, extends the danger to more
than just the officers involved. If the public feels all law enforcement is to be purely a police affair and that they are not involved, then crimes will (and do) occur in
broad daylight and nothing will be done to prevent or even to report the.

The classic case of the public's failure to intervene is the Kitty Genovese murder, where scores of citizens hear her screaming and some saw her repeatedly stabbed,
but no one did anything to help her or to summon the police. Somehow it must be
communicated that citizens can no longer leave law enforcement to duly sworn officers. They need to see that their cooperation is necessary for their own protection.

Bouza (1990), Muir (1977), and Sparrow et al., (1990), all of whom have
reported on a major city police department in their books, concur that cops must
have the involvement and cooperation of the community if they are to effectively maintain the law. Communities that are closely knit, watch strangers, and feel
that others will back their actions have less crime problems than those areas that
are disorganized and rely exclusively on the police to maintain order.

The last decade has been marked by a trend toward community-assisted policing. This approach not only facilitates understanding and improved relations between public and police but has been successful in reducing neighborhood crimes (e.g., Glensor, 1992; Walker, 1992).

❖ WAYS OF GETTING THE PUBLICS' COOPERATION

Making arrests for crimes already committed is not proving to be effective in keeping the crime rate down. With the recognition of the failure of traditional police methods, the emphasis is now changing to crime prevention. If this new model of law enforcement is to be successful, the backing and cooperation of the public are needed. The implementation of this approach will require departments to find ways and techniques to reeducate citizens to view law-enforcement officers as professionals who need the public's help to be fully effective.

Once the public accepts the need for their cooperation if crime prevention programs are to work, then citizens involvement in self-protective activities can be initiated. One such program developed to promote a partnership between police and the public is *community-oriented police.*

Muir (1977), who followed 28 young police officers over a period of a year, observed that in lower-class districts officers often served as counselors and gave advice on repossession, insurance matters, getting ripped off at the store, and how to get help with a child's school problems. To be able to do this, the officer had to have some mastery of the law and know something about the red tape in their community and how to cut through it.

Muir gives the example of a young officer who had won the officer-of-the-year award several times from a local newspaper because of his unpaid service to local youth groups. This same officer spent much of his free time finding ways to raise money so that other officers could be paid for working with juveniles.

Being a good cop usually means being a good talker or, as some cops put it, "bullshitter." A good bullshitter can instruct, summarize, manipulate, and inspire. It means the street cop can express facts and emotions in colloquial language that the citizen can understand. Muir (1977) found that the most professional officers in his study were also those who were the most eloquent in talking with people.

"Developing the beat" is the term that Muir uses for police officers establishing relationships with the people on their beat. This meant getting to know the citizens by name and what their concerns were and making an attempt to correct situations that were community annoyances. This resulted in citizens giving information and interceding in crime prevention and other forms of cooperation. All of which lowers the stress on the officers involved.

Community-oriented policing is called by a variety of names: the Houston Police Department has Neighborhood Oriented Policing; Newport News Police and San Diego Police call it Problem Oriented Policing (POP); Flint, Michigan, is Community-based Policing; Baltimore has Citizen Oriented Police Enforcement (COPE); and Reno has Community Oriented Policing and Problem Solving (COPPS). The following section takes a look at the Reno program.

❖ RENO'S COMMUNITY-ORIENTED POLICING AND PROBLEM SOLVING

The Reno Police Department had distanced itself from the community by its emphasis on a high number of arrests and citations and lack of attention to what the citizens saw as their needs. (This program is described in three papers: Bradshaw, et al., 1990; Glensor, 1992; Weston, 1991). Relations between the police and the public were not close, so despite the growth in population of the city of Reno and loss of officers, the citizens voted down a tax increase to hire needed officers.

To implement the new program, the department decentralized into three operational areas each under a deputy chief. This provided better communication within the units. Neighborhood Advisory Groups (NAG) were formed to discuss with the police the problems as the people in the neighborhood saw them and possible solutions. Under the new philosophy, less emphasis was placed on making arrests and more on finding and correcting the underlying problems that lead to conditions producing a need to arrest people. The final models, then, for the Neighborhood Advisory Groups (NAG) depended on the nature of the neighborhood served.

A Media Advisory Group was developed to improve relations with the media, which had been seen as "unfair, biased, and sensationalized," thus contributing to the department's poor image. This gave the police an opportunity to communicate with the public about programs and projects as they evolved.

Surveys were done to measure attitudes toward the police at various points in the program development. These report cards on police activity showed a rapid improvement in the department's image. The third try at a tax increase was passed and this allowed the department to hire 88 more officers.

The authors list 20 programs that improved community relations, and we will describe four of them as examples of the kind of thing that a department can consider doing to improve community relations.

1. *Eviction program.* Properties in one area were deteriorating due to drug sales and prostitution. The landlords were afraid of lawsuits if they evicted the guilty tenants. With the police cooperating with HUD, evictions were possible and there was a significant drop in complaints.

2. *Abandoned vehicles in stead.* Community–police cooperation led to the towing of over 100 vehicles that had been abandoned in the area. Volunteers in the community provided the tow trucks.

3. *Neil Road foot patrol.* An area with a high proportion of Hispanics that was experiencing gang problems had foot patrols assigned, with one officer of the patrol being bilingual. After the start of the program, gang activity subsided.

4. *Homeless coalition.* Reno has 200 to 300 "hardcore" homeless, which produced complaints from downtown businesses. A coalition of downtown property owners, members of the city government, social service agencies, hospitals, and the police was formed to work on a solution.

❖ SUMMARY

For a number of reasons the public misunderstands the nature of law enforcement. These reasons include movies and TV misrepresentations and the news media's tendency to look with concern on police actions. What the public wants in the way of services is often different from what a law-enforcement agency sees as its mission. Good relations with the public will significantly lower the dangers and the stress of police work. Departments are now moving toward community-oriented policing to get more cooperation from citizens. In places where it has been tried, it lowers tensions, improves community relations, and raises citizen involvement in crime prevention.

OFFICERS RECLAIM AVENUE'
Neighbors Hail Police Who Retook Streets
by Bill Bryan
Of the Post-Dispatch Staff

Three months ago, Annie Pride, 70, was afraid to leave her home of 40 years in the 3700 block of Aldine Avenue. Her neighbor across the street, Grace Hayzlett, 77, was scared to leave her home, too.

Rick Green, 42 a businessman down the street, was hesitant to walk to the auto parts store around the corner on Martin Luther King Drive.

The residents of the 3700 and 3800 blocks of Aldine, in the Jeff Vander Lou neighborhood, were virtual prisoners in their homes and businesses, frightened by young men who gathered idly on the street at all hours, drinking their beer and wine, dealing their crack, and intimidating passers-by. Vandalism and car break-ins were routine.

Today, thanks to St. Louis Police Officers Ron Hasty and Tim Kavanaugh, the two blocks of Aldine have been returned to the residents. The officers, through constant, vigilant enforcement, ran off the undesirables. Along the way, the officers also helped to close some crack houses on the street and got heaps of litter removed from vacant lots.

"These two guys have done an unbelievable job," said Green, owner of Max German Meats, a neighborhood institution at 3836 Aldine for 70 years.

"I was afraid to walk to Jerry's auto parts round the corner, and I had customers who wouldn't even come here. Now, nobody's loitering in front of my place, and the vacant lot next to my building is clean.

"These two policemen cared about our area. We've never had that before."

Pride said the two officers had improved the area "100 percent."

"I was always harassed and picked on," she said softly at the front door of her small, red-brick home. "The youngsters around here were terrible.

"But I feel safe now."

Hayzlett added: "It sure is a lot different around here, now. I feel safe."

continued

continued

"The change makes you feel kind of good," said Hasty, 30, and outgoing 6-year police veteran with bright red hair. "These people have to live here or work here, and we have to work here for eight hours a day, so whatever is bad for them is bad for us."

Kavanaugh, 28, and also a 6-year veteran, lets Hasty do all the talking.

The two officers got the idea to target the two blocks of Aldine, just a small part of their beat, after they were told to come up with a COPS project. COPS stands for Community Oriented Policing, or Community Oriented Problem Solving, depending on who in the Police Department is talking.

Hasty and Kavanaugh said they chose Aldine Avenue because they were bothered by the sudden death of a baby at a "crack house" in the 3700 block. "We thought, 'This is enough.'"

Hasty and Kavanaugh began by taking a "zero tolerance" approach to the loiterers on the street. "We wouldn't let anyone congregate," Hasty said.

We leaned on them constantly," Hasty said. "Basically, I guess you'd have to say we intimidated them."

As for the crack houses, "We sat in front of them in our patrol car and ate our lunch," Hasty said. "Our presence hurt their business.

"Eventually, they moved out."

"The two officers also persuaded the owner of a junkyard—after several warnings, summonses, and arrests—to clean up unsightly debris. And they got the city to remove hundreds of liquor, wine, and beer bottles from a vacant lot next to Max German.

The neighborhood today is still a montage of vacant lots, boarded-up red brick buildings marked with spray-painted gang graffiti, and a few neat bungalows and red-brick flats. "But you should have seen it before," Hasty said.

Another appreciative resident is Larry Dotson, 47, who runs a towing service for McCall's Auto Sales and Service at 3717 Aldine.

"There used to be a lot of trouble around here with stealing, drugs, whooping, and hollering," Dotson said.

"People kept breaking in here. I was afraid to work late. Our customers were scared to come here."

"Now, I'm not afraid to work late, and the customers don't mind coming here anymore."

Harry Loebner, 55, owns Jerry's Auto Supply nearby at 3869 Martin Luther King Drive and an apartment building in the 3700 block of Aldine that was taken over by drug dealers.

"The drug dealers are gone now, thanks to these two policemen, who deserve some praise," he said.

˙Repritned with permission of the St. Louis Post–Dispatch, copyright 1993.

Two police officers chat as they patrol a high-crime area in the projects. (Photo from the *Columbia Missourian*)

QUESTIONS

1. If you witnessed the verbal abuse of a suspect, would you report it to a superior officer? What would be the likely reactions of your fellow officers if you did?
2. Examine your own expectations of what a police officer's job is like. What has contributed the most to the picture of law enforcement you now have?
3. Consider that you have a beat in a low-rent district with a group of citizens who are hard working and basically law abiding. What are three specific things you might do to improve relations with this community?

REFERENCES

Bouza, A. V. (1990). *The Police Mystique: An Insider's Look at Cops, Crime, and the Criminal Justice System*. New York: Plenum Press.

Bradshaw, R. V., K. Peak, and R. W. Glensor (1990). Community policing enhances Reno's image. *The Police Chief*, October, 61–65.

Brown, M. K. (1981). *Working the Street: Police Discretion and the Dilemmas of Reform*. New York: Russell Sage Foundation.

Glensor, R. W. (1992). *Community Oriented Policing and Problem Solving*. Report available from Reno (Nevada) Police Department.

Muir, W. K. (1977). *Police: Street Corner Politicians*. Chicago: University of Chicago Press.

Sparrow, M. K., M. H. Moore, and D. M. Kennedy (1990). *Beyond 911: A New Era for Policing*. New York: Basic Books.

Walker, S. (1992). *The Police in America*. New York: McGraw-Hill.

Weston, J. (1991). Community oriented policing: An approach to traffic management. *Law and Order*, May, 32–36.

11

❖

Testifying in Court:
On the Firing Line Again

A security station at a courthouse manned by two court security officers using a metal detector and an x-ray scanner. (Photo from the files of the *Columbia Missourian*)

❖ OBJECTIVES

1. To identify the sources of stress confronting the officer in dealing with the judicial process, attorneys, and judges.
2. To describe techniques for effectively coping with court-related stress.

❖ INTRODUCTION

Just when you thought it was all over—and it may have been 6 months ago since you last thought about the case—you are called to testify in criminal court. You locate the case file, search your memory for the details you left out of the report, try not to confuse specifics from similar cases, and in your imagination begin a long series of appearances in which you make every blunder possible.

Frustration with the judicial system is one of the more commonly acknowledged sources of stress external to the law enforcement organization (Stratton, 1978; Territo and Vetter, 1981). Rulings by the court are viewed as too lenient, compelling evidence is excluded, charges are plea bargained, offenders are prematurely released on bail, and civil rights suits may be brought against the officers themselves (White et al., 1985).

Although most officers will make only a few court appearances in their career, some who specialize in certain types of cases, such as child abuse, sexual assault, and drug traffic, may be called on regularly to give testimony. Anxiety when preparing to give testimony is routine. A common negative experience is the use of unfair pressures and tactics during cross-examination by the defense attorney, which leaves the officer feeling that he or she is on trial rather than the defendant.

But testifying *is* law-enforcement work, no matter how tempted the officer may be to avoid testifying by losing the subpoena, calling in sick, or supporting a plea bargain. And like any other aspect of law enforcement, the officer needs to be trained, equipped, and mentally prepared to deal with the situation. In this chapter we will first examine the sources of stress frequently experienced by those who have testified and then present recommendations for officers who are preparing for an appearance in court.

❖ GETTING READY TO TESTIFY

Many times an arrest is made on the basis of probable cause. However, since the court must convict on the basis of "beyond reasonable doubt," the prosecutor may be unwilling to accept a case for prosecution. Prosecutors are usually elected officials, and many of them do not want to take on cases in which conviction is not practically guaranteed. Sometimes this is for political reasons, but it may also be considered that a particular case is a poor use of limited resources. The officer may be very sure, based on what he or she has seen, that the person arrested is a bona fide perpetrator. In general, however, the court system gives every advantage to the defendant, who is presumed innocent until proved guilty.

Many officers think that after the case report is written the case is closed for them. However, in order to distribute case overloads, some prosecutors may return the case to the police department with a request for more information and statements. Even after additional information and more time into the case, it may still not be pursued. After a few circuits between offices, it often simply gets "lost."

The timing of court may also be a problem, especially for officers who work the graveyard shift. During the time they would normally be asleep, they may be called to court to testify, only to find out that other testimony took longer and they must wait or return again the next day. Interference with sleep and prolonged alertness take their toll on motivation to perform well, concentration, mood, and accuracy of memory. One officer states:

> Our department has a 12-hour shift schedule for the graveyard shift, and court is usually maintained on a rotating schedule that just accidentally matches ours. That means that whenever we bust someone, it's guaranteed that we'll have to lose either sleep or off-duty time to testify. We usually have to appear in the morning, just a few hours after we get off, so there's no use trying to get to sleep. Waking up half-rested is even worse. Half of the time we get called in only to have testimony postponed to the next day or the next. By that time, I'm no good to either the court or on the job.

Scheduling of court appearances may be a special problem in small departments. Court appearances are often scheduled when the officer needed to testify is off duty, since nobody would be left to cover calls if testifying during duty hours. For county deputies, constables from small towns, or forestry and game wardens, traveling long distances to the courthouse is not uncommon. Reimbursement for travel expenses and off-duty time spent testifying can sometimes be sparse, further increasing the undesirability of testifying.

Sometimes an officer may need to be prepared to testify in a series of graduated court experiences over a period of months or even years. For example, an appearance might be necessary for a deposition, an omnibus (show cause) hearing, followed by an arraignment, grand jury, and possibly an appeal. In all these situations the facts and details in the testimony must be consistent and identical. In complex cases with multiple defendants, the officer may have to testify on several occasions while undergoing an onslaught from several different defense attorneys who are attacking every minor discrepancy in his or her memory.

When the officer is finally ready to attend court, he or she may find that, frequently, prosecutors will not have looked at the case more than 20 to 30 minutes before the initial hearing. This is not because the prosecutor in the case does not want to present a strong case, but because a burgeoning caseload does not leave enough time. Some departments estimate that from 20% to 25% of the time the officer has had no contact with the prosecutor to review relevant information, questions, and strategy.

❖ TESTIMONY: FACTS ONLY, PLEASE

Of the estimated 44 typical objections that attorneys can make to answers, nearly 90% are due to the testifying officer not appreciating the boundaries of testimony. These problems most commonly arise from attempts to draw a conclusion or from nonresponsiveness (Rutledge, 1979).

Officers do not usually classify as experts in court unless they have specialized knowledge of accident scene reconstruction, narcotics, ballistics, fingerprinting, and the like. Typically, they can only provide facts to the court, not state opinion. For example, an officer cannot draw conclusions and testify how drunk a driver is, but must confine testimony to observable facts and symptoms of drunkenness. If conclusions, speculation, inferences, or conjecture is given, defense will usually object and the judge will declare that portion of the testimony stricken from the court record.

Nonresponsiveness refers to not answering directly and precisely the question the officer was asked. This most often occurs when the officer tries to anticipate the answers to questions, to "mind-read" what the officer thinks the attorney is really asking, or wants to give the court some important information they have not yet been asked about.

Both attorneys will attempt to systematically elicit information from witnesses to carefully build a legal argument, but prosecution and defense pursue this in different manners. The questioning process used in the adversarial system can be perplexing to a novice officer in court. The prosecutor will often ask open-ended questions that allow the officer to provide necessary elaboration: "Would you describe the condition of the victim when you arrived on the scene?" On the other hand, the defense will phrase questions that require a yes or no and use the limited answer to build an argument. Some of these questions may strike the officer as being like "Do you still beat your wife?" Although the officer may feel the urge to explain and tell more, he or she must answer specifically only what is asked, without elaboration or explanation.

An officer who had been on the force less than a year had to shoot a knife-wielding assailant in order to protect himself and a victim. Although the shooting was justified and he received clear support from peers and administration, he still felt some guilt and self-doubt under the questions posed by the press and friends of the now paralyzed perpetrator. In court, he was restricted to answering only those questions posed by the attorneys:

> I wanted to tell them everything that led me to make the decision to shoot the perp. There was so much that I thought they should know, and it was driving me nuts to just sit there on it and not be able to explain—to have to wait for the D.A. to ask the right question so I could explain. I knew I had done the right thing, I followed procedure exactly, I did what I had been trained to do, and I just wanted to tell my side of the story. I wanted everyone to understand what had happened.

❖ TESTIFYING: RELIVING THE EVENT

Testifying in court can also require detailed descriptions of situations, which can have the effect of forcing the officer to relive traumatic events. In an attempt to discredit the officer by showing emotional reactiveness or instability, the defense may dwell on unnecessarily disturbing or irrelevant details in order to evoke feelings or reactions. This is another reason that debriefing following a traumatic incident is so important—so that the officer will have resolved the event's emotional impact and can present relevant case information in court without succumbing to tactics calculated to arouse intrusive emotions. It is a difficult but important adjustment for an officer to make in recognizing that the public may never know (or want to know) what enforcement is like in the streets.

> And every one of those clashes had taken place out there in the streets, in the basements, on the rooftops, in the alleys, in that hidden land where the lawyers and the reporters never had to go, where the stakes were literally mortal and the room for hesitation and uncertainty no wider than a neuron, no more durable than a synapse. They were on you in seconds, and over you in a heartbeat. And whatever you did, no matter how frightened or how brave you were, the issue would always end up discussed in the club-room serenity of a court of law, by men and women who met for drinks when it was over, detached, privileged, and protected acolytes of cold-blooded justice, who didn't know, and didn't care, about you or what you had been trying to do. (Stroud, 1987, p. 195).

❖ TESTIMONY: THE DEFENSE ATTORNEY AS ENEMY

The adversary (defense attorney) is paid to discredit the officer and make him or her look bad. Some officers have described testimony under cross-examination by the defense attorney as being on trial themselves. The intent of the defense is to question certainty, memory, accuracy, consistency, and even the officer's credibility and integrity. The officer may be asked to justify exactly what he or she did and why he or she did it. It is not enough to see a crime, but in many cases the officer must prove what he or she saw!

For some officers who are much less frequently involved in court testimony, dealing with the defense attorney can be particularly challenging. Security officers, game and forestry officers, and corrections officers may not have the same routines for dealing with evidence as police officers, and the discrepancies are often framed as insufficient training and flawed practices. In other relatively new areas of enforcement, such as toxic waste enforcement, the concept of "standard" procedures is still being developed, and officers are challenged at every step. The intent in questioning again is to exhaust them or the jury or to make them appear unknowledgeable or underprepared.

Defense may examine step by step the chain of evidence until the officer's judgment, performance, and testimony appear to become the focus of the court rather than the defendant's crime. The spelling, grammar, wording, and organization of reports may be scrutinized in more detail and critiqued more strongly than the officer's sixth-grade English teachers ever grilled them.

One officer reported losing a DWI case that went to trial because he mistook the color of the vehicle during testimony, which lead to the defense attorney questioning every single sentence in the report. "And did you mistake this sentence...?"

A determined defense attorney may review past testimony the officer gave in other cases in an attempt to determine whether there is anything that might suggest bias on his or her part or at least create doubt in the mind of the jury about his or her credibility. Discovery motions may be made to examine the officer's personnel record to find out if there have been any complaints, reprimands, or other questionable behavior that could be related directly or indirectly to the case. Some attorneys simply want to get the officer to react emotionally to them so that they can elicit that same reaction during testimony—in front of the jury.

One officer had several pretrial encounters with the defense attorney, who had seemingly done everything to annoy and irritate him. When the officer finally took the stand, the attorney attempted to elicit anger by asking several rapid fire questions and then asked whether the officer was angry. The officer smiled at the jury and replied, "not yet, but it appears that you're trying to move me in that direction." The officer joined the jury in brief laughter that stopped that tactic. During cross-examination the officer may have fantasies of the interrogation he or she might put the defense attorney through if he or she ever had reason to stop the attorney for drunk driving.

Defense may object at every opportunity, partly to suppress damaging evidence, but also to interfere with the officer's thinking, concentration, and memory. It also serves to distract and confuse the jury as they try to attend to the officer's statement, the defense objections, the judge's sustaining or overruling, and the officer's return again to his or her statement.

During a hearing involving a campus security officer's testimony against a custodian who aggressively harassed a young college student, the officer was continually questioned about his training as a "police officer" and his investigative and evidentiary procedures. Although he was well trained in his security field, he became more flustered by being inappropriately compared with another specialty. By the time he was asked questions about the facts in the case, he was obviously on the defense, which is what the attorney wanted.

❖ ADDITIONAL FRUSTRATIONS

Some cases are personally important to the officer, such as those that involved a particularly heinous crime (e.g., sadistic child sexual abuse) or even a chase, personal assault, or torn uniform. If the officer takes the case personally, there is risk of compromising integrity by overstating the case in court—a situation seldom overlooked by defense and the judge. It is essential that testimony be given in a completely unbiased manner. Honesty and integrity are essential. The officer will have to reappear in the same court with same judge for years and cannot risk loss of credibility.

One police officer from a small town described his disgust at having to arrest the same criminal several times for similar offenses because the judge kept letting the perpetrator go. This led to an intense desire to "get the guy":

> Every time I would arrest the guy, the damn judge would let him go. I remember one time the guy got let off again, and when he was walking out of the court room he looked at me with this smirky smile on his face. That really pissed me off. He knew that when he was arrested again that he would just get let off again. When I would arrest him he would sometimes say, "I don't care. You know that Judge Moynihan is going to let me go anyway. The joke is on you, pig." I was so pissed that I felt like giving up entirely or getting this guy for good. I would look for him because wherever he was, there was trouble.

Appeals can be very frustrating. One officer described intense demoralization following a case that dragged on for nearly a year in court. Even after convincing the supervisor that the suspect was worth going after, successfully searching for more evidence in which the suspect admitted the crime to a friend, providing convincing testimony to 23 people on a grand jury, and sentencing him to prison—after one year the state supreme court overturned the conviction. Months of thorough and dedicated work became fruitless. The officer even considered resigning at that point.

❖ MAKING USE OF OUTSIDE EXPERTISE

Many officers are reluctant to accept suggestions or training in many areas from people who are not also officers. This often holds true in training for testimony as well. It is important to remember that, as much as officers have expertise in law enforcement, other specialists may have perspectives, information, and skills that can be very valuable. It may be more useful to consider other professionals as part of a team.

One approach to teamwork in preparation for court is the First Witness Program for child abuse in Duluth, Minnesota. The investigating officer meets with the abused child in a small and comfortable room. The officer wears a headphone for communication with the social worker or psychologist and prosecutor, who view the interview through video in a separate room. At any time in the interview, the observers can suggest additional questions to the officer in order for important areas to be covered. There are several advantages to this program:

1. Most relevant information can be obtained at one time without further recalling trauma for the survivor.

2. A tape is available for evidence that provides both factual and emotional content.
3. The tape serves as a means for reviewing and preparing the case.
4. The prosecutor can decide at the time whether there is sufficient information available to prosecute.
5. The prosecution team is formed early in the case and can ensure coordinated effort.

Having an attorney as a part- or full-time legal advisor to the police department has been suggested by some officers. This would enable officers to have ready access to a consultant who can answer their questions, help identify areas of strength and weakness in information, and provide realistic challenge to their testimony. Information about court procedures, rationale for plea bargaining, dealing with defense tactics, and understanding judicial process would be helpful. The attorney could also assist in conducting departmental training and provide debriefing after court.

The Federal Law Enforcement Training Center (FLETC) in Glynco, Georgia, has a program designed to enhance the courtroom skills of officers. The three and a half day training program is staffed by a team of lawyers and instructors who provide practice through a mock trial. Video and constructive verbal feedback are given to help officers relax under pressure, present a confident image, understand the strategy behind questioning, clarify their role and obligations, and present concise and accurate information (White, 1992).

As with most police work, during the court process you must maintain emotional composure, no matter how threatening or frustrating the case may be. Even during breaks and adjournments, you may need to be a source of support to witnesses or survivors, and you will likely be under the scrutiny of bystanders or media. Be careful of your expressions and comments in this public forum. This makes it especially important to find a place, time, and trusted people with whom you can blow off steam about the case. This is valuable not only for emotional release and support, but to review the case and your testimony to learn from mistakes. Again, the team concept is important, because your testimony can be viewed from several perspectives and more ideas are available about what to do differently next time. And there will always be a next time!

❖ RECOMMENDATIONS FOR PREPARING FOR A COURT APPEARANCE

Have your reports in order. Be prepared from the beginning by developing a well-organized and complete style for writing reports (Ross and Plant, 1978;

Rutledge, 1979). These reports will often be the basis for your recall as well as cross-examination. Avoid slang and jargon in writing. While it can be convenient to use police notation or shorthand, it can be confusing to the jury to be confronted with a collection of abbreviations:

At approx. 1200 hrs, 6 June 92, comp. obs. Susp #1, AKA "Speeder," att. to enter R/R entrance of warehouse at 4th and Main under S/C. Susp #1 had parked gray Chevy van IFO the garb. dump. at the r. of the bldg N/B on 5th., while Susps #2 & #3 watched from the veh.

Complete reports as soon as possible after the incident.   Memory degrades a great deal and becomes contaminated with other information within the first 24 hours. Your intent is to inform, not entertain, impress, or confuse. Write detailed, accurate, complete sentences without using pretentious or overly formal language, such as "The undersigned officer returned to the assigned unit whereupon the complainant approached and made contact with the assigned officer and his designated partner." This could simply be written, "I went back to my patrol car where the complainant met my partner and me."

Draw pictures.   A picture can be worth a thousand words, and worth even more when helping refresh your memory. Draw a sketch of the situation layout or room arrangement, label items and people, use arrows to show movement, and numbers to show sequences of actions. Properly title and date the drawing as a supplement to your written report.

If possible, use a memory device.   You may want to develop some type of memory device or strategy to make sure you can recall accurate and complete information under intense examination. For example, if you had seven reasons why you stopped the defendant for probable cause, you might create an acronym (D.A.B. R.E.S.M.) from the key words:

1. Drug dealer was known.
2. Address was known trafficking center.
3. Bag was put in jacket pocket and ran when police approached.
4. Resisted when apprehended.
5. Eyes were pinpoint.
6. Speech was slurred.
7. Movements were clumsy.

Make maximum use of evidence available.   Whenever possible, make sure that the original "best evidence" is available for court, rather than sitting in an evidence locker, described in a report, or merely represented in a photograph.

When presenting evidence, demonstrating an action, or explaining a diagram, make sure you do not block the view of the jury. If you are writing or drawing, make sure the display is large enough to be clearly seen by the jury. While pointing to something, look at and talk to your audience rather than at the item. Check the evidence before taking the stand so that important evidence is not misidentified. Rutledge (1979) gives the example of officers who reported recovery of a stolen Sony TV, only to find it was a Sanyo; another who described a .38 Smith and Wesson only to find that it was defined in evidence as a Colt.

Know the people you have to deal with. When possible, know the "players" in the court drama, their styles, tactics, and personalities. It can be useful to know that a particular attorney usually starts with a friendly and complimentary approach to an officer and then quickly switches to rudeness and accusations. You may want to find out whether the judge has any idiosyncrasies that you should know about. Some judges are easily offended, have strong expectations about exactness of answers, and may be merciless in their reprimand of a witness who strays from the court's expectations.

Prepare ahead of time with the prosecutor. Whenever possible, meet with the prosecutor ahead of court. You will need to tell in more detail the information you have that should be drawn out in questioning. You may need to give the prosecutor ideas how to word questions so that information will be admissible and not be considered hearsay or something that will be objected to. Find out what questions you will be asked and how you can best present that testimony.

Do positive mental rehearsal. The few nights before testimony can be difficult if you replay a "worst-case scenario" for your testimony. Remember that your body reacts to what your mind is thinking—stressful thoughts, stressful body. This kind of self-inquisition can decrease your appetite, make you withdrawn or irritable, and severely interfere with quantity or quality of sleep. Sometimes a recurrent "tension dream" will appear and even interfere with the brief respite of sleep.

To counteract this negative mental rehearsal, don't try blocking thinking about it—that usually makes it more persistent. Instead, visit the courtroom ahead of time, walking around and sitting in various locations to get a sense of perspective from attorney, jury, judge, and witness positions. Later you can visualize the courtroom and take a mental tour of the area. Sit in each seat, including the judge's.

Practice the deep relaxation and deep breathing skills we discuss in Chapter 17 while doing this and associate the setting with confidence and comfort. Recall feelings of confidence and assertiveness in the past and bring them with you into this image of the courtroom. This practice is a good opportunity to use the anchoring techniques described in previous chapters. Imagine the relaxed assertiveness of your posture, the confidence and loudness of your voice.

Picture the defense attorney trying to frustrate you while you repeat to yourself, "I am providing the best information I can for the court." Imagine the judge and jurors listening with interest to your testimony. Feel the satisfaction and relief of leaving the witness stand and leaving the courtroom. Practice imagery that elicit feelings of success, confidence, integrity, and assertive comfort.

Carefully review the case. There is no substitute for case review and even practicing by role play to deal with expected questions and challenges on the facts. In effect, you must become an expert on a case you may have been involved with long ago. In court, you are expected to have near total recall with no flaws or inconsistencies. Although it is most impressive to be able to answer all questions from recall, it is permissible to request to review case material (which will be called into evidence) to refresh your memory and testify more accurately.

If you do not understand a question, ask the attorney to repeat or restate the question. If you need a moment to think about a question, say so. Review your report so that you appear more knowledgeable than the defense attorney, who has rigorously studied it looking for flaws. You should be able to demonstrate good knowledge of the case and communicate that information clearly and succinctly. Remember, *you* are not the one convicting the defendant, the *facts* are.

At the same time, it is impossible to anticipate every question and challenge that will be posed to you. Furthermore, no case is ever perfectly prepared with virtually all procedures followed. When these flaws are discovered, do not try to explain them away or cover them up. Acknowledge your errors and learn from them. If asked a question that you do not know the answer to, state "I don't know." Do not bluff or fill in memory blanks with speculation.

Address your remarks to the jury or judge, not the defense attorney. You should always address yourself to the decision makers in the court room, whether this is the judge or jury. It can be difficult for a jury to stay attentive throughout hours or days of testimony, so it is important that you hold their attention. Be respectful, alert, and animated, let your voice be easily heard, use moderate gestures to match your words, and use eye contact with the jury. Speak at a normal pace, but slowly enough so that the court reporter will not have to ask you to slow down.

The defense attorney will attempt to have you direct your comments directly to him or her, hoping that the lack of attention to the jury will detract from your impact on them. It is important to address the jury with your answers. Look at each of them while giving your answer as if you were in a personal conversation with them. Even when the defense might say "would you please speak up, I didn't hear you," continue looking at the jury and simply speak louder.

Assume a version of Murphy's law to be in full operation in the courtroom: If anything can be misinterpreted and misunderstood, it will be. To minimize this problem, make your statements clear, concise, audible, and factual. Be careful in your use of pronouns to be clear to whom you are referring. For example, how clear would it be to a jury member who hears, "When they approached him, he hit him first." Who hit whom? Make the referents clear.

Don't play the defense attorney's number game. Do not let the defense get you involved in playing a numbers game in testifying. For example, if you are asked whether you are "45% certain about what you saw" or "was the distance 100 feet," you may be getting set up for testifying with an accuracy that cannot be supported. It is best to reply that you cannot give percentages of certainty because you have no reference point for such an estimate. Measurements such as speed, distance, height, weight, and number of items should be phrased in terms of ranges rather than a specific number.

Your task is to provide the facts, not draw conclusions for the judge and jury. Defense may try to get you to overextend your role by asking you to speculate about motives, outcomes, or other events you did not directly observe. Avoid such entrapment by noting the phrasing of such questions: assume, guess, suppose, might it be, don't you think, didn't you suspect, theorize, likely, presume, infer, imply, and isn't it possible. Generally, it is best to refuse to speculate, indicating that you do not know would only be offering your personal ideas and that you prefer to let conclusions be drawn by the jury.

Learn to qualify yes–no answers. When you want to explain your reasons for an action but are limited by the nonresponsiveness restriction, you might tempt the defense into asking you for elaboration. For example, when you are asked a yes or no question, give it with a qualification, such as "of course," "absolutely," "not at first," "most definitely," or "yes, initially." This usually requires an elaboration to clarify your answer. An officer who was attacked by the defense attorney for using particularly foul language in an arrest admitted, "yes, of course I used that language." When the "of course" was questioned, the officer explained that in his experience as an officer, street criminals were more responsive to rough language. When he had used milder language, it usually resulted in resistance or a chase.

Some judges may see this form of qualification as an attempt to evade the nonresponsiveness restriction. In that case the judge will instruct you to confine you answers to "yes" or "no" and "not qualified."

Watch where you talk. Be cautious of discussion or comments that can be publicly overheard regarding a case in which you will be appearing. Private opinions, inflammatory comments, biased attitudes, and controversial statements can return to haunt you during court if they make their way to the defense attorney. Be courteous to all citizens in the courthouse since some of them may be jurors.

TABLE 11-1	CHECKLIST FOR TESTIFYING IN COURT

1. Review the case to refresh your memory in detail.
2. Reexamine the evidence so it can be quickly, clearly, and accurately identified.
3. Rethink the scenario so that each step of the events and procedures is clearly in mind.
4. Visit the courtroom and become more familiar and comfortable with the suroundings.
5. Role play and use imagery to rehearse your confident and knowledgeable testimony.
6. Meet with the prosecuting attorney to share information and discuss strategy. Identify probable areas of challenge.
7. Know the players in court, their roles, tactics, and idiosyncracies when possible.
8. Have a good team or other support system for emotional release and debriefing.

It is generally best to avoid contact with the defense attorney, especially if it may be a public encounter.

A checklist to refresh your memory about preparation for testifying in court is given in Table 11-1.

S U M M A R Y

Court appearances by officers can be a source of concern for the following reasons, 1. the timing is often inconvenient, 2. there are restrictions on how much an officer can say in answer to questions, 3. it may revive unpleasant memories, 4. defense attorneys use tactics that may make the officer look bad.

Various methods can be used to prepare for court appearances such as making careful notes at the time of the incident, preparing ahead of time with the prosecutor, mental rehearsal, and being prepared for the defense attorney's tactics. A summary checklist for testifying in court is given in Table 11-1

E X E R C I S E

Consider the following situations and work out a statement of what you will say to yourself or what you will do to keep yourself calm.

1. You're dealing with a defense attorney and you feel his game plan is to make you look stupid or inadequate. He has just asked you a question to which you don't have an answer.
   a. You say to yourself_____
   b. You say to the attorney_____

2. The defense attorney implies that you haven't done enough investigation on this particular case.
   a. You say to yourself_____
   b. You say to the attorney_____
3. The defense attorney is on one side of the room and the jury is on the other. You are looking at the jury as you answer. The attorney says, "I can't hear you."
   a. You say to yourself_____
   b. You say to the attorney_____
4. You need help preparing to testify in an important case. Two people you seek help from are:
   a. _____
   b. _____
5. Two things you can do to convince the jury of the validity of your testimony are:
   a. _____
   b. _____

REFERENCES

Ross, A., and D. Plant (1978). *Writing Police Reports: A Practical Guide*. Schiller Park, IL: Motorola Teleprograms.

Rutledge, D. (1979). *The New Police Report Manual*. Flagstaff, AZ: Flag Publishing.

Rutledge, D. (1979). *Courtroom Survival: The Officer's Guide to Better Testimony*. Flagstaff, AZ: Flag Publishing.

Stratton, J. G. (1978). Police stress: An overview. *The Police Chief 45(4)*, 58–62.

Stroud, C. (1987). *Close Pursuit: A Week in the Life of a NYPD Homicide Cop*. New York: Bantam.

Territo, L., and H. J. Vetter (1981). Stress and police personnel. *Journal of Police Science and Administration 9(2)*, 195–208.

White, M. A. (1992). Testifying in criminal court: A training program for law enforcement officers. *The Police Chief 59(11)*, 32–34.

White, J. W., P. S. Lawrence, C. Biggerstaff, and T. D. Grubb (1985). Factors of stress among police officers. *Criminal Justice and Behavior 12(1)*, 111–128.

12

❖

Special Job Assignments:
Undercover

❖ OBJECTIVES

1. To understand the physical and psychological dangers of undercover work.
2. To recognize the ways the stress of undercover work affects the officer.
3. To understand the ways of minimizing the negative effects of undercover work.

❖ INTRODUCTION

The use of undercover operations to gather information involving criminal activity is likely to increase rather than decrease over the next decade. Marx (1988) discusses the expansion of undercover operations against an ever-widening list of offenses. White-collar crime, foreign business's trade violations, dumpers of hazardous wastes, corrupt civil servants, and traffickers in endangered wildlife are some of the offenses he lists for which undercover operations may produce the best evidence against those engaging in illegal activities.

This means an increasing number of law-enforcement personnel will be exposed to the special hazards of going undercover to gather information on which prosecutions can be based. To gather this information, officers must for varying periods of time act convincingly as if they were someone else: a druggy, a janitor, a jewel thief, a dishonest business man, and so on.

Besides the physical and psychological dangers of going undercover where the agent only acts a role for a short time, there are additional problems that arise when an agent has to go in deep cover, that is, an assignment where he or she has to develop another personality that exists over a long period of time. The assignment becomes especially dangerous to the adjustment of the agent if that role demands the agent to act in ways that are markedly different from his or her regular behavior and attitudes.

For example, if the agent who before the assignment kept regular hours, associated only with law-abiding citizens, and took part in many family activities is put into a role with irregular hours and associating with persons with psycho-pathic behavior, there will be difficulties both in getting into the role and later in getting back into the old law-abiding behavior.

Even taking on short-term assignments in which the agent has to act like someone else may present long-term problems. One administrator who has observed undercover operations said

> The longer the person is undercover the more they get to see the perspective of the so-called dirt bag. The dirt bag's ideas start rubbing off on them. At first it's rather uncomfortable. But then it becomes like acting, so in fact we've forced the agent into a multiple-personality situation to start off with. Then, when they come out, we give them another short-term assignment with another personality, so when they come out it becomes difficult for them to separate themselves from those identities. I mean its hard for them to quit the acting even if they want to.

As this administrator points out, if the agent is left undercover too long, the new role as a criminal may become so normal that the person has difficulty going back to the more normal behavior that existed before the assignment.

Many occupations require a person to develop certain attitudes and behaviors in order to function well in the roles demanded by that line of work. For instance, if a rookie is to become an effective officer, he or she will need to learn a set of behaviors and develop certain attitudes toward the job and public that let him or her function. In a small sense, the new officer has to become another person to perform effectively.

This need to develop a new public personality is true of doctors, lawyers, social workers and teachers. There are certain expectations people have of them that they need to live up to in order to be a success in their occupation. We have discussed previously that an effective officer has good verbal skills (can bullshit the suspect); is suspicious, observant, and cynical; covers for other officers; and has a good deal of bravery in dangerous situations. These are all characteristics expected of a good officer.

Going into deep cover goes a step further in what it requires of the individual. When done well, going undercover creates something very much like a multiple personality in the officer, since the role he or she takes can become so real that it is difficult to give it up. It may become more valid and real to the individual who has gone undercover than the role that was left behind.

For example, in the case where the officer is going to gather information on organized crime, he or she is asked to act the role of a crook to the fullest. The role must be played so well and so completely that there is minimum danger the crooks will break the cover. This role exceeds anything an actor has to do on the stage, since an actor only gets bad reviews. The officer, however, could and sometimes does end up dead when he or she doesn't play a convincing role.

❖ PSYCHOLOGICAL HAZARDS

Our observation is that the conflicting roles may have some aspects in common with a psychiatric diagnosis of multiple personality disorder. The American Psychiatric Association lists its formal diagnosis of mental disorders and personality disturbances in a handbook used by all psychiatrists called the *Diagnostic and Statistical Manual of Mental Disorders, third edition*. The current diagnostic criteria for multiple personality disorder (DSM III-R, p. 272, 1987) are:

A. The existence within the person of two or more distinct personalities or personality states (each with its own relatively enduring pattern of perceiving, relating to, and thinking about the environment and self), and

B. At least two of these personalities or personality states recurrently take full control of the person's behavior.

To some extent, we are all who others think we are. That is, we get feedback that we are a certain kind of person and begin to think of ourselves as being that person. It is difficult, if not impossible, to pass oneself off as a "tough guy" if no one is willing to respond to us as one. In deep cover, the operator has to take on certain personality characteristics to pass as who he or she says he or she is, and others begin to respond to that new person. This new person can become very real and carry over into the officer's off-duty life.

One officer reported that his negative reaction to police officers, which developed when he was in deep cover, carried over after he returned to regular status and had to report to the station house daily.

> I had never smoked a cigarette, even through high school, I was always into sports. I was undercover 3 years before they brought me into the office. It was finally when they were reeling me in and bringing me into the office I started smoking. I have ever since. But I don't smoke on weekends. I can take a 6-week vacation and don't

smoke. But, when I get in that police car, detective car, to drive, I've got to have a cigarette. Nicotine has got nothing to do with it. It's totally stress. The point I'm making is I got to the point I didn't want to be around police officers. I wanted to separate myself so much it makes me nervous to have to come to the office. Being around cops and having to be one is a stress situation. I've been asked how undercover work affected me. People say to me, you're teaching these classes and you seem very normal. Well, I'm still dealing with it. I'd just quit smoking if I didn't have to come to the office.

Mike Himmel, an officer who had been undercover for a number of departments over an 8-year period, said:

The way I got into undercover was by accident. It was acting to me. I got to live a life-style that was different than what I grew up with. You're forced to live two different life-styles. You're the family person at home, and when three o'clock in the afternoon comes you're the biker, hell bent, putting up that act, that personality. You are forced to live another life.

Relationships develop in the new role, and to carry out the assignment, the agent has to act like a friend to the suspects. To do this usually requires developing a cover, which includes values different from those of the officer's regular life. The undercover operative eats, drinks, gambles, and makes deals with the criminal element. This close association can easily slide over into a real liking for the people that the operator is going to have to testify against. The agent may even begin to take on the values and beliefs of the people he is working with (e.g., Marx, 1988; Daley, 1978).

Some officers have suggested that the identification has some similarity to the Stockholm syndrome they see in people taken hostage. That is, hostages, if held for a period of time, can become supportive of the hostage taker and even try to protect him from the law-enforcement officers who are trying to rescue the hostage.

Working undercover, lying becomes a way of life that can lead to the officer becoming confused about who he or she really is. There is danger that the operator will become what he or she pretends to be and degenerate into a criminal. Marx (1988) points to the addictive quality of being an agent. They get caught up in the sense of power, intrigue, and excitement. Added to this is the fact they are playing this role under protected status; that is, they can do illegal things legally. This can cause decay of the officer's moral standards, leading to corruption. As an example of this kind of corruption, Marx (1988) cites the case of New York City's Special Investigating Unit, an elite narcotics force. While the unit made many arrests and seized large quantities of drugs, of the 70 detectives, 52 were indicted for corruption.

Farkas (1986, p. 433) cites an FBI report on 76 agents who had considerable time undercover. Their major psychological reactions "were paranoia, changes in attitudes toward certain laws, sympathy for the views of the criminal target and 'corrosion' of the agent's value system."

Farkas in his study of 82 current and former undercover officers from the Honolulu Police Department, who had an average of 13 months undercover, found the results given in Table 12-1.

During the undercover assignment, certain psychological reactions occurred often or always in a fair number of members of the Honolulu Police Department undercover division. Several of these changes have survival value for someone trying to pass in a dangerous situation: oversuspiousness and nervous tension or anxiety. These emotional reactions return to almost normal levels after the assignment is completed. Feelings of loneliness and isolation stay unusually high after the assignment is over, suggesting that the officers involved have trouble relating to others in the same way they did before the event.

Excessive use of alcohol also increases. We believe this is the result not only of the need to relieve tension on the assignment, but is also due to the fact

TABLE 12-1   PERCENT OF RESPONSES TO PSYCHIATRIC SYMP-
TOMS AT THE TWO HIGHEST LEVELS OF ENDORSEMENT

Symptom	Before (%)	During (%)	After (%)
Not sleeping well	6.1	28.3	7.0
Loneliness/isolation	19.4	37.0	37.5
Excessive use of alcohol	3.7	19.7	12.5
Drug abuse	0.0	1.2	1.4
Relationship/marital problems	11.3	27.6	14.2
Lack of energy	2.4	10.0	7.0
Sadness	7.3	13.3	5.4
Low self-esteem	7.2	13.5	4.1
Crying spells	0.0	2.4	2.7
Nervous tension or anxiety	13.3	39.0	9.6
Guilt	7.2	11.0	6.9
Feeling of emptiness	3.7	12.3	7.0
Self-doubt	6.1	18.5	1.4
Confusion	7.3	19.7	4.3
Experiencing self "unreal"	7.7	21.2	2.8
Disorientation	2.5	13.7	1.4
Oversuspiciousness	15.2	44.0	19.5
Suicidal thoughts	0.0	0.0	0.0
Poor concentration	0.0	26.2	4.2
Poor memory	1.2	21.0	2.7
Hearing voices	1.2	0.0	0.0

that in many undercover operations the agent drinks to keep up an image with the group he or she is trying to infiltrate. On many assignments, the agent spends a lot of time in bars or other situations where it is expected that alcohol and drugs will be used. Mike Himmel reports his undercover experience as follows:

> We were drinking a lot, regularly. It helped with the stress. Each of us were doing 30 to 40 buys a month. Every 2 or 3 months the whole squad would get just falling down drunk. Nobody would plan it, it seems things would just click and we'd go on a major drunk. The drinking is not only from the stress but it's something you can do legally.
>
> You've got to understand you're in this atmosphere, where you've got all these people around you doing drugs. Remember you're playing that you're a dealer or taking care of a lady. You can't take drugs, but at least you can sit around and drink all of the time. So you always have a drink in your hand. Nowadays, we train the agents to always have something in their hand but to make it last. Back then in 1975, when I started undercover, it was a whole different world.
>
> As administrators, we got to take this into account. We've got to salvage these people. We forced them into that schizophrenic life-style.

A number of other symptoms increase that don't seem to have any survival value for the undercover agent, but that are a result of the increased tension of being in hazard for a long period of time. Farkas (1986) reports that these symptoms occur 5 to 6 months after the officer goes undercover. These symptoms are not sleeping well, sadness, self-doubt, confusions, feeling self "unreal," disorientation, poor concentration, and poor memory. It is notable that after the agent has come out from the undercover assignment most of these symptoms return to being very close to what they were before the agent went on the assignment.

Relationship and marital problems also increase, but much of this is likely to be due to the time spent away from home. The officer may come and go at odd hours and if in deep cover may only get home on an occasional weekend. Added to the strain in the relationship is the fact that most undercover agents cannot talk about their assignments to their family. In fact, the spouse, without knowing what the operator does, may have to become a coconspirator and also falsify facts and create a cover story for the absence of his or her spouse. Living a lie, when the spouse does not know the truth he or she is hiding, places an extra strain on the relationship.

On occasion the individual working undercover is thrown into the company of attractive members of the opposite sex, and in some situations a sexual relationship follows. If the spouse finds out about this, she or he will feel betrayed and more damage is done to the marriage.

Because of the irregular contacts and degree of secrecy about the agent's assignment, the spouse feels left out and may begin to build a life around being a single parent. When a spouse is out of the family, the remaining spouse often learns to live without him or her. Instead of welcoming the partner back, the spouse may find the returning partner is an intrusion on the new patterns of behavior that have been established.

❖ PHYSICAL HAZARDS OF UNDERCOVER

There are a number of physical dangers. The most obvious is that an officer who is discovered to be an undercover operator can be tortured or killed (e.g., see Levine, 1990). But there can be other reasons for the criminals to kill the undercover operator besides the discovery that he is an officer. The lawbreakers are also tense and suspicious and can overreact when they see a deal going bad. When they see something as a threat, they may shoot first and consider the alternatives later.

Additionally, the crooks may be greedy and, in the case of a drug deal, decide to take the drugs and the money. Case 1 that we report here is an example of the dealer getting greedy. It is appropriate for an agent to be suspicious and anxious in such a situation. Case 1, given by Mike Lyman, who was undercover with various agencies for 11 years, emphasizes this need for suspiciousness on the part of the agent.

CASE 1

DON'T TRUST ANYONE

The guy I was trying to get to deal so I could arrest him was a button man for an organized crime figure. A made guy. He had come to Oklahoma City at their request to set up prostitution and drug operations through a huge bar called Claudio's. A T&A bar where at any one time 15 girls were dancing. They also had hot tubs in the back room. Real fancy.

He was insulated like all made guys are, with all these punks working for him. He never handled a drug deal personally. So, they had 15 years of trying to get him, but the agency had never gotten him on anything but a charge of tax evasion, which hadn't stuck. So I had to figure out some way that he would do business directly with me.

We decided I'd go in as a jewel thief from Kansas City who had a big load to get rid of. To get ready, I went around to jewelers and pawn shops in the city and collected jewels and expensive watches. I got explanations from the jewelers what everything was. They gave me a short course on being an expert on jewels. It was then I learned about Gem Printing, a way, well, it's the DNA of diamonds. Every diamond has its own pattern.

I met the guy we wanted to get through an informer who had been one of his previous guys who he had left out to dry. He got arrested and prosecuted. When he finally got out of jail, he was mad and wanted to get back at him.

So one noon at lunch time, the informer introduced me to him at his club as a burglar from Kansas City who had just made a big hit and had some stuff to sell.

That put him totally at ease because we weren't asking anything of him. I was the bad guy that had stuff to sell. The reason for the jewelry was that none of his stooges knew anything about jewelry, but he was an expert on it. He even carried one of these little eye things around with him so he could check it out. When we made the setup, we knew he would have to inspect it personally.

At lunch, when we were introduced, he brought some of his girls over and I got a free lap dance and a table dance. You know that kind of thing. So we got acquainted that way. I knew I couldn't ask him outright for dope, because he'd just have one of his stooges sell it to me. We stayed away from the discussion of dope altogether but arranged for a meeting at a Howard Johnson's.

At this point the reader might ask how he or she would be feeling about what is happening. What would be your emotional reactions to being in this situation? How would you be handling your tensions?

My tension level when making these deals was always high. It wasn't any higher because I was involved with organized crime, cause you can get killed by anybody. Whenever you go into these situations, you're always in the "getting killed mode." Your switch is either on or off. It doesn't matter if you're undercover to a crack freak, a dealer, or a made man from the Mafia, you're still in the "getting killed mode," so all of your senses and resources just have to be at peak. You're hyperalert, but at the same time you have to be hyperrelaxed as far as the other guy is concerned.

I got pretty good at acting relaxed when I was under tension, but it didn't get that way overnight. I must have been doing undercover 5 years before I got really good at looking relaxed and yet be watching everybody and see if they were watching me. But you have to look like you're not paranoid, like you're not watching.

When we met at the Howard Johnson's, he wanted to inspect the merchandise, and I had brought the things we had which I said were part of much larger haul. He was examining the watches and the rings and he holds up one ring and says, "This ring's never been worn. What's the deal with this?"

I said, "I don't have any idea. Look, I just took the stuff. I don't know anything about anything."

He sat there and just stared at me for maybe 10 seconds and I stared right back. And then he goes on to another topic. It was the weirdest deal. He was reading me. He looked right behind my eyes into my head. Apparently, something clicked and he said this is OK.

We agreed on $65,000 for the jewelry. He was willing to give me 25% of the value. We agreed to meet in 3 to 4 days and complete the deal. I haven't mentioned any dope, so at this point its a straight deal. I'm the crook. He's completely at ease. I mean, if I'm a cop, why am I trying to sell him stuff? It was really a sweet deal.

On the way out the door when we're packed up and done, I stopped and said, "Listen for your information I had a cocaine connect in K.C. and the guy got busted. I'm not going to do any more business with him at all. Just in case you're interested, I'm interested in another connect." I said, "But you probably wouldn't know about that."

He said, "Of course, I do. How much are you interested in?"

I said, "I'm used to buying about half a pound at a time, but I'll take whatever. I don't know anybody, so I'm very reluctant to trust anybody."

Immediately he bit. He said, "Why don't we trade cocaine for your jewelry?"

We talked about how much for the jewels. I told him, "Listen, you wanted to see my sample, I need to see your sample before you have me show up with all my stuff."

And he said, "O.K." We agreed to meet at 7 on Saturday morning at Country Kitchen. After the meeting, he got the informant aside and said, "Why don't we just set the deal up and kill Mike and then we'll split the jewels two ways. We'll put his body in a U-Store-It place for a few months and then dispose of it."

The informant tells me about the double cross. So we know we have to change our plans. Now, the informant could have gotten greedy and taken the deal, in which case I would have been dead.

We thought the dealer might send a stooge with the sample, but lo and behold the yellow Cadillac drives up and he's in it by himself. I open the door and he says here's your sample, and hands me a packet with an ounce of high-grade cocaine. I arrested him on the spot. He got 10 years and the informant had to go into the witness protection program.

It might be of value for the reader to go back and think through what his or her reactions would have been in a situation similar to Mike's.

1. How do you act relaxed while still being hyperalert?
2. What would you have said when the dealer asked about the ring that had never been worn?
3. Note the indirect way that Mike led the dealer into committing himself to the drug deal.
4. Knowing your death had been planned on this deal, how might you react to your next undercover assignment?

❖ PROBLEMS COORDINATING DIFFERENT AGENCIES

The criminals are not the only hazard the officer faces. Because he or she is undercover, not even the members of his or her department know about the assignment, much less many of the other agencies that might have a hand in investigating the particular crime the agent is working on. The Drug Enforcement Agency (DEA), the FBI, and state agencies may be involved, but have no coordination in terms of who has who planted. That means that our agent may be arrested by members of another agency and in the heat of the moment in some cases be roughed up or even killed. On rare occasions, even the public gets into the act and may take vigilante action, in which the agent gets hurt. All these possibilities reinforce the feeling undercover agents have that they cannot trust anyone and that everyone is a potential enemy.

The Missouri State Highway Patrol has attempted to solve this problem by coordinating undercover work in the state through regional drug task force units. These units are made up of the undercover agents of municipal agencies, county sheriffs, and the state highway patrol, as well as the DEA. In a many of these cases the federal government is cooperating with the program as well. This means that at least one agency knows all the undercover agents working in a particular area. This kind of coordination makes it possible for an individual undercover agent to be used in another area where he or she is less likely to be known; for example, an agent may be taken from Lake of the Ozarks to make buys in Springfield, or an individual comes from Springfield to Lake of the Ozarks to make buys from a drug dealer who has come over from St. Louis.

Previously, if an agent from one agency was working to develop evidence against another individual, there was no way to know if the target was an agent from another agency. In some situations, an undercover officer has become a target because he was associating with known drug pushers. With the regional coordinating setup, this is less likely to occur. In the case of Missouri, an individual assigned in the State Highway Patrol drug control unit handles the undercover operations, coordinates all the regional units as well, and knows who the undercover agents are.

❖ PROBLEMS WHEN COMING OUT FROM UNDERCOVER

The role the agent has been playing is often hard to give up. In many cases a multiple personality has been created, and in some cases the new personality has some advantages over the old personality. The new role may allow the officer to be freer and less responsive to a conscience and provide him or her more immediate rewards. One of those rewards is the adrenaline rush from danger, and once back in the old role as police officer the ex-agent may take undue risks or engage in illegal acts to bring him or her back in contact with the personality he developed when undercover. The following story from Mike Himmel, an ex-undercover agent, illustrates the addiction that some operators develop for the adrenaline rush.

CASE 2

THE ADRENALINE RUSH

I was at multifederal survival school for undercover agents in Boulder, Colorado. I was on a deep cover assignment. You know, we were riding the motorcycles and had long greasy hair. We had psychologists who were making observations. They'd go to dinner with you, they'd listen to you talk. What was interesting, was you're supposed to work in teams, you know, take your partner everywhere. The psychologist said to me, "I've been watching you guys and I'll bet you'll run in and do a quick deal now without even taking your partner."

Later he came back to us and he said, "I'll bet you don't even carry a gun on a lot of your deals." And he was right, because it wasn't something I made a conscious decision about. But it started me thinking. Yeah, I've run in and made a deal without backup.

He talked about the type of person that gets in this line of work anyway. The adrenaline rush of it is a high in itself. And what he said was that, after being in it for so long, subconsciously we were making a decision to get the rush back. We had become too complacent. It was an everyday activity now, so we were trying to make it a little more exciting. Not really consciously making that decision.

The insights he gave me about the risks I was running probably saved my life. The training we received as far as weapons and undercover techniques was interesting, but wasn't stuff that we basically didn't know already. It was the knowledge that I was going to keep taking more risks, so I went back and started carrying my gun, and started taking my partner with me whenever I went out to make a deal.

If the assignment has been deep cover with organized crime, when the agent comes out there may be danger of retribution. The agent is now a witness, a danger to be eliminated. FBI Agent Joseph Pistone (1989), better known to the Mafia as Donnie Brasco, had a hit contract out on him after he came out from undercover and was beginning to testify against the men he associated so closely with for 6 years.

We mentioned corruption and decay of morals because of the associations the agent must make. This may show up in a disregard for the law when the individual returns to a regular assignment. Colleagues may pick up on this change in attitude and behavior and respond differently, increasing the agent's feelings of isolation.

❖ IMPLICATIONS FOR STRESS MANAGEMENT

Selection. Individuals who are to be sent into undercover operations need to be carefully selected. Individuals who do any kind of undercover work need to have certain characteristics: flexibility, a sense of independence, and a strong sense of self. In addition, for deep cover they need to be street smart, not something that you can teach them in a short-term training program at the academy.

Ostrovsky and Hoy (1990), who wrote a book about Ostrovsky's experiences as a member of the Israeli undercover organization, the Mossad, describes the careful way they go about screening their agents. Besides days of written tests and intense interviews, the candidates are subjected to a series of real-life tests on the street to find out how creative they can be in solving problems and how skillful they are at convincing others.

Ostrovsky was taken to downtown Tel Aviv, given no ID, and the following instructions, "See that balcony on the third floor over there? I want you to stand here for three minutes and think. Then I want you to go to that building and, within six minutes, I want to see you standing out on the balcony with the owner or tenant, and I want you holding a glass of water" (page 40).

On some occasions the Mossad candidates were arrested by the police and beaten in an attempt to get them to break their cover stories. While we wouldn't suggest anything as drastic as this, role plays to test the candidates creative potential would be appropriate.

Making sure the agent fits the role in terms of background personal history also adds to the chances that the assignment will be carried out successfully. This may mean speaking Italian, Spanish, or other appropriate languages like a native or knowing life on the streets where the suspects were raised. For investigators of white-collar crime, the officer who goes undercover may have to be very knowledgeable about art, computers, or investment scams.

Information about undercover work.   In the group of Honolulu undercover officers that Farkas (1986) studied, 29% said they had received no information about the nature of their assignment before they were sworn in. Fifty-eight percent of this uninformed group felt such information would have been helpful in adjusting to the assignment. The FBI warns all volunteers about the risks and dangers. They are also shown a video of the "60 Minutes" story on Livingston, an FBI agent who had problems coming out from undercover after two and a half years posing as a distributor of pornography. Livingston's problems resulted in his being fired after 17 years service with the agency (Marx, 1988).

There are limits to what an agent should be told before taking an assignment. In order not to broadcast too widely what is taking place, it would be better to give full information to the agent only after he or she has been selected and has agreed to go undercover. But enough information can be given so that the volunteer can appraise the hazards of the assignment and decide if he or she has the necessary courage to undertake the task.

Developing the role.   The role should be as close to the agent's previous life as is possible to construct it. This includes keeping the names similar. Buckwalter (1983) recommends using the same first name and a last name that starts with the same initial. This prevents the agent from responding inappropriately when by accident someone calls out his real name.

The agent must rehearse the role until he or she is completely comfortable in answering questions in that role. If tools or special uniforms are required, Buckwalter suggests that they be used so as not to arouse suspicion. The main thing is that the agent feels reassured that everything has been done to provide a cover that is real, and he or she can live without constant worry about being discovered.

The problem we introduce here is that the best roles for doing the job required are the ones the agents can most completely get into, which raises the problem of how to help them out of the role when the time comes. That is, the more completely you create a multiple personality, the more difficulty you will have in debriefing the agent on termination of undercover work.

Maintaining contact.   In the Farkas (1986) study, one main complaint of the agents was loneliness and isolation. An examination of Table 12-1 shows this continues after the agent comes out from undercover. A second factor is the one we have been discussing, losing contact with a previous identity. The new role may become more real to the agent than what he or she was before the assignment. Finally, there is the growing mental disruption caused by the assignment: the confusion, forgetfulness, and taking of undue risks. These symptoms also provide clues to the controller (the officer maintaining contact with the undercover agent) as to when the operator is ready to be brought out from undercover.

Several kinds of continuous contact appear to be necessary if the agent is to weather the experience in good emotional condition. Marx (1988) recommends that the officer who is the controller or handler of the undercover agent be of equal rank, someone who knows the undercover situation and can act as buffer between the agent and the agency. The agents in charge of the ongoing case need to have contact with the undercover operator to reinforce the fact that he or she is part of a team with responsibilities to the project. The undercover agent is never allowed to forget who he or she is in reality.

Finally, some departments require the undercover agent to have regular contact with a psychologist. Again, the psychologist must be street wise and understand what the undercover agent is going through. The psychologist needs to be aware of the danger signs that indicate that the agent is becoming too attached to the undercover role or to the criminals with whom he or she is associating.

Coming out from undercover.   When a case is going well, there will be a tendency on the part of the administrator monitoring the undercover activity to keep the agent in as long a possible. There will be a conflict between the value of the information being received and the mental health of the agent. The priority should be given to the mental health of the agent, because an agent who begins to make mistakes can lose the case. Even if the agent does not lose the case at this point, the defense may concentrate attention on the agent's mental health and try to prove that there were errors in judgment sufficient to damage the case. Factors the defense lawyer might dwell on are errors made because of lack of concentration due to being undercover too long; the taking of unnecessary risks by the agent, which resulted in the agent committing felonies in making the case; or any signs that the agent felt that he or she was above the law and that laws did not apply to what was done when undercover.

The following is the report of an ex-agent who now trains undercover agents and consults with other agencies on how to manage officers who are undercover.

The way we're dealing with undercover agents now is to have them see a psychologist when they're under and during the time they're coming out. Back when I first went undercover, we really didn't understand much about the stresses and nothing in the way of psychological support was available.

I had been undercover 4 years before I started getting any attention from psychologists. By then I was having some psychological problems caused by the job, and the psychologists basically said I was a mess. We had a judge in Kansas City who looked at the police officers and looked at the bad guys and said in court, "I can't tell who the good guys are and who the bad guys are."

We were to the point where we would take needles and put fake tracks on our arms if we had to buy heroin. The dealers would ask, "where are your needle marks." You're almost getting too deep in it when you're taking pins and needles and putting holes in your arms and stuff. I mean, there are real chances of infection. But that's what it took to make the drug buys. It was part of the acting of it.

But as far as coming out of it in those days, we didn't have any support. That's why I think so many had trouble. When I was with the drug squad, we had one officer released for perjury on the stand, one officer was released for getting involved in a bunch of stolen tires, and we had another one released because of attempted rape of another undercover female officer. You could just see that the inner workings of that unit were so deep we were starting to eat each other.

Recognize that the agent will need time off to reorganize his or her personality and perhaps some retraining in standard procedures and ways of looking at the law from a regular law-enforcement point of view. Counseling by a professional is recommended in order to help the person make the transition. As we have been suggesting throughout this chapter, it may be necessary for the counselor to treat the ex-undercover agent as if a multiple personality exists. To prevent some of these problems, the FBI does not allow an agent to go under again for 3 years after coming out (Marx, 1988). We don't know if this would be acceptable to some of the agents who resent going back to regular law-enforcement work after their experiences undercover, but it is worth considering as a way of protecting the agent's mental health.

One agent we interviewed gave another slant to the problem of coming out from undercover.

One of the problems of coming back to regular life is what I call the pedestal. You've got to understand you've got a guy who's gone to all the police courses and had special training, plus he's had our own 4-month program where we teach him what he needs to know to be an effective undercover agent. And he's got the support group around him, his field supervisor, his sergeant, and his surveillance people. And they're constantly reinforcing his ego, telling him he's doing a good job, constantly supporting him.

After you've done that for 18 months or 2 years, you've made a star out of this guy. You've put him on the pedestal. And that's what you want. You've got to keep his motivation up. You know there are peaks and valleys. He'll get depressed about stuff and you work him through that. But you've always got to be reinforcing him because he's got to go out there and do business. He's got to go out and produce some numbers, some stats. If he doesn't, we'll all be out of work.

Then all of a sudden, some agencies end an operation and they have the big "coup de grace." You got the big buy bust days, and it's even heightened, he's got his name in the paper, he's brought into the department and he's the star. But just a bit later, he's one of a hundred blue suits. He has to totally change from that stardom to being one of another hundred. He's not special anymore, there's no big support group around him anymore. He's just competing with the other people in his squad. And they basically just want to see if he'll sink or swim. There's a lot of pressure on him there. He lost his stardom status and that's a hell of a personality change to put up with. They're the center of attention, then they're just one of a hundred. In a big department they could be one in a thousand. He's just a number, nobody even knows him.

SUMMARY

Besides the physical dangers involved in undercover work there are the emotional-psychological hazards to the agent. The agent becomes addicted to the adrenaline rush of risk taking. More subtle, but probably more dangerous, are the problems involved in changing from the role required on the assignment back to regular law enforcement.

Problems can be kept to a minimum by (1) careful selection of agents, (2) good preplanning with the officer, (3) careful monitoring of the agent while undercover, and (4) good procedures for bringing the agent back into the department.

EXERCISE

Buckwalter (1983) lists five types of undercover assignments:

1. *In the area*: The officer passes as a worker or service person who belongs in the area.
2. *Employment*. The officer takes a job in a firm to investigate theft, embezzlement, or the like.
3. *Infiltration*. This would be the deep cover assignments we have been discussing.
4. *Spying*. In this country, this is usually counterespionage, both industrial and governmental.
5. *Personality impersonations*. This is the taking on of the role of a person who actually exists.

Consider each of these types and discuss which you would be good at, how you would create your role, and what stresses you would expect to experience in this role. Think about possible ways you might manage the stress in each of these situations.

REFERENCES

Buckwalter, A. (1983). *Surveillance and Undercover Investigation*. Boston: Butterworth Publishers.

Daley, R. (1978). *Prince of the City*. Boston: Houghton-Mifflin.

Farkas, G. M. (1986). Stress in undercover policing. In James T. Reese and Harvey A. Goldstein (eds.), *Psychological Services for Law Enforcement*. Washington, DC: U.S. Government Printing Office.

Levine, M. (1990). *Deep Cover*. New York: Dell Publishing.

Marx, G. T. (1988). *Undercover: Police Surveillance in America*. Berkeley: University of California Press.

McCarthy, B., and M. Mallowe (1991). *Vice Cop: My Twenty-Year Battle with New York's Dark Side*. New York: William Morrow.

Ostrovsky, V., and C. Hoy (1990). *By Way of Deception*. New York: St. Martin's Press.

Pistone, J. D. with R. Woodley (1989). *Donnie Brasco: My Undercover Life in the Mafia*. New York: Signet.

13

❖

Women
in Law Enforcement

Officer reporting assignment completed. (Photo courtesy Duluth, Minnesota, Police Department)

❖ OBJECTIVE:

1. To recognize the dilemmas both female and male officers face regarding the woman's role in law enforcement.
2. To identify myths about women in law enforcement.
3. To recognize that despite women's demonstrated competency they face many barriers.
4. To identify ways that negative attitudes toward female officers are manifested.

5. To identify ways individuals and organizations can combat negative stereo-types and sexual harassment to make the policewoman's work environment more hospitable.

6. To identify unique ways that women contribute to effective law enforcement.

❖ INTRODUCTION

Women have been involved in certain aspects of police work for well over 100 years. However, duties initially assigned to women were clerical and custodial in nature. Their duties included court visitations, assisting male officers in cases involving women and children, and social work functions. In 1915 the National Association for Policewomen was established to help develop the role of women in policing by searching for better standards for women in law enforcement (Bell, 1982). By the early 1920s, over 200 cities had appointed women to official police duties within their police departments (Balkin, 1988). However, these positions were still usually restricted to cases involving women and children or clerical duties.

During the 1960s, the civil rights movement led to charges of discrimination by police departments based on sex. Court rulings led to withholding funds from departments discriminating against women (Milton, 1972). Consequently, departments were forced to change their official policies. However, as we will discuss later in this chapter, the attitudes of the establishment toward women did not change as quickly as the policies.

In this chapter we will discuss the myths presently held about women in policing. We will present empirical evidence that disputes these myths by showing that women are as competent as men in law-enforcement activities. Additionally, we will discuss a number of barriers women in law enforcement face, the dilemma female and male officers face regarding the woman's role in law enforcement, and the unique contributions women make to the profession.

Many of the myths about women in policing presented in Table 13-1 remain a major barrier to the equality of sexes in law enforcement. These myths are a product of the social structure, the stereotypically masculine view of police

TABLE 13-1   MYTHS ABOUT WOMEN IN POLICE WORK

1.	Women are not physically strong enough for police work and therefore require the protection of male officers.
2.	Women are too emotional for police work.
3.	Women shouldn't being doing the dirty work, it is unfeminine.
4.	Women are unable to handle volatile and dangerous situations.
5.	Female officers do not have the required leadership skills.

work, and the unwillingness of both male and female officers to accept women as equals. Following is a description of the research on the competency of women in police work and attitudes toward female officers.

❖ COMPETENCY OF AND DISCRIMINATION AGAINST FEMALE OFFICERS

Critics of women in police work often argue that women are unfit for police work for a number of reasons (see Table 13-1). Overall, they argue that women simply cannot perform as well as men in a number of critical areas of law enforcement. However, research over several decades has clearly indicated that women perform as well as men or better than men in almost every aspect of the job (Balkin, 1988; Bell, 1982).

One study of 16 female and 16 male officers matched on demographic variables was conducted in 1975 in St. Louis county. Observations on patrol, departmental statistics, and reports by civilians and department members indicated that women performed as well on patrol duties as did their male cohorts (Sherman, 1975). However, a few differences emerged. For example, female officers handled service calls and domestic disputes better than men, but were involved in more car accidents. Similar results were reported by Sichel and colleagues (1978) in their study of 41 policewomen and 41 policemen in New York City. Many other studies have also demonstrated that females are competent patrol officers (for an extensive review, see Balkin, 1988).

Women are often held to even higher standards of performance than are their male counterparts. When interviewed, a number of female officers described unusually stressful assignments given to them to see "if they could hack it." A veteran female officer described her first assignment:

> I remember my first assignment was as an undercover drug agent in the projects. I knew that this was different because nobody was ever assigned undercover in the projects right after they were hired. I was the first woman hired by our department and I was told that they were going to find out if I could hack the pressure of being a police officer. I knew that this wasn't fair. They wouldn't get away with it these days because of the sexual discrimination laws. I know that other female officers get the same kind of stuff, only it's not as out in the open.

Another female patrol officer describes how she is held to a higher performance standard:

> Every time one of us female officers makes a mistake its "because we are women." When one of the guys makes a mistake, it is just a mistake—everybody makes mistakes. But when a woman makes even a small mistake, we are accused of being

incompetent. It's like we have to be perfect and even then it isn't good enough. I feel like I'm always having to prove myself. The women officers have to be much more careful to avoid any scrutiny. It's like some of the men are looking for a reason to be breathing down our necks.

Although laws have made different standards for male and female officers illegal, discrimination has not gone away, but rather has become more implicit than explicit. For example, during interviews women law-enforcement officers reported getting more verbal reprimands from male supervisors than they thought their male counterparts did. The message that the female officers have to prove themselves worthy remains as part of the system, which causes additional sources of stress for female officers.

Other real-life stories of female officers provide vivid examples of the explicit and implicit discrimination against female officers by demands for higher standards of performance (e.g., Taubman, 1987). However, perceptions of male and female officers may vary on this topic, as described later in this chapter, where male officers describe using more lenient discipline with female officers to avoid accusations of unfair sex bias.

❖ ATTITUDES TOWARD FEMALE OFFICERS

Despite weighty empirical evidence that women are competent officers, attitudes toward female officers' performance varies a great deal. Research regarding citizens' attitudes and officer attitudes will be examined separately.

Citizen Attitudes. A number of studies have shown that citizens generally accept policewomen as equally competent and capable. For example, in the St. Louis county study (Sherman, 1975), citizens felt just as safe when their calls were answered by policewomen. In fact, they felt that female officers were more sensitive and responsive to their needs than male officers. Additionally, citizens in the New York City study (Sichel et al., 1978) felt that the female officers were more respectful, pleasant, and competent. Furthermore, citizens held a higher regard for the department after their experience with the female officers. Overall, citizens appear to have positive attitudes about women in law enforcement. For a more extensive discussion of citizen's attitudes, see Balkin (1988).

The culture or ethnic group in which the citizen is raised is an important factor in attitudes toward the female officer. Some cultures from various parts of the world have differing views of a woman's role. Several women officers have described incidents where men from foreign cultures have refused to cooperate or even talk to them because they did not accept the woman in a professional role. It is important for the officer to understand that cultural values may affect the reactions of citizens during interactions.

Police Attitudes.   Attitudes of policemen toward female officers have traditionally been negative. Even after studies in which women officers were found to be equally competent (e.g., the St. Louis study), policemen reported negative attitudes about the ability of female officers. In the face of evidence to the contrary, male officers maintain negative attitudes about the performance of their female counterparts. Balkin (1988) describes a number of studies in which it was found that male officers felt that women were incompetent and unfit for police work.

Policemen's attitudes have been shown to become worse after working with female officers (Glaser, 1983). Some research has shown that older male officers have more negative attitudes (Weisheit, 1987) and that younger male officers who have undergone law-enforcement training with female peers have more favorable attitudes. This trend toward acceptance is expected to continue as women officers become the norm.

Negative attitudes get expressed toward female officers in a number of ways. Sexual harassment is one common way that men express their dislike of female officers (this is further described in the following section on sexual harassment). Wexler and Logan (1983) studied stress in female officers and found that male officers made cutting remarks about women in their presence, refused to speak to female officers, and questioned female officers' sexual orientations. One female officer who was interviewed described how the men in her department were constantly inquiring about female officers' sexual orientations:

> For some reason the men in the department want to know if the women are lesbians. It's like you're OK if you're married, but if you're single, they think you're a lesbian. If they think you're lesbian, then you really are under scrutiny.

The negative attitudes of policemen toward policewomen result in explicit and implicit discrimination. These examples show how prevalent discrimination currently is in police departments, even though discrimination is against the law.

Why do men have negative attitudes toward policewomen? One reason may be the sex-role expectations of women as passive caretakers, which is clearly reflected in the research of the resistance to women in police work in the 1800s. Ehrlich (1980, p. 79) states that "the integration of women into police patrol work as coworkers threatens to compromise the work, the way of life, the social status, and the self-image of the men in one of the most stereotypically masculine occupations in our society." If such is the case, the perseverance of negative attitudes becomes a defense mechanism for the male officers' own insecurities.

Policemen often feel that the female officer is a handicap because they feel the need to protect women. Several male officers have described an "instinct" to look out for and protect the female officers in many situations. Rather than protecting themselves in a fight, they reported constantly looking over their backs to make sure that the female officer was protected first, which didn't happen when working with male officers. Male officers are not to blame for such behaviors, because societal sex roles clearly have supported men for being protective of women.

However, the research clearly supports the notion that women can handle themselves and that it is the male's desire to protect the female officer that is the problem for the policeman. The female officers feel that they don't need any more protection than any other officer, regardless of sex. This desire to protect female officers is more likely a result of the socialization of men to protect women and children than a reflection of the female officer's incompetence.

In summary, the attitude of policemen toward female officers is one of the most persistent obstacles to career advancement and job satisfaction. Clearly, these attitudes do not come from observation and experience with female officers, but rather from preexisting attitudes and values (Balkin, 1988). Some have even suggested that "the only trouble with women in policing is men in policing" (Lehtinen, 1976, p. 55).

❖ SEXUAL HARASSMENT

Sexual harassment is one of the most commonly reported sources of stress among female officers, and research has found sexual harassment to be rampant in law enforcement (e.g., Balkin, 1988). Policewomen report that comments and actions of male colleagues, supervisors, and administration create a hostile environment and make them feel uncomfortable. This problem has grown as women have increasingly entered the traditionally macho world of police work. Often harassment comes in the form of snide comments about women in the policewoman's presence, unwanted inquiries into the sexual orientation of the policewoman, treatment as sex objects, unwanted physical contact, or intentional provocation to try and make the female officer respond emotionally. Several types of sexual harassment are described in Table 13-2.

Female officers have a much higher dropout rate from the occupation than do male officers (Harman, 1990). Part of this increase in resignations may be caused by male officers making the working environment so hostile that policewomen choose to avoid such stress. The policemen then often say, "I knew she couldn't hack it." Male officers sometimes work hard to get women to act in ways consistent with their stereotypes.

TABLE 13-2   TYPES OF SEXUAL HARASSMENT

1. *Gender harassment:* sexist statements and behavior that convey insulting, degrading, and/or sexist attitudes

2. *Seductive behavior:* unwanted, inappropriate, and offensive physical or verbal sexual advances

3. *Sexual bribery:* solicitation of sexual activity or other sex-linked behavior by promise of reward

4. *Sexual coercion:* coercion of sexual activity or other sex-linked behavior by threat of punishment

5. *Sexual assault:* assaultive behavior and/or rape

Adopted from Paludi & Berickman, 1991

One female officer describes her experience when she was the first woman to be hired by a municipal department.

> The guys made fun of me all the time. Sometimes they would say stuff directly to me or they would say it to each other loud enough so I could hear it. I remember them leaving cartoons on my locker so I would see them. I felt so damn angry, but I didn't know what to do. I refused to become one of the boys and they didn't like it. I still see this stuff going on 15 years later.

❖ STOPPING DISCRIMINATION AND HARASSMENT

There are a number of things that administration and individuals can do to ensure that women are not forced to work in a hostile environment, but rather are respected as equal law-enforcement officers. As individuals, officers must fight inaccurate and destructive stereotypes used to discriminate against female officers. For example, individuals can be explicit about their support for police-women by letting others know that they will not tolerate sexist, degrading remarks. This can be especially effective if male officers openly show their support of females in the department, thereby serving as role models for other male officers.

Another way individuals may attempt to stop discrimination or harassment against themselves is to utilize the legal systems. A recent increase in the number of legal cases against departments and individual perpetrators (Erez and Tontodonato, 1992) reflects the degree to which this method has been effective.

There are a number of alternatives that the individual can use to stop harassment, such as sending the harasser a letter by registered mail, speaking with union officials or other employee advocacy organizations, using the media to expose the problem, or contacting state government officials under whistle-blowing statutes. It is recommended that employers include in employee handbooks information on resources for employees who feel they are being harassed, along with clear departmental policies on reporting and discipline. Additionally, a separate packet that contains valuable articles and resource information (see references and additional readings at the end of this chapter) should be made available to all employees.

Higgenbotham (1988) describes a number of ways a police organization can combat sexual harassment. The first step is to establish a clear policy identifying the conduct that constitutes sexual harassment. A grievance process should then be clearly outlined. This grievance procedure must be accessible and confidential so that employees feel comfortable stepping forward. A number of persons of both sexes should be assigned as grievance counselors to reduce the anxiety of reporting. Mandatory investigations should be carried out and fully documented, with remedial or punitive measures mandatory for guilty parties. Most importantly, administration should be clear about its intolerance of sexual harassment and work to create a friendly and supportive work environment for both police-women and policemen.

❖ THE DILEMMA

The introduction of women into professional roles in law enforcement and the multitude of associated problems have led to a number of dilemmas for both female and male officers. Both sexes have reported during our interviews with them a number of situations where difficulties exist, and that attempts to elimi-nate problems of sex bias and harassment have created dilemmas that serve to perpetuate the problems.

Policewomen's Dilemma

The concept of defeminization has been described by Berg and Budnick (1986) as one such dilemma. Women are forced to try to find a balance between a police officer role (which has traditionally been associated with male character-istics) while maintaining the role of a woman. This can be very difficult to find a balance, as one veteran female officer describes:

> I had to assimilate more of the male characteristics in order to be accepted by every-one. I did this by being less sensitive, bantering and playing back and forth with the other male officers, and trying to depersonalize comments about women like I was one of the guys. This was tough, though, because I still wanted to be seen as a female. It's like you are one of the guys in order to fit in, but you're really not. I think that it is important for me to retain my female personality outside the police culture.

Although female officers feel as though they need to emulate a male officer to be accepted, doing so may cause them to be seen as a career threat by other male officers. This can lead to unfair characterizations of female officers as being "bitches" or "lesbians" (Berg and Budnick, 1986).

Women police officers have also described a tendency to refrain from reporting incidents in which they were sexually harassed or discriminated against because they didn't want to appear as though they were using the grievance inappropriately to get what they wanted. Women who report violations are sometimes seen by other officers, both male and female, as being nasty and manipulative. This has caused a great deal of stress for some female officers, because they would rather take the harassment and discrimination than be stig-matized by their self-assertive behavior. However, false accusations have occurred in an attempt to get revenge or gain power in some cases.

Finally, the increased emphasis on sensitivity training has led to increased problems for some women law-enforcement officers:

I think the overemphasis on sensitivity training has led to the sexes being treated differently. In some ways it has been a real setback for us, since it sometimes leads to us being singled out. I know of one department where male and female officers are not allowed to go to coffee together anymore, since sensitivity has turned into oversensitivity. Everybody is afraid to be around each other because they might say or do something that is politically incorrect. Everyone is paranoid.

Policemen's Dilemma

Similar dilemmas exist for male law-enforcement officers as well. One such dilemma is that male supervisors sometimes feel as though they must give preferential treatment to female officers out of fear that women will lodge complaints of sex discrimination. For example, during an interview one male supervisor explains:

I work very hard to treat men and women equally. But I sometimes think twice about disciplining women and give them an extra chance because I don't want it to look like I'm being tougher because she is a woman. If it were one of the guys, I wouldn't worry about it as much. I want to avoid being accused of discrimination, so I have to bite my tongue.

Another dilemma, which is related to the one just described, is that men have reported an uncertainty of how to act around women officers. During interviews with male officers, it was clear that male officers chose to avoid contact with female officers because they were afraid that they might say or do something inadvertently that wasn't politically correct. This reflects an oversensitivity described by some of the female officers earlier in this chapter. Unfortunately, this leads to a sense of segregation for both sexes.

According to Martin (1990), officers must depend on each other for protection and support at critical times. Men depending on men represents a form of "male comradery." However, relying on a woman for protection and support goes against traditional socialization, and for some men it feels "unmanly." Consequently, male officers seem to be in another "catch-22" when working with female partners.

It is important to understand that inherent differences in the way that men and women communicate may indeed be the source of some of these problems. For example, men tend to show acceptance and affection toward others by teasing, but women tend to personalize this (Glass, 1992). Glass provides excellent suggestions for both men and women on how to improve communications in general, but especially around sensitive areas such as sexual harassment.

❖ UNIQUE CONTRIBUTIONS

There are a number of strengths and unique contributions that policewomen add to law-enforcement departments. Some have argued that emphasizing these strengths has supported stereotypes and undercut arguments for equality (Balkin, 1988). However, here they are intended to highlight the importance of women's contributions. Balkin (1988) outlines several contributions, some of which are discussed next.

As discussed earlier, the public reacts favorably to women in police departments. They see women as more sensitive, pleasant, and equally competent. Therefore, female officers can play an important role in public relations. This has become increasingly important with the current trend toward an emphasis on community relations, an increased recognition of the service aspect, and movement toward police professionalism (Lord, 1986).

Policewomen are better at de-escalation of potentially volatile situations for a number of reasons. First, women are better communicators and often rely on negotiation and verbal exchange rather than physical force. Second, it is often considered heroic to hit a policeman, but cowardly to hit a policewoman. Third, male officers are perceived as more threatening to the public than female officers. Finally, policewomen are less interested in saving face or keeping the macho image than are male officers.

An example of what we are taking about is the following reaction of a male police officer to the effect of women in his department.

> Policing has changed in the last 13 years. When I started, a measure of how good a cop you were was by how good a fighter you were. Nowadays, if you're big and you're bad, they want you there in case they need to be protected, but that's not how we measure how good a police officer you are. What we're seeing is the result of having women and smaller men on the force. If you can talk a guy into coming along peacefully that's just as good an arrest as if you have to knock him unconscious.
>
> Sometimes the reactions you're getting from the bad guys are emotional, they're afraid they're going to get beat up, or they're afraid of what's going to happen after you get the handcuffs on them. At six foot seven and two hundred pounds, they're afraid of me. I have to do everything I can to make them understand that I'm a professional dealing with them. Whereas you get a female out there, this big bad guy he's not worried about getting beat up. So he's not so scared.

Female officers have been shown to handle domestic disturbances more effectively (Sherman, 1975). However, one veteran female officer said that a drawback is that the male will think the policewoman is always on the female's side during a domestic dispute. Consequently, she always talks with him first to get his side of the story. Overall, the female officers have been shown to be more patient and understanding and show more concern in family fights (Homant and Kennedy, 1985).

Child and female victims often respond better to female officers than to men. Therefore, female officers are valuable members of investigative teams of crimes against the person. Other areas of unique contributions include undercover work, public education programs for domestic violence and rape, and peer counseling for female colleagues.

SUMMARY

Women are increasingly entering into police work as a chosen career. Research has clearly demonstrated that women are as competent in police work as male officers. The public has responded favorably, although the negative attitudes of male officers remain a problem, though current trends show that this is changing. Sexual harassment is one common way negative attitudes are expressed, causing a considerable amount of unnecessary stress for female officers. Individuals and organizations can take active steps to reduce sexual harassment and promote a healthy work environment for both male and female officers. Policemen also perceive a number of added stressors associated with working with female officers. These issues have caused a number of dilemmas for both men and women in law enforcement. Policewomen make many unique contributions to law enforcement and will assume a greater role in policing in the future.

EXERCISES

I.   Imagine that you are a new officer in an urban police department that has a significant number of female officers. After a couple of weeks on the job, it becomes clear that the male officers do not approve of female officers and consequently make inappropriate comments in your presence. You feel uncomfortable with this and want to speak up but are afraid to.

1. How would you handle the issue?
2. What are the consequences of not speaking up? Of confronting the officers?
3. What are your responsibilities as a fellow officer?
4. How are your stereotypes about women going to affect your decision of what to do?

II.   Now imagine that you are a new male officer in the same department. You have come from a traditional family and have been taught since early childhood to respect and protect women. You are assigned a female partner who you like and feel is a good police officer. However, you notice that you are always nervous that she is going to get hurt, so you only let her handle nonvolatile situations. She has become upset with you for being sexist and discriminatory.

1. Are you discriminating? If so, in what ways?
2. What is the motivation for your behavior?

3. How do you solve the conflict with your partner?
4. Describe other situations where similar conflicts could arise.

REFERENCES

Balkin, J. (1988). Why policeman don't like policewomen. *Journal of Police Science and Administration 16*, 29–387.

Bell, D. J. (1982). Policewomen: Myth and reality. *Journal of Police Science and Administration 10*, 112–120.

Berg, B. L, and K. J. Budnick (1986). Defemininization of women in law enforcement: A new twist in the traditional police personality. *Journal of Police Science and Administration 14*, 314–319.

Ehrlich, S. (1980). *Breaking and Entering: Police Women on Patrol.* Los Angeles: University of California Press.

Erez, E., and P. Tontodonato (1992). Sexual harassment in the criminal justice system. In I. L. Moyer (ed.), *The Changing Roles of Women in the Criminal Justice System: Offenders, Victims, and Professionals* 2nd ed. Prospect Heights, IL: Waveland Press.

Glaser, D. F. (1983). *Male police officers' attitudes toward working with female police officers.* Unpublished doctoral dissertation, California School of Professional Psychology, Los Angeles.

Glass, L. (1992). *He Says She Says: Closing the Communication Gap between the Sexes.* New York: G.P. Putnam's Sons.

Harman, A. (1990). Report from the International Conference for Policewomen. *Law and Order*, April, 56–59.

Higgenbotham, J. (1988). Sexual harassment in the police station. *FBI Law Enforcement Bulletin*, September, 22–29.

Homant, R. J, and D. B. Kennedy (1985). Police perceptions of spouse abuse—a comparison of male and female officers. *Journal of Criminal Justice 13*, 29–47.

Lehtinen, M. W. (1976). Sexism in police departments. *Trial 12*, 52–55.

Lord, L. K. (1986). A comparison of male and female peace officers' stereotypic perceptions of women and women peace officers. *Journal of Police Science and Administration 14*, 83–97.

Martin, S. B. (1990). *On the Move: The Status of Women in Policing.* Washington, DC: Police Foundation.

Milton, C. (1972). *Women in Policing.* Washington, DC: Police Foundation.

Paludi, M. A., and R. B. Berickman (1991). *Academic and Workplace Sexual Harassment.* Albany, NY: State University of New York Press.

Sherman, L. J. (1975). Evaluation of policewomen on patrol in a suburban police department. *Journal of Police Science and Administration 1*, 383–394.

Sichel, J. L., L. N. Friedman, J. C. Quint, and M. E. Smith (1978). *Women on Patrol—A Pilot Study of Police Performance in New York City.* New York: Vera Institute of Justice.

Taubman, B. (1987). *Lady Cop.* New York: Warner Books.

Weisheit, R. A. (1987). Women in the State Police: Concerns of male and female officers. *Journal of Police Science 2nd Administration,* 15, 137–144.

Wexler, J. G., and D. D. Logan (1983). Sources of stress among women police officers. *Journal of Police Science and Administration 11,* 46–53.

ADDITIONAL READINGS

Cole, D. (April 19, 1989). Don't just stand there. *New York Times,* "A World of Difference" supplement.

Dunham, R., and G. Alpert (1989). *Critical Issues in Policing.* Prospect Heights, IL: Waveland Press.

Martin, S. E. (1990). *On the Move: The Status of Women in Policing.* Washington, DC: Police Foundation.

Moyer, I. L. (1992). *The Changing Roles of Women in the Criminal Justice System: Offenders, Victims, and Professionals,* 2nd ed. Prospect Heights, IL: Waveland Press.

Poole, E. D., and M. Pogrebin (1988). Factors affecting the decision to remain in policing: A study of women officers. *Journal of Police Science and Administration 16,* 49–55.

Weisheit, R., and S. Mahan (1988). *Women, Crime, and Criminal Justice.* Cincinnati, OH: Anderson Publishing Co.

14

❖

Stress
and Cultural Diversity

While the passenger kneels, an officer checks a car that collided with an ambulance. The driver left the scene of the accident and was later arrested. (Photo from the files of the *Columbia Missourian*)

❖ OBJECTIVES

1. To identify the stressors unique to culturally diverse groups in law enforcement.
2. To describe the strengths of a culturally diverse police organization.
3. To describe steps toward becoming multicultural.

❖ INTRODUCTION

The very nature and composition of the workplace and workforce are changing as a result of cultural diversity. From the late 1800s to the early 1900s, large groups of immigrants entered the United States from Ireland, Russia, Poland, and Italy. Having different customs and languages, they were not quickly assimilated. They worked hard, often in the face of overwhelming adversity, to gain a position in the steel, coal, and auto manufacturing industries. By the 1960s, the struggle for independence and recognition of rights for these disenfranchised white groups had been largely attained. The stage was now set for similar "outsiders" to seek acceptance.

The United States has long been thought of as a melting pot in which immigrants and ethnic minorities are somehow assimilated into the American fabric and thereby lose their unique characteristics. Instead, what has developed is a "mosaic society" in which nearly every city has its own ethnic communities, each with its own identity, concerns, values, and other cultural characteristics. For example, by the year 2000 English will be a second language for the majority of people residing in California. In the next 20 to 25 years, it is projected that Hispanics will surpass blacks as the largest minority. In 1988, over 30% of New York's residents were not born in the United States. In addition, San Francisco was one-third Asian, Detroit and Miami were nearly two-thirds black and Hispanic, respectively (Dicken and Blomberg, 1991).

By the year 2000 it is estimated that native-born, white U.S. males, who have dominated the workplace for generations, will be in the minority. Women will make up about 47% of the workforce, with immigrants and nonwhites holding another 26% of all jobs (Nussbaum, 1988). Eventually, it will be nonsense to speak of "minorities" at all; the term will be so relative to the composition of each community.

There are several reasons for this increasing diversity and the need to consider it in the management of police organizations. At this time, most law-enforcement organizations are still predominantly white, Anglo, male. According to the Bureau of Justice Statistics (Reaves, 1992), in 1990, 92% of officers were males, 83% were white, and 10.5% were black; Hispanics represented about 5.2% and other minorities such as Asians and Native Americans comprised about 1.3%. As demographics change and if talent is normally distributed in the population, we would expect that gradually staffing would proportionally represent the local community.

There is also the awareness that organizational performance can be improved by hiring the best candidates available. It is already recognized that minority officers often have better understandings of their own cultures and are more rapidly accepted into the communities they patrol than dissimilar ethnic officers. Finally, various laws have simply made it illegal to discriminate against various groups. Successful lawsuits have been made against offending officers, as well as the administrators and departments who did not intervene to stop it.

The need to respect, understand, and work closely with multicultural communities was clearly shown in the reaction to the legal decision on the Rodney King beating and conflicts between Korean and black residents in Los Angeles. Police officers are ultimately the ones who are designated to intervene in such high-risk and complex situations, and departments must have officers prepared for such events.

Most minorities have either not been hired or have simply been relegated to the lower ranks of organizations. When they aspire to more responsibility or promotion, they hit the "glass ceiling" (Morrison et al., 1987), an invisible barrier of prejudice and misunderstanding by the dominant culture that makes it difficult for women and minorities to advance in an organization. In 1988, women received only 66% of the wage that men earn for the same job. Of all workers earning minimum wage or less, women compose two-thirds of this group (Erlich, 1986). The result is a gross underutilization of human resources that police organizations desperately need.

The advantages of ethnic diversity in law-enforcement agencies are listed in Table 14-1.

❖ THE MINORITY OFFICER

Besides the stresses we have been discussing that all law-enforcement officers face, special stresses are placed on the minority officer by a number of sources; family and relatives, the minority community, other officers, and in some cases department administration. Much of our discussion will refer to black officers

TABLE 14-1   ADVANTAGES OF ETHNIC DIVERSITY

1. *Cost-effectiveness*. Organizations that have learned to cope with and utilize diversity generally have become more productive and have lower levels of absenteeism and turnover.

2. *Human resource development*. When a department becomes known for its fairness and as "a good place to work," it becomes easier to attract highly talented and qualified people from diverse groups.

3. *Acceptance by community*. Diverse departments are better able to understand and interact with diverse communities than are more restricted departments.

4. *Creativity*. Different perspectives are gained for problem solving, creativity, and innovation. From multiple cultures come multiple viewpoints that generally provide more thorough planning and solutions to problems.

5. *Flexibility*. By adapting its mechanisms to a more diverse work force, the police department becomes more flexible. This enables a more rapid response in addressing itself to the unique needs of communities.

because that is the population we have had the most contact with. That their experiences are representative of what other minorities face is supported by feedback from other regions of the country.

The first thing a minority going into law enforcement has to face is their own family's reactions. These reactions may be based on dislike of police and what they represent in the minority community or it may be similar to what a white officer faces in terms of the family's concerns about his or her welfare.

A representative example of family reactions comes from a black policewoman who came into the field 14 years ago when there were still few blacks and even fewer women. She reports the following reactions of her family.

> My mother and father's negative reaction wasn't with the fact that a member of the black race was going to be a police officer; their feelings were more "my daughter is taking a dangerous job and I don't want her to get hurt."
>
> My parents saw the work as having more risk than if I had become a counselor or something like that. My sister didn't really care. She said, "If it's what you want to do, OK. If you choose it, you can handle it."
>
> My brother is a street person and he had an "Oh my God, why would you want to do that. It's such a sell out occupation. You'll be doing whitey's work for him." He just down talked it a lot and said demeaning things....He eventually adjusted because it's me, but he still doesn't like police officers. But he gets in trouble with the police and goes to jail. He's had a lot of problems, like he's a drug user and stuff like that.

We hear comments from administrators on the difficulty of recruiting black officers. The recruiting officer has to make a case for working with law enforcement. We suspect that part of the problem lies in the attitudes of the black community toward police, which generalizes to community members who talk about joining the force. Again a black female officer gives some representative reactions as she talks about her impressions of how other blacks react to seeing a fellow black dressed in blue.

> How the other black people accept me as a police officer depends on their age. The older black people think it's wonderful we're making those inroads. And since I was the first black woman to get on the police force, they respect me. They say, "I'm really scared for you, I wouldn't want my daughter to do it, but I'm happy for you."
>
> But there are younger people who think you're a sell out. They hate the police and they say they don't care what color you are. We hate you because of that. I can remember, in '84, we were going to a call on Sexton Road, and it was a domestic disturbance with a black family. The fight had erupted out of the house and they were now fighting on the porch. This guy sees me come and immediately calls me a black bitch and tells me to get off his porch. He don't want no black cop in his house. Then he turns to the white officer who was with me and asks him to come on in.

❖ PREJUDICE IN THE POLICE DEPARTMENT

Besides family and community pressures, minority officers need to contend with department resistance to minorities. Examples of how bad the prejudice and hostility of white officers could be are given in the book *Black in Blue* (Alex, 1969), a study of the New York City Police Department in the late 1960s. Resistive antagonism has decreased considerably, but most black officers who have been in law enforcement for more than 15 years can remember how difficult is was when they joined the force. The difficulty of dealing with hostility was worsened by the small numbers of blacks who were in most departments.

The recruiting and hiring of large numbers of black police officers are relatively recent phenomena. The National Advisory Commission on Civil Disorders report showed that, given the percentage of the population that was black, they were grossly underrepresented in most police departments. For example, in the 1960s in Detroit, blacks were 39% of the population, but only 5% of the sworn officers. This has improved markedly in many places (Walker, 1992). In Detroit, 57% of the officers are now black. Some other examples of increased hiring of black officers are Atlanta, 56%; Washington, D.C., 41%; and New Orleans, 33%. Some cities with large black populations still trail far behind. Oklahoma City has only 4% black officers.

A black officer talks about how things were when there were only a few black officers in a department:

> In '75 when I took this job it was really stressful. The community didn't want me here, the white officers didn't want me here, so what was I doing here? It was terrible. I'd go to the shift meeting at night, I was working the midnight shift 11 to 7. I was being trained by someone who didn't appreciate blacks. He pretty much set the tone at shift meeting. They'd sit there and they'd tell racist jokes. They'd talk about spear chukkers and things like that. Right in the shift meeting and just laugh. It wasn't the upper administration, it was just the rest of the officers. Nobody ever addressed it and of course as a new officer I wasn't going to do anything. I had to complete my probation year, I wasn't going to make any trouble because I wanted to make it through.
>
> I'm pretty accepted now, but I feel I had to work twice as hard as a white. You really have to get out there and show them who you are. That you can think, that you're resilient, that you won't back down. People would try me, test me, to see just how far they can get. Now they know, now I think they respect me.

The chief and the officers around him were often prejudiced and contributed to the problems that black officers had in adjusting to the job. But there were members of administration, often at the intermediate level, who were active in trying to make sure that blacks became fully integrated into the department.

Nobody tells racist jokes in front of me anymore. We went to administration a few times. There have been new procedures put in place. The Captain came down hard on some people and it set a different tone around here. Administration in this department won't tolerate racism anymore. Officers have said to me, I do fear you. I do feel you have power.

The biggest stress for me anymore isn't a black thing, it's a blue thing. You're in a uniform, black, white, or whatever, and there's the public attitude of "I don't care for you." There's a hate there, an attitude. You know what I mean. On the flip side, I've had situations work for me because I was black.

Our deputy chief has done a good job of recruiting minorities. Things are much easier for black cops because we have the same percentage of blacks on the force as we have in the community. I'm not sure how we're going to do when he retires.

The deputy chief mentioned, when asked about the early days, reported the following incident:

We had a black officer who was hired here back in the early '70's when we only let black officers work the black area of the city. I had talked with him and we thought it wrong that he could only work the black district. He decided one day, when as usual he was assigned to cover the black district, he wasn't going to go out. The white officers rotated the districts and he wanted to rotate just like they did. His Captain told him, sorry you work the black district, that's your assignment.

He said Ok, then I'm not going to go out. I won't leave the station. I'm not going to work that district. You can fire me, do what ever you want to do, but I'm not going out. I want to be treated like everybody else. The powers that be got real disturbed and got on the phone to find some way to deal with him. They couldn't get any support from the city administration to fire him, so when they got done he rotated like everyone else. The thing was that in the white community when he started to rotate it was absolutely unnoticed. It was police resistance that was keeping him in the black district, because it was the way it had always been done.

A white officer on the topic of treating the black officers with respect said,

I was never aware of the black male officers having the problems with the white officers that the black females officers did. You can't get away with much or they'll run over you, beat you up. Literally. The black male officers who have done well were low key. Maybe too low key.

For example, we had a black officer who was a sergeant, he had been in the department 18 years. When I came here in the early '70's, he had just been promoted. Two or three years later they had a captain vacancy and John had seniority. He had everything going for him. He did fine on every test. Then at the last minute, when they got ready to pick the candidate, they made a new requirement that he couldn't meet. I can't remember what it was, but it knocked him out of the running.

I got with John the day that it happened. I tried to get him to file a discrimination complaint. The climate was ripe for it. You'd have to know John, but he didn't want the attention. He just wouldn't do it. He could have won but he wouldn't do it.

Earlier in this chapter we indicated that progress has been made in increasing the number of black officers in many cities like Atlanta and New Orleans. We believe this is only because of administrators who were willing to take some risks in the recruiting and retention of black officers. Again the deputy chief talks about how progress was made.

The real push to hire black officers came from '82 on. The present chief and I had gotten into a position where we had some power, and we decided that we were going to hire any black that made the final list. Any of them. What we did that was critically important was to drop the ranking that we had done. You know, 1 to 14 based on test scores and take the top candidates. If you make the eligibility list, we just put you in alphabetical order. You're qualified or you're not. That helped, because if you picked a black for a new position, some people would argue, "Hey this black candidate he's number nine. Hot damn there's eight more ahead of him." We felt those points didn't mean anything, if a person made the list they're qualified.

The same deputy chief gave another illustration of the problems of dealing with administrators who were out to keep blacks off the force in talking about a black female officer who was given a rough time by her Field Training Officer (FTO).

She was assigned to a training officer who didn't like blacks. I didn't have anything to do with where she was assigned. She would ride with him and he would make insulting remarks about blacks. At the time I had no support in the department, I couldn't get her off with another training officer. I couldn't have anything done with him. The major in charge of patrols was in cahoots with the FTO to get rid of her.

The FTO wrote a memo that I had to send on, which they had evidently agreed upon. The memo asked that she be dismissed as a result of poor probationary performance. Well, she and I had been talking about her problems, so I knew what was going on. So I took the memo and wrote in big red letters across every word of it, "This memo is a very serious violation of the chain of command, and I am in total disagreement." And signed my name. That meant they couldn't use the memo in the way they had intended without my bringing them up on charges of violation of the chain of command.

I didn't want her riding with him anymore because I knew he was going to destroy her. So I did what had never been done before; I pulled her out and put her in a car by herself and told her, "Here's what you got to do. Always answer your radio. Don't go code 7. Go to all calls, but don't piddle around. When an officer is making a traffic stop, I want them to look down the road and see your car setting as backup. Just making sure they're safe. When they're done, just drive away. They'll know you were making sure they were all right. Also coop up. When you see one in a parking lot, drive over, talk to them. Bitch about the administration, talk about the weather, don't stay to yourself. They're not going to be against you if they'll be looking you in the eye talking to you.

❖ RECRUITING

Because of black citizens' general resistance to police, it is hard to get individuals from the black community interested in joining the force. Even if they're interested, there is likely to be too much trouble from their peers in the community An active program of recruitment is required. An administrator talks about recruitment.

> The civil rights movement affected everybody. Captain Barbee pushed hard to get us to hire black officers. It was the mid seventies when we really started to hire black officers. Dye, the black chief, came in '82 and put some teeth into our hiring of black officers. We went to black colleges and different criminal justice programs in colleges here and in other states. We had a 60-hour college credit requirement, and we weren't willing to reduce the requirements for blacks at all. No shortcuts. Other than if they made it through all that, we would hire them. Still will today. We don't hire any blacks that don't meet all our qualifications.

In an attempt to recruit bright, qualified, career-oriented officers, the St. Paul Police Department under Chief William Finney has proposed changing the requirements for application as an officer in Minnesota. In the past, the POST Board required extensive testing, 2 to 4 years of college, and a criminal justice degree. The new proposal is designed to draw on a larger pool of minority and mid-level career changer applicants by recognizing any 4-year degree. While the typical 8 to 12 weeks of skills training is still mandatory, some departments are exploring the possibility of developing an internal cadet program. The cadets would be paid to work, explore the career fit, and obtain training leading to officer status.

❖ KEEPING BLACK OFFICERS

Holding qualified black officers can be a problem because of the current pressure on federal and state agencies to have staff with a proper mix of minorities. A qualified black candidate is likely to be heavily recruited. Some local police departments may have the feeling that they are screening and training minority personnel for other agencies. An officer in personnel reports with a mixture of pride and annoyance,

We've hired double the number of black officers you see in the department right now. One of our female black officers is just now leaving to go to law school. It's the quality of people we're getting. One has recently gone to the federal prison system. We sent him to a school and they spotted him and recruited him. The highway patrol just recruited one away from us. It makes me just furious when they do that. A good qualified black officer who wants to move on we'll just lose them. The federal agencies can offer them more. Or a private business comes in and offers them more money and they're gone.

❖ CONTINUING CONFLICTS BETWEEN BLACK OFFICERS AND ADMINISTRATION

All is still not well and problems continue to exist in departments. A black officer can use race to scare or pressure administration because of fear of what happens when the human rights commission gets involved. Administrators complain that it makes it very hard to fire an inadequate officer. Our impression is that under present circumstances administration will do everything in their power to bring black officers up to the level they should be at. We are also aware that not all black officers will agree that the department is giving blacks with borderline skills any special attention. Again an administrator speaks.

I think black officers who are unhappy just want to use the black issue to get an advantage to get promoted or get better assignments. I talk with them and ask what's the problem. They say it's just not fair. Well, what's not fair? It's just not fair. And you can't get anything more specific.

Or they say, "This is little Dixie. There's prejudice. There's the good old boy system."

"Like what?"

"Well you know all the whites stick together."

"How is that adversely affecting you?"

"Well, you can't get any promotion."

"What promotion?"

Nobody can name anything you can do anything about.

We need all the black officers we can get. We need black officers up in the ranks. I'm totally against any shortcuts. If they don't meet every qualification, forget it. We've got really good black officers here. We do have a few really prejudiced black officers. I'm just amazed. We have one who is one of the most racist individuals I'm ever met. He tells other black officers, "You're thinking like whitey." He comes in and tells me, you're hiring black officers who go and think like a white. They've gone to white college, criminal justice program, you're not hiring blacks.

We had a black officer last year who didn't make it through probation. Talk about dotting i's and crossing t's, we knew we would be examined to the nth degree and we were. The black officers came in to see me, that he wasn't being treated fairly and on and on. Everything was just wrong with what we were doing. We watched it closely to be sure he had every opportunity. He wasn't doing his reports. He just wouldn't do his police reports. He'd do a vandalism and 3 days later we still wouldn't have the report. A black officer sat down with him and said let me show you how to do it. How can he not do a police report and blame it on whitey. After the black officer had worked with him and saw that he wouldn't do the work, she went to other black officers and told them that protesting was just bullshit. That if he would do those things he would be ok. But he wouldn't. I think it would be a disservice to blacks to back off the requirements for all officers. It's an insult to them.

Some minority officers have dealt with the pressure by becoming tougher in dealing with members of their ethnic group, in an attempt to prove themselves to white officers. In a 1980 *Detroit Free Press* article, a black officer who had been described as a "good black police officer" had died. During his years of service, he had developed a reputation of being much tougher on blacks than other fellow officers. Over the duration of his career he had killed 20 men. At his funeral—no one attended (Warren and Ingram, 1983).

❖ NATIVE AMERICAN OFFICERS

To many Native Americans groups who reside in North America as sovereign nations, working in criminal justice is like living a double life. While their primary motivation in encouraging entry to the profession is to divert their youth from destructive life-styles and enhance the pride of their people, they must also contend with being viewed by other community members as "sellouts" or "apples"—"red on the outside and white on the inside."

The laws governing the many tribes in North America are as varied as the tribes themselves. Some are uniquely native, while others are a conglomeration of native and white-negotiated rules. In still other cases, white rules have been clearly imposed and little exists reminiscent of native law. Especially in these latter situations, native people feel little obligation to live by laws that are alien to them or represent subjugation. The officers who must enforce them have often reconciled the dilemma by trying to live harmoniously in two very different cultures.

❖ STRESS FROM CROSS-CULTURAL CONTACT

To officers who have had little experience with members of minority cultures, working in their communities may be stressful. For example, a white officer who had little background experience with Native Americans but who was assigned to a district heavily populated with them, found himself having culture shock:

One of the first things I learned as a [white] kid was to look someone in the eyes to prove that you were being honest with them—averted eyes mean that you were hiding something. It's completely different with Indians.

One of the first times I questioned a kid on the street we had stopped for questioning, he wouldn't even come close to making eye contact. I *knew* from that he was guilty and demanded that he look me in the eyes. The more he resisted, the more I was convinced he had done something wrong.

I later found out that I was the one who was wrong—I really jumped the gun and misinterpreted his behavior. I didn't know that these people showed respect by averting their eyes. He was showing me respect and I kept hassling him. I was too embarrassed to go back to him and apologize. I really felt stupid, here I was trying to work with their community and I couldn't even communicate with them. I learned quickly, but it was usually from more mistakes I made.

Like time—they deal with time different than a lot of whites do. I think of time as exact and specific, I try to be exactly on time. When I plan to meet with indian people at the community center, for example, I know that the meeting will eventually happen, but after everyone arrives at their own pace. It was hard for me not to impose my judgments on them that they were doing it "wrong." I've learned a lot from them, and about myself and my culture, and it's made me a better officer.

Contact with Native-Americans, of course, is only one situation that officers may have problems with because they do not understand the behavior of the citizens that they have to deal with. To prevent misunderstandings that can result in anger or resistance, officers need to learn at least the basics about cross-cultural differences. Cultures may differ greatly in their use of gestures and other nonverbal behavior, role expectations toward gender, behavior toward elders, perception and use of power, drive for achievement, decision-making style, and many other social conventions that white, male, middle-class people simply assume to be correct.

For example, the ok gesture made with the index finger and thumb is considered an offensive gesture by Russians, Greeks, and Brazilians; to the French it signifies something worthless; and to the Japanese it means "money." Another example: Many officers want to keep a safety distance between themselves and citizens and find touch too intrusive. When dealing with Middle Eastern people, who prefer a very close personal distance, or Hispanics, who often touch to establish contact and show receptiveness, the officer who pulls back physically is seen as rude and abrupt.

Language and social convention are also highly influential in establishing a cooperative relationship. For example, the United States uses a "low-context" language that leads the speaker to be very specific and directive and get right to the point. While this mode of communication is highly appreciated by people of Swiss and German backgrounds, people from "high-context" cultures may take it as brash, rude, and pushy.

Traditional Japanese often speak in broader contexts and more abstract fashion to avoid offending another person; directness is often viewed as being ignorant and impolite. Arabs and Chinese may spend considerable time just getting to know someone before they will discuss important issues at all. Some Native American tribes do not address individuals directly but through others, who indirectly give or obtain information.

While these methods may not be seen as efficient for the officer to use in emergencies or for the short term, they are mandatory to learn and appreciate if cooperative relationships are to be developed within diverse cultural communities.

❖ CHANGING ATTITUDES, CHANGING ORGANIZATIONS

Cultural awareness programs should focus more on understanding these cultural nuances and how they can be used to enhance the contact made with citizens from different cultures. However, many attempts to reduce minority–majority misunderstandings have had mixed results. The encounter and sensitivity groups of the 1970s dealt with differences in a direct and often confronting manner. Sometimes this approach brought people together, but often the intensity was threatening and accusatory and entrenched them in their biases, while forcing them to publicly pretend reconciliation.

Administrators should also be cautious not to automatically assign their minority officers to be the cultural sensitivity trainers for the department. While this might be considered a compliment to place them in an instructional role, it is another example of discriminatory selection on the basis of race rather than performance and may convince the officer that he or she is again a representative rather than a person. In addition, officers may be less willing to openly explore their own biases because they do not want to appear prejudiced in the presence of a minority trainer (Hennessy, 1993). Furthermore, some officers find that white officers who are culturally sensitive may be more effective and believable role models for other white officers. Probably the best criteria is simply to choose the best qualified people who are interested in the task.

A primary objective in cultural diversity training is to challenge *ethnocentrism*. This refers to the belief that one's own culture is the best, should be the reference point for all decisions, and may be imposed on others. People who are high in ethnocentrism are convinced of the superiority of their culture and use their cultural standards to measure the worth of other cultural practices and beliefs. This often leads to arrogance and contempt and intolerance of people and customs that are different. Many white Americans are surprised to discover that many of their cherished beliefs and proud accomplishments in American culture have been made through contributions by people from other cultures.

In effect, much of the behavior of discrimination can be legislated out of law enforcement by clear policy and consistent consequences. In contrast, it may be impossible to change attitudes and beliefs solely through rules. To alter unrealistic expectations and distorted perceptions about minorities, appreciating and understanding the cultural differences may create more favorable conditions for relating. A summary of what minority employees want is given in Table 14-2.

Making changes in law-enforcement organizations and the way cultural diversity is approached is not the same as simply being "politically correct." While such terms as "coloreds," "blacks," and "people of color" may be in fashion from time to time, minority groups still must deal with the same discrimination that name changes do not affect. Attitudes in favor of diversity cannot simply be mandated or prescribed—they must be experienced, felt, understood, learned, and practiced. As Gordon (1992) accurately observes,

> What is odd about the PC [politically correct] people...is their dopey belief that people can be bullied into being kind, good, and sensitive to each other, never speaking thoughtlessly to, or thinking unkindly of, people whatever their race, religion, country of national origin, sex, or sexual habits.

Although change is often a slow and difficult process and some small group may secretly hold onto their prejudices, there are some actions that can be taken to move your department toward diversification.

1. *Mentorship.* Provide mentorship to minorities to give them the same opportunities to develop their talents as other personnel. This usually involves a senior officer who recognizes strong talent in new officers and provides them with occasions to build their skills.

TABLE 14-2   WHAT MINORITY EMPLOYEES WANT

- To be valued as unique individuals, as members of ethnically diverse groups, as people of different races, and as equal contributors.
- To establish more open, honest working relationships with people of other races and ethnic groups.
- The active support of white males in opposing sexism and racism.
- To be valued for what they do and are capable of, rather than just on their appearance or other superficial characteristics.
- For organizations to proactively address work and family issues.
- To be seen as peers, not as "those people" or the enemy.
- To have others understand and appreciate their cultural contributions and assets.

Source: Loden and Rosener, 1991. *Workforce America!* Homewood, IL: Irwin.

---

2. *Orientation*. Many women and minorities do not have experience negotiating the "good ol' boy" network that so many white males have grown up with. Provide information and orientation to "the way the system works," much as white officers will have to come to understand the subtleties of minority communities.

3. *Policies*. Equal opportunity should not just be represented in policy regarding hiring practices, but should cover the challenges that arise from such diversity. Enforced practices regarding harassment and discrimination send a strong and clear message about what the department values.

4. *Practices*. Diversity can be supported by offering networks, newsletters, and groups for officers. Benefits packages and flextime may be appreciated by officers who want to give equal time to child rearing. Teams and committees, especially those for planning and policy, can be comprised of diverse members.

5. *Diversity training*. Organizations in business are finding that diversity can be implemented with fewer conflicts as a result of training regarding differences and similarities. Different groups can share perceptions, needs, and information about their unique perspectives.

In addition to the sources of stress we have been discussing, Debro (1983) suggested that minority officers experience more stress than others due to the following:

1. Being constantly reminded of their minority status
2. Expectations that they are (or should be) more aware of and tolerant toward minority issues within their community
3. Expectations that they should join a departmental organization that represents their minority interests (which becomes another barrier between them and the majority)
4. Expectations that they should become members of some formal and traditional criminal justice organization (whose policies they may not completely agree with)
5. Slower promotional opportunities that support the impression that there are discriminatory processes at work

SUMMARY

Members of minority groups have faced considerable resistance to employment in law enforcement from their families and from members of law enforcement agencies. However, the situation has improved in many cities as recruitment policies have changed and members of minority groups now made up a significant percentage of the officers. Tension continues between officers from minority groups and administration in places and cultural awareness programs are needed to help both sides recognize differences in attitude and life style. A person does not need to be politically correct to appreciate the advantages to departments of having ethnic diversity among their staff.

QUESTIONS

1. Think of a time when you were an outsider, when your talents were unrecognized or unappreciated. How did it feel to be different and on the outside? How would being included have made a difference?

2. Think of the stereotypes you have of different groups: racial, religious, gender, age, disabilities, nationalities, affectional preferences, and so on. Where did you learn these stereotypes? Can you think of exceptions to them?

3. What are some things your culture takes for granted that may be very different in other cultures? Consider such things as eye contact, gestures, relationship toward older people, dealing with authorities, loyalty toward family, reputation, and so on.

REFERENCES

Alex, N. (1969). *Black in Blue: A Study of the Negro Policeman.* New York: Appleton-Century-Crofts.

Debro, J. (March, 1983). Minority stress: A case of dual identity in law enforcement. *The Police Chief 50*, 106–115.

Dicken, B., and Blomberg, R. (1991). Immigrants—Can they provide the future labor force? *Public Personnel Management,* Spring, 91–100.

Ehrlich, E. (1986). 9 to 5 and then some: More women are moonlighting. *Business Week,* August, 41.

Gordon, J. (1992). Rethinking diversity. *Training,* January, 23–30.

Hennessy, S. M. (1993). Achieving cultural competence. *The Police Chief,* August, 46–53.

Loden, M., and J. Rosener (1991). *Workforce America!* Homewood, IL: Richard D. Irwin.

Morrison, A., R. White, E. Van Velsor and the Center for Creative Leadership (1987). Breaking the Glass Ceiling: Can Women Reach the Top of America's Largest Corporations? Reading, MA: Addison-Wesley.

National Advisory Commission on Civil Disorders (1968). *Report.* New York: Bantam Books.

Nussbaum, B. (1988, September 19). Needed human capital. *Business Week*, 100–103.

Reaves, B. R. (1992). *State and Local Police Departments, 1990*. Washington, DC: Bureau of Justice Statistics.

Terkel, S. (1992). *Race: How Blacks and Whites Think and Feel about the American Obsession*. Garden City, NY: Doubleday.

Walker, S. (1992). *The Police in America*. New York: McGraw-Hill.

Warren, A., and R. Ingram (1983). Police stress in black and white. *The Police Chief 50*, 112–115.

15

❖

Small Departments and Rural Law Enforcement

Officer plows up a field of marijuana. (Photo from the files of the Missouri State Highway Patrol)

❖ OBJECTIVES

1. To understand that the nature of stressors differs for rural versus municipal law enforcement.
2. To identify the unique characteristics of working in a rural setting that cause stress.
3. To identify ways of reducing the stressors associated with work in rural settings.

❖ INTRODUCTION

Working as a law-enforcement officer in a rural environment is a great deal different from working in a municipal district. Rural law enforcement constitutes a large proportion of the law-enforcement profession. Officers from many organizations such as state police, county sheriff deputies, customs and immigration officers, conservation agents, border patrol officers, small town police officers, and FBI and DEA agents all work in rural settings. However, very little consideration has been given to the unique characteristics and demands of working in rural settings compared to working in large metropolitan areas (Sandy and Devine, 1978). Consequently, issues regarding the unique characteristics of rural patrols are often given limited attention in research and training.

The purpose of this chapter is to describe a number of sources of stress that are caused or exacerbated by work in rural settings and/or small departments. It is important to acknowledge that working in small departments in rural areas is not identical to working for a federal or state agency in rural areas. Although some of the unique stressors are the same, some are unique to small departments. Throughout this chapter the reader should compare and contrast the differing effects of the stressors on those who work for small departments versus those who work for federal or state agencies.

❖ ISOLATION

The most prominent characteristic of working in rural areas is isolation. Officers are often aware that backup units are many minutes and miles away. Officers in metropolitan areas more frequently encounter dangerous situations, but may be less stressed by them because of the accessibility of backup officers. However, conservation agents, officers from small municipal departments, border patrol, and state police often work alone in large geographical areas. This isolation can often lead to feelings of insecurity for officers (Sandy and Devine, 1978).

During routine stops in metropolitan areas, surrounding officers often drive by the location of the stop to communicate their availability for support if it is needed. In rural areas, vehicle stops are often in isolated areas where there is limited visibility at night, no backup for miles, and no citizens to serve as witnesses or sources of support for the officer. Some officers have reported that the absence of any witnesses can be particularly troublesome, because the testimony of the officer becomes more significant. Unlike crowded urban areas, rural areas offer little chance that any witnesses can help to provide evidence.

Calls such as bar fights and domestic disputes that would automatically require more than one unit in metro areas are answered by single officers in rural areas or in small departments. Rather than using backup as a safety precaution, it is often used only when the situation is unmanageable for one officer, and then help does not arrive immediately. This can be very stressful for officers who are being physically confronted by perpetrators. One officer describes his experience:

> Not having backup nearby is always on my mind. I think about it more when I am going into a bar fight or a domestic disturbance. But even when you make a routine traffic stop and something just doesn't seem right, you look for cues about whether or not backup is required—like how many there are, if you know them, whether you need to search the vehicle. You always have to make the decision about whether or not to call backup. When it's late at night, then someone is going to have to get out of bed to come and back you up. If you call for help a lot, then some of the guys start to give you shit for being a wimp. Some of the guys pride themselves on never having to call backup.

There are effective strategies for officers without backup readily available to help relieve the stress. Some officers devise strategies for de-escalating volatile situations to buy time until backup arrives. Others communicate at regular intervals on the radio with other officers and dispatch to let them know if the situation has a high potential for escalation. Each officer should consider devising his or her own strategies for handling situations without backup as a means of reducing the anxiety associated with working alone in rural areas or in small towns.

❖ BOREDOM

The rural officer typically has fewer calls during the course of a shift than officers working in highly populated areas, especially during late night shifts. Boredom in law enforcement leads to job dissatisfaction and decreased self-esteem in some officers (Sandy and Devine, 1978). Officers sometimes begin to feel badly about themselves because they don't feel as though they are contributing services for pay when they are inactive for a majority of the time, leading to a decreased sense of competency. This conflicts a great deal with the stereotype of what the job should be which is based on metropolitan law enforcement (Sandy and Devine, 1978).

In many rural areas there are no 24-hour stores where an officer can go to be in bright lights and visit with people to remain awake and aware. Rather, rural officers are left with dark, quiet communities with very little action to keep them interested, which makes staying awake and alert during night shifts more difficult. Suggestions provided in the chapter on shift work can help the rural officer to cope with this difficulty.

Long stretches of boredom are sometimes interrupted by high-risk calls that require the officer to instantly be energetic and focused. Once the call is over, the officer is then faced again with long periods of boredom. Sudden changes in activity from one extreme to the other lend to the unpredictability of work activities, which can be stressful for some people. Additionally, officers often need to talk with someone following a stressful event. For those in rural settings this is often not possible. Rather, the officer is left without any peer support for an extended period of time, if peer support is available at all.

In addition to the lack of activity, a restricted range of activity also leads to boredom. Officers in rural areas are less likely to get a wide range of calls, which helps to keep the job interesting and challenging. Rather, most of the active time is spent doing the same kind of work. The activity frequently observed in rural areas or small communities involves lost pets, keys locked in cars, domestic disputes, DWI arrests, minors consuming alcohol, vehicle accidents, and routine traffic stops. Rarely does the officer get involved in interesting cases of crimes against the person (e.g., sexual assault), white-collar crimes, robbery, homicide, arson, organized crime, kidnapping, or large-scale drug cases. Answering the same kinds of calls all the time can lead to job dissatisfaction.

❖ LIMITED RESOURCES

Small law-enforcement agencies are often forced to operate on a limited number of resources. For example, small communities can rarely afford the latest innovations in law-enforcement technology that are available in larger departments or in federal or state agencies. Rather, small departments may have a limited supply of equipment that is outdated or worn out. In one case a small community would not allocate funds for a new squad car (there was only one) even though the current cruiser had over 200,000 miles on it. The car would quit running, not start, and had a top speed of 70 miles per hour. The city council decided that the city could simply not afford a new car. This same lack of financial resources has led to the use of outdated or faulty equipment such as radios, investigation equipment, bullet proof vests, and mace.

The opportunities for continuing education can be quite limited because the small department cannot afford the expenses or to have an officer gone (Sandy and Devine, 1978). For many small communities where crime is not a major problem, city administrators can be quite reluctant to make a financial commitment to improving the quality of training and equipment for law-enforcement agencies. This can also lead to a decrease in a sense of professional identity, since the department may not be viewed as important by city administrators.

Another difficulty caused by a lack of financial resources is the limited amount of time the city's prosecuting attorney is allowed to spend on each case. At times, limited consultation with the prosecutor leads to poorly prepared cases, mishandled evidence, and eventual dismissal of the case. Furthermore, this may lead to a greater tendency to plea bargain cases or drop charges to save the money required to go to trial. These are examples of how limited finances can preclude the quality of services and the safety of the officers and community residents.

A limited number of officers in small communities can have an adverse impact. Officers may find it difficult getting vacation time simply because there aren't enough officers to cover. During special events the officers may be required to work unusually long hours without much time off. One chief of police of a small community was forced to plea bargain almost all the criminal cases simply because the city could not afford to have an officer away testifying.

❖ ABSENCE OF ANONYMITY

A substantial source of stress for officers working in rural communities is the inability to shed the "cop" perception of others. For example, one of the authors is still referred to as the "cop" in a small town where he has not worked as a police officer for 5 years. The person becomes known as the "cop" and is seen as such even off duty. This is very stressful for some officers, because they feel as though they are on duty every day of their life. People continue to make complaints, ask about cases or incidents, and treat officers differently than other citizens when they are off duty. This can be extremely bothersome and stressful.

Officers feel as though they can't "let their hair down" and be normal citizens because others will be judgmental of them. One officer describes his inability to go out and have a good time without later consequences.

> I feel like I can't even go up to the local pub and have a beer after work like everyone else can. The next time I am making a DWI arrest someone will come up and say "I saw you drinking last night. What the hell makes you think that you can drink but we can't? You damn hypocrite." It just seems like you have to keep some image up even when you are off duty. It really restricts what I can do for fun. I have to leave town and go where nobody knows me or else I have to put up with the crap later. In school my kids are the "cop's kids" and my wife is the "cop's wife." They shouldn't have to put up with that crap either!

Officers in urban areas do not have this problem to the same extent because their professional identity is unknown for the large part when they are off duty. Consequently, off-duty behavior of officers from rural communities is held to a higher standard.

❖ CONFLICT OF INTEREST

It seems that in rural areas or small communities everybody is related to or knows everybody else, which can cause a problem for the law-enforcement officer. Nearly everyone that an officer comes in contact with during routine police operations, he or she knows in another setting. Preexisting relationships with law breakers can cause a great deal of stress because the officer is forced to make decisions about whether to arrest or cite an individual with whom he or she may have to deal with in a different context later. For example, one officer we interviewed was ordered by the chief to drop charges against the owner of a large business because of the business owner's political influence in the small community. During interviews, another officer described a case in which a relative of another officer was involved. Charges were not filed because the arresting officer was afraid of the dissent it would cause within the department.

Political interests can interfere with the objectivity of carrying out investigations. For example, one officer interviewed reported that his chief of police ordered officers to *not* investigate further a burglary of one of the local businesses when a city council member's son became the prime suspect. Additionally, another supervisor called a friend to warn him that his daughter was under an investigation for selling drugs. Similar conflicts of interest are by no means uncommon in small communities nationwide, as people inevitably are more likely to have preexisting relationships with community members.

Sandy and Devine (1978) described a tendency to hire "local boys" who have gone through law-enforcement training as police officers in the community in which they grew up. These officers can have difficulty overcoming preconceptions about the community and its citizens. Additionally, these officers are more likely to have existing relationships of one kind or another with nearly everyone in the community. Sandy and Devine describe an incident in which an officer was called to his former high school principal's house because of a domestic conflict. The ability of the officer to assert himself as an authority figure was greatly compromised by his preexisting relationship with the people involved. The former principal refused to respect the authority of the police officer since he knew of him as a former student. Situations like this can lead to frustration on the part of the officer, with the possibility of escalation of the situation if the people involved refuse to cooperate.

❖ LIMITED PROFESSIONAL DEVELOPMENT

Rural law-enforcement agencies often operate on limited budgets. Consequently, opportunities for continuing education are sometimes unavailable. This leads officers to a sense of stagnation in their job, with little opportunity to continue to develop their professional careers. Even when officers in small departments receive a promotion, they often continue to do the same job they did before. The only thing that changes is their title and a modest increase in salary. This is unlike larger departments that assign new and challenging duties to those who receive promotions.

Additionally, small rural departments are highly unlikely to have separate divisions that officers can choose as an alternative. For example, larger departments have divisions of prevention and education, investigation, drug enforcement, homicide, and public relations, to name a few. Lateral moves allow officers in these departments an alternative when they feel they need a change in their duties. These opportunities for diversity are almost nonexistent in smaller departments.

Because advancement within small departments is rare, there is less emphasis on performance evaluations and accountability of services. Since officers are not competing for promotions, administration is often less concerned with evaluating the performance of officers. What results is an ambiguous set of expectations with less formal guidelines for what constitutes acceptable behavior. Administration may be less concerned about the technicalities of paper work and following proper procedure. Instead, the department is at risk for becoming ruled by an autocratic chief who may be less concerned with fairness than with his or her own interests. In such cases, clear grievance procedures may not exist, and officers who complain about the way they are treated suffer more discrimination from those in control. Consequently, officers may experience more job dissatisfaction and anxiety about limited options for changing employment and problem solving.

❖ LACK OF PEER SUPPORT GROUP

Officers from small communities may have very few friends who are in law enforcement. The opportunities to seek out peer support are more limited. An important outlet for dealing with stress is the peer support group of other officers (Sandy and Devine, 1978). Unlike urban areas where large numbers of officers participate, there is seldom enough support available from the limited number of officers to allow the peer support groups to be formed.

❖ HIGHLY ARMED PUBLIC

Rural law-enforcement officers perceive their contacts to be more highly armed and dangerous than those encountered in urban settings (Sandy and Devine, 1978). While certain areas of inner cities are saturated with firearms, rural citizens are more likely to have guns for hunting and self-defense than the average urban citizen. Therefore, the rural officer must be more aware of the potential use of firearms by citizens resisting arrest. However, with the increase in violence in urban schools, and the like, this awareness is critical for all officers.

❖ COPING WITH STRESS

A study conducted by Fain and McCormick (1988) examined the coping styles of rural officers with those of urban officers in Louisiana. Although the sources of stress are often different for rural officers, there appears to be no difference in the way rural and metropolitan law-enforcement officers cope with the stress. Furthermore, coping styles were unrelated to demographic variables such as age, years of experience, rank, or education. It appears that sources and levels of stress may be different for rural and urban law-enforcement personnel, but there is a consistent pattern in the way officers attempt to deal with the stress.

SUMMARY

Our discussion of the unique sources of stress is by no means exhaustive. Each individual varies in reactions to various stressors. While some officers experience very little stress working in rural areas or small departments, others who are less comfortable working on their own under isolated conditions may experience a great deal of anxiety. Likewise, departments vary a great deal in their organization and support from the community. Some rural departments function quite well and do not have problems associated with the sources of stress described.

Many of the sources of stress cannot be eliminated because they are inherent in the nature of rural law enforcement (Sandy and Devine, 1978). However, the attention given to these issues in the training of new officers has long been inadequate. By better understanding the unique aspects of work in rural settings, officers can better understand their own role and reactions to work in this kind of environment. Additionally, a commitment at the organizational and individual level to combat or minimize these stressors would do much to improve the job satisfaction and quality of services provided by rural law-enforcement personnel.

EXERCISES

1. Imagine that you are working in a rural area and you receive a call at 3:20 A.M. about a car full of people acting suspicious in an alley behind the bank. You approach the vehicle.
   a. What cues would you look for to determine if you needed backup?
   b. When would you feel that you needed backup?
   c. How would you react to the suspects while you waited for backup to get there?
   d. What if you were called to a domestic dispute?
2. Refer to the domestic abuse situation described earlier in which the officer was called to his former principal's house.

a. How could this officer overcome his inability to assert himself as an authority figure?

b. What could this officer have done to prepare for a situation like this?

REFERENCES

Fain, D. B., and G. M. McCormick (1988). Use of coping mechanisms as a means of stress reduction in North Louisiana. *Journal of Police Science and Administration 16,* 21–28.

Sandy, J. P., and D. A. Devine (1978). Four stress factors unique to rural patrol. *The Police Chief,* September, 42–44.

SUGGESTED READINGS

Riser, M. (1974). Some organizational stresses on policemen. *Journal of Police Science and Administration 2,* 156–159.

United States Department of Justice (1982). *Criminal Justice in Rural America.* Washington, DC: National Institute of Justice.

16

❖

Stress Management:
An Overview of Methods
and Techniques

❖ OBJECTIVES

1. To provide an overview of stress management methods and techniques.
2. To identify the basic conditions for practicing these techniques.
3. To describe a comprehensive list of activities for stress inoculation.
4. To present two rationales for helping select appropriate techniques.

❖ INTRODUCTION

Unique to law enforcement and other emergency service occupations is the continuing presence of high-stress events. The impact of these may vary by longevity in the occupation or stage of career development, but stress is pervasive in the law enforcement profession (Violanti, 1983). Unlike occupations in which many stressors can be eliminated, avoided, or reduced, police officers only have the option to learn more effective strategies for coping with stressors. This approach to stress management can be likened to inoculation, through which officers become more resistant to the effects and more resilient under the strain (Ganster et al., 1982; O'Neill et al., 1982).

This is not to say that officers do not already have and use a variety of stress management techniques. But as some studies have reported (Ball, 1986; Violanti and Marshall, 1983), most methods for coping with stress that have been learned are either insufficient to deal with the intensity and frequency of law-enforcement stress or the methods increase and complicate stress rather than alleviate it. Frequent but ineffective coping includes emotional blocking, withdrawing from the spouse, alcohol, drugs, sleeping aids, behavior problems, and cynicism.

The techniques presented in this chapter and the next are quite varied, but have been selected because they are relatively straightforward to learn and have been effectively used by officers and other emergency personnel. Chapter 17 will describe the techniques in much more detail.

❖ THE PROBLEM OF CATEGORIZING
STRESS MANAGEMENT TECHNIQUES

There have been many attempts to categorize various stress-management techniques, but there is no widely accepted classification at this time. As we have discussed in previous chapters, stress is a mind–body problem. It produces symptoms that are both mental and physical, and should be dealt with from such a two-fold perspective.

Some techniques place an emphasis on reducing physiological symptoms such as muscle tension. These include biofeedback, spot checking and scanning, deep breathing, progressive relaxation, anchoring, and exercise. Others emphasize quieting the mind, such as thought stopping, positive self-talk, cognitive rehearsal and desensitization, autogenic training, imagery, and meditation.

Effective stress management requires learning how to voluntarily produce both physical relaxation and mental calm. Whichever techniques you finally decide to implement, it is important that they be practiced regularly until they are mastered and built into your life-style—as much as stress is currently built into it.

Because a positive attitude toward the techniques is an important ingredient in their regular practice and successful application, requiring all officers to use any one technique is discouraged. Furthermore, no single technique works equally well for everybody. Some stress-control methods, although very effective, may be viewed by more traditional officers as too esoteric (e.g., meditation or yoga), while other techniques (e.g., imagery and self-talk) are considered mundane. It would be more valuable to assist reluctant officers to identify effective coping methods that they are currently using and assist them in refining or expanding their application. The models presented at the end of this chapter can assist in matching techniques with the needs and styles of different individuals.

Most of the techniques discussed have been found to reverse the stress physiology described in Chapter 3. During deep quieting of mind and body, respiration slows remarkably, often from an average of 12–14 breaths per minutes to as low as 4–6. In addition, oxygen consumption decreases, heart rate slows, and blood pressure decreases (Benson, 1975; Curtis and Detert, 1981). After they have been startled or stressed, the heart rate of meditators returns to normal much more quickly than that of nonmeditators (Goleman, 1980).

Daily relaxation breaks have also been found to significantly decrease stress symptoms and enhance performance and satisfaction. They can reduce frustration levels, feelings of work overload, type A ("workaholic") behavior, and anxiety. Physical energy is rated higher, concentration is deeper, problems are managed more effectively, efficiency increases, and there are greater feelings of self-confidence and self-control (Goleman and Schwartz, 1981; Lester et al., 1984; Peters et al., 1977).

❖ BASIC CONDITIONS FOR PRACTICING TECHNIQUES

Like any other skill, proficiency in voluntary relaxation requires time for practice, proper instruction in the technique, and adopting it into your life-style with regular practice. Much of each day is filled with multiple cues to "get prepared," "tense up," and "fight or run." It is not surprising that so many officers experience high blood pressure and muscle tension discomfort resulting from a chronic state of arousal and bracing. If what we practice daily is reacting tensely to stimuli and cues all around us, then we get very good at becoming tense. The tension builds gradually until we think our normal state is one of being anxious, nervous, and uncomfortable.

Stress-coping practice provides a needed skill so that we can choose to release unnecessary muscle tension and quiet our minds. When we are relaxed, thinking is clearer, movements are faster and smoother, and attention can be paid to things other than our own arousal and discomfort. But relaxation does not come easy. We have spent years conditioning ourselves to the cues in our environment to "tense up"! We must give ourselves equal time and practice to unlearn tension and relearn real choices.

The techniques presented have been tried and tested by police officers, emergency medical technicians, crisis workers, air traffic controllers, and other professionals who work in high-stress occupations. Most of these techniques can help you to accomplish the following objectives:

1. Decrease the overall level of residual tension in your daily life; lower your normal level of tension.
2. Enhance your "early warning system" by lowering your threshold of awareness, thereby increasing your sensitivity to subtle increases in tension.
3. Increase the rebound or recovery time within which you relax back to your normal level of arousal after a stressful period.

4. Increase voluntary control over your tension level so that you can regulate the optimal degree of tension.

These techniques work effectively, but if they were that easy to implement, you would probably be using them already. They require practice, and practice requires time. One of the first requirements is to give yourself permission to work slowly, carefully, and with discipline to master a new skill. Do not pressure yourself to immediately understand or produce results. In the authors' experience, it takes about 2 weeks of daily practice for most people to begin to notice the effects of relaxation training. In the beginning the techniques will require a significant amount of time, but once mastered they will require much less time to keep them functional—a little like marksmanship practice.

The purpose of stress-coping training is to be able to quickly and effectively apply it on the job, but it will take a while getting to the point where it responds on demand. For the beginner, several suggestions can make learning easier and quicker.

1. *Protected time*. For many of the techniques you will need to create a block of time sufficient for deep relaxation or concentration in which you will not be interrupted. In the beginning, about 20 to 30 minutes should be enough, about the same amount of time you would need for a physical workout. Even the expectation that you could be interrupted at this early stage of practice will interfere with your release of residual tension. Consider that you already have certain times and places at home where you cannot be bothered (e.g., bathroom or bedroom). You will need to let family members or others know that your time for relaxation is just as important as other special times. Put out a "Do Not Disturb" sign and take the phone off the hook. In the beginning you may also want dim lighting so that there is less visual distraction.

2. *Loosen up*. Loosen your tie and belt, remove your shoes and glasses, and loosen any other clothing that is restrictive. Tight clothing can become uncomfortable when you are resting quietly for long periods. Also "loosen" your attitude and do not be too critical of yourself; generate an attitude of curiosity about each practice session.

3. *Balanced posture*. Sit in a comfortable chair that provides good support for your back. While you may be tempted to lie down, that posture is associated with sleep and you may become drowsy. A slightly reclining or upright posture is associated with relaxed alertness. Keep your arms and legs uncrossed so that they will not restrict your circulation and it will not be necessary to shift from posture to posture. Your head can rest against the back of the chair or wall or just remain comfortably upright.

4. *Starting cue.* Create for yourself a word or phrase that can serve as a cue or "permission" for you to really take time out and enter your relaxation. Phrases like "This is my time" or "Breaktime" or "Timeout" can serve the purpose.

5. *An "allowing" attitude.* Most of the time we "force" reactions, "try" to respond, and "make" things happen. Trying too hard will only get in your way with relaxation training and many other techniques. It is a bit like taking a trip. You must have the destination in mind, but few people drive down the road with hands clenched on the wheel reminding themselves continually where they are going. For relaxation training, you can have the intention to relax and then just allow yourself to respond to the technique and enjoy the trip. You need high motivation to persist and strong self-permission to allow yourself to respond.

6. *Monitor your changes.* At the beginning of practice, notice the symptoms of stress or at least your general level of arousal. This will be the base line for comparison after you have completed your practice. Some people prefer to rate their tension level on a 1–10 scale before and after practice as a way of keeping track of performance and improvement. Be careful, however, not to let this useful attention become a compulsive goal that distracts you from the benefits of relaxation.

❖ STRESS INOCULATION

In describing how people contracted diseases, Louis Pasteur often said, "It's not the 'bugs,' its the battleground [host]." This can also be said for stress. Like inoculations for disease, you can make yourself more resistant to the effects of stress. Each of the following items is considered to be an important aspect of life-style that can inoculate us to be more resilient under stress. Although it can be very challenging to completely overhaul our life-styles to master all these components, they can be an ideal toward which we strive. Assess the extent to which you have adopted (or need to adopt) these into your life-style to become more stress resistant.

1. *Relaxation.* Practice some kind of deep muscle relaxation procedure for 20 to 30 minutes daily to increase bodily awareness, reduce residual tension, control anxiety, and develop voluntary control. Brief scanning and release of muscle tension several times during the day can also prevent chronic accumulation of tension. A variety of effective techniques is available, including progressive muscle relaxation, biofeedback, autogenic training, imagery, breathing exercises, yoga, t'ai chi, and massage.

2. *Exercise.* Participate in some kind of cardiovascular fitness activity at least

three times a week for 20 to 30 minutes that requires exertion to the point of perspiring. Steady, rhythmic activity is best, including biking, swimming, walking, stepping, jogging, cross-country and water skiing, rope jumping, jazzercise, and snowshoeing.

3. *Nutrition.* Eat a regular, balanced diet with high fiber and low fat. Drink plenty of water each day. Take time to eat slowly and enjoy your nourishment. Minimize salt, sugar, caffeine, and alcohol intake. Be cautious of fad diets, high-energy foods, and other quick-fix alternatives to good nutrition.

4. *Sleep.* Regularly get about 8 hours of complete rest. Develop a ritual or regular procedure in preparing for sleep. Read or reflect on peaceful thoughts or interesting ideas and take them into sleep. Resolve arguments before going to sleep.

5. *Mental discipline.* Practice a technique for developing concentration, clearing the mind of distracting or intrusive thoughts, and focusing attention. These can be done in conjunction with physical relaxation techniques such as meditation, biofeedback, and self-hypnosis. Other techniques for developing concentration include marksmanship, martial arts, pottery, and related arts.

6. *Self-regulation.* This skill can be learned from a combination of physical relaxation and mental discipline. It involves the ability to voluntarily control stress-related physiological processes such as muscle tension, anxiety, heart rate, blood pressure, and pain perception. This skill can be learned in biofeedback, yoga, and self-hypnosis.

7. *Self-esteem.* Find ways of acknowledging, appreciating, and rewarding your personal qualities and efforts. Develop intrinsic sources of reward so that your esteem is not dependent on external circumstances or outcomes. Personal compliments on a job well done, positive self-statements, positive imagery, and reflecting on learnings and personal growth can contribute to self-esteem.

8. *Support.* Establish a clear, confidential, reliable, and trustworthy network of people as a support system. They can provide direct, honest, and accurate feedback, as well as care and concern, encouragement and enthusiasm, understanding and acceptance.

9. *Career clarity.* Periodically review your career directions and goals, and why you are doing what you are doing. Seek commitment, challenge, and control in your work. Set clear and attainable goals and create reasonable plans to reach them.

10. *Time management.* Based on your values and goals, set priorities and schedule your time to accomplish what you want and need to do. Make sure you build in protected time for relaxation training and meditation or reflection, family and social time, and slack time for unexpected events. Identify and

reduce time wasters. Find out what events prevent you from making the time necessary to implement effective stress-management techniques.

11. *Mental stimulation and creativity.* Keep learning! Read about and discuss ideas that excite you, preferably from a variety of fields. Use your creativity to view a problem from different perspectives, train your intuition, learn to redefine problems as opportunities. Learn and fine-tune subtle skills from more experienced and expert officers.

12. *Recreation.* Engage in hobbies, sports, and leisure time activities that provide a change of pace from your usual work. These should be refreshing or entertaining in themselves, not just more work. They may include photography, painting, studying languages, travel, gardening, inventing, woodworking, puzzles, music, and coaching athletics.

13. *Philosophy.* Reaffirm the values that underlie your daily living. Through meditation, prayer, contemplation, or reflection, consider the meaning of your life and work. Consider using a journal entry at the end of the day to record your reflections. Read some of the great spiritual or philosophical literature from different cultures. Celebrate holidays and special events with true meaning.

14. *Humanness.* Keep your sense of humor and absurdity. Enjoy your (and other's) human faults and foibles. Remember that no one is perfect and that you probably learn more from your mistakes than from your successes. Don't spend your life trying to live up to lists like this one.

❖ SELECTING AN APPROPRIATE TECHNIQUE

No single stress-management technique works for everyone, and many people utilize several alternative techniques under different conditions. The important point is to use the most effective technique for the right reason. Your choice of technique may be based on your preferred sensory mode or your unique combination of stress-related symptoms.

The sensory mode approach was popularized by the pioneering work of Grinder and Bandler (1982). Their neurolinguistic programming (NLP) theory proposes that we all have preferred ways of representing external reality in our minds, and these are based on the three primary perceptual modalities of vision, hearing, and touch/feeling (kinesthetic). While almost everybody uses all three modes, Bandler and Grinder suggest that each of us has a preferred mode that is strongest and on which we most rely. To use a stress-management technique that is most aligned with our preferred modality is thought to make learning and application easier.

To identify whether your preferred style is visual, auditory, or kinesthetic, consider the following:

1. When you misplace your car keys, how do you recall where you left them? Do you use your visual memory to review mental pictures of where you placed them? Do you ask yourself questions, talk yourself through recalling the event, and perhaps recall the sound of the keys striking a type of surface when being set down? Do you re-create the memory of kinesthetically moving through the space you were in, noticing temperatures, textures, and tactile locations?

2. How do you best learn something new? Do you like to visually learn by reading, observing, and creating images and models of information? Do you prefer to listen to lectures or have discussions or study with music in the background? Or do you learn best with hands-on experience in which you physically enact the activity?

3. Perhaps your hobbies and pastimes reflect your modality preferences. People who have a strong visual preference often watch more TV, enjoy photography, paint landscapes, enjoy window shopping, and are sensitive to a well-decorated home. Auditory preferences are often found in listening to music, studying foreign languages, and talking with friends. Kinesthetic styles are found in athletics and manual skills such as woodworking and ceramics.

If you find that you do not have a consistently preferred style, the distinction among related stress-management techniques may not be as important. However, if you identify a preferred modality, certain stress-management techniques may be easier for you to learn. Table 16-1 on page 224 presents some techniques associated with each preference. For example, if you prefer a kinesthetic style, you might find progressive relaxation, yoga, aikido, breathing, or a hot bath works best.

It is important to remember that many of these techniques lend themselves to multiple modalities. For example, in progressive muscle relaxation (PMR) you may repeat the tension–relaxation directions to yourself (auditory), as you imagine a tense color in your muscles gradually changing to a relaxed color (visual), and enjoy the feeling of the tension dissolving into the heaviness and warmth of deep relaxation (kinesthetic).

A second model (Table 16-2, page 225) for selecting an appropriate stress-management technique is adapted from the work of Davidson and Schwartz (1976). It is based on the two dimensions: somatic or physical anxiety and cognitive or mental anxiety. Somatic symptoms might include racing heart, perspiration, stomach upset, muscle tension, and the like. Cognitive symptoms include difficulty concentrating, memory problems, distractibility, flight of ideas, intrusive thoughts, and so on. Symptoms on both of these dimensions can be considered as ranging from low to high.

There is a rationale for the techniques included in each of the resulting four combinations of symptoms.

1. *High somatic–high cognitive:* This combination indicates that you feel wound up both physically and mentally; therefore, an activity that requires your attention and physically discharges tension is most appropriate. A high-action sport such as tennis, racquetball, aikido, swimming, fast dancing, or bag punching would provide this kind of release.

2. *High somatic–low cognitive:* In this case, the mind does not require calming, but the body is experienced as tense and uncomfortable. The primary objectives of techniques in this grouping are to relax the body and teach voluntary self-regulation. This area would include the techniques of progressive relaxation, autogenic training, biofeedback, yoga, deep breathing, and hot bath.

3. *Low somatic–high cognitive:* This is the area where you may have experienced a deeply tired and relaxed body, but where your mind is still working and racing. This condition is often the one that most interferes with sleep. The objective for this quadrant is to hold the attention, focus it, and wear it down through repetitive activity. The time-worn technique of counting sheep is one that thoroughly involves the visual (imagining sheep), auditory (counting), and kinesthetic (imagining them jumping over a fence) modalities. Other examples include reading a book, doing intricate carving or needlepoint, or working on a puzzle.

TABLE 16-1

Preferred modality	Techniques
Visual	Guided imagery
	Photography
	Biofeedback (visual)
	Healing imagery
	Visual fixation
	Cognitive rehearsal with imagery
Auditory	Autogenic training
	Counting down
	Positive self-talk
	Music
	Biofeedback (auditory)
	Singing/chanting
Kinesthetic	Progressive muscle relaxation
	Breathing
	Yoga/t'ai chi
	Exercise
	Massage/whirlpool

TABLE 16-2

	Somatic Anxiety (physical anxiety)	
	Low	High
Low	Meditation Prayer Breathing Reflection	Progressive relaxation Autogenic phrases Biofeedback Massage Whirlpool bath Yoga/t'ai chi
Cognitive anxiety (mental anxiety)	4.	2.
	Imagery Self-affirmations Thought stopping Reading/watch TV	Jogging Swimming Biking Aikido Punching bag
High	3.	1.

4. *Low somatic–low cognitive:* The last area is not as problematic as much as it is an opportunity to take advantage of a nonstressed state to refine awareness or fine-tune responses. Meditation, breathing, imagery, prayer, reflection, and contemplation all respond well to this quiet condition.

It may be likely that you will find this model guiding your activities over the course of an evening. For example, you might come home feeling both physically and mentally energized (Table 16-2 quadrant 1) and go jogging or for a bike ride to discharge the tension. When you return home, you might take a hot shower and sit down in chair to relax from the workout (quadrant 2). Later you could watch television, read a book, or have a conversation (quadrant 3). Finally, upon going to sleep, you might reflect on the day and focus on a pleasant image as you go to sleep (quadrant 4).

It is important for you to trust your own experience in experimenting with these techniques rather than taking anyone else's word about what is the "best" technique—including ours. Each officer is slightly different in values, tolerance to stress, personality, and other factors that affect which technique will be more interesting and how well it works. There is no substitute for practicing and fine-tuning the techniques that can be built into your life-style that will keep you more relaxed, aware—and alive. Some principles for practicing stress-management techniques are summarized in Table 16-3.

TABLE 16-3 PRINCIPLES FOR PRACTICING STRESS-MANAGEMENT TECHNIQUES

1. Experiment: there is no single stress-management technique that works equally well for every body.
2. TANSTAAFL: There ain't no such thing as a free lunch—mastery of all effective techniques takes work.
3. If you don't take time to take care of yourself now, you'll have to make at least twice as much time when you get sick.
4. A technique must be adopted into your life-style in order for it to be useful to you throughout your life.
5. You can learn a lot about yourself by discovering how you keep yourself from changing when you need to.
6. Time will pass anyway—it just depends on how you use it.

Chapter 17 will describe in more detail some of the specific physical and cognitive techniques you can use to quiet body and mind.

SUMMARY

Stress management techniques can emphasize physiological symptoms such as muscle tension or mental symptoms such as negative self-talk. Practice in a protected environment is needed to become proficient in the use of stress management methods which should be used as part of an overall program of stress inoculation. An individual can best chose appropriate methods by understanding his or her own personality style.

QUESTIONS

1. If you were going to begin a committed relaxation training program, where would you be able to practice according to the recommended conditions for practice? What adjustments might you have to make with others?
2. If you rated yourself on each of the stress-inoculation skills, where are your strengths? Where do you need more attention?
3. Based on your method of recall, learning style, and pastimes, what sensory modality is probably strongest for you? What stress-management techniques would be a good match for your preferences?
4. Using the Davidson–Schwartz model, what techniques would probably be the best for your combination of somatic and cognitive anxiety?

REFERENCES

Ball, S. (1986). Self defeating behavior patterns in law enforcement officers. In J. T. Reese and H. A. Goldstein (eds.), *Psychological Services for Law Enforcement*. Washington, DC: U.S. Government Printing Office.

Benson, H. (1975). *The Relaxation Response*. New York: Avon Books.

Curtis, J. D., and R. A. Detert (1981). *How to Relax: A Holistic Approach to Stress Management*. Palo Alto, CA: Mayfield.

Davidson, R. J., and G. E. Schwartz (1976). Matching relaxation therapies to types of anxiety: A patterning approach. In J. White and J. Fadiman (eds.), *Relax: How You Can Feel Better, Reduce Stress, and Overcome Tension*. Confucian Press.

Ganster, D. C., B. T. Mayes, W. E. Sime, and G. D. Tharp (1982). Managing occupational stress: A field experiment. *Journal of Applied Psychology 67*, 533–542.

Goleman, D. (1980). Meditation helps break the stress spiral. In J. D. Adams (ed.), *Understanding and Managing Stress: A Book of Readings*. San Diego, CA: University Associates.

Goleman, D., and G. E. Schwartz (1981). Meditation as an intervention in stress reactivity. *Journal of Consulting and Clinical Psychology 44*, 456–466.

Grinder, J. and R. Bandler (1982). *Reframing: Neuro-Linguistic Programming and the Transformation of Meaning*. Cupertino, CA: Meta Publications.

Lester, D., L. A. Leitner, and I. Posner (1984). The effects of a stress management training program on police officers. *International Review of Applied Psychology 33*, 25–31.

O'Neill, M. W., W. B. Hanewicz, L. M. Fransway, and C. Cassidy-Riske (1982). Stress inoculation training and job performance. *Journal of Police Science and Administration 10*, 388–397.

Peters, R. K., H. Benson, and D. Porter (1977). Daily relaxation response breaks in a working population: I. Effects on self-reported measures of health, performance and well-being. *American Journal of Public Health 67*, 946–953.

Violanti, J. M. (1983). Stress patterns in police work: A longitudinal study. *Journal of Police Science and Administration 11*, 211–216.

Violanti, J. M., and J. R. Marshall (1983). The police stress process. *Journal of Police Science and Administration 11*, 389–394.

17

❖

Stress Management: Physical and Psychological Techniques

1. To describe the major techniques that can be useful in reducing or coping with the physical and psychological symptoms of law-enforcement stress.
2. To identify the advantages, disadvantages, cautions, and contraindications for the use of these methods.

❖ INTRODUCTION

We present a variety of stress-management techniques in this chapter which have been selected because they have been found by officers to be effective in relieving tension. Individuals react differently to relaxation methods based on their physiology and personality. Thus, you need to keep in mind that one of the goals of stress management is to find those methods which work for you. Detailed descriptions will be presented to provide an opportunity for you to experience which techniques work best for you in your specific situation.

❖ SPOT CHECKING AND SCANNING

In the beginning, it may not be practical to find a quiet place for 30 minutes once or twice a day to recline and practice deep muscle relaxation or meditation. In some ways, it may even be more beneficial to start by using much briefer techniques several times, distributed throughout the day. A study conducted by one of the authors on the use of time showed that most people have many brief snatches of time that cumulatively comprise as much as 2 hours a day. These periods are often ignored and wasted: riding an elevator, slow traffic, stop light, sitting in the car or at a desk, having the telephone placed on hold, waiting in line, waiting rooms, bathrooms, and so on. There are hundreds of times each day when 15–30-second periods are available for use.

Spot checking is a helpful way to place reminders in our environment for us to relax, rather than attend to all the other cues to become tense. It consists of placing colored, 1/4-inch adhesive labels (available at most office supply stores) on various objects such as the phone or radio, desk drawer, siren switch, and file drawers. Each time a dot is noticed it is a reminder to take just a few seconds to do a quick relaxer.

1. Repeat a brief reminder to yourself that you, too, deserve some self-care. You might say, "this is my time to relax and take care" or "timeout!"
2. Take a deep breath. On the inhalation, say to yourself, "I can …" On the exhalation say "…feel relaxed."
3. Quickly scan your body from head to toe to notice any excess tension from posture or unnecessary bracing. Release any tension by letting go or shifting posture.
4. Return to your work with less residual tension and slightly more alert.

The regular use of spot checking and scanning helps generalize your cues for relaxation. It also keeps your overall arousal level low so that it is less likely to have accumulated by the end of the workday. When mastered, the scan and release can be done very quickly and eventually becomes unconscious and automatic in response to stress.

❖ DEEP BREATHING

Breathing—sounds easy, but that is only because we seldom pay attention to it. Although it is regulated by our autonomic nervous system, we can also exercise some degree of voluntary control over it. Meditation and yoga practitioners consider the breath to be a bridge between the conscious and unconscious and a major goal for mastery.

Under stress, people have a dramatic change in their pattern of breathing. A startling sound, deep concentration, anger, fear, or anxiety can cause us to gasp, hold our breath, or breath rapidly. When this occurs, the natural rhythm of the diaphragm, the large sheet of muscle in the lower abdomen that contracts and causes inhalation, is suppressed by intense thought or emotion. With tension, respiration moves from the deep, slow breathing of the lower abdomen to the rapid, shallow breathing of the upper chest.

You have probably witnessed people who have become anxious and hyperventilated—breathing so fast that the natural oxygen–carbon dioxide balance is changed. They experience difficulty breathing, tingling sensations in their fingers and toes, ringing or buzzing in the ears, and a sense of impending dread. Their thinking is clouded, muscles become tense, emotions are panicky, and vision becomes increasingly tunneled.

Consider the experience of Officer Owens, a new patrol officer who had been recently hired in his home town. This was his first call on domestic violence involving a weapon. He was anxious about the call and also wanted to prove himself and make a good impression.

> We had just received a domestic call and were on our way with an ETA of 3 minutes. I think that was the longest 3 minutes of my life. At first I didn't know what was happening. I felt very self-conscious, and that I couldn't get enough air. I rolled down the window and started breathing faster but that didn't seem to help any. I noticed that my fingers were beginning to tingle, I could feel my heart pounding, and I guess I thought I was having a heart attack.
>
> My partner noticed that I was shifting around and asked if I was alright, but I felt embarrassed and told him I was OK. By then I noticed that my vision was beginning to get sort of cloudy or greenish around the edges, and I knew I must be dying or something. I just couldn't think. He noticed that my feet were pushing on the floor and that I couldn't breathe and must have recognized that I was hyperventilating.
>
> He pulled over, calmly told me what was happening, it was OK, and that I needed to breathe into a bag to get more carbon dioxide. I felt pretty ashamed that I had lost control, but he said that he'd experienced it before too, and now I would be able to recognize it easier.

Emotional anxiety is often defined by the physical presence of muscle tension and occurrence of rapid, shallow breathing. Such disabling emotion can be reversed by voluntarily engaging the opposite reaction—deep breathing and muscle relaxation.

Breathing exercises may sound easy, simply because we do it automatically, but they can be highly complex, and experienced meditators can spend years developing subtleties in breathing. The purpose behind experimenting with and practicing breathing exercises is to gain voluntary control over it when the stress response kicks in. By regular practice, you can quickly become alert to early gradual increases in anxiety and return your breathing to normal.

One of the easiest ways to practice this kind of technique is to simply sit quietly, breathe, and observe the process.

1. Notice the cooling sensation of the air as it moves past your nostrils. Many people associate this sensation with invigoration, refreshment, or preparing for action as the inhalation reaches its limit.
2. Then allow your inhalation to naturally pause a moment. Holding the breath or gasping can occur when startled or concentrating, as when aiming a weapon. This is usually done unconsciously and is associated with some degree of tension.
3. Then let yourself breathe out, all the way, without forcing the breath. Notice the warmth of your breath on your nostrils, the association of slowing down, and heaviness and sinking as muscles relax. Pay particular attention to the relaxation in the jaw, neck, shoulders, and abdomen.
4. At the end of your exhalation, let the breath pause again for a moment. Use this pause to increase your sensory awareness of the relaxed heaviness you can feel.
5. After four or five cycles of this breathing, pay more attention to the rhythm of rising and falling in the lower abdomen as breathing continues. You might focus your attention on the imagery of waves of air rolling into your lungs, expanding, and allowing your lower abdomen to extend.
6. Finally, each cycle (inhalation–pause–exhalation–pause) can be simply counted from 1 to 10 repeatedly, especially if you want to use breathing as a focus for meditation.
7. To make the practice a bit more varied and creative, some people like to vividly imagine inhaling sunshine, fresh outdoor fragrances, or even pleasant sounds.

Practicing breathing exercises can be done virtually anywhere, for a few minutes or for up to a half-hour. Such drills can increase sensitivity to subtle body tensions, increase control over breathing (actually, reestablish deep breathing), and be used to focus mental concentration and attention. Practiced briefly throughout the day, they can prevent residual tension from accumulating (Jencks, 1977; Schafer, 1987).

❖ PROGRESSIVE MUSCLE RELAXATION

Also called deep muscle relaxation and neuromuscular relaxation, progressive muscle relaxation (PMR) was developed by Edmund Jacobson (1978) in the 1920s. He recognized that emotional anxiety was directly related to muscle tension and concluded that, to reduce the anxiety, simply get rid of the tension! He designed a series of simple, easily practiced tension and relaxation exercises. Progressive muscle relaxation is among the most widely practiced and most effective stress reduction techniques in the world, with about an 80% success rate.

This practice is ideal to increase awareness of the subtle levels of tension we carry around. By tensing various areas of the body and then releasing the tension very, very slowly, you can learn to sense gradual increases in tension while they are still at a low level. Tense each area of the body tightly, feeling the tension and appreciating the pressure, and knowing that you can increase it—and let it go. Don't let go too quickly. Let it slowly ease out as you notice the gradual changes from tension to relaxation. After releasing the tension, focus on the relaxed sensation for 15 to 20 seconds before moving on to the next body area. You may want to associate a color with the tension and imagine the tense color changing to a relaxed color as the tension drains out of your body.

The following areas for relaxation can be recorded into a cassette player or just read off a piece of paper until they become memorized.

1. Clench left fist
2. Clench right fist
3. Bend left wrist upward
4. Bend right wrist upward
5. Flex biceps by bringing your arms to shoulders
6. Shrug shoulders
7. Wrinkle forehead
8. Close eyelids tightly
9. Press lips together
10. Press tongue against roof of mouth
11. Push head against back of chair
12. Press chin down to chest
13. Arch back
14. Take deep breath and hold it
15. Pull in stomach
16. Tense stomach as if to be hit
17. Tense buttocks
18. Tense thigh muscles by lifting feet
19. Point toes upward
20. Curl toes downward

When you have completed the relaxation sequence, pay attention to how you feel in this relaxed state. Notice how slow, deep, and rhythmic your breathing and heart rate have become. Enjoy the feeling of warmth and heaviness in your extremities and deep in your abdomen. When you are ready, give yourself a different cue or phrase to return to your daily work, refreshed and alert.

To become highly skilled in PMR, you will need to practice for about 20 to 30 minutes daily for several weeks. This focused practice enables you to fine-tune your awareness of muscle tension and voluntarily release it before it creates anxiety, muscle tension headache, or cramp. You will find that you will be able to relax more and more quickly and be able to do so outside your practice situation. At this stage of practice, you are ready to "streamline" and "operationalize" your new skill.

On the job you will want to make deep relaxation available quickly without having to practice for 20 or 30 minutes. This can be done by streamlining the practice mentally. When you have mastered the muscular tensing and relaxing, just *imagine* the sequence of tensing and relaxing and notice that your thinking of the procedure can produce the same relaxation!

There is an interesting demonstration of this effect. Interlace your fingers together, keep the base of your fingers together and separate the tips of your fingers. As you notice the space between the fingers, repeat to yourself, "Fingers come together." Notice what can happen to your fingers when you concentrate on this thought. It is simply a demonstration of how your mind and body can cooperate when you allow them to do so.

After a few more weeks of using imagery to complete PMR to a deep level of relaxation, begin counting slowly from 10 (normal tension) down to 1 (deep relaxation). The duration of time between each number counted can be as long as needed. Building this skill will enable you to "count yourself down" to relaxation in about 10 seconds—enough time to prepare yourself for most situations.

Finally, you should begin to actively practice (if you haven't by now) in your natural workplace. You might count down while riding an elevator, sitting in a patrol car, or waiting for a red light or during the many other 10-second opportunities you have throughout your day. In the final stage of mastery, PMR is described as *differential relaxation*. This means that only those muscles that are required for a particular action are tensed, while the rest of the body is relaxed and alert, conserving its energy until needed. A way to practice this most refined form of relaxation is to periodically scan your posture and voluntarily release any tension unnecessary to carry out the activity or maintain your postural alertness.

❖ CAUTIONS FOR RELAXATION TRAINING

There are very few contraindications for relaxation training, but there are some comments worth noting. If you have diabetes, seizure disorder, migraines, or heart condition or are on medication, be sure to check first with your physician to make sure that relaxation will not adversely affect your condition. Some people are able to relax so deeply that the dosage for some conditions may need to be monitored or lowered.

Tense the muscles for only 2 or 3 seconds, then begin relaxing. Tensing for more than 5 seconds, especially the legs or back, may produce muscle cramps. If the muscle does spasm, breathe deeply, massage or lightly stroke the muscle with your fingertips, or stretch it in the opposite direction to reduce the contraction.

If you tend to fall asleep, listen to what you are telling yourself—you need more sleep! Don't practice relaxation training when you are tired. Although it can be used to fall asleep quickly, you must first stay awake long enough to learn it well. Practice when you are awake and alert, and do not use a reclining posture when drowsy.

Memories are not stored only in our brains, but seem to be stored in our muscles as well. As muscle groups that have been chronically tense become loosened, sometimes the memories associated with the tension-producing situation also come back. When this happens, neither avoid nor focus on the memory. Just return to the image and the feeling of your muscles tensing and relaxing. If they persist, talk them out with your support system.

Finally, when you begin to develop high sensitivity to your musculature and other parts of your body works, you may become aware of some sensations unnoticed before. These are normal, but have been largely unconscious, since we tend to focus our attention on outside events most of the time. The sensations might include feeling your pulse in your fingers and toes or feeling "streaming sensations" as tiny muscle fibers twitch as they let go. Occasionally, the quality of your relaxation might be so deep that you may momentarily feel as if your whole body is asleep or floating, but this is merely a brief decrease in tension and bodily position sense. Most of these signs are simply positive indications of how deeply you are learning to release.

Exercise

Remember the last time you checked yourself out in a full-length mirror? You probably were not just checking creases in the uniform, you were making the comparison with that unforgiving image inside your head that has just the right size and shape for chest, arms, waist, and legs. You might recall repeating to yourself that you will never (repeat, NEVER) let yourself lose that muscle tone or develop a paunch. It is the image that holds most of us to our activity level—that is, until fatigue, balancing work and family schedules, winding down after duty, and other events we never planned divert us.

The usefulness of exercise is not restricted to looking good, however. The feelings we get from slamming a door, throwing a pillow across the room, or punching a wall (provided the stud is missed) attest to the secret satisfaction from a physical discharge of energy. When regularly discharged in constructive exercise and physical activity, it promotes energy, strength, agility, flexibility, endurance, and general well-being; when pent up and unexpectedly and explosively expressed, it can become abuse and brutality.

Physical fitness does not develop from engaging in just any physical activity. Some are better than others, depending on your level of fitness, age, and objectives. For example, jogging, swimming, skiing, biking, and skating provide the best cardiovascular exercise, weight control, strength, and endurance. Calisthenics and weight training provide the best muscle definition and strength. Agility is enhanced by skiing, tennis, biking, and handball.

Psychologically, exercise can have strong benefits. Solitary activities can permit time for reflection and personal time without interruptions and demands from others. Team sports can enhance high-spirited teamwork and cohesiveness that transfer to the job setting. In addition, making progress with your own training, seeing an activity to completion from beginning to end, can be a satisfying contrast to the unending piecemeal work of law enforcement. Research has also found that endorphins, pain killing substances in the brain, are produced with intense exercise and produce a state of relaxation and feeling of well-being (the "runners high").

As noted before regarding other stress-management techniques, there is little use in practicing exercise on a sporadic basis. There are some cautions, however, before starting a dedicated and regular exercise program. The American College of Sports Medicine (1986) recommends that an exercise screening (e.g., stress electrocardiogram) be conducted for people who are over age 45 or have symptoms or risk factors of coronary disease. Such conditions and risks include diabetes, musculoskeletal diseases, high blood pressure, use of certain medications, rheumatic fever, obesity (more than 20% over your ideal weight), smoking, shortness of breath, leg cramps after climbing stairs or walking a few blocks, or arthritis. A thorough physical examination by a physician trained in sports medicine or exercise physiology is recommended.

For strenuous exercise to have cardiovascular benefit, the heart should be operating at between 60% and 80% of its maximum output. The average heart rate is about 70 to 75 beats per minute (bpm), whereas a well conditioned athlete has a resting pulse of about 60 bpm and a sedentary person has 80 to 90 bpm. The difference between a conditioned and unconditioned heart working to pump blood through your system is that the latter must beat about 30,000 times more a day (Rice, 1987)!

An informal calculation of your exercise *target heart rate* can be calculated by subtracting your age from 220 (the maximum attainable heart rate). For example, if your age is 30, your maximal heart rate is 190. Exercising at 60% to 80% of that should put your target heart rate at between 114 and 152 beats per minute. As age increases, the target rate required for training effects decreases.

For example, a 40-year-old-officer needs a target range of 108 to 144, and a 50-year-old needs 102 to 136 bpm.

Generally, you should start at the lower end of the target rate and gradually increase your performance as your fitness improves. Cardiovascular endurance tends to decrease after 48 hours, so schedule 20 to 30 minute workouts about every other day. To keep from over-or undertraining, monitor your pulse in your neck every 5 minutes. Overtraining can result in increased risk of injuries, restlessness, difficulty going to sleep or staying asleep, soreness, appetite loss, gastric problems, or heart rate not returning to normal within an hour after exercise. In addition, overtraining can interfere with motivation to train at all. In some cases, prolonged training at a high level, followed by injury in which training is impossible, can produce feelings of frustration, agitation, and depression.

Some light or periodic exercise can be done in the normal course of daily work: walking through neighborhoods, climbing stairs, standing instead of sitting, and isometric tension by pulling on the chair seat or steering wheel. While these can be useful to temporarily raise your energy level during shift work, they are not the same as regular training. Training can be *aerobic* (using the large muscle groups over long duration, while not overextending your oxygen intake) or *anaerobic* (short duration, all-out expenditures of energy). The first includes the many exercises we have already discussed (e.g., biking, skiing, and rope jumping), while the latter is found in sprinting to catch a purse snatcher.
Some general considerations for exercise can be recommended.

1. Get a checkup and an exercise prescription for starting your activity program.
2. Schedule time on an every-other-day basis. You may alternate exercise with some other refreshing activity.
3. Start gradually and avoid overtraining, appropriately warm up and cool down.
4. Dress appropriately for the season and exercise. Do not wear rubberized clothing in an attempt to work off more weight. It will just be water weight lost (it returns just as quickly) and overheating can be serious.
5. Trust your body. When you feel the need to slow down or stop. Don't push your limits unless you are in excellent condition.
6. Be careful not to get caught up in more competition—with your own high goals or others. Use exercise to feel good, socialize, stay fit, and reduce tension.
7. Reward yourself for the effort; buy or do something special for maintaining your program and attaining your goals.
8. Periodically monitor and record your progress. But be careful not to get too compulsive. Use the record to follow your progress and detect cycles or problem areas in your training.

9. Set reasonable and attainable goals. Start with losing 5 pounds, jogging a mile in 10 minutes, or going up a long flight of stairs without getting winded. You are more likely to stay motivated and keep track of your progress with small wins.

Departments might consider scheduling exercise and relaxation time into the officers' daily routines. For example, the FBI, Bureau of Alcohol, Tobacco and Firearms, and Inspector General's Defense Criminal Investigative Service allow agents to use up to 3 hours of duty time per week for exercise, workload permiting (Caldwell and Dorling, 1991). The calories burned per hour of exercise is given for different activities in Table 17-1.

TABLE 17-1

	Activity (150-lb. person)	Energy Output (calories per hour)
Light activity	Sitting down	100
	Driving a patrol car	120
	Standing	140
	Working around an office	180
Moderate activity	Biking (5.5 mph)	210
	Gardening	220
	Canoeing	230
	Golf	250
	Lawn mowing	250
	Bowling	270
	Rowing	300
	Swimming (0.25 mph)	300
	Walking (3.75 mph)	300
	Horseback riding (trot)	350
	Volleyball	350
Vigorous activity	Table tennis	360
	Ice skating	400
	Wood chopping	400
	Tennis	420
	Water skiing	480
	Snow skiing	600
	Handball	600
	Biking (13 mph)	660
	Running	900
	Walking up stairs	1100

Source: President's Council on Physical Fitness and Sports (1976), p. 8.

❖ BIOFEEDBACK

One of the more efficient and rapid ways to learn to attend to the physiological changes we are learning to regulate in relaxation training is through *biofeedback training* (BFT). This refers to the feedback of information about specific physiological processes by the use of highly sensitive sensors attached to the body. This is really no different than the use of a thermometer that tell us when our temperature is too high or the "mood ring" that changes color with skin temperature.

The advantage of biofeedback is that we receive immediate information (often in less than a 25th of a second after it occurs) about stress-related physiology so that we can learn to identify and change it. This is usually accomplished by attaching sensors to monitor heart rate, brain waves, blood pressure, skin temperature, muscle tension, and electrical conductivity of the skin. Biofeedback uses devices similar to those employed by a polygraph, which also measure stress reaction. Feedback is usually in the form of a tone, lights, or dial indicator that informs us that arousal is decreasing.

Unfortunately, biofeedback is usually not a do-it-yourself technique, but requires special equipment and a trainer who can properly instruct you in the use of the instruments and procedures. The idea behind biofeedback is that, once you can identify the internal sensation or experience that corresponds to tension or relaxation, you can learn to voluntarily elicit your relaxation response at will. For example, with a heat-sensitive thermistor on your fingertip, you can "think" your hands warmer so that anxiety does not appear in a cold, clammy handshake during an undercover encounter.

Biofeedback has been successfully used for migraine and tension headache, pain control, muscle tension and anxiety, high blood pressure, teeth grinding, ulcers, sleep disorders, phobias, stuttering, dermatitis, and anxiety (Gatchel and Price, 1979; Olton and Noonberg, 1980)

While the application of biofeedback is beyond the scope of this chapter, this technology is a powerful way to quickly learn to monitor your physiology and to learn when your relaxation technique is really producing an effect. Biofeedback is usually available through psychologists, counselors, physical therapists, and chiropractors. Initially, sessions may be several times a week until you can produce a consistent and stable response; then they require daily practice of related relaxation training exercises like the ones described in this chapter. A small biofeedback unit would be feasible for use in a police department after officers are initially trained in its use.

❖ BUILDING AND ANCHORING RESOURCES

Lucky rabbit's feet and "worrystones" are only superstitious reminders of the actual potential we carry inside us for self-confidence. *Anchoring* is a technique that was developed in the discipline of neurolinguistic programming (NLP) to help trauma survivors confront their fears while anchoring them to feelings of self-confidence (Grinder and Bandler, 1982), based on the principle of associative learning—that if two events are paired together, one tends to elicit the other. It is also based on the concept of "reciprocal inhibition" (Wolpe, 1973) in which anxiety can be significantly reduced by decreasing muscle tension. In this case, you can intentionally construct an association for relaxation, comfort, and confidence to be used as a calming influence when under stress.

A cue can be of any kind—visual, auditory, or kinesthetic—that anchors us to the association. For example, we may recall the face of a respected mentor, remember the encouraging words of a friend, or recollect the feelings of a deep relaxation exercise. The touch on the shoulder by a friend is an anchor or cue to generate the feeling of reassurance. When we elicit this anchor, the stronger it is, the more its associated relaxation interferes with the production of anxiety.

Kinesthetic anchors tend to be preferred in counteracting stress because they can compete with the intensity of physical emotions. A simple cue is to touch the forefinger and thumb together and associate this with an intense emotion. To build this anchor, vividly recall (see, hear, and feel) an incident when you most felt relaxed, calm, confident, and secure. When the experience is most intense, touch your fingers together as a reminder to anchor the association. Think of several other similarly useful experiences, and anchor them when the recollection is most intense. This stacking or accumulation of anchors makes the association more intense.

To test your association, shift your attention to some other activity that elicits different feelings. At some point, touch your fingers together and notice how strongly your anchor recalls the positive feelings. Whenever you have strong feelings of confidence, continue to build this resource by anchoring them. When you are preparing to enter a stressful situation, the feelings of confidence and calmness are right at your fingertips.

❖ THOUGHT STOPPING

Following disturbing or traumatic events, troubling thoughts in the form of words (e.g., self-talk, recalled conversations), images (e.g., accident scenes), or feelings (e.g., phobias or unreasonable fears) may intrude into awareness. While these will generally pass within a few days of a crisis, in some cases they may persist uncomfortably for weeks. This kind of internal activity goes on all the time and comprises the modes by which we think. However, when the content is disturbing and we are not able to turn it off, it can be a nearly inescapable source of stress.

The technique of *thought stopping* was introduced by Bain in 1928 and used by Wolpe (1958) to reduce the effects of intrusive or obsessive thoughts.

Negative thoughts seem to precede uncomfortable emotions, and if the thoughts can be controlled, then the stressful feelings can be avoided or reduced. When the negative thinking is only cognitive and has not been translated into avoidant behavior, the success rate of this technique is more than 70% (Davis et al., 1982).

The strategy for this technique is not to initially avoid the intrusive thinking—such struggling sometimes make it persist even stronger. For example, close your eyes for a moment and try not to think of a polar bear [pause]. Notice how trying to block a thought out sometimes makes it even more prominent.

Follow this sequence:

1. Allow yourself to intentionally focus in detail on the obsessive thoughts for a given period of time, for example, 15 minutes. During this period, indulge yourself—give full attention to the thoughts.
2. Then interrupt the thoughts by shouting the word "STOP!" or "NO!" aloud in your mind, and empty your mind.
3. Finally, redirect your attention to some other pleasant thought or substitute more positive self-talk.

If this does not work satisfactorily, you may add an *aversive* aspect to the practice. Aversive conditioning attempts to link the intrusive thought with an unpleasant or even painful stimulus. By learning to associate the pain with the thoughts, your mind becomes conditioned to avoid the thoughts, and they are no longer intrusive. If you decide to use this modification of the technique, insert the following at stage 2:

> Place a rubber band around your wrist. At the instant you say "STOP," pull the rubber band back and snap it smartly on your wrist. The stinging sensation is usually sufficient to make the associated thoughts aversive.

❖ CONSTRUCTIVE SELF-TALK

Our minds are continually active to some degree, and one of the more common processes we experience is an inner chatter as we talk to ourselves, comment on circumstances, or replay memory recordings of past conversations. Most of the time this is no problem, but when the thoughts become intrusive or excessively self-critical or produce anxiety by anticipating negative consequences, we need to constructively change them (Meichenbaum, 1977). Even with training in coping skills, officers are prone to rate themselves more critically in performance than objective observers rate them, and they should be aware of this tendency (Sarason et al., 1979).

Self-talk is particularly prominent just before and after important events or traumatic situations. If we preoccupy ourselves with talking about past failures and mistakes, all the things that can go wrong, and all the signs of stress reaction, we will create that stress reaction. Even after a critical event is over, many excellent officers are more silently critical of themselves than a supervisor could ever be.

Positive self-talk can be used to reduce anxiety, control anger, and learn that our thinking controls our feelings (Mahoney and Thorenson, 1974; Novaco, 1975). The following are examples of some phrases that officers have found to be useful substitutions for the critical self-talk that they used to experience:

1. *Preparation for a stressful event:*
   I've done this before, and I can do it again.
   This is a good time to make a plan.
   This could be a tough situation, but I believe in myself.
   I'll stay focused on what I need to do.
   This will be a good opportunity to practice my calming techniques.
   I'm going to do all right. I'll be ok.
   I know exactly what procedures to follow.
   It's easier once I get started.

2. *During a stressful event:*
   This will last only a little while.
   It'll be over soon.
   Just a little longer—I can take it.
   Where am I feeling tight? I can relax it.
   One thing at a time.
   I don't have to take this personally.
   Tomorrow I'll be able to look back on this.
   Concentrate on breathing. Relax.
   I've survived worse before.

3. *Following a stressful event*
   I did it—I made it through!
   I felt more comfortable than I did last time.
   I'm getting a lot better at this.
   I'm lucky—It could always be worse.
   I got through this without losing my cool.
   It's getting easier to turn off worry.
   I've got some new ideas for next time.
   I'm doing better at this all the time.

These statements can be written on a sheet of paper and carried as a reminder for review until they become part of your automatic thinking. Feel free to change and add to them as needed. The most easily forgotten of all coping skills is to reinforce your own successes. Be sure to recognize, compliment, and reward your efforts in taking more constructive action with your self-talk. This will help you to remember your coping skills when you are next confronted with a stressful situation.

❖ COGNITIVE REHEARSAL AND DESENSITIZATION

Anxiety about how well one will be able to handle an upcoming situation coincides with how much stress is perceived (Alkus and Padesky, 1983; Jacobi, 1975). Officers can become anxious about and obsessively rehearse doing something wrong, receiving criticism, being investigated, being suspended or fired, being seen as vulnerable or weak, or being sued.

There is a thin distinction between what we call worry and what may be useful review or rehearsal in preparing for a problem situation. Both go on in the mind using imagery, self-talk, and feelings. This reflection becomes worry when the critical thoughts and negative feelings intrude into our experience when we really want or need to concentrate elsewhere. In contrast, rehearsal is an opportunity to replay situations to see what we can learn from them—how to improve our responses for the next time; they are more constructive and optimistic.

In addition, we can prepare ourselves for future stressful events by mentally rehearsing them while at the same time eliciting our deep relaxation response. This desensitizes us to the event emotionally, while enabling us to practice what we might say, do, and think to ourselves. Remember that we do not automatically react anxiously to situations—we have simply learned to react that way—and we can unlearn it. Role playing and rehearsal has been shown to be effective when the portrayed situations are highly similar to those actually encountered by the officer (Sarason et al., 1979).

The principle by which we can unlearn reactions was discovered in 1950 by Joseph Wolpe, a South African psychiatrist. Recall that the two branches of the autonomic nervous system cannot both be activated at the same time; they will interfere with each other. The stress-activating sympathetic branch can be blocked by activating the relaxation response in the parasympathetic branch. Wolpe (1973) called this interference "reciprocal inhibition," referring to the reciprocal or counteractive effects of one on the other. In practical terms, this means that, when you can voluntarily elicit a relaxation response in reaction to a stressful event, the event is no longer (or at least is much less) stressful.

A prerequisite for using this technique is the ability to voluntarily relax deeply. You should have developed a strong relaxation response by practicing any of the various techniques presented in this chapter. Mastery of the coping skill of cognitive rehearsal and desensitization usually takes about 1 to 2 weeks of regular practice. Once learned, the desensitization can be used immediately before or after the distressing event.

To use desensitization, you will need to think of a situation in which you want to feel more relaxed. Here is an example of a typical sequence for a stressful situation such as initial intervention in domestic violence:

1. Start by identifying 15 to 20 scenes in the scenario, and rate them from 5 (low) to 100 (high) regarding how anxiety producing they are. These ratings are called subjective units of discomfort scaling (SUDS). Place these in a hierarchy from low to high. Generally, there should be a 5- to 10-point increase in ratings as you go up the hierarchy. Make adjustments in ratings by adding or deleting scenes.

2. With the hierarchy of scenes ranked by SUDS, now take 10 to 20 minutes to induce your deep relaxation response.

3. When your relaxation is at its deepest level, refer to your list of scenes. Start with the lowest SUDS scene. Imagine the scene as vividly as you can *while remaining deeply relaxed*. Replay it three or four times while enjoying your relaxation, calmness, and confidence.

4. When you have rehearsed the scene several times and maintained your deep relaxation, go on to the next scene. Again, vividly rehearse the scene while eliciting your relaxation response. Move on to the next scene when ready.

5. Do not try to progress too rapidly through scenes. It may be sufficient to complete between three to five scenes per practice session. If you experience any discomfort, stop the rehearsal and deepen your relaxation; then return to the scene. If the discomfort persists, create an intermediate scene with a slightly lower SUDS and master it first.

6. When you start each practice session, start again with a brief deep relaxation exercise. Then begin imagery with the first scenario while you maintain relaxation, moving to where you left off at the last session. From there, proceed slowly and comfortably as instructed in steps 3 and 4.

The following is a hierarchy used by an officer in becoming desensitized to domestic violence calls. Notice that the scenarios combine a "distance" theme (e.g., getting closer and closer) and an "intensity" theme (getting more intense). The last scenario in the hierarchy may also be a "worst-case" scenario, rather than a positive ending, so that you can become overtrained or more highly desensitized.

1. (SUDS = 5) You receive a call from dispatch that a violent domestic is occurring at an address in your patrol area.
2. (10) You reach down and switch on the lights and siren. You feel the car accelerate as the familiar streets pass by.
3. (20) You are 10 blocks from the address.
4. (30) You are 8 blocks from the address.
5. (40) You are 6 blocks from the address.
6. (50) You are 4 blocks from the address.
7. (60) You are 2 blocks from the address.
8. (65) You pull next to the curb a few houses away from the address. You get out of the car and look and listen carefully.
9. (70) You and your partner split up and approach the door from different angles. You hear loud yelling from inside.
10. (75) At the door you stand to the side and announce yourselves. The shouting stops.
11. (80) The door swings open and an angry-faced man with a torn shirt yells at you to go away and that it's none of your business.
12. (85) You openly gesture and tell him to return inside. Entering, you carefully glance behind the door.
13. (90) The living room is a mess and there is a woman in the corner crying. Her hair is mussed, clothes torn, and her lip is swollen and bleeding.
14. (93) The man starts yelling again, waving his arms, and tells you to leave. He begins to move toward a baseball bat in the corner.
15. (97) When you move to redirect him from the bat, he lunges toward it. You intercept and take him to the floor. You see your partner moving toward the woman, who is now up and coming toward you with a table knife.
16. (100) You and your partner struggle with the disputants. After you restrain and cuff them, you feel the pain in your hand where you have been cut by broken glass.

Other situations to which officers might consider desensitizing themselves include several noted as among the highest stressors (White et al., 1985): performance evaluations, officer fatality or injury, child fatality and abuse, killing someone, IAD investigation, aggressive crowd confrontations, physical assault, delivering bad news, receiving a "standard" rating, inadequate supervisor support, dysfunctional peers, and public criticism. Remember that the purpose of desensitization is not to make you feel limp and passive or stop having feelings of concern for others, but to assist you to reduce your anxiety so that you can think and react faster and calmer.

❖ AUTOGENIC TRAINING

Around the turn of the century, a physiologist, Oskar Vogt, coined the term "autohypnosis" to describe the self-induced state of relaxation in which subjects reported decreased fatigue, tension, and stress symptoms. Following Vogt's work, in 1932 a German psychiatrist, Johannes Schultz, noted that subjects developed two distinctive sensations: heaviness and warmth in the extremities and torso. The feeling was the result of muscular and vascular relaxation and, therefore, increased blood flow to the arms and legs.

Autogenic training (AT) was subsequently popularized and thoroughly researched by Schultz and Luthe (1959). Autogenic refers to *self-generated* experiences and particularly refers to the relaxation response. To the warmth and heaviness sensations, Schultz and Luthe also added the sensations of slow and deep respiration and heart rate and coolness of the forehead. They discovered that, by suggesting that subjects create the sensations, a self-induced autohypnotic state could be achieved for profound relaxation (Luthe, 1969).

Although the original formulation of AT took as many as 200 sessions in which a single phrase was boringly repeated for weeks at a time, current research shows that a more varied set of statements can fortunately produce similar results.

Adapted from AT, the sequence of instructional statements presented next can be read or listened to on a tape recorder. Regular practice of this exercise is from 10 to 40 minutes, from one to six times per day. Repeat the instructions slowly to yourself, moving slowly, and repeating them several times as you allow your body to learn to respond to the suggestions. Notice the key themes of heaviness and warmth in the extremities and abdomen, calm and regular heartbeat and breathing, and cool forehead. Interspersed among these are other suggestions for relaxation and self-care.

> This is my time to relax and take care.
> I can feel quiet.
> I can begin to feel quite relaxed.
> I imagine my arms becoming heavy and warm.
> Warmth and heaviness are flowing into my arms.
> My body feels quiet, relaxed, and comfortable.
> (*Repeat the warmth and heaviness suggestion several times.*)
> I feel quiet and relaxed.
> I imagine my legs becoming heavy and warm.
> I can feel warmth and heaviness flowing into my legs.
> My body feels quiet, relaxed, and more deeply comfortable.

(*Repeat the warmth and heaviness suggestions several times.*)

I feel more quiet and relaxed.

My heartbeat is calm and regular.

My breathing is slow and relaxed.

My body feels quiet, relaxed, and more deeply comfortable.

(*Repeat several times.*)

I feel deeply quiet and relaxed.

My abdomen feels warm and relaxed.

The whole center of my body feels relaxed and quiet.

My whole body feels quiet, comfortable, and relaxed.

(*Repeat several times.*)

I feel more deeply quiet and relaxed.

My forehead is cool and calm.

My mind is still and quiet.

My body is warm and relaxed.

(*Repeat several times.*)

My whole body feels calm, relaxed, and comfortable.

My mind is quiet and still.

I am quietly and comfortably alert.

(*Repeat several times.*)

(When you are ready to conclude the exercise:)

I can feel energy and alertness flowing through my body: through my arms and legs, shoulders and hips, torso and head.

I feel light and energized and can take my comfort and relaxation with me, as I return to my work refreshed.

(*Focus on the details around the room, stretch, and slowly arise.*)

❖ IMAGERY: WHAT YOU SEE IS WHAT YOU GET

We are making pictures in our mind's eye all the time: sometimes to recall where we misplaced the keys, to match faces seen before, or to imagine what a scene will be like when we arrive. Our bodies react to stress whether real or imagined, so we can turn this natural ability into an asset by adjusting the content to be more pleasant and relaxing.

Imagery is ideal for taking a "mini-vacation" to some distant and pleasant location, real or imaginary, from a few minutes to 20 or 30. Some people prefer actual places where they have been before, like walking in a flowered meadow on a mountain side, or a path through the forest by a quiet pool or misty waterfall, or along a long stretch of beach. Other people like to let their imaginations become more creative and imagine drifting like a cloud or flying, swimming in the ocean like a porpoise, or going to an imaginary place or time.

If spontaneous imagery is difficult, find a photograph that is pleasing and has relaxing associations. Nature photography, especially landscapes, are often preferred, but any picture will do. Allow yourself to imagine that you can walk right into the picture. Notice all the qualities of the scene that greet you and absorb your attention. Eventually, your memory of the setting will serve as well as the picture.

In any of these scenarios, the experience can become more powerful by also attending to the other senses in addition to imagery. Notice the sounds, temperatures and textures, fragrances and tastes. You may find that you can create a favorite refreshing place, a sanctuary in your imagery, and can make it increasingly vivid by examining it for more detail each time. Remember to keep a relaxing theme to the imagery or you will just be stimulating your stress response much the same as your work does.

❖ MEDITATION

Meditation often conjures images of yogis contorted into pretzellike shapes or people staring mindlessly off into infinity. It is important to realize that each of us moves through several states of consciousness many times a day. Most of these occur so briefly that we do not notice them or when we are tired or distracted, so they occur without awareness. While most people can identify such states as sleep, drowsiness, hyperalertness, and coma, there are over 20 distinctly different states of consciousness (Tart, 1969). Each of these states enables us to access different experiences or resources, for example, enhanced concentration, vivid memory, creative imagination, or pain control. Not all these are obviously useful in relation to law enforcement, but several are strongly related to relaxation and mental health.

Most officers who have experienced even a low-level traumatic event have probably noticed how active the mind becomes after the incident. The scene is replayed repeatedly, roles and actions are rehearsed, feelings are reactivated, and the internal chatter of self-talk goes on incessantly. While some of this "instant replay" may help us to analyze and learn from experiences, most of this mental activity activates arousal, interferes with sleep, and increases irritability. We have as much difficulty turning off our mental tension as we do letting go of our muscular tension. Meditation is the cognitive equivalent of progressive muscle relaxation; PMR relaxes the body, and meditation voluntarily quiets the mind.

Meditation, as used in this book, is simply a focused state of attention in which we learn to voluntarily create an internal experience that is useful. This internal state may enable clearer concentration for vividly recalling a crime scene, eliminate distractions while preparing for action, decrease pain perception when injured, or just turn off the internal chatter when we want some peace and quiet for relaxation or sleep.

The practice of meditation does not require any particular religious beliefs, special practice clothing, unusual postures, or loud chanting. While myths about meditation are popular, it will not turn your brain to putty or make you vulnerable to spirits, nor will it help you levitate or give you ESP. It simply involves giving yourself enough time (the same 20 to 30 minutes as for any other relaxation training) to learn the discipline of quieting your mind.

As with PMR, certain conditions are more conducive to effective practice. In the beginning you may want to set a timer for about 20 minutes, since meditation can involve distortion of time perception. Later you may develop a strong sense of timing and a timer may be unnecessary. In addition to the conditions noted for PMR, it is important for your torso and head to be erect, but not rigid. This is because a slumped posture can interfere with the depth and evenness of breathing, which is a central feature of meditation. Sitting in a straight-backed chair that gives support to the lower back may be the best posture. The posture should be balanced, mouth lightly closed, and breathing should be through the nose.

After a comfortable and upright posture has been found, you will need to find a focus for your attention. Some people prefer a kinesthetic focus, such as the sensation of alternating coolness and warmth as the air moves in and out the nostrils or the rising and falling of the abdomen with each breath. Others like an auditory focus, as in repetitively counting their breaths from 10 to 1, or repeating a silent phrase, such as the words "relax," or "one," or the sound "om" (which has no meaning). Still others favor a visual focus such as a sunset, flower, symbol, or even a spot on the floor. Generally, background music (especially with lyrics) is discouraged, although natural sounds (e.g., wind or water) may be pleasant.

In meditation, the mind is often characterized as a "curious monkey" or a "blundering ox." Neither of them is well disciplined and tends to wander endlessly and carelessly. The purpose of meditation is to increase your voluntary focus for attention and to provide discipline for your internal monkey and ox. This is not easy. When you try to just pay attention to one thing—your focus—you will struggle with 10,000 other things competing for your awareness. You may remember that you forgot to let the dog out, that you must pick up groceries on the way home, the tires must be rotated, and your shift will change next week. The challenge is to keep returning to the single focus. Do not try to rush through the meditation; if you can't let go of feeling time pressured, do it another time. When you are finished meditating, take several deep breaths and slowly stretch. Since blood pressure and heart rate are decreased, rise slowly so you will not feel light-headed.

As with PMR, meditation has few contraindications. Again, medical conditions may need to be monitored since stress physiology often decreases in arousal following regular meditation. It should also not be practiced following a large meal, since you want your blood flow to focus on digestion rather than flowing to the extremities. Meditation should not be done following intake of caffeine, nicotine, or alcohol since these alter attention and concentration. Finally, if meditation works well for you, more is not necessarily better—prolonged meditation (for more than 3 hours) can produce mild disorientation and depressed mood and interfere with sleep.

SUMMARY

This chapter has covered in detail a variety of stress relieving techniques that can be used for a number of different purposes. Physiological techniques such as spot checking, deep breathing and progressive muscle relaxation often are useful during or immediately after a stressful event. For regular, long-term prevention approaches to stress such methods as exercise, autogenic training, imagery, and biofeedback are highly recommended. When stress interferes with your on the job performance or intrusive thoughts make you tense constructive self-talk, thought stopping, and progressive desensitization are often useful.

QUESTIONS

1. If you were going to place dots in your environment for Spot Checking, where would you place them?
2. Do a quick scan of your body right now! Where do you notice postural tension? Let it go and readjust your posture to be more relaxed and balanced. What does it feel like?
3. Make your own list of coping statements. What phrases would you like to affirm to yourself before, during, and after a stressful event?

REFERENCES

Alkus, S., and C. Padesky (1983). Special problems of police officers: Stress-related issues and interventions. *Counseling Psychologist 11(2)*, 55–64

American College of Sports Medicine (1986) *Guidelines for Exercise Testing and Prescription*, 3rd ed. Philadelphia: Lea and Febiger, 1986.

Caldwell, D. S., and W. Dorling (1991). Preventing burnout in police organizations. *The Police Chief 58(4)* 156–159.

Davis, M., M. McKay, and E. R. Eshelman (1982). *The Relaxation and Stress Management Workbook*. Oakland, CA: New Harbinger.

Gatchel, R. J., and K. P. Price (1979). *Clinical Applications of Biofeedback: Appraisal and Status*. New York: Pergamon.

Grinder, J., and R. Bandler (1982). *Reframing: Neuro-Linguistic Programming and the Transformation of Meaning*. Cupertino, CA: Meta Publications.

Jacobi, J. H. (1975). Reducing police stress: A psychiatrist's view. *In Job Stress and the Police Officer: Identifying Stress Reduction Techniques*. Proceedings on Symposium, Cincinnati, OH, May 8–9. Washington, DC: US Government Printing Office.

Jacobson, E. (1978). *You Must Relax*. New York: McGraw-Hill.

Jencks, B. (1977). *Your Body: Biofeedback at Its Best*. Chicago: Nelson Hall.

Luthe, W. (1969). *Autogenic Therapy, 6 vols*. New York: Grune and Stratton.

Mahoney, M. J., and C. E. Thorensen (1974). *Self-control: Power to the Person*. Monterrey, CA: Brooks/Cole.

Meichenbaum, D. (1977). *Cognitive Behavior Modification*. New York: Plenum.

Novaco, R. (1975). *Anger Control: The Development and Evaluation of an Experimental Treatment*. Lexington, MA: D. C. Health.

Olton, D. S., and A. R. Noonberg (1980). *Biofeedback: Clinical Applications in Behavioral Medicine*. Englewood Cliffs, NJ: Prentice Hall.

President's Council on Physical Fitness and Sports (1976). *Exercise and Weight Control*. Washington, DC: The Council, p. 8.

Rice, P. L. (1987). *Stress and Health: Principles and Practice for Coping and Wellness*. Belmont, CA: Wadsworth.

Sarason, I. G., J. H. Johnson, J. P. Berberich, and J. M. Siegel (1979). Helping police officers to cope with stress: A cognitive-behavioral approach. *American Journal of Community Psychology 7*, 593–603.

Schafer, W. (1987). *Stress Management for Wellness*. New York: Holt, Rinehart and Winston.

Schultz, J. H., and W. Luthe (1959). *Autogenic Training*. New York: Grune & Stratton.

Tart, C. T. (1969). *Altered States of Consciousness: Book of Readings*. New York: Wiley.

White, J. W., P. S. Lawrence, C. Biggerstaff, and T. D. Grubb (1985). Factors of stress among police officers. *Criminal Justice and Behavior 12*, 111–128.

Wolpe, J. (1973). *The Practice of Behavior Therapy*. New York: Pergamon.

Wolpe, J. (1958) *Psychotherapy by Reciprocal Inhibition*. Stanford, CA: Stanford University Press.

18

❖

Developing Support Systems

❖ OBJECTIVES

1. To recognize the importance of giving consideration to officers' emotional reactions to stress.
2. To understand some reasons officers have for denying and avoiding their emotions.
3. To introduce effective ways of using officers as peer counselors.

❖ INTRODUCTION

Traditionally, law-enforcement officers strive to accept and live by the myth that they solve other people's problems and are not supposed to have any of their own. It is as if recognizing that they have problems like anyone else makes them unfit to be a professional caretaker—a law-enforcement officer (Fisher, 1986).

In their training, officers are encouraged not to get too emotionally involved in dealing with citizens. They are to strive to remain objective. That is, they observe things happen but do not let themselves respond to the anger, hate, pain, or sorrow. Officers too often interpret this message as an injunction not to feel anything.

Two studies of police officers in Virginia found that they encountered an injured adult three times a month, a life-threatening bleeding every 3 months, an injured child every 2 months, a severe assault victim every 45 days, and a dead person every 2 to 3 months (Capps, 1984; Terry, 1981). This kind of regular encounter with tragedy requires exceptional coping techniques and a strong support system.

Police officers are required to deal with situations that are very painful, but ones in which they must inhibit emotional expression. For example, officer Schwartze is working an accident in which a 3-year-old boy is killed by a drunk driver. As she helps to remove the dead child's body from the car, she notices that her hands are shaking. She feels sadness for the family of the child. As she looks up, she sees the drunken man walking around unhurt in a daze. She feels her face getting hot with anger. She quickly reminds herself to act professionally and she continues to extract the broken youngster. To public bystanders, she is an emotionless officer who is just doing her job.

Earlier we talked about people pain and how it affects officers, recognizing that to do their job officers need to find ways of not responding to the swamp of emotion in which they frequently find themselves. The danger to the officer is the generalization of this nonfeeling in crisis situations on the job to family affairs and life away from the department.

Fisher's (1986) experience as a police psychologist is that during marital or family problems officers who have adopted the detached approach deteriorate emotionally to a greater degree than other officers. Officers who cannot accept their feelings of anger and sadness are much more likely to find themselves dysfunctional on the job. They are also more likely to have accidents or hostile encounters with citizens. As we have made clear in this book, it is impossible to avoid the effects of stress produced by the emotions raised by the people pain that officers must deal with as part of their job.

Built-up tension from unexpressed emotions can lead to a number of difficulties:

1. The officer may develop chronic physical problems due to prolonged stress reaction.
2. The officer may have limited energy since it takes energy to sit on feelings—energy that could be better put to use solving problems or attending to what is happening around him or her.
3. When an officer has built-up tension or anger, it can be acted out inappropriately and explosively on people who resist arrest.
4. Tense or angry officers are prone to see more hostility in citizens who have been stopped for some reason, such as a traffic violation.

❖ PROBLEMS WITH LAW-ENFORCEMENT SUPPORT SYSTEMS

About 85% of officers involved in shootings return to their departments to informally talk out the incident with other officers within 48 hours. Officers without proper training were helpful in 59% of the cases, but in 41% of the cases surveyed, inept responses by other officers were actually a source of aggravation (Lippert, 1981; Nielsen and Eskridge, 1982).

There are a number of reasons why law-enforcement officers might not be giving adequate support to other officers who have either just been in stressful situations or are dealing with built-up frustration and unexpressed emotions. Knowing these reasons can help officers understand one another better and build a foundation for providing support when it is needed. Reluctance to provide support is often due to the following:

1. Need to protect the male image
2. Tendency to want to top each other's war stories
3. Training to ask questions and not respond to the emotions
4. Activation of officer's own tensions and anxieties
5. Need to support the rightness of what another officer has done

Protection of the male image. Early in their development, boys learn that there are certain things that you do not do if you are to earn the respect of the other boys. A boy who cries easily or is too sensitive to teasing soon finds that he is either the target for practical jokes or is rejected as a companion. Because so much that boys do relies on teams on which each person's contribution to success is important, the team members must be able to count on everyone carrying out their assigned role.

Men learn as boys to avoid things that are seen as "unmanly" or outright "feminine." This is summed up in the phrase, "real men don't eat quiche." Tannen (1990) in her book *You Just Don't Understand: Women and Men in Conversation* reports on her study of the differences between men's and women's communication styles. It is a lifelong pattern with men that they do things together and not talk about feelings. Women, on the other hand, spend a considerable amount of time comparing and sharing feelings about things. It is not that men do not have feelings, but that they do not show a lot of consideration for other's feelings or become obviously sympathetic.

In some police departments this avoidance of emotions can be carried to the extreme. In a department one author did training for, a chief expressed disbelief when he was told that some of his men were having a strong emotional reaction to seeing a fellow officer commit suicide in the day room and that maybe arrangements should be made for some counseling. He indicated that the officers in his department were stronger than that and "could get by without any of this fancy psychology."

Somewhere in the back of this rejection of posttraumatic reactions, the chief did have a point. An officer who gets too concerned about all the pain around him or her could soon become burned out and ineffective. An officer who approached everyone with consideration rather than suspicion could easily end up getting manipulated by others or even killed.

More so than men in general, officers are suspicious of other officers who are too sensitive to their own and other people's feelings. There is a belief that if you have a partner or a backup who is too excitable you could end up in trouble, because the partner might lose emotional control and not be able to hold up in a crisis. Many of the rules of behavior men regulate their lives by go back to the team games, which was a major learning experience for most of us.

This difference in emotional reactions may lie at the heart of some of the suspicion of women as partners, which is discussed in more detail in Chapter 13. The norm that has developed is that "to be a credible cop, you must keep up a strong front, regardless of the circumstances, and not show too much fear, anxiety, or caring." The agreement seems to be, "I'll protect your masculine image, if you'll protect mine." Many woman officers appear to have adopted these rules as a condition for being accepted by male officers.

The nature of working in law enforcement is that most officers will continue to hide their negative emotions from others. We have no reason to believe that the masculine norms in our society will change quickly. On the other hand, officers need a confidante with who they feel free to discuss their anger, fear, hate, and disgust. This can be either another officer who shares his or her feelings, a friend, or a family member. The most frequent citizen is likely to be a spouse or lover, but as discussed elsewhere, this seems to be a problem for many officers. They don't want their spouse worrying about them and know that some of the stories about what happens to them would arouse anxiety.

Male officers, despite everything we have said about emotions and their expression in this book, are not likely to become highly expressive. Caution in emotional expression is still going to be the norm. But officers need to have someone they can trust to talk to or just let off steam around. We recommend sending up trial balloons. That is, share an emotion with someone who seems sympathetic. If he or she listens, shows understanding, and then responds with a similar feeling or example of a problem he or she has, you are probably on pretty safe ground if you wish to share deeper feelings about some topic. Over a period of time, you check out and see if this person is going to be part of your support system.

Topping each others war stories. A complaint we have heard from officers who have just been through a harrowing event is that, "So I started to tell how I had disarmed the perp when another officer says, 'You think that was a hot one to handle, wait till you hear what happened to me!'" Not only does the officer not get to explore what just happened, but is left with the feeling that he or she may be a bit of a wimp for thinking that what happened qualified as a serious situation. On the other hand, the other story tellers get an opportunity to work on some of their own emotional material, but only if it is made into a joke or merely a story.

Do not assume that you have to top any story you hear. Recognize that in the aftermath of a crisis the officer involved needs an opportunity to vent. If you wish to add your own story, hold off until the officer talking about the recent event has had time to explore what happened. Keep in mind that anyone who has been in a dangerous situation has a need to talk about the event in order to discharge the tension and to make sense out of what happened.

Questions and answers without emotion. Officers are taught to ask questions to find out the facts of a case. The reports they file are supposed to contain hard information and not the emotions surrounding the situation. Officers become skilled at following the details of a story. What they do not get good at is following the feelings of the person telling the story in such a way that the person telling the story feels that his or her emotions are important. After a stressful event, however, the emotions are often what is important to that person, not the facts.

When individuals have survived a stressful situation, they are under pressure to talk about it and may want to repeat the story to everyone they meet. Good interrogators know that this is true of criminals, also, and that if given the chance immediately after a crime many of them are likely to confess. That is, they feel a need to tell their story, and if the interrogator listens well, he or she will hear the emotional signs that the suspect is about to break.

The interrogation stance is one of the hardest habits to break for an officer who wants to be a helper. It becomes so natural to interrogate someone for the facts that not asking questions seems artificial. We would suggest that learning to respond to emotions and to paraphrase what the other person says is a good technique for helping the others. This provides an opportunity for them to discharge some tensions.

Strong feelings in others arouse tension in us. Hate, grief, and fear in one person tend to make other people tense. Many men were taught early in their lives to handle other people's strong emotions by ignoring or minimizing them. It is as if not responding to them will make them disappear. Because many men practice hiding emotions, when an officer has them and they do not go away, he may see himself as different and not one of the team. He becomes suspect in his own mind: "Am I really tough enough to do this job?"

One way officers deal with difficult emotions is with grim or "gallows" humor. This mode of managing feelings was popularized with the movie *M.A.S.H.*, in which daily encounters with the horrors of war were coped with by viewing war as absurd, playing practical jokes on each other, and minimizing the seriousness of the impact. Not confined to television, this diversion can be a relatively normal and healthy outlet for police, rescue units, emergency rooms, crisis clinics, and other emergency services. It should, however, be combined with more direct expressions of emotion.

Support of the rightness of another officer's behavior.   Officers do support one another. The problem is that it is not always the most useful kind of support. Officers often have a need to support the rightness of what the other officer has done without letting that person deal with the emotions or conflicts connected to the event. An officer in the day room may say, "Good going killer," or "Well, that's one less scum bag to worry about." If the officer does talk about the shooting and shows a normal posttrauma reaction, even though the other officers understand, they will do what they can to shut down the emotions. "You followed procedure, it's a clean shoot so don't worry about it."

❖ PEER COUNSELING

Support and employee assistance programs work. They have been found to increase productivity, reduce absenteeism, decrease grievances, reduce disciplinary action, and improve the morale of employees. Similar corporate programs through Equitable Life Insurance Corporation have shown a decrease in medical visits from 24 to 6 annually. At New York Telephone, stress-related programs cut the rate of high blood pressure from 18% to half that; the company estimates it is saving about $130,000 from reduced absenteeism. The FBI Employee Assistance Program reported in 1981 that of 45 employees seeking assistance, 27 were self-referrals, 28 returned to full duty, and all but 3 responded favorably to intervention (Capps, 1984).

A solution increasingly relied on by police departments is to train officers as peer counselors. Trained officers can provide immediate help after traumatic critical incidents, as well as provide long-term support for officers who have built up cumulative stress. Another important aspect of having a peer-support system is that it creates and reinforces norms that the department is a safe place to "unload" feelings. It provides a clear message that officers not only take care of each other's physical safety, but are also concerned about their emotional well-being.

It can be made either mandatory or strongly recommended that all officers talk to a peer counselor after events that are known to cause stress to most people. This would include shooting incidents, particularly harrowing accidents and violent confrontations. It can also be made available on request for officers who feel that they have been building up tensions for whatever reason and they would like to talk about them.

Levitov and Thompson (1981) found among officers with an average of almost 11 years service on the force that 59% would seek psychological help if it were available. Of their sample, 29% reported that they were experiencing high or above average amounts of stress. We would have expected the percent willing to seek help to be lower due to the suspiciousness of officers toward outsiders. It is our experience that it takes awhile for a psychologist or counselor to win the confidence of officers by proving that he or she really understands what officers are up against and knows the inner workings of a department.

It is a big step for an officer to schedule an appointment with a professional psychologist or counselor, but a much smaller step to talk casually with another officer. Thus the alternative, which is being used in an increasing number of departments over the last 10 years, has been peer counseling. In this system, volunteers are given a 3-day intensive training program in counseling and are then available to talk with any officer who feels the need to ventilate on problems in general or process a particularly stressful critical event.

The Los Angeles Police Department, the Los Angeles County Sheriff's Department, and over 40 departments throughout California have trained officers to work as volunteer counselors. One developer of the California Program (Klein, 1989) feels that these trained helpers can handle stress, posttraumatic stress, relationship problems, and chemical dependency.

The perception of the trainers (Klein, 1989; Klyver, 1986) is that police officers are bright, motivated individuals with much experience with the issues that are likely to be brought up in a session. This, coupled with their sociability and ability to talk easily with people, makes them very good candidates to be trained as helpers.

There is some disagreement as to whether officers need to be screened before they are trained. Klyver (1986), working with the LAPD, believes the only requirements are that the officer be willing to be available, not be currently in personal therapy or the subject of a departmental investigation, and have the approval of the volunteer's commanding officer. Our experience on a much smaller sample is that officers who have not resolved their own posttraumatic reactions will likely have problems as counselors. Those who are having residual problems should not be trained until such problems are resolved. We recommend that part of the screening be that those chosen for training be experienced officers who can take a nonjudgmental role in dealing with the problems of others.

In spite of their natural skills as helpers, almost all officers have some behaviors that get in the way of their being effective helpers.

1. They tend to interrogate and ask a lot of specific questions that get in the way of exploring the problem in the client's own words and at his or her pace. As Charles F. Kettering once said, "a problem well stated is a problem half-solved."

2. Knowing something about the problem area, the helper too often jumps to conclusions and gets closure too early on what is happening. The helper must learn to relax, be patient, and allow the entire story to come out at the client's pace.

3. The helper may give advice too early. It is as if the helper feels pressured to come up with a solution as fast as possible and believes peer counseling will be a failure if an answer cannot be given to the client quickly.

We also need to keep in mind that most officers who seek help are basically stable, normal people who are reacting to extraordinary circumstances. Therefore, they need temporary help and not long-term counseling or psychotherapy. For those officers who may need long-term counseling, arrangements need to be made with a knowledgeable professional to give backup coverage.

The LAPD peer counseling program was initiated in 1981 and has been highly successful. In 1984 they reported using 69 peer counselors to provide services to 191 officers over 469 hours of service. The majority of time (70%) was spent on dealing with issues involving personal relationships, such as family stress and divorce, job discipline, and career advancement problems (Capps, 1984). By 1986, Klyver (1986) reported percentages of problems for the LAPD as follows:

1. Job concerns, 32.4%
2. Relationship, 29.4%
3. Disability, 12.9%
4. Death, 11.8%
5. Alcohol, 6.5%
6. Financial, 3.3%

Wagner and Brzeczek (1983) are particularly concerned about the relationship with alcoholism and suicide, since police officers have a higher rate than the general public. One statistic they cite is that a Chicago police officer is five times as likely to take his life as a citizen of the city. We would hope that making help more readily available will help prevent some suicides.

Any use of peer counselors needs to be organized in such a way that the officer seeking help feels safe in talking about personal concerns or problems. While a helper cannot have the legal privilege of confidentiality, it would in any case very seldom be needed given the nature of problems that officers talk about. On the other hand, officers do need to know that what they say will not be passed on to anyone in administration. It would be well if the chief or other top administrator could grant limited confidentiality to the helpers and that only criminal acts and serious misconduct would need to be reported, with the definition of serious misconduct being left intentionally vague.

❖ HONING YOUR SKILLS AS A HELPER

When you are providing support to another officer, do not be in too much of a hurry to advise without first hearing the concerns connected with the situation. If you have had a similar incident, after hearing what the officer with the problem has to say, sharing the emotions from your experience can be very helpful.

TABLE 18-1   SAMPLE INSTRUCTIONS TO HELPERS IN TRAINING

- You will be counseling with people who have something in common with you. The business of being a law-enforcement officer is one that is frequently misunderstood by others, including many professionals. Your similarity of background with other officers seeking help is more likely to convince them that they can trust you and believe that you really understand. That belief creates good rapport and makes it much easier for the officer to talk openly about concerns and problems.

- Your focus during these sessions will be on the concerns of the officer who has asked for help. The officer will have faced situations that were unusually stressful. As the helper, you will know about possible reactions to these stresses and ways to help your client deal with them. You will not be expected to diagnose or treat complex problems. Confidentiality will be a requirement in these situations.

- During these training sessions, we will occasionally be talking about some things that have happened to us that are not general knowledge. We ask that each of you make a commitment to confidentiality about anything personal you hear during the training. This means you will not refer to anyone or anything you hear in these sessions in a way that could identify a member of the training group.

CASE EXAMPLE 1

A suicide has just taken place in an officer's car. The officer had answered a call saying there was a man threatening suicide in a graveyard. The officer in answering the call had left his vehicle to search the area, at which time the man who had been threatening to commit suicide crawled into the officer's car and held himself hostage with a gun to his head. Other officers arrived, and the one whose car was occupied attempted to talk the man out of committing suicide. He was unsuccessful and the man shot himself in the head, splattering blood all over the inside of the patrol car.

Consider that the officer comes up to you in the day room and wants to talk about what just happened. He says, "That was a bitch out there. I don't know what I could have done to save him. I tried everything I knew how to do. The bastard really messed up my car."

Here are some possible responses.

1. I'm a bit confused about how you're feeling about this. Help me understand it better.
2. It sounds like you've got mixed feelings about this. You're feeling both angry and helpless.
3. What do you mean you tried everything you knew how to do? Are you thinking there's something you might have missed saying?
4. It's really frustrating to try everything you can and then still have the guy kill himself.

TABLE 18-2   COUNSELING COMMUNICATION SKILLS

1. Be clear with the officer seeking help as to what you will be doing. It must be plain you are not making judgments about what the other person is experiencing. Like any professional helper, you need to be permissive about what are acceptable reactions to stress, such as startle responses, sleeplessness, short temper, and nightmares.

2. With some officers you will discuss the goals of counseling if this is to be more than a one session affair. What is going to be the direction, purpose, and focus of future sessions?

3. Be an active listener; let the officer speak. Don't be overactive. It's natural to want to talk and offer a lot of help, but let the client lead the discussion and follow his or her lead.

4. Express empathy, care, and concern for the person. You need to create an atmosphere in which the officer can be open about fears and weaknesses.

5. Use open-ended questions, exploring, and circular questioning to help the officer fully express ideas and feelings. Be cautious not to unduly influence the officer with your own values, interests, or needs.

6. Respond to expressed and implied feelings (confusion, frustration, ambivalence, resentment, excitement, etc.). While these may be uncomfortable, they need to be expressed in order to deal with the stress involved.

7. Attend to minimal cues. Be aware of nonverbal behavior that may reflect ambivalence, conflicts, or concerns. These may or may not be conscious to the officer.

8. Examine barriers, difficulties, and risks involved in confronting problems.

9. Summarize and integrate diverse information. It can be difficult for the officer in the middle of a crisis reaction to think clearly about what's going on. You may need to help simplify, organize, and pull together the information you have been hearing.

10. Know your limitations; listen, use what skills you have, but don't hold off on using your knowledge of possible referrals that may be needed by the client.

While many of us have been concerned about training officers to work with those in trouble, Watson (1986) feels the emphasis should be on preventive counseling. He recommends that all personnel in the department, including the chief executives, get preventive counseling on a once-a-month basis. He also concludes that there is a need for family and spouse support groups to better the officers home life.

TABLE 18-3   OPENING STATEMENTS IN PEER COUNSELING

1. What would you like to work on today?

2. What do we need to talk about today?

3. What are your goals for our meeting today?

4. What do you expect to happen during our meeting?

5. How can I best help you?

6. Come up with two of your own opening statements. What would you like to hear that would encourage you to express your thoughts and feelings?

TABLE 18-4   CLOSING STATEMENTS IN PEER COUNSELING

1. I have enjoyed talking with you today. I hope you see things a little more clearly now. Good
    luck and take care.
2. What might you do differently next week as a result of what we talked about today?
3. How has our talk today been helpful to you?
4. Today we talked about these experiences, _____, _____, and these feelings,
    _____, _____, that you had as a result of the experiences. I wonder what stands out
    the most for you now.
5. Come up with some closing statements of your own.

What we present in Tables 18-1 through 18-4 is not intended as training to be a peer counselor, but as an introduction to the kinds of things that peer counselors will be expected to know and do. Before an officer can work as a peer counselor, he or she needs to undergo a minimum of at least 24 hours of training.

SUMMARY

Law-enforcement officers, particularly male officers, often avoid expressing negative emotions such as grief, fear, and rage. Yet the expression of these emotions in an appropriate setting can help the officer deal with the stresses of the job. Talking to outsiders who do not understand the nature of law enforcement often does not help. One solution is to train officers as peer helpers who can listen to and give guidance to officers who are having problems. Another solution is for the department to do a better job of educating spouses about the nature of the work and teaching them how to give better support during stressful times.

EXERCISE

Late in the afternoon of June 20th an off-duty officer, Skip Zurn, was attending an out-of-door family picnic with his wife's family. An argument between Dave, Skip's 27-year-old brother-in-law, and Bob, Skip's father-in-law, developed. Both men had been drinking during the afternoon. Skip's wife asked him to mediate the argument, which he did successfully; both men separated. Later Dave left and got a large-caliber handgun from his nearby house. He came back and restarted the argument with his father. Not knowing about the gun, Skip once more tried to break up the argument. Dave ordered Skip to "mind his own business." Skip continued his approach, talking with both men. Dave yelled, "I told you to keep out of this," drew the handgun from under his shirt and fired a single round. The round struck Skip in the upper torso, killing him. The responding officer, Vince Williams, was a close personal friend of Skip's.

Consider that Vince has come to talk to you.

1. How will you open the conversation?
2. What emotions are you expecting him to be feeling?
3. What might you say to encourage him to talk about it?
4. What are your own feelings likely to be about the incident?
5. How might this influence how you could relate to what Vince is feeling?
6. What might you say at the end of the talk that might be helpful to Vince?

REFERENCES

Capps, F. L. (1984). Peer counseling: An employee assistance program. *FBI Law Enforcement Bulletin 53*, 2–8.

Fisher, C. R. (1986). Some techniques and external programs useful in police psychological services. In J. T. Reese and H. A. Goldstein (eds.,) *Psychological Services for Law Enforcement*. Washington, DC: U.S. Government Printing Office.

Klein, R. (1989). Police peer counseling: Officers helping officers. *FBI Law Enforcement Bulletin*, October, 1–4.

Klyver, N. (1986). LAPD's peer counseling program after three years. In J. T. Reese and H. A. Goldstein (eds.), *Psychological Services for Law Enforcement*. Washington, DC: U.S. Government Printing Office.

Kroes, W.H., B. L. Margolis, and J. J. Hurrell, Jr. (1975). Job stress in policemen. *Journal of Police Science and Administration 2*, 145–155.

Levitov, J. E., and B. Thompson (1981). Stress and counseling needs of police officers. *Counselor Education and Supervision 21*, 163–168.

Lippert, W. (1981). The cost of coming out on top—emotional responses to surviving the deadly battle. *FBI Law Enforcement Bulletin 50(12)*, 9.

Nielsen, E., and D. L. Eskridge (1982). Post shooting procedures: The forgotten officer. *Police Produce News*, July, p. 41.

Tannen, D. (1990). *You Just Don't Understand: Women and Men in Conversation*. New York: Ballantine Books.

Terry, W. C., III. (1981). Police stress: The empirical evidence. *Journal of Police Science and Administration 9*, 61–75.

Wagner, M., and R. J. Brzeczek (1983). Alcoholism and suicide: A fatal connection. *FBI Law Enforcement Bulletin*, August, 8–15.

Watson, G. (1986). Thoughts on preventive counseling for police officers. In James T. Reese and Harvey A. Goldstein (eds.), *Psychological Services for Law Enforcement*. Washington, DC: U.S. Government Printing Office.

19

❖

The Work–Family Stress Connection

❖ OBJECTIVES

1. To show the interactive nature of work and family stress.
2. To identify the sources and symptoms of stress on the family.
3. To explore techniques that families can use to reduce stress.
4. To describe ways in which the department can assist the family to moderate work stress.

❖ INTRODUCTION

Officers' commitment to a law-enforcement career and department has been described as a "de facto marriage…in sickness and in health, till death do us part" (Kroes, 1988). Commitment to the job sometimes even supersedes that to the family, and the job has been referred to as a "jealous mistress" that negatively affects the marriage and family (Niederhoffer and Niederhoffer, 1978).

Working in law enforcement has an impact on individuals that causes stress on officers' families. Some of the consequences of being an officer that can cause maladaptive behaviors in the marriage have been variously identified (Maynard and Maynard, 1982; Nordlicht, 1979; Stenmark et al., 1982) and include cynicism, lack of long-range plans, authoritative and insensitive demands, dishonesty and infidelity, excessive drinking, insecurity regarding spouse's safety, insufficient communication with spouses, inattention to children, intense involvement with co-workers, isolation from community and spouse, irregular schedules, lack of outside interests and involvements, limited family time, double income family pressures, moonlighting, overprotectiveness, physical fatigue, aggressive displacement, and concern over weapons in the home. High levels of alcohol and drug abuse, depression, and other maladaptive behaviors are also related to familial and marital discord.

❖ LAW-ENFORCEMENT STRESS ON THE FAMILY

Work–family conflict is reported more often by married officers (as opposed to single parent or divorced), those who exhibit strong type A characteristics, and those who report having less of a social support system. There is an interaction between work and family such that officers who report more conflicts between work and family demands think more often about leaving the job and are also more dissatisfied with work. Those with more work–family friction also admitted more symptoms of burnout and alienation from work, more psychosomatic symptoms, negative feelings, and higher frequency of negative life-style and health behaviors (Burke, 1988).

The public perception of what most stresses officers (e.g., personal risk or weapons) is not necessarily related to what really bothers police families the most (Hageman, 1978; Maynard and Maynard, 1982). In one study, spouses and children were most disturbed by disruption of family activities due to shift work, schedule changes, on-call and emergency hours, and anxiety and frustration over promotional practices. These events also interfered with the family members developing close friendships with people who were not connected with law enforcement. Many wives found themselves being caught between isolation from friends outside the profession and emotional separation from their spouses.

Previously, we talked about the tendency of officers to detach themselves from emotional responses and to become overly objective, which in turn may influence their marriages and family life. Kroes et al. (1974) found that 98% of the 81 officers they surveyed reported that their work did have an adverse effect on their marriage. About 83% of administrators voiced similar concerns. The amount of detachment from feeling has been found to be related to length of time on the force: as length of time in the career increases, the detachment as a coping mechanism becomes part of the officer's personality (Alkus and Padesky, 1983; Hageman, 1977). The wives of rookie officers said their husbands rarely shut themselves off from feelings, whereas the wives of veteran officers felt that their husbands often did.

However, the detachment process from negative community attitudes and stress may begin as early as 3 months after starting work (Kroes, 1974), and as many as 70% to 80% risk marital breakup during the first 3 years (Rogers, 1977). The process often involves the young officer closely identifying with and relying on peers, combined with distancing from the family in order to protect them from the negative aspects of the job. The self-imposed isolation from the family tends to undermine trust and increases alienation—unless it is caught and resolved.

In addition, family members often see themselves as outsiders to the department. This barrier can foster an antagonistic and competitive relationship with the department and peers, who are often seen as having antifamily sentiments. Too many officers believe, "no one but another officer can really understand what I think and feel; what it's like to be a cop and deal with this stuff day after day." As a result, they tend to identify with and relate more intimately with their peers and become more distanced from their families (Reiser, 1974). Some spouses even perceive that the department harbors antifamily sentiments (Maynard and Maynard, 1982). Male–female police teams and the strong intimacy and support that partners share can be particularly troubling to an insecure spouse.

Furthermore, officers and their spouses appear to have different ways of dealing with job pressures. In a survey of about 130 police couples from several parts of California, Maslach and Jackson (1979) found that 80% of the wives sought out organized groups and activities as a source of support, while only 10% of the men did so. The men preferred to keep their reactions to themselves, share with a close friend or partner, or "decompress" while "drinking with the guys."

Although the spouse may initially overlook the inconveniences and slights and take pride in the officer's profession, such acceptance usually changes. As the officer learns to adjust to the pressures of work by increasing work time commitments and detachment, these personality changes are taken home and begin to affect the marriage; that is when the spouse's attitude usually begins to change. The tension mounts in the family setting, tension that the officer then takes to work. It is difficult for an officer to leave a family dispute at home and then try to not let such feelings be an influence when intervening in a domestic call. The work and family contexts begin to feed each other (Besner and Robinson, 1984).

These stress factors are not limited to individuals who work in law enforcement. In a project titled the National Study of the Changing Workforce by the Families and Work Institute, the effects of work on family life were explored. In spite of the impression that the 1990s have spawned a new generation of males who help out at home, the study found that younger males (under 25) were no more inclined to assist with cleaning, cooking, shopping, or paying bills than are older men.

This National Study of the Changing Workforce found strong conflicts between job and family dependents, with 87% of the adults surveyed having family responsibilities at home that have implications for work policies. They concluded that, when there is a conflict between work and family, the family was more than three times as likely to suffer than was job performance. Rather than refuse overtime, avoid travel, reduce output, or argue with a supervisor, people were more likely to forego time with family, leave home duties undone, or experience bad moods. Two-thirds of the nearly 3,000 workers complained of inadequate time with their children, and even when they were home they were often too exhausted to become involved (Shellenbarger, 1993).

❖ FAMILY SAFETY

Because of the nature of the citizens that some law-enforcement personnel work with, there may be cause for concerns about the families' safety. Here is an example from the perspective of a probation/parole officer:

> Every day I leave work I have to check the parking lot and rear view mirror and see if one of my clients might be following me home. I take care to drive a different way every few days, and have never listed my address or phone number. One of our probation officers had a problem only a few months ago when his house was repeatedly vandalized and he received threatening phone calls. I don't want that to happen to my family and it's always in the back of my mind. It's not like it really preys on me, but it's like checking your equipment each day, it's a routine to be prepared. It sometimes even crosses my mind when I go shopping or to a movie or out to dinner with my family—I don't want any of my clients knowing what my family looks like, I don't want to have to worry about them.

An extreme case of law-enforcement assignments causing problems with the family was shown in a study of undercover officers assigned to Narcotics/Vice, Criminal Investigation, or Criminal Intelligence Divisions. In these situations, strain to family and social relationships was common (Farkas, 1986). Relationship and marital problems were noted by about 28% of the 82 current and former undercover officers. The problems were generally due to secrecy, isolation, and loneliness. Unable to fully associate with friends and family, 41% of the officers reported "great changes" in their relationships. Although the most intense stressors were experienced during the undercover assignment, comparison of pre- and postassignment symptoms showed that many did not have a reduction of symptoms back to the preassignment level. In addition, lasting symptoms were noted involving feelings of guilt, poor concentration, low self-esteem, emptiness, and sadness. These reactions frequently complicate attempts to relate effectively with one's family.

❖ DIVORCE

In a review of studies reported by Terry (1981), the rate of divorce for several police departments was between a low of 17% and a high of 37%; both are considerably higher than the national average of 13.8%. A large-scale study of 29 departments involving 2,300 officers found that 37% of the officers reported serious marital concerns (Blackmore, 1978). In a report on police wives, Webber (1976) cites the divorce rate exceeding 50%.

Studies from the 1960s contrast strongly with these more recent reports. A mid-1960s study of the Oakland Police showed that only 7% of the 285 respondents were separated or divorced (Skolnick, 1966). Only 2% of the 1969 Denver Police Department surveyed were divorced (Bayley and Mendelsohn, 1969). One of the largest studies (Watson and Sterling, 1969) involved a late 1960s study of over 7,000 questionnaires to 294 police departments. They found that only 2% of the participants reported being divorced.

While there is some debate as to whether police officers are more frequently divorced than the general public, our own experience is that the divorce rate is high and directly related to the stresses and strains of law enforcement. If a wife or husband is unhappy with the law-enforcement partner's emotional responses or the dangers the partner faces, he or she can hardly be part of the good support system the officer certainly needs.

Second marriages of officers, in which both partners know better what to expect, often fare better than first or second marriages in the general population (Rogers, 1977). In a NIOSH report cited by Terry (1981), 26% of officers who were married prior to joining the profession subsequently divorced, while only 11% who married after joining were later divorced. However, the stress on police families is so clear and consistent that it has been referred to as a "high risk lifestyle" (Depue, 1981).

❖ MARITAL INTIMACY

In a study by Goodman (1990) of 199 male officers, time off due to family problems was one of six significant predictors of officer burnout during his career. We have observed that marriage can be both a creator of stress as well as a reducer of stress, depending on the couple's relationship. This is supported by Rogers (1977), who reports that family stability is one of the better predictors of success or failure in police work.

It is the quality of relationships, not simply that they exist, that determines whether a relationship moderates the effects of stress (Gotlieb, 1984; Graf, 1986; Pearlin et al., 1981). In both marital relationships and close friendships, it is the willingness of the officer to seek out and accept support and the interest, concern, availability, and persistence of the support giver that make a difference.

In contrast to common sense, marital intimacy and satisfaction are not directly related to each other in law-enforcement marriages. Marital satisfaction was less related to perceived stress and more to an officer's perception of his wife's satisfaction with his career (Lester and Guerin, 1982). A curvilinear relationship has been discovered between the two; that is, too much or too little intimacy is related more often to marital dissatisfaction. Excessive intimacy is thought to reflect overdependency and enmeshment between spouses. Without clear individual boundaries, spouses can become more worried about each other, strive to protect each other, overinterpret what is good for the other, and increase jealousy regarding the closeness between partners (Elliott et al., 1986).

It would be useful for officer families to find a way to monitor the level of intimacy or cohesiveness as a way of knowing when to moderate this source of stress. They might identify and agree on "red flags" that would signal under- or overinvolvement. The former signs might include not talking, decreased sexual intimacy, increased frequency of irritability and arguments, fewer activities together, and not going home often after work shift.

Overinvolvement might include making several phone calls to each other each day, repeated requests and manipulations for reassurance, persistent worry and rumination, and feelings of jealousy. Most importantly, spouses should seek to have open and frequent communication in which they can express and check their expectations with each other.

The personality style useful in criminal justice is a double-edged sword. The very qualities that make an officer successful on the job are the ones that make for poor parents and spouses. On the job it is highly functional to strictly control feelings and maintain detachment, become suspicious, interrogate others, and be prepared for continual sources of threat. This readiness obtains cooperation and respect from the public and enables rapid and efficient response to danger—it keeps the officer alive. In the family setting these same behaviors distance members from one another, undermine trust and open communication, and create tension. A criminal investigator for the Virginia Office of Attorney General wrote of his ordeal in confronting the discrepancy between the effectiveness of his work and home behaviors. In a sensitive and thought-provoking disclosure, he described a family argument in which he decisively intervened (Southworth, 1990, p. 21).

> Take for example, the day my wife was trying to get our son to wash the dishes. They were locked in a battle of wills. After I walked into the kitchen, I evaluated the situation and immediately took control. I admonished my wife for being bossy, talked with my son about responsibility, and told everyone else to leave the room so that the job could get done.
>
> In less than 5 minutes, I issued a warning, dispersed the participants in the dispute, and got the job done. I acted like a good trooper. The problem was that I still had to live with these people. I could not get into my patrol car and drive

away. Predictably, my wife and I argued, my daughter defended her mother, my son sulked, and I justified my actions like a good trooper. Everyone was upset, all because I took control.

❖ EFFECTS ON CHILDREN

Officers routinely see child abuse, molestation, abandonment, drug and alcohol abuse, teen prostitution, torture, and murder. They try to block out thinking about the risks to their own children, but often and unintentionally become overly protective, restrictive, and suspicious.

The children of police parents are often challenged with expectations that are unfamiliar to other children. They experience the bind of being children, yet are often held to the same standard as their parent. When they misbehave, as all children do, they are reminded, "you should know better, your father/mother's an officer."

In families that experience high stress because the officer experiences emotional exhaustion, the children are often described as feeling more anxious and isolated and as getting into more conflicts. Compared with nonstressed families, the children are four times more likely to look to the nonpolice parent for support, the officer is twice as likely to experience distance from the children, and the couple is twice as likely to have disagreements about how the children should be raised and disciplined (Maslach and Jackson, 1979).

Parents are often identified by their role rather than by personal characteristics. When there are media reports of corruption involving the police, the children are faced with teasing, jokes, and harassment (Hurrell and Kroes, 1975).

Teen-agers in particular are subject to the stresses in a criminal justice family. Whereas officers often note their satisfaction in dealing with children and old people, they routinely express frustration in handling juveniles. This is partly due to the natural independence that juveniles want from adults at their age, but also because the officer has to deal with more rebellious youths who intentionally defy and test authority or engage in delinquent acts.

The officer's own teen-age children are often not appreciated at home after a long day of dealing with testy street youths. Instead, they are greeted with suspicions, distance, and directives. This tends to make them counterreact to their parents with more defiance. Another vicious and self-defeating cycle begins, and the officer finds himself or herself getting a double dose of exhaustion on and off the job (Maslach and Jackson, 1979).

While most adults believe that quality of time spent with children is a reasonable way to cope with time demands, most younger children think in terms of quantity (Means, 1986). Children can react strongly to parental absence and decreased family activities due to shift work, nonverbal signs of stress, tension between parents, and worry about parent's safety.

In addition, children often suffer at the tactless inquiries and jokes of peers, struggle to live up to higher expectations, and withhold information from parents who would disapprove of their behavior and associations with "problem" peers. Parenting may be mostly carried out by one parent, or, worse, the parents may have incompatible styles and values of parenting, and the child becomes confused and caught in the middle. In some cases, the officer carries an authoritarian demeanor home and into family relationships, where it eventually creates resistance, defiance, and conflict (Nordlicht, 1979).

❖ THE MAN BEHIND THE WOMAN: THE SPOUSE OF THE WOMAN OFFICER

Nearly all the literature covering police marriages view the spouse as the wife. Increasingly, women are entering the profession, breaking the "glass ceiling," serving in all roles, and being promoted to higher levels in the organization. This presents a unique set of problems to many husbands who must contend with the following challenges:

1. Many husbands are often expected to be seen as the "head of the household" and assertively in charge of all matters. For women police officers who spend a full day countering public and fellow officers' expectation of the same, they are not receptive to becoming "the little woman" when they get home.
2. Many husbands are highly protective of their wives. While they may have resigned themselves to their wive's career choice, many of them worry silently about their safety. While wives of officers may have the outlet of an auxiliary or support group, most men do not attend these. They feel out of place as one of a very few men in a group of women—probably good empathy training for what their wives feel on a male majority force—and not a source of support.
3. Husbands are very aware of the sexual harassment that occurs in the workplace—especially in the criminal justice system, both from clients/criminals and from other employees. They find it difficult to allow their wives to take care of themselves. Well-intentioned suggestions or offers or attempts to intervene in harassment are often taken by the woman officer as a lack of confidence in her abilities. She may withhold sharing certain events of the day in order to avoid distressing her husband or being deluged with advice.
4. Husbands must deal with the role change that usually occurs when their wives move to shift work. Husbands must do much of the housework, child care, shopping, and other tasks traditionally left to the wife or mother. They must deal with role conflict, ambiguity, and overload at home equivalent to that of the officer at work.

5. Husbands of women officers become concerned that their spouses will become hardened by such work, especially if they have narcotics, vice, and homicide assignments. They fear that their wives will eventually become emotionally insulated as a way of dealing with trauma and that marital intimacy will suffer.

6. Women officers working daily with other men is also threatening to many husbands. They can become jealous of the close relationship between partners and the degree of sharing that is done with people other than their mate. Reports of affairs by male officers often add to their anxiety, and they can become suspicious of their spouses' relationships. Several women officers noted that they did not have the freedom of male officers in "going out with the guys" after work to wind down because this socializing would be too stressful to their husbands.

The increasing numbers of women officers place more men in this perplexing situation. As the trend toward a gender-balanced work force continues, it is likely that there will be more attention given to support for husbands. As part of the orientation process, nonofficer husbands should be fully informed of and set realistic expectations about the unique stresses they may face.

❖ FAMILY MEETINGS

Family meetings are an effective way to explicitly and regularly deal with stresses and teach children how to constructively use family resources. Since stress on the officer affects the whole family, we advise that the whole family be involved when problems are being discussed. Even when parents try to shield very young children from concerns and disputes, the children invariably sense nonverbal components in the parents' behavior. As children become older, they need to know what the concerns are, have input into the decisions that affect them, and be heard as members of the family.

Family meetings can be scheduled on a weekly basis for perhaps an hour, not only to discuss stresses, but also parenting issues and problems at school. They should not be only problem focused, but should also include recognition and compliments for cooperation and jobs well done. Members need to have the opportunity to express their definition of problems, disagree without being put down, and experience family decision making. In addition, the rule could be made that any member could call a special meeting if the situation warranted.

When family members, especially children, feel that they have some degree of control over circumstances, they are less likely to resort to indirect or manipulative maneuvers to influence outcomes. More importantly, it provides them with positive and constructive experiences in directly dealing with realistic family problems—what better way for parents to teach their children about raising a family. Several considerations should be kept in mind for using family meetings:

1. Schedule problem-solving discussions when everyone's energy is high. Trying to be focused, calm, rational, and attentive is less likely immediately after work due to fatigue or agitation. Even if you come home to be welcomed by a problem, unless it demands immediate attention, call a time-out and set aside a specific time after everyone is rested.

2. Separate problem-solving activities from other family activities. It is important to devote time to talking and listening. In addition, other activities can be engaged in without detracting from them with other concerns.

3. When discussing problems, listen to suggestions from everyone. These discussions create the expectations for dealing with other problems, establish norms for expression, and demonstrate the value of listening and understanding.

4. Keep the focus on one problem at a time. At the beginning, define exactly what the problem or topic is and what solution or decision is needed. Let this guide the discussion.

5. Keep the discussion positive and constructive. Although the problem statement and effects on each other may be painful, after the statement, shift to the changes people want to make. Avoid going back over old problems or blaming.

6. Periodically review and evaluate how the family meetings are going. How satisfied are members? What needs to be kept and what needs to be changed?

❖ DEPARTMENTAL INTERVENTIONS

Departments have developed a variety of ways to help spouses set realistic expectations about work and become more a part of the support system. Orientation to the department can be an important initial message of inclusion and belonging for the police family. Such a program might include tours of the department, riding along in patrol cars, instruction, and attending conferences on law enforcement and the criminal justice system (Besner and Robinson, 1984; Paulson, 1974; Stratton et al., 1982). Other common programs and services include the following:

1. Orientation for new officers and their families should fairly present the duties and risks faced by workers. Ride-along programs, tour of unit facilities, sitting in the operations center, presentations on ID and lab proce-

dures, and so on, can provide a realistic picture of daily work, rather than having family members rely on their imaginations.

2. The department can establish a communication system that spouses can turn to in an emergency to get current information. Many spouses compulsively monitor a police scanner during working hours and have a remarkably rapid communication network with each other when incidents occur. A department hotline can provide immediate and accurate information for spouses during crises.

3. Critical-incident debriefings should be held for families as well as for the officers involved. It may be useful to hold separate sessions for the officers directly involved, but at some early point the families should also be included. Without family involvement, the officer may find tentative resolution to the crisis only to return home to a traumatized family.

4. Spouses can join groups made up of other officer's spouses to work with community problems such as assisting crime victims, battered mates, and abused children. This enables them to safely but directly relate to the world that their spouses deal with daily. This common experience can facilitate communication and becoming more a "part of the team."

5. Counseling and support groups can be conducted for spouses, couples, and families to discuss frustrations and problems common to criminal justice marriages and the job.

6. It has been suggested by some departments that employment screening include an interview with and even testing of the spouse, since marital adjustment is so strongly intertwined with work performance and job stress. Reluctant or uninformed spouses might be encouraged to further discuss the effects of stress with their mates before the officer continues the application process. This suggestion poses a series of legal and personal privacy questions, but highlights the importance of marital adjustment to officers.

7. Workshops to teach effective stress-management techniques can be held for both officers and families. This instruction can have the dual benefit of helping family members understand why an officer needs quiet time to unwind and can also be used by them during periods of family distress.

8. Spouses and even older children can learn gun safety and self-defense to help them understand and feel more comfortable with the officer's work.

9. Frequent departmental activities such as picnics, sporting events, rallies, and holiday events would help the families feel more a part of the law-enforcement team.

10. Spouses may be able to direct much of their frustration into lobbying and political activism for better working conditions and benefits, public recognition, and support of politicians favorable to criminal justice—something that officers do not often feel comfortable doing.

An example of such a comprehensive program is the one reported by Stratton et al. (1982) for the Los Angeles County Sheriff's Department. Using many of the ideas just listed to create a "mini academy" for orienting and training spouses over eight sessions, they obtained a highly favorable response from wives. An immediate evaluation of the program showed 100% of the 400 participating wives rated it highly (Stratton, 1978). All the deputies whose wives attended the program also believed that their spouse benefited from the program, although only 40% believed it positively affected their marital relationship. In a 5-year follow-up evaluation of the program, however, there was no significant change in the divorce or remarriage rate of officers who participated. It was concluded that providing information to the spouses alone did not have as much effect as it would have if the orientation had focused more on the couples and families.

Some departments sponsor a Marriage Encounter Program in which spouses learn to more openly and clearly communicate feelings in words and writing through highly structured exercises (Fisher, 1986). The activities emphasize awareness and labeling of feelings, acceptance of differences, and looking at spousal differences as complementary. Originally intended for marriages that had "plateaued," the program can also be used for new police families to establish healthy expectations and ways of relating. Couples can negotiate house rules for relating and supporting each other during a stressful period. As one officer stated:

> I just didn't know how to say it—to tell my family I needed some time alone before they swamped me with their affection. I've been around people all day, talking, investigating, and the last thing I want is to get overrun with people when I get home. I mean, it's not like I don't love my kids and wife, but I just need time and quiet. What I used to do was just let the kids climb over me, my wife would start telling me all about her day, and I'd just keep nodding and turn them off. When I finally told them that I just needed a half hour or so to wind down, they understood. I could kick myself for not having talked it out sooner. Now, we save the late evening for debriefing each other's day.

Or another couple who realized that sometimes men and women have different needs in a conversation:

> I'm so used to quickly gathering information, making decisions, and giving directions that when my wife would start telling me about her frustrations during the day, I'd quickly jump in with "so why don't you...." After my suggestions, she'd just keep talking about the problem, so I'd either give more suggestions or eventually feel like she wasn't listening. Then I found out in our support group that most women don't want quick solutions, they want to be listened to. Since I learned that (and it's been tough changing), it takes the pressure off me to give suggestions, and she likes my listening.

Such programs often use stimulus video tapes to provide initial information for discussion. For example, Kirkham (1976) prepared a series of training films on personal, family, and social issues in police marriages. The films presented the unique issues for police wives who were attempting to form their own identities while coping with the realities of danger, husband's contact with other women, his "marriage to the job," and competition with the strong bonding and intimacy between officers.

Finally, spouses of officers can greatly benefit from much of the same counseling training that peer counselors receive. The training is very similar and involves such skills as active listening, responding to content and feeling, asking what the spouse wants from you, assertively setting limits, and willingness to ask for outside help when needed. Such training helps them better understand how their spouses are reacting and what they can do to provide constructive support.

❖ WHEN THE FAMILY NEEDS PROFESSIONAL HELP

We have already noted that it is particularly difficult for officers to ask for help from professional counselors. In the family there are often strong norms that mitigate against reaching out for family intervention as well. It can be easier to deny the existence of problems, that stress symptoms are "just a stage the kids are going through," or to identify a single child as being a problem child separate from the family process and parent's job. To many officers it is just too embarrassing to acknowledge that their child is showing conduct problems or the family needs help.

Asking for help is viewed somehow as an admission of weakness, vulnerability, and that they cannot do the job; "If you need it, you must be unfit for this kind of work." Officers often have the belief that they ought to be able to take anything—and so should their family. They sometimes worry that if the family shows signs of stress then they have failed as a spouse and parent as well. However, many officers recognize the need and quietly seek consultation. During a study of death notification stresses and strategies, for example, Eth, Baron, and Pynoos (1987) noted that several of the 50 male and female officers participating in the survey unobtrusively talked with the authors about marital discord.

Most marriage and family counselors concur that the family is a complex social system; one in which all members are connected to each other. Major events rarely occur in isolation. When a young child is defiant to a teacher at school or a teenager goes with the wrong crowd, there is a chance it is related to other events occurring in the family. This is not to say that the police family is "sick, bad," or "wrong" but simply that the child often becomes the symptom carrier for the family. It may not be safe for a child to argue with a parent, but a teacher is much safer; likewise to the officer, the wife may be a safer target for anger and complaints than to police administration.

There are several signs that are serious enough to indicate that the family should meet with a professional to examine itself, and explore the possibility that the behavior is a reaction to family stresses:

1. Depression or suicidal themes in letters, songs, poetry, drawings, or said in angry outbursts.
2. The children having close association with exactly the kind of people whom the parents are most against.
3. Abuse of alcohol or drugs.
4. "Perfect children" who seem to have no problems, never get in trouble, are a perfect mold of family expectations, and have no distinctive lives of their own. This concern is often overlooked because the child is "so good," but in fact may show the same facade to the family that the officer shows to the public.
5. Children showing recurrent behavior problems such as stealing, vandalism, fighting, truancy, promiscuity, etc.
6. Children's Academic performance that fluctuates with family tensions.
7. Persistent somatic complaints such as headaches, stomach problems, fatigue, and vague illnesses that appear during stressful periods in the family.
8. Extramarital affairs.
9. Emotional or physical abuse.

❖ POSITIVE EFFECTS ON THE FAMILY

It would be a serious mistake to think that stress only produces negative effects on the family. Although in much of this book we have highlighted the dangerous aspects of stress which are essential for the officer to be aware of, there are positive aspects as well.

As noted above the family is the primary medium through which social learning occurs and culture is transmitted. This provides a particularly powerful vehicle for family members to create a family process that is more supportive, resourceful, and stress resilient than the average family. However, like special operations units, this requires training above and beyond the normal implicit activities that most families engage in.

Most people with whom the authors have worked, in and outside the criminal justice system, readily acknowledge that they never learned or were explicitly taught effective stress management techniques in their family. Usually, people learn implicitly, even unconsciously, how to deal with stress by observing other family members cope. The mandate for officers to deal with stress more effectively means that they must more openly and explicitly discuss sources, symptoms, and methods of coping. This enables all family members to deliberately examine their beliefs and techniques.

Intense stress or crises may require the officer to let down the normal facade of imperviousness and reach out to the available support system. Willingness to receive support from others can contribute to the precedent in the officer's life and a norm in the department of asking for help when it is needed. During crises the officer and family come to deeply appreciate the resources and friendships available. These contacts can establish new acquaintances, reaffirm and renew older relationships, and provide reassurance that care and concern are obtainable.

At the Los Angeles Police Department, for example, of the 104 disability pensions granted in 1981, it was discovered that 63% were related to stress or psychological disability. In response to an 82% increase in applications for disability pensions over a one year period, the LAPD experimented with a "home visit" program. This service was designed for officers and their families to help them deal with their concerns over trauma, injury, disability, recovery, finances, and separation from the normal work environment. Although there were unforeseen problems with this program in terms of staffing and policy, most officers were favorable toward the intent of the program (Petrone & Reiser 1985).

Stress also pushes the family beyond its normal coping skills. It requires them to become more creative and resourceful in the way they manage schedules, take time for themselves, set priorities, reassess values, and appreciate diversity in each others' styles. Struggling with the hardships of stress can increase member's resiliency, tolerance of stress, and confidence that they can survive such strain. During the process of the officer's learning new skills (e.g., progressive relaxation, meditation), other family members often become curious and may adopt the techniques, or at least become familiar enough to call on them in the future.

Families in which members have been distanced from each other can be drawn together during stressful periods. The common enemy of stress makes them more reliant and interdependent on each other. Children who have been locked into defiant relationships with their parents may shift their anger outward toward the stressor and seek reassurance from their parents. It becomes an opportunity for the members to reassess and reaffirm their closeness. As a family they can see the daily stresses as part of a larger pattern over which they can identify positive outcomes. In this larger scheme the stressors may be seen as less of a threat and more of a challenge. In the same way that an officer becomes stress inoculated, the family can foster "psychological hardiness" (Kannady, 1993).

SUMMARY

The stress of criminal justice occupations requires the officer to emotionally detach in order to be protected from the strain of human pain. Such detachment also places strain on the family resulting in marital distress, alcohol abuse, extra-marital affairs, child misbehavior, and divorce. In turn, family problems can affect work performance. Marital intimacy and work performance have a curvi-linear in that over- or under-dependent relationships increase stress on the marriage during times of work stress. Individual family members, especially the children, may carry the stress symptoms for the family and require family meetings or professional help. The department can also help moderate the effects of stress through ongoing orientation, training, and support programs. Stress can also increase the resiliency, skill level, and cohesion of families.

QUESTIONS

1. If you were faced with the dilemma of choosing between loyalties toward the job or your family, what would you decide? Would you always decide the same way for all issues?

2. If you were the spouse of an officer, what would be your primary concerns? How do you think such worries would affect your relationship? What might the department do to reduce such concerns?

3. If you emotionally detach in order to protect yourself from the stresses of work, how could you intentionally go about "reattaching" your emotions before you go home to those who need your intimacy?

4. If you are in a relationship, what signs can you and your partner agree on as indicators of relationship stress? What will you do when either of you notice them?

5. Imagine that your family shows several signs of stress and that your attempts to manage it on your own have not worked. How would you approach your family suggesting family counseling? How would you feel about admitting such a need? What would your objectives be for counseling?

REFERENCES

Alkus, S., and C. Padesky (1983). Special problems of police officers: Stress-related issues and interventions. *Counseling Psychologist* 11(2), 55–64.

Bayley, D. H., and H. Mendelsohn (1969). *Minorities and the Police: Confrontations in America.* New York: The Free Press.

Besner, H. F., and S. J. Robinson (1984). Police wives—The untapped resource. *The Police Chief* 51, 62–64.

Blackmore, J. (1978). Are police allowed to have problems of their own? *Police Magazine* 1(3), 47–55.

Burke, R. J. (1988). Some antecedents and consequences of work–family conflict. *Journal of Social Behavior and Personality 3(4)*, 287–302.

Depue, R. L. (1981). High-risk lifestyle: The police family. *FBI Law Enforcement Bulletin*, 50, August 7-11.

Elliott, M. L., R. D. Bingham, S. C. Nielson, and P. D. Warner (1986). Marital intimacy and satisfaction as a support system for coping with police officer stress. *Journal of Police Science and Administration 14(1)*, 40–44.

Eth, S., D. A. Baron, and R. S. Pynoos (1986). Death notification. Paper presented at the annual meeting of the American Psychiatric Association, Washington, D.C.

Farkas, G. M. (1986). Stress in undercover policing. In R. T. Reese and H. A. Goldstein (eds.), *Psychological Services for Law Enforcement*. Washington, DC: U.S. Government Printing Office, pp. 433–440.

Fisher, C. R. (1986). Some techniques and external programs useful in police psychological services. In J. T. Reese and H. A. Goldstein (eds.), *Psychological Services for Law Enforcement*. Washington, DC: U.S. Government Printing Office.

Goodman, A. M. (1990). A model for police officer burnout. *Journal of Business and Psychology, 5(1)*, 85–99.

Gottleib, B. (1984). Social support and the study of personal relationships. Paper presented at the Second International Conference on Personal Relationships, Madison, Wisconsin.

Graf, F. A. (1986). The relationship between social support and occupational stress among police officers. *Journal of Police Science and Administration 14(3)*, 178–186.

Hageman, M. J. C. (1977). Occupational stress of law enforcement officers and marital and familial relationships. Doctoral Dissertation. Pullman, Washington, Washington State University. 114 p. (NCJ 44610).

Hageman, M. J. C. (1978). Occupational stress and marital relationships. *Journal of Police Science and Administration 6(4)*, 402–412.

Hurrell, J. J., and W. H. Kroes (1975). Stress awareness. In W. H. Kroes and J. J. Hurrell (eds.), *Job Stress and the Police Officer: Identifying Stress Reduction Techniques*, pp. 234–245. Proceedings of Symposium, Cincinnati, OH, May 8–9, 1975. Washington DC: U.S. Government Printing Office.

Kannady, G. (1993). Developing stress-resistant police families. *The Police Chief*, August, 92–95.

Kirkham, G. (1976). *Police Marriage: Personal Issues*, and *Police Marriage: Family Issues* (motion pictures). Kansas City, MO: Calvin Laboratories, 22 min. color, 16 mm (NCJ 38485 and NCJ 38486).

Kroes, W. (1974). Psychological stress and police work. Paper presented at the Third Annual Symposium of the American Academy of Stress. St. Charles, IL.

Kroes, W. H. (1988). *Broken Cops: The Other Side of Policing*. Springfield, IL: Charles C Thomas.

Kroes, W. H., B. Margolis, and J. J. Hurrell, Jr. (1974). Job stress in policemen. *Journal of Police Science and Administration 2*, 381–387.

Lester, D., and T. W. Guerin (1982). Further explorations of police officers' satisfaction with their marriages. *Psychological Reports 50(2)*, 608.

Maslach, C., and S. E. Jackson (1979). Burned-out cops and their families. *Psychology Today*, May, 59–62.

Maynard, P. E., and N. E. Maynard (1982). Stress in police families: Some policy implications. *Journal of Police Science and Administration 10(3)*, 302–314.

Means, M. S. (1986). Family therapy issues in law enforcement families. In R. T. Reese and H. A. Goldstein (eds.), *Psychological Services for Law Enforcement*. Washington, DC: U.S. Government Printing Office.

Neiderhoffer, A., and E. Neiderhoffer (1978). *The Police Family—From the Station House to the Ranch House*. Lexington, MA: Lexington Books.

Nordlicht, S. (1979). Effects of stress on the police officer and family. *New York State Journal of Medicine 79(3)*, 400–401.

Paulson, S. L. (1974). Orientation program for the police family. *Police Chief 41(3)*, 63–64.

Pearlin, L. I., E. Menaghan, M. A. Lieberman and J. T. Mullan (1981). The stress process. *Journal of Health and Social Behavior 22*, 337–356.

Petrone, S., and M. Reiser (1985). A home visit program for stressed police officers. *The Police Chief*, February, 36–39.

Reiser, M. (1974). Some organizational stresses on policemen. *Journal of Police Science and Administration 2*, 158–159.

Rogers, K. (1977). Marriage and the police officer. *Police College Magazine 14(1)*, 40–42.

Shellenbarger, S. (Sept. 3, 1993). Work-force study finds loyalty is weak, divisions of race and gender are deep. *Wall Street Journal*, B1–B2.

Skolnick, J. (1966). *Justice without trial*. New York: Wiley.

Southworth, R. N. (1990). Taking the job home. *FBI Law Enforcement Bulletin 59*, 19–23.

Stenmark, D. E., L. C. Depiano, J. C. Wackwutz, C. D. Cannon, and S. Walfish (1982). Wives of police officers: Issues related to family job satisfaction and job longevity. *Journal of Police Science and Administration 10(2)*, 229–234.

Stratton, J. G. (1978). Police stress—an overview. *The Police Chief 45*, 38–42.

Stratton, J. G., B. Tracy-Stratton, and G. Alldredge (1982). The effects of a spouses' training program: A longitudinal study. *Journal of Police Science and Administration 10(3)*, 297–301.

Terry, W. C. (1981). Police stress: The empirical evidence. *Journal of Police Science and Administration 9(1)*, 61–75.

Watson, N. A., and J. W. Sterling (1969). *Police and their opinions*. Gaithersberg, MD: International Association of Chiefs of Police.

Webber, B. (1976). The police wife. *The Police Chief 43*, 48–49.

20

Administration's Role
in Combating Police Stress

❖ OBJECTIVES

1. To recognize the limitations of administrators' abilities to modify the law-enforcement system.
2. To suggest a variety of ways in which chief administrators could lessen the distress that officers experience.

❖ INTRODUCTION

The evidence we have produced in previous chapters illustrates the many ways in which police work is stressful. Most of the material in this book has been addressed to showing law-enforcement officers how to prepare themselves mentally for stress and providing them with techniques that they can use to lower stress's negative effects on them. We would like to close with two chapters that give consideration to what administrative actions might be taken to prevent and minimize the adverse effects of some of the stress produced by the system.

First, we must recognize some limitations as to what an administrator, such as a police chief or a sheriff, can do to change the conditions under which officers must work. Being a law-enforcement administrator can be a very frustrating job. The police department is a bureaucracy within a larger bureaucracy. By the nature of the way bureaucracies are structured, they do not make changes or modifications to their procedures easily.

Once the top administrator makes a decision to modify the system, he or she must get the cooperation of the various levels of staff under him or her, including the front-line troops. At any point, the administrator's desires may be sabotaged by passive resistance or union rules. Above the administrator, the changes may be disrupted by a council member, the mayor, or a city manager.

The bureaucracy ensures that there will be continuity over time. You can count on consistency in how the system operates from one year to the next. Although sometimes this can be a plus (because it prevents the introduction of radical, untried ideas), we have seen that large corporations like IBM and General Motors can get into real difficulties because they cannot introduce innovations at the same rate as smaller companies.

The system in which law-enforcement administrators must make their decisions is set up in a way that limits the administrators' effectiveness by preventing them from making the changes they might want to. A number of factors are responsible for these limitations. One factor is that often the administrator, particularly in police departments, has to share power with the unions, who often resist changes in the organization. For example, the chief administrator in many cases cannot put who he or she wants into support positions, due to limitations imposed by union rules.

A second level of resistance is from civil service procedures controlling personnel decisions, which, while eliminating certain bias and political influence, further tie the administrator's hands when it comes to hiring and firing. A third factor is the public, which serves as a watchdog and, as we have seen, can go beyond written and oral complaints and take to the streets to protest police actions.

The limitations placed on the police administrator's freedom of action will vary from agency to agency and city to city depending on the factors we have just mentioned. Given these limitations, what can an administrator do to improve the working conditions and ensure that officers will not fall victim to burnout or disability due to stress reactions? We will suggest a number of approaches for the administrator's consideration, with the assumption that at least parts of these approaches may be implemented in even the most bureaucratic system.

Considering the limitations on administrations' actions, we will suggest eight areas of law-enforcement agency procedures where modifications would lead to stress reduction for officers.

❖ SUPERVISOR TRAINING

Individuals get into law enforcement because they have a high personal need to be in this line of work. To most officers, it is a profession, not just a job. The great majority are motivated by a desire to fight crime and to be of service to the public (Meagher and Yentes, 1986). In most cases it is possible to become an officer only after surviving an intensive selection process in which the candidates' work histories, mental health, and physical condition are carefully evaluated. Usually, only the most fit candidates make it through this culling process. Consequently, police departments start with the best material that is available to them.

When these select candidates complete their training and are given their badge and issued a gun, they enter employment enthusiastic about their new profession. Rookie officers often feel high self-esteem for being trusted with the responsibilities of enforcing the law and are committed to doing their very best to warrant this trust. When given the opportunity to work as professionals and provided with appropriate supervision, officers will, in most cases, work hard to live up to expectations.

Implications for administration.   Many studies (e.g., see Adlam, 1982; Beutler et al., 1988; Pugh, 1986) report that, within 3 to 5 years of entering the field, many officers become cynical and pessimistic about their work. We have reported in previous chapters that the time it takes for officers to become skeptical about their work depends on a number of factors: (1) the particular stresses they face, (2) the extent to which the legal system backs them and rewards them with convictions for their good arrests, (3) their zone of stability, and (4) their support system.

Much of the loss of enthusiasm is the result of changes that occur as officers realize that doing a good job on the street may not be what brings departmental rewards and praise. The street officer finds the evaluation of his or her performance is based on a search for failure to follow department rules or negative reports from citizens. Thus, officers feel they are being slammed for mistakes, but not rewarded for being an effective law enforcer and giving good service to the community. For example, an administrator is more likely to hear from a citizen who is angry about being stopped for driving fast than citizens who are happy the officer found their child or rescued their cat.

Advanced training for patrol sergeants on how to supervise and how to educate the officers under them would be a major contribution to improving the morale of patrol officers. Supervisors are in the best position to recognize good accomplishments and how to reward them. They can hand out the "at-a-boys" that do so much to keep self-esteem high. In addition, they could learn to keep reprimands for minor infractions to a minimum without jeopardizing their role as disciplinarian. They could also serve as a source of support and an advocate during times of stress.

A second very important role, which could be improved by further education of patrol sergeants, relates to their function as educator and advisor to the officers under them. For example they can (1) teach the officers "verbal judo," that is, how to use words to control citizens behavior, (2) show the officers the laws that apply and when to use them, and (3) explain the nature and characteristics of the particular public they serve.

Finally, the most important role of the supervisor could be that of a role model. Modeling appropriate behaviors is one of the most effective ways of teaching behaviors. For example, rookie officers are likely to treat people the way they see their supervisors doing it. Additionally, supervisors who practice what they preach are likely to be much more respected both by the officers they are supervising and the upper-level administrators.

❖ MISUSE OF SUPERVISOR AS RULE ENFORCER

One reason there are so many rules covering the behavior of police officers is the need to contain the tremendous discretionary power that they have on the street. It's as if an officer who shines his shoes and always reports on time and uses politically correct language won't take a bribe or abuse a prisoner. The history of policing shows that controls of this nature have not prevented corruption. What overly structured regulations do is cause officers to live in fear of breaking some departmental or legal provision. Because of the rigor with which regulations are enforced in many departments, the violation of rules is so common that there is much cooperation among officers to cover up each others infractions.

Implications for administration. Patrol sergeants may have been chosen for the job for the wrong reasons. That is, those officers selected for promotion may have been very good at sticking to the regulations, but they are not necessarily the officers who were best at working with other people. Those who are promoted may also be good test takers. However, these two characteristics do not provide a necessary background for giving orders and encouraging good performance.

We would suggest that the job description be examined to determine if what the patrol sergeant is being asked to do is really in the best interest of what the department needs. Officers need to be promoted on some basis that takes into account the department's need for someone who can (1) educate the patrol officers and supervise in a way that encourages self-esteem, (2) act as an appropriate role model, (3) be sensitive to the patrol officers' experiences of stress, and (4) communicate effectively.

❖ USING WHAT OFFICERS KNOW

The day-to-day (or night-to-night) contacts the officers have while on their beat provide them with the opportunity to gain much information about the condition of their patrol area. Besides their observations on the physical state of their beat, they also will often know the mood of the people and what problems the local citizens see as lowering the quality of their lives.

Not every officer, of course, is aware of the problems in his or her area. However, many officers, as they work the street, build up a great deal of knowledge about what is going on in their section. They know how well the city is taking care of potholes, where the derelict cars are a blight on the streets, and how the homeless are faring. It is an often unacknowledged fact that police officers have information that would be of value to those leaders who are interested in having a well-run community with happy, cooperative citizens.

Implications for administration.   The first obstacle to using this information is selling its significance to the city leaders. Mayors and city managers may have trouble realizing how valuable this information can be unless someone in the department is able to make a case for it. If these city leaders could be sold on the importance of the police as a source of valuable information, the police could do a better job of meeting the community's needs. This adds to the value of the police department.

The next question is how to get useful information from the police department into decisions about how the city is run. Even if there is good communication between the police chief or sheriff and the mayor or county commissioners, there still remains a major block to information from street cops getting to the appropriate administrator. This step depends on the department's middle management, particularly the sergeants. Promotions based on present criteria often lead, as we have pointed out, to conservative management. Sergeants are likely to be suspicious of new ideas and lack imagination about innovations that might improve the quality of life in a community and the police department's relation with it.

One movement introduced to improve policing is the concept of *team policing* (Walker, 1992). This is an attempt to bring the police closer to the community by decentralization. This puts decision making into the hands of middle-level managers in charge of neighborhood teams. The decisions about police operations are made by team members on a collaborative basis. Officers are allowed to participate in the making of policies.

Most of these programs were badly implemented and are not much used at this time. We would suggest a variation of team policing as a way of making better use of what officers know.

The Japanese, using the ideas of the American Demming, involved their workers in improving the job and the quality of their products. The process is based on the premise that the worker on the line dealing with the manufacture of the product has more insight than management into what needs to be done to improve the product and the job situation. Peters (1987) has recommended that U.S. industry copy the Japanese in this area. Quality circles are useful, however, not only for improving the manufacturing of products, but also for civil service agencies like the police department. We are aware that some police agencies use participative management, an idea that needs more widespread utilization.

The key idea is to get officers involved in decisions that influence their immediate territory and tap into their knowledge of the community and their creative skills. A quality circle would consist of 8 or 10 officers in a squad working a designated area of the community and the sergeant in charge of that squad. The group would meet once a week for an hour or two to identify, analyze, and solve problems in their territory. The sergeants would need about 20 hours of training to learn the techniques of encouraging a participative approach to problem solving.

The chief of police would be the one to make the decision to begin the program and would decide how many circles to implement. It could be as few as one. If a decision is made to start such a project, union leaders will have to be included in the planning. The areas chosen for experimentation should be those where the sergeants will be enthusiastic about trying something new.

The chief needs to be sure that the officer placed in charge of carrying out the program wants it to work and will openly support its implementation. The chief also needs to be sure to either implement the suggestions that come out of the meetings or explain why they cannot be implemented.

Using the ideas generated in quality circles should not only improve the quality of life in the community that the squad serves, but it may also raise the esteem of the officers who are allowed the opportunity to provide the information that leads to change. Like everything else we have discussed, it will require some changes in attitude from top to bottom in both the police department and the leadership of the city.

❖ DEALING WITH OFFICER DISCRETION

For the officer on the street, much of what happens is unpredictable. There is an aura of danger to much of what an officer is exposed to due to the fact that people's behavior cannot always be anticipated. Because "shit happens," what an officer does cannot be covered by rules that dictate specific behavior.

In addition, the need for discretion grows out of the fact that in criminal law the definitions of crimes are vague (LaFave, 1965). LaFave argues, "The exercise of discretion in interpreting the legislative mandate is necessary because no legislature has succeeded in formulating a substantive criminal code which clearly encompasses all conduct intended to be made criminal and which clearly excludes all other conduct" (pp. 69–70).

Patrol officers make a number of on-the-street discretionary decisions. LaFave (1965) lists the following:

To stop, question, or frisk a suspect
To arrest or write a traffic ticket

To patrol an area more intensively than normal

To conduct a high-speed pursuit

To use a particular tactic to maintain order

To use physical or deadly force.

As an illustration of differences in the use of discretion on the last item, Milton et al. (1977) notes that the police in Birmingham, Alabama, shot and killed citizens at a rate of 25 per 1,000 officers, compared with 4.2 per 1,000 in Portland, Oregon.

Given this discretionary nature of much of police work, some commitment has to be made by the department's leadership to trust that officers will obey the spirit versus the letter of law as they perform their duties. Some young officers may work harder to keep the streets clean than do older officers, who feel that taking a chance will only result in a reprimand if it goes bad and no reward if it goes well. Thus, they give up enforcing the law and giving service to the extent that they once did.

Stroud (1987), in his book on the week of a New York City Police Department homicide cop, talks about an officer who is transparent on his way to becoming invisible as a way of avoiding doing anything that might call attention to himself and the possibility of discipline. Other writers talk about this phenomenon (e.g., Muir, 1977; Brown, 1981) of officers avoiding breaking the regulations and getting a reprimand by not doing anything or at least by doing as little as possible.

At some point an assumption must be made that most individuals who become officers are essentially honorable people who want to do what is required of a good officer. By the nature of law enforcement, officers must be given considerable discretion as to which laws to enforce and which not, when to take action and when to hang back. Given that many events are unforeseeable or that a situation can quickly become hazardous, officers must often make decisions in the heat of the moment. Sometimes these decisions do not follow the rule book exactly or lead to an outcome different from what the officer expected. The intent of the officer becomes an important factor.

For example, officers do not write tickets for going 1 or 2 miles per hour over the speed limit. However, situations often change rapidly and discretion becomes more automatic. If during the traffic stop the officer begins to feel as if his or her safety is jeopardized, action must be taken. When does one use a night stick, mace, draw the gun?

Implications for administration. Sparrow et al. (1990) believe that officer's behavior should be judged on the bases of reasonableness of their actions under the circumstances in which they find themselves. They suggest that the Procedure Manual may be too frequently used as a weapon to prove specific transgressions and punish the officer even when he or she had good intentions. It is this behavior that leads to officers losing their motivation to do the best possible job and consequently slacking off on their enforcement of some laws and not giving services to civilians. Sparrow et al. feel the heavy emphasis on the Procedure Manual should be tempered. Instead, a more global base for judgment should be developed that takes into account the reasonableness of the action under the conditions in which it occurred and the motives of the officer into consideration.

In summary, administrators need to give recognition to the fact that police work is unpredictable and full of unexpected incidents that cannot be covered by precise rules. As a result, supervisors need to be trained to accept and even encourage creative reactions from their staff. Finally, they need to place more emphasis on evaluating the circumstances under which infractions occur.

❖ PUBLIC RELATIONS

Good public relations are important to police departments in a number of ways: aid to officers in trouble, quick reporting of crimes, cooperation in investigations of crime, and active prevention of criminal activities are some. The starting place for good public relations is the street officer. For too long, police departments have had the attitude that officers should take care of all problems. The social problems that the police have been given the mandate to manage have become so widespread that the public has got to take some responsibility for their own welfare and the prevention of crime.

Implications for administrators. Police officers need to know the people in their area better and be given the power to make changes the community members can see in order to encourage their cooperation. Some way needs to be found to encourage creativity by officers in improving relations with the community they serve. If an officer comes up with a good way to interact with the public or give a better service that improves relations, this officer's behavior needs to be encouraged.

Suggestions. Patrol officers need to be encouraged to find ways of gaining the respect and cooperation of the public. Some of this could be accomplished by providing services such as getting derelict cars moved off the street, getting rid of graffiti, or getting street lights replaced. The officers could be true public servants working with prevention, checking buildings when people are gone, and setting up street watches. Officers who wish to get even more involved could work with teen-agers with the intention of breaking up street gangs.

Any human being can become a victim of a posttraumatic stress reaction. Given the number of situations an officer deals with that places him or her in contact with death and brutality, we can expect that most officers will at one time or another have very strong emotional reactions that can interfere with their performance or job satisfaction. We have covered this more completely in Chapter 18, which dealt with the use of officers as peer counselors. Administration needs to be attuned to those situations when more than peer counseling will be required.

Besides acute symptoms that come from traumatic events, such as shooting and disasters, day-to-day stresses build up and result in adverse consequences such as divorce, substance abuse, and even suicide. These are all symptoms of stress that push the officers beyond their zone of stability. These officers can often benefit a great deal from appropriate counseling services.

Graf, in the *Journal of Police Science and Administration* (1986), reports that two-thirds of the officers in his sample indicated that they felt they never (or almost never) deal successfully with work hassles, and they did not feel confident about their ability to handle work-related problems. They felt that sharing their concerns with other officers would lead to being seen as weak or inadequate. Despite this suspicion of the reactions of their fellow officers, 60% had at least one other person they could talk to about their problems.

If a professional such as a psychiatrist, psychologist, or counselor is made available, we can assume that many officers, at least at first, will resist discussing their personal problems for a number of reasons: they have an image of strength to protect and admitting to problems they cannot handle might hurt this image; outsiders do not understand what it is like to be a police officer and cannot be of much help.

That the situation may not be as hopeless as the statements of some officers would suggest is found in a study by Levitov and Thompson (1981) of 250 officers in a major metropolitan area in the southern United States. They found that 59% of the officers said they would seek assistance for personal problems if it were available.

Implications for administration.   Much remains to be done in providing counseling services for officers. If the chief administrator decides to make the professional services of a psychiatrist or psychologist available, that professional must have credibility with the street cop. If the professional is not an ex-officer, this respect can often only be gained by riding with officers and getting insights into their life. An alternative choice is to provide peer counseling.

For officers involved in serious situations known to produce posttraumatic stress reactions, it should be required that they see a counselor within 24 hours. This would include not only shooting incidents but any event that is markedly beyond the ordinary, such as a plane crash, a particularly appalling auto accident, or a murder where the body is grossly violated.

To ensure that a defense lawyer does not use treatment against an officer, the department may have to take steps to protect them. It has been observed that some defense lawyers may use previous psychological help as a weapon to discount an officer's testimony. If the officer can say that all officers involved in certain situations are *required* by the department to see a counselor, it should remove the stigma implied by the lawyers' questions.

When we discussed undercover work, we noted the particularly stressful nature of living a role in such a dangerous situation. We would remind the administration that there should be ongoing monitoring of the officer by a psychologist while he or she is undercover and close follow-up after the officer terminates his or her undercover work.

If the city has an Employee Assistance Program or Preferred Provider Contract, we suggest that it would be more beneficial if one provider is assigned specifically to work with the police department. The counselor needs to have the necessary knowledge to work with officers. We have found that a random assignment to therapists who don't understand the peculiar stresses of law enforcement does little to encourage officers to work with them on personal problems.

❖ OFFICER PHYSICAL FITNESS

On joining the force, most officers pass a stringent medical examination that screens out individuals with medical conditions. Those who go to an academy for longer training must take physical education for several hours a day so that when they start the job they have a good capacity to endure. Once on the job, however, many slack off and may do little more than walk from the door of the station to their automobile. One report (Getz, 1990) states that 56% of officers are overweight and 86% do little or no exercising.

Officers are also notorious for their eating habits, which may be regular, but consist largely of quick foods with a heavy loading of salt and fat. This, coupled with the stresses of the job, leads to hypertension, clogged arteries, and generally poor physical conditioning. Getz (1990) cites a U.S. Department of Health study showing that law enforcement has the highest rate of heart disease, diabetes, and suicide out of 149 professions.

There is more than the physical danger of the poor health of the officers involved. In the case of Parker versus the District of Columbia, a jury awarded half a million dollars to a man who was shot twice during an arrest. The jury found the district guilty of deliberate indifference to the physical training of its police officers. The jury reasoned that if the officer had been physically fit he could have overpowered the suspect instead of shooting him. This would appear to set a legal precedent that an officer must be in good enough physical conditioning to do his or her job.

About 25% of the nation's police departments have a fitness program. Some of the reasons for resistance to putting them into place are (1) fear of litigation from officers who cannot meet the standards, (2) opposition from unions and others who see fitness programs as a way to retire older officers, and (3) the expense of setting up a total program, including screening and fitness training.

Implications for administrators. Given the amount of absenteeism, disability retirements, and loss of trained officers to heart attacks, plus the new possibility of lawsuits if unfit officers have to resort to maximum force inappropriately, administrators must consider ways of improving the physical fitness of their officers.

Arliss (1991) reports that the New York City Police Department has a fitness program consisting of a number of elements. They measure each officer's risk factors with a personal history, blood pressure, and cholesterol screening. Each officer who undergoes the testing is counseled concerning his or her risk factors and possible ways to minimize their damage. Nutritional education is given, and if the officer is interested, there are NYPD Cardiovascular Fitness Centers to provide modern exercise equipment and instruction. The fitness centers are funded by the New York City Police Foundation.

For cities without much in the way of funds, it is suggested that local universities and hospitals may provide the needed expertise and perhaps even inexpensive screening programs. The basic program would include screening for hypertension, cholesterol, and endurance, followed by counseling on changes in life-style and nutrition. If at all possible, physical fitness programs should be made available for the officers. The minimum usually suggested is 30 minutes of aerobic exercise (swimming, jogging, stationary bicycle, rowing machine, etc.) at least three times a week. Finally, a regular fitness test requirement (every 6 months) needs to be instituted to ensure that officers maintain their conditioning.

❖ VERBAL SKILLS FOR OFFICERS

Muir, in his *Police: Street Corner Politicians* (1977), notes that the best officers are those with the greatest ability to "bullshit." These officers can talk an angry person down, quiet a victim, or question a suspect by the clever use of words. Muir found that he could predict by their interest before they joined the force which individuals would be the best at this. If they liked debating and talking to convince others, they had the raw material to become good at dealing with others.

In addition, it took experience over time to hone this skill with words.

Bradstreet (1986), the director of psychological services for the Austin Police Department, feels that becoming a silver-tongued talker is as important as marksmanship or learning parts of the penal code. A good talker can (1) calm citizens, (2) interview people for information, (3) reduce call backs on family disturbances, (4) handle crisis calls such as hostage negotiations, (5) reduce the complaints about rude officers, and (6) reduce the need for physical force.

Implications for administrators. Bradstreet (1986), in his paper on developing silver-tongued officers, recommends finding the most commonly used verbal skills that officers use and teaching them to new officers. This would include giving the new officers background on the types of citizens they will be dealing with, making clear to them what goals and major approaches are needed in different situations, and finally using a lot of practice in role-playing the common situations that the officer is likely to encounter. The latter would include dealing with accident victims, angry spouses, suicidal persons, and street interrogations. Chapter 10 gives some guidelines as to what methods should be covered in this kind of training.

SUMMARY

In any agency there is resistance to change both within the department and in the bureaucracy in which it exists. Sometimes the road blocks to change or innovation are people, but often they are the regulations of the agency itself.

Even within a structured system, however, there are possibilities for positive change that will alleviate stress on the officers and help them become more effective. Some actions the agency director should consider are (1) better selection and training of first-line supervisors, (2) finding ways to use what officers know about their area, (3) more rewards for officers when they do a good job, (4) improved relationships with the public, (5) better counseling for at-risk officers, (6) required physical exercise programs, and (7) more training for officers in verbal self-defense.

PROJECT FOR ADMINISTRATION'S CONSIDERATION

As you have been reading this chapter, you have probably rejected a number of these suggestions without needing to think about them. Some of them, however, may have looked as if they had possibilities for making your department less stressful for officers at the same time that it would improve their effectiveness on the street. Go back over the eight suggestions and find the one that would seem to give the department the least difficulty in carrying it out.

1. Write yourself a goal statement of what you would like the outcome to be if you implemented this change.
2. Now indicate specifically what steps will need to happen to make this a success.
3. What will the time periods be for each step?
4. Who will need to be involved at each step of the process?
5. What kind of resistance will you get at each step?
6. Consider what steps you can take to get the cooperation of anyone who resists or how you can overcome their resistance in some other way.
7. Write down the various things that will happen if you implement the suggestions. List both positive and negative factors.

REFERENCES

Adlam, K. R. C. (1982). The police personality: Psychological consequences of being a police officer. *Journal of Police Science and Administration 10*, 344–349.

Arliss, R. M. (1991). Healthy hearts for New York city cops. *The Police Chief*, July, 16–22.

Beutler, L. E., P. D. Nussbaum, and K. E. Meredith (1988). Changing personality patterns of police officers. *Professional Psychology: Research and Practice 19*, 503–507.

Bouza, A. V. (1990). *The Police Mystique: An insider's Look at Cops, Crime, and the Criminal Justice System*. New York: Plenum Press.

Bradstreet, R. (1986). A training proposal: Developing silver-tongued officers. In James T. Reese and Harvey A. Goldstein (eds.), *Psychological Services for Law Enforcement*. Washington, DC: U.S. Government Printing Office.

Brown, M. K. (1981). *Working the Street: Police Discretion and The Dilemmas of Reform*. New York: Russell Sage Foundation.

Getz, R. J. (1990). You can't afford not to have a fitness program. *Law and Order*, June, 44–50.

Graf, F. A. (1986). The relationship between social support and occupational stress among police officers. *Journal of Police Science and Administration 14*, 178–186.

LaFave, W. R. (1965). *Arrest: The Decision to Take a Suspect into Custody*. Boston: Little, Brown and Company.

Levitov, J. E., and B. Thompson (1981). Stress and counseling needs of police officers. *Counselor Education and Supervision*, December, 163–168.

Meagher, M. S., and N. A. Yentes (1986). Choosing a career in policing: A comparison of male and female perceptions. *Journal of Police Science and Administration 14*, 320–327.

Milton, C. H., J. W. Halleck, J. Lardner, and G. L. Albrecht (1977). *Police Use of Deadly Force*. Washington, DC: The Police Foundation.

Muir, W. (1977). *Police: Street Corner Politicians*. Chicago: University of Chicago Press.

Peters, T. (1987). *Thriving on Chaos: A Handbook for a Management Revolution*. New York: Knopf.

Pugh, G. M. (1986). The good police officer: Qualities, roles, and concepts. *Journal of Police Science and Administration 14*, 1–5.

Schowengerdt, G. (1984). Human services professionals for smaller departments. *The Police Chief*, January, 29–31.

Sherman, L. W., C. H. Milton, and T. V. Kelly (1973). *Team Policing: Seven Case Studies*. Washington, DC: The Police Foundation.

Sparrow, M. K., M. H. Moore, and D. M. Kennedy (1990). *Beyond 911*. Basic Books.

Stroud, C. (1987). *Close Pursuit: A Week in the Life of an NYPD Homicide Cop*. New York: Bantam Books.

U.S. Department of Justice (1977). *Neighborhood Team Policing*. Washington, DC: U.S. Government Printing Office.

Walker, S. (1992). *The Police in America*. New York: McGraw-Hill.

21

❖

Modifying the Stress Culture through Organization Development

❖ OBJECTIVES

1. To identify the "change drivers" to which the modern law-enforcement organization must adapt.
2. To recognize the limitations of a traditional top-down approach to management.
3. To describe effective strategies for organization change that can lessen stress on officers and lead to healthy organizational culture.

❖ INTRODUCTION

As we have seen in previous chapters, much of the stress in law enforcement is generated by the nature of the work and the workplace. It is the obligation of police administration to honestly and critically examine the structure of the processes of the organization, identify and reduce or eliminate the sources of stress, and develop the workplace as a healthy environment (Ayres and Flanagan, 1990).

The very culture of law-enforcement organizations, like those of business, health care, and even the military, is currently in upheaval. Traditionally, the structure and processes of law enforcement have been paramilitaristic, top-down, and autocratic. It has been among the several service organizations that provide a stabilizing force that maintains the status quo in society. The effectiveness of a structure, however, is not determined by its internal consistency, but by how effectively it interacts with its external environment and accomplishes its purpose.

❖ THE CHANGE DRIVERS

Law-enforcement agencies' external environment is made up of political, demographic, technological, and social forces. These are the factors that drive agencies to make changes, and the relationships among them are producing change at an unprecedented pace characterized as "turbulent" and "chaotic" (Naisbitt, 1982; Peters, 1987; Stacy, 1992).

Instead of being able to plan a year ahead, law-enforcement organizations must conduct strategic planning for the next 3 to 5 years. Large organizations in metropolitan areas, as part of the city planning process, must sometimes plan as long as 10 to 15 years in the future. At the same time that long-range plans are required, there is greater uncertainty and ambiguity about the future. This means that any planning done must be with the idea that it is ongoing and must be continually revised.

Several sweeping changes are already beginning to affect law-enforcement organizations (Boyett & Conn, 1991).

1. Hierarchical organizations are flattening out. Layers of administrative overhead are expensive, slow to react, and impede the free flow of communication. Traditional pyramidal structures are downsizing, increasing the span of control of managers and increasing the range of duties of personnel. There is more delegation and decentralization of decision making.

2. Upward mobility and promotion in organizations are becoming limited. With reduced administrative levels due to downsizing, career plateauing will occur more frequently. The "career ladder" is becoming more of a career "lattice" or "network" that involves the potential to move in all directions. Rather than seeking unlikely promotions, officers can be given other rewards, such as higher involvement in the organizations decision-making processes regarding innovation.

3. Technology is increasing in its complexity and availability. Given the growing use of computers and the ready availability of large amounts of data, organizations now have the ability to search for information and organize it much more efficiently than was once possible. To remain viable, law-enforcement organizations must become computer literate and information-wise, as well as deal with nationwide information networking that

will challenge old turf prejudices. It also means that centralized administration will find it nearly impossible to "be on top of everything."

4. The "melting pot," where different ethnic groups become blended together into an American composite, has more accurately become a "mosaic society" of various minicultures. Police need to recognize and appreciate these differences in dealing with various communities and use this diversity in staffing the organization. Lack of such understanding will restrict the effectiveness of police efforts. With women and people of color entering the work force at unprecedented rates, by the year 2000 the white male worker may comprise only a minority of the total work force.

5. Communities are becoming more consumer minded in their expectations of quality in products and services, including those provided by law enforcement. They expect courtesy, immediate response and decisive action, direct access to supervisors and administrative decision makers, and responsiveness to their unique needs. Police departments are becoming more community and neighborhood based in their services.

6. There is a growing awareness of the need to change "paradigms" or the way we think about problems. The reactive mode of waiting until problems occur and then taking disciplinary action is changing. Departments are becoming proactive and problem or solution focused and are drawing on management models from business and science.

❖ THE CHANGING PYRAMID

One major change confronting law-enforcement organizations is the challenge to the traditional, authoritarian, bureaucratic, hierarchical pyramid structure that comprises most departments. Law-enforcement agencies have generally modeled themselves after the organizational structure set by business and the military. These top-down designs have fixed functions and role relationships and rely on policy and formal controls to regulate consistency.

The 1960s and 1970s saw attempts by the Presidential Task Force Commission on Law Enforcement and Administration of Justice and the National Advisory Commission on Criminal Justice Standards and Goals to reexamine and revise organizational structure and processes. Programs such as management by objectives, cost–benefit analysis, and zero-based budgeting were advocated. However, most of these found limited acceptance, and the bureaucracies generally resisted further revision and endured.

Bureaucracies are receiving renewed criticism that they are inefficient, dehumanizing, and underproductive. Their structure is viewed as disempowering officers (see Table 21-1). As law-enforcement tasks become more complex and officers become better trained and educated, the authoritative structure is less appropriate. Modern officers are more able to think independently, they are concerned about the effects of stress on themselves and their families, and they are more interested in career and personal development. In addition, there are other serious limitations to the bureaucratic model (Archambeault and Weirman, 1983).

Rewards (e.g., recognitions, citations, promotions) are based on individual performance rather than on the team cooperation that is necessary to the modern law-enforcement organization. The old individualism also promotes manipulation, self-interest, competition, and scapegoating. In other cases, rewards and other incentives are not clearly tied to performance at all. The Public Agenda Foundation found that 45% of workers do not believe that pay and performance are linked (Perry, 1988). Other experts assert that as much as half of current incentive plans do not work well.

Administration and officers are often placed in an adversarial relationship, as evidenced by the role of police unions, grievances and lawsuits by officers, discrimination claims, and collective bargaining agreements. In a nationwide survey of employees in large companies, most thought upper management was less receptive to ideas and gave less respect than 5 years earlier. Even when employees were willing to share ideas, only 45% of employers regularly used surveys to access important feedback (Denton, 1991). This situation creates a negative work environment in which loyalty to the organization is undermined and attitudes of dissatisfaction are carried into the community.

TABLE 21-1   SOURCES OF DISEMPOWERMENT IN ORGANIZATIONS

Many rules and regulations governing decisions

Highly established work routines

Low variety of tasks

Approval needed for nonroutine decisions

Limited contact with senior officials

Low participation in programs, conferences, meetings, or problem-solving task forces that affect job

Low opportunities for advancement

Many rewards for reliability and predictability, or arbitrary rewards

Authoritarian, high-control supervisory style

Lack of opportunities for forming networks

Rewards not based on innovation or creativity

Emphasis on failures

Impersonal bureaucratic climate

Top-down or poor communication

Highly centralized resources

Limited training

Using a military rank structure, new recruits start at the bottom and aspire to attain a higher rank. This promotional sequence is often the primary means of obtaining status and has taken on a nearly obsessive sentiment that pervades the organization (Burke, 1989). Childers (1991) describes the "99% rule" in which each department can only have one chief; the remainder of the personnel are all subordinates. When an officer reaches a career goal or promotion is no longer possible, boredom and career plateauing can occur.

Giving people specialized work assignments is a standard procedure in bureaucracies. These narrow work assignments have the effect of limiting the exchange of information, constricting perspectives, restricting training, and resulting in career dead-ends.

Career dissatisfaction often results in job turnover, which in turn is costly, interferes with continuity of tasks and programs, and adds to the demoralization of those who stay. It is estimated that as high as 16% of officers voluntarily resign, with rates directly related to increasing size of the bureaucracy (National Manpower Survey: Police, 1978). Mid-career officers who worked in law enforcement for 9 or more years, but who were passed over for promotion, experienced job dissatisfaction. They did not lose hope—until they were passed over for a second time (Cooper, 1982).

There are signs of organizational burnout much the same as those for individuals. Some indicators include time problems such as absenteeism, late attendance, untimely reports, and leaving early. Clerical and data entry errors, misplaced documents, and nonresponding to correspondence also signify stress. Less obvious and unobtrusive indicators are decreasing frequency of notes in the suggestion box, higher bottled water or coffee consumption, and even higher usage of toilet paper. More serious signs include complaints of rudeness and sarcasm, as well as allegations of brutality, corruption, underenforcement, and harassment. Eventually stress levels are reflected organizationally in higher rates of accidents, sick leave, health care costs, and turnover (Caldwell and Dorling, 1991).

❖ PARADIGM CHANGE

A paradigm is a working model or way of thinking about something. A model conveniently simplifies a complex situation so that we can understand it, and it guides attention to those things that are considered important. However, a model also restricts our looking at the situation from alternative perspectives and may leave out unexpectedly valuable information altogether (Barker, 1992).

Senge (1990) proposes that organizations can have the equivalent of a learning disability imposed by their paradigms that seriously interfere with creativity, innovation, decision making, and problem solving. To overcome this potential disability, a shift to *systems thinking* is recommended, a model that is currently finding strong application in business, industry, health care, education, and military settings.

Several assumptions underlie this paradigm (Nadler and Hibino, 1990; Senge, 1990):

1. The "parable of the boiled frog" described earlier in this book can also refer to the inattention by management to the subtle and gradual processes that can have significant impact. Police administrators should identify those hassles that are minimal when taken alone, but combine to produce an oppressive work situation.

2. Past experience may be of limited benefit when we are entering a period of change and new challenges. In fact, our old paradigm may restrict seeing new opportunities. Police departments should promote an organizational culture in which the education, independence, and diversity of available ideas can be tapped.

3. Tradition and an orientation toward dealing with crises have trapped us into seeking quick fixes for our problems. Quick fixes usually involve "satisficing," or taking the first alternative available, and that seldom works effectively or for long. In an attempt to placate irate citizens, maneuver politically, and attain segmented goals, the chosen solutions eventually become sources of additional problems themselves. Administrators must live in the short term, but plan for the long term.

4. Change is ongoing, and adaptation and being proactive will likely dominate organizational planning for years to come. As Peters and Waterman (1982) found in their examination of "excellent companies," 5 years later, two-thirds had lost their position, and some were failing. There is no end point, no winning position, no final outcome—only ongoing change in which participation must be complete (Brown, 1991).

5. Understanding connectedness and how parts of a system are related and affect each other are more important than seeing parts in isolation or blaming and scapegoating.

The police department is one part of a highly complex social system that comprises the community. In years past, at best most planning considered only those agencies and people to whom the department was accountable, such as the mayor and county commissioners. Today, the concept of stakeholders is appropriate for identifying community linkages. *Stakeholders* include individuals, groups, or organizations who have an effect on or are affected by the decisions of the police department. Community-based police work shifts from what police managers and politicians want to an accurate assessment of the needs of the community as citizens express them.

Finally, problem-solving procedures need to undergo a change in paradigm. Typically, it is the symptoms that are the focus for intervention: When the violation occurs, apprehend the offender and give a citation. Symptomatic treatment, however, does little to alter the process that produces the problems. Problem- or cause-oriented police work seeks to identify the source of the problem and alleviate it. Alternatively, if there seems to be no apparent way to work forward from a problem definition, perhaps the real problem is in the way it is framed. In this instance you can identify a desired solution and work backward to build a plan.

Traditional organizations have held to the *scalar principle* of management, otherwise known as the chain of command, or that each officer has one and only one supervisor, from top to bottom of the organization. While this might hold for simple and traditional tasks, the generalists of modern departments may have different supervisors for different assignments. For example, as an investigation shifts from the specialties of one bureau to another, the officer might also shift supervisors who have the needed expertise for guidance. This arrangement is similar to the matrix-style organization found in very flexible business organizations that must respond to rapidly changing conditions by forming teams comprised of diverse personnel. As the problems change, their roles change (Brown, 1991).

❖ ORGANIZATIONAL CULTURE CHANGE

Culture, in an organizational sense, refers to the consistent patterns of assumptions that underlie its key beliefs, values, norms, and practices and that are taught to new members as the correct "way we do things here." Culture is the perspective that administrators and officers use as a reference for determining what is relevant, making decisions, relating to the community environment, and concluding what the right action is (Schein, 1984). The idea that organizations have culture came out of the discoveries in the late 1970s that there was something about the way they operated that often made the difference in whether they were successful in dealing with a rapidly changing environment. Strong cultures, where nearly all managers share consistent values and methods, can enhance cost-effectiveness and performance (Kotter and Heskett, 1992).

The law-enforcement culture, as discussed in earlier chapters, places a premium on being in control of the situation and emotions, being completely informed, and following the dictates of rank and protocol. We have also seen that such attempts at extensive control and rigidity have resulted in a less adaptive police organization and constitute a specific stressor to personnel at all levels.

The visible manifestations of culture include the uniforms and insignias, symbols, slogans, war stories, ceremonies, and layout of offices. The invisible level of culture, however, is the more deeply valued and believed in component that is shared by organization members. It is the operating assumptions of this deeper level that must be questioned and challenged. As an officer related, culture is hard to change:

> We were told that after the new shakeup in administration we'd be doing things differently—more democratically. So I figured that I'd tell the chief about some ideas I'd kept to myself for quite awhile that I thought would work in community outreach. When I told my partner, he suggested that I be careful. Anyway, I went to the Chief's office, part of his new "open door" policy, and started to give him my ideas. Before I got it all out, he cut me off and said "we're already working on it." His body language and tone both said we were done. I think that's the last time I'll try that. I don't know that anything is different, and I still haven't seen the community outreach stuff change.

This story, when told to peers, is the stuff of which culture is composed and how it is communicated to others. If that department was seriously overhauling its management paradigm, the exchange might have been different. The chief might have encouraged the officer to express and elaborate on the idea, share what had already been considered, and ask for reaction to it. The initiative of the officer could have been complimented and she might have been offered a part in planning that project. Had this occurred, the stories that create culture might have been different.

Heroes are also part of a cultural heritage. They are chosen to exemplify the desirable actions and characteristics of the cultural model; they show how to do the right thing. When individual behavior in a team effort is rewarded, the message is clear that teams are not as important as individual limelighting and risk taking. Heroes can be those people and teams who do things differently, challenge the norms, suggest innovative ideas, and work effectively as a team. They should receive the recognitions for their joint contributions.

Ceremonies are planned special events conducted for the benefit of an audience. Group cohesiveness is increased by a team's efforts being appraised favorably by outsiders, such as the press and community members. Such ceremonies communicate what is valued, what the outcomes and rewards of behavior are, and reinforce organizational norms. When a department understands its community connections, the stakeholders are part of the ceremonies; when a new policy is implemented, opportunities are made to demonstrate rewards for performance in the new direction.

Deal and Kennedy (1982) have described four cultural types based on the level of uncertainty of decisions and the speed with which feedback is received regarding the success of the decision. Law-enforcement organizations historically embody a category described as the "macho, tough guy" culture. This entails high-risk decisions and quickly learning whether the decisions were correct. The stakes can be high in this kind of culture, there are many unknowns, and a serious mistake can have high impact on the person and organization. While the autocratic style of many administrators is an attempt to maintain control and accountability in this unstable kind of environment, it often has a paradoxical effect. Valuable information needed by administration is filtered out, group cohesion becomes "group think" that impairs decision making with its enforced conformity, and "CYA" becomes the mode of operation.

Every human system develops ways of protecting itself and coping with stress, and law-enforcement organizations are no less talented. The issue is whether the adaptive processes make the system more adaptive and innovative in problem solving or whether the adaptations themselves become a burden and part of the continuing problem. There is often a difference between managerial theories "espoused" and those actually in use (Argyris, 1985; Argyris and Schon, 1982).

This idea is similar to Kilmann's (1989) concept of a culture gap, in which there is a variance between the actual and ideal culture of an organization. The discrepancy results in a set of confusing, contradictory, and perhaps conflicting messages to personnel and the public. Self-protecting "defensive routines" are implicitly implemented in organizations to avoid embarrassments, conflicts, and uncomfortable situations.

To create a more open and responsive culture, the message must be clear that all personnel are encouraged to question and challenge "why we do things the way we do?" Police managers have a relatively high need for security, a reasonable concern since the average tenure of chiefs is only about five and a half years (Enter, 1986: Rawlins and Daumer, 1987). This task requires high confidence, self-esteem, and openness on the part of administration to receive doubts and questions about cultural norms.

Yet this very questioning leads to the processes that allow an organization to identify dysfunctional norms and modify them as necessary. Even if a benevolent autocrat makes changes that the officers might like, the internal mechanism of organizational self-regulation has not been activated. There must be participation at all levels of the organization for the cultural change to occur. Open discussions with officers should center on what kind of organizational structure, policy, and procedures would work better. Task forces or ad hoc committees can be formed to review needs and make recommendations or decisions. Broad participation ensures that the changes are owned by everyone.

Renewed attention to quality of performance, job satisfaction, and healthy organizational culture has lead to several studies of such organizations. Peters and Waterman's (1982) examination of excellent organizations found eight attributes that characterized the most successful ones. In contrast, some of the least successful were found to have top-heavy, centralized decision-making structures where "everything is important." In one unfortunate organization, a new process required review and approval by 223 separate committees before it could be put into practice! We give the 6 most relevant attributes of successful organizations in Table 21-2.

For the most part, these eight recommendations do not require cost or high technology; they are not gimmicks or formulas. They require only time, effort, and commitment by management to apply the principles and learn by systematically experimenting and experiencing.

❖ THE LEARNING ORGANIZATION

Learning occurs by finding discrepancies and making adjustments, by finding out what prevents and enhances attainment of goals (Argyris and Schon, 1982; Senge, 1990). The learning organization and learning teams are those that have an expanding capacity to actively learn from experience and shape their own future. Whereas most organizations may review progress at an annual planning meeting and spend the remainder of the year dealing with issues of control, the learning organization attempts to shift concern from control to ongoing learning.

The broad interest in implementing total quality management (TQM) is partly grounded in Japan's success with it and America's fascination with quick fixes. For example, when quality circles were used by U.S. firms, the organizations missed the main point: They focused on forming teams rather than on development of team learning skills. The Japanese concept of *kaizan*, organization-wide commitment to continuous improvement, underlies much of what TQM and related methods are about. Attending a few workshops is unlikely to

TABLE 21-2   CHARACTERISTICS OF "EXCELLENT" COMPANIES

1. *Bias toward action.* Successful organizations spend more time doing than talking about it. If something is researched, surveyed, planned, or discussed, it should be related to action.

2. *Close to the customer.* Customer-driven organizations are those that know the needs, values, problems, and concerns of their stakeholders.

3. *Autonomy and entrepreneurship.* Innovation and change are encouraged by stimulating dialogue rewarding efforts, encouraging diversity, and championing ideas. Keeping teams small and cohesive can contribute to a sense of belonging and adaptability.

4. *Productivity through people.* The organization is not the methods and rules, it is the people who make it work. Productivity and quality of performance occur by enlisting and inspiring people and involving them in decisions. Low to moderate levels of conflict are encouraged rather than suppressed.

5. *Hands on and value driven.* Successful organizations know what they value, believe in, and stand for. Vision and mission statements are understood, relevant, and meaningful to employees. Management is personally involved with people and issues at all levels.

6. *Stick to the knitting.* The most successful organizations do what they do best. They are highly focused on the specialty they know and understand.

produce change. Change comes from understanding, commitment, and action (Gordon, 1992).

The key idea to the learning organization is what Argyris (1985) calls "double loop learning" in which there is continuous attention to the feedback generated by experience. It involves a sort of "helicopter thinking" in which teams in the organization shift to a metaphorical position above themselves and examine how they define and solve problems. They are then in a position to better alter their approach to problem solving (McGill, Slocum, and Lei (1992)).

From an organization development perspective, there are several essential things administrators and administrative teams can do to transition to a learning organization (Senge, 1990; Kouzes and Posner, 1991):

1. Inspire and build a clear mission and shared vision of the kind of organization toward which your department is moving. Communicate the vision in ways that enlist the commitment of others, by appealing to a common purpose, for example. The vision can energize people and sustain their efforts during stressful periods, and they must see how their actions are tied to the future state.

2. Empower people who are aligned around the common vision. Empowerment means giving officers the skills, information, and authority to make discretionary decisions, initiate actions, and be accountable. It also involves acting on suggestions and involving people in the decisions that affect them.

3. Challenge the status quo, question the norms, and identify the underlying assumptions. Obviously, this entails risk and must be modeled, encouraged, and rewarded by administration. This can also involve looking at problems from different perspectives, including diverse personal styles on administrative teams, and looking for exceptions to the rules (thereby creating better rules).

4. Administration must "walk the talk" by modeling in their own behavior the changes they are proposing, maintaining congruence between the espoused and actual management practice. It may also involve "managing-by-walking-around" in which discussions are held with others about values and beliefs, core beliefs are strongly expressed, and priorities are clearly demonstrated in action.

5. Develop teamwork by recognizing and rewarding team, rather than individual, effort. Form ad hoc committees, task forces, and administrative teams to carry out important work. Delegate the power they require and publicize and celebrate their accomplishments.

6. Practice reflective learning at all levels, whereby attention is not given only to the problem, but to how the problem is formulated, approached,

and solved. Encourage identification and exploration of learning, decision-making, and problem-solving styles.

❖ PROFESSIONAL DEVELOPMENT

Restricted opportunities for promotion and the competition for scarce positions require a refocusing for officers on alternative career development paths in the department. Bardwick (1986) suggested that the pyramidal structure of most law-enforcement agencies makes plateauing inevitable before the age of retirement. By restructuring and reducing the number of hierarchical levels in a department, the importance of promotion is likewise reduced. She recommended that officers direct their attention laterally to task challenges, rather than vertically to promotion.

There is also evidence that small, cohesive team units can counter stress as well as promote a sense of belonging and identity. It appears that the effects of informal peer relationships and less rigid structure may maintain job satisfaction despite lack of promotion (Billings and Moos, 1982).

While promotion, pay, and security will often delay or prevent job dissatisfaction, they may not provide the motivation and incentive for higher performance and creativity required by new law-enforcement organizations. Mentoring, such as the Field Training Officer Program may provide such an enhancement. The FTOs, as more experienced officers, orient and assist newer officers to become familiar with the department and community, refine skills, and learn subtleties attained after years of service. This relationship becomes the core for transmission of culture and a way of keeping top management informed. Much mentoring has been related to higher motivation, performance, and job retention (Waller, 1991; Wilson and Elman, 1990).

In 1973, the Report on Police by the National Advisory Commission on Criminal Justice Standards and Goals recommended that all police departments should require a 4-year degree by 1982. While that goal has been approached but not met, the Police Executive Research Forum (PERF) reported that it found an increase in education from 12.4 years in 1967 to nearly 14 years currently. PERF went on to reinforce the college degree as a minimum requirement, supervisory positions requiring 60 credits, and all administrators to have bachelor's degrees (Ayres and Flanagan, 1990).

There is a dilemma, however, with promotion of education for officers. With education usually comes higher need for achievement and status. But, as noted, promotional opportunities are becoming increasingly limited. In addition, well-educated officers find it increasingly difficult to maintain both work and family, encounter occasional harassment by less educated but more experienced senior officers, and experience job frustration and career plateauing sooner and frustration with the rigidity of traditional police organizations. The resolution of this bind is to modify the organization to take advantage of the larger human resource pool generated by additional education.

Other alternatives to promotion that challenge officers' creativity and abilities include serving on advisory groups in the community, serving on committees in the department, writing for a department newsletter or newspaper, conducting training programs, serving as "devil's advocate" in meetings, enhancing computer networking capabilities, participating in recruitment and hiring, conducting surveys, or exploring the feasibility of suggestions coordinating retreats or programs on special topics. Many of these activities are stimulating opportunities for officers to upgrade their skills and learn new competencies, which has the effect of upgrading the resource pool of the entire organization.

❖ COPING WITH TRANSITIONS

That things appear the same from day to day is more illusion than fact and more a comment on our rigid expectations than in their nature. Some degree of change is always occurring in organizations, but it is usually the larger transitions that are noticeably disruptive to people. Organizational transition to a new desirable state can be initially as stressful as the old condition that is being left behind. Yet, as Maddock (1982) wrote:

> To cherish traditions, old buildings, ancient cultures, and graceful lifestyles is a worthy thing, but in the world of technology, to cling to outmoded methods of manufacture, old product lines, old market or old attitudes among management and workers is a prescription for [organizational] suicide.

Transitions are hard on people, and changing traditional ways of doing things is difficult. At an insurance company, 485 teams were created to develop cost-saving measures. One of the most creative ideas was projected to save $40,000 per year and simply involved inserting the paper sideways into the FAX machine. By doing so, it cut transmission time by 15% and thereby cut costs. However, implementation was doubtful because it involved changing a habitual behavior.

Perhaps more than anything else it is the uncertainty about their personal future that concerns most employees. What will happen to their job, role, and type of tasks with which they feel comfortable? The change process is often characterized as a three-stage sequence (Bridges, 1991; Lewin, 1951); from "unfreezing" or disengaging from the past, transition through a "neutral zone," and finally "refreezing" or reestablishing the new paradigm and organizational culture. The following recommendations may assist during these disruptive periods:

UNFREEZING

1. Identify a highly desirable future state for the organization toward which efforts can be directed.
2. Provide people with legitimate, irrefutable feedback and information that disconfirm beliefs about the adequacy of the current structure and motivate the need for change. Provide data and contact with community members or others who need a more responsive system.
3. Announce and predict a period of turbulence and disruptions to avoid people being taken by surprise.

TRANSITION

1. Help people identify exactly how the change will affect people, their positions, roles, and tasks. Conduct open discussions about the adjustments that may be necessary.
2. Explore what stakeholders have to lose with the new system. Acknowledge losses openly and sympathetically and expect overreactions and grieving. When possible, find ways to compensate for the losses.
3. First sell the problem that is the reason for the change—then sell the solution, the planned change. Design temporary systems to contain the confusion and disruption.
4. Provide plenty of information and keep people updated. To the extent that information is withheld or delayed, the rumor mill will compensate with misinformation. Use workshops and training to provide new skills and details.
5. Keep the change package as a coherent whole, rather than presenting one change after another. A series of unexpected changes can exhaust people more than a large one. Set short-term goals and checkpoints to monitor progress.
6. Manage by walking around. Talk with people about their reactions and what kinds of problems they are having, and elicit their ideas for the future.
7. Restructure work areas to reflect teamwork and interdependence, rather than individualism.
8. Talk about the transitional process and how it affects people. Provide supervisors with the information and skills they need to effectively support people.
9. Use a transition monitoring team to follow the issues and needs for the transition. The team can review plans before announcements and provide a checkpoint for rumor control.
10. Support people changing old behaviors and attitudes by encouraging innovation and creativity. Make sure they are not punished for intelligent and sincere efforts that fail.

1. Symbolize the new identity. Recognize that everything can mean something. Take the opportunity to recognize new decor, parking space, computer terminals, use of equipment and space, and the like.

2. Plan small wins. This results in quick victories that reassure believers in the change, convince doubters, and confound critics.

3. Be consistent in policy and procedure. Don't reward old actions and reactions by preaching teamwork and then rewarding individual contributions, preaching risk taking but then rewarding conservatism, preaching feedback but rewarding silence.

4. Establish policies and procedures that reinforce change. Tie rewards to accomplishments of new goals. Celebrate successes at arriving at a new beginning.

While we cannot avoid stress, we can reduce it, use it as a motivator, and develop hardiness toward it. We can also create the kinds of organizations that don't add insult to the injuries that go with the job in police work. As Toffler (1990) advised, "our moral responsibility is not to stop the future, but to shape it...to channel our destiny in humane directions and to ease the trauma of transitions."

SUMMARY

A number of forces are pushing for change in the way that law enforcement agencies are run. Among changes that are likely are less of a hierarchical management structure, broader work assignments at the lower levels, and a greater involvement by officers in decisions about the departments functions. These changes will demand that the officers involved be more highly educated and better trained. The chapter closes with suggestions for unfreezing out-of-date organizational systems and making the transition to the more effective organizational structure.

REFERENCES

Archambeault, W. G., and C. L. Weirman (1983). Critically assessing the utility of police bureaucracies in the 1980's: Implications of management theory Z. *Journal of Police Science and Administration 11*, 420–429.

Argyris, C. (1985). *Strategy, Change and Defensive Routines*. Marshfield, MA: Pitman.

Argyris, C., and D. Schon (1982). *Theory in Practice*. San Francisco: Jossey-Bass.

Ayres, R. M., and G. S. Flanagan (1990). Preventing Law Enforcement Stress: The Organization's Role. Washington, DC: Bureau of Justice Assistance of the Office of Justice Programs, U.S. Department of Justice.

Bardwick, J. (1986). *The Plateauing Trap*. New York: Bantam.

Barker, J. A. (1992). *Future Edge*. New York: William Morrow.

Billings, A., and R. Moos (1982). Work stress and the stress-buffering roles of work and family resources. *Journal of Occupational Behavior 3*, 215–232.

Boyett, J. H., and H. P. Conn (1991). *Workplace 2000: The Revolution Reshaping American Business*. New York: Dutton.

Bridges, W. (1991). *Managing Transitions: Making the Most of Change*. Reading, MA: Addison-Wesley.

Brown, L. P. (1991). Policing in the 90's: Trends, issues and concerns. *The Police Chief 58(3)*, 20–23.

Brown, W. J. (1986). Organizational assessment: Determining the state of a police organization. *Journal of Police Science and Administration 14(4)*, 267–284.

Burke, R. (1989). Career stages, satisfaction, and well-being among police officers. *Psychological Reports 65*, 3–12.

Caldwell, D. S., and E. W. Dorling (1991). Preventing burnout in police organizations. *The Police Chief 58(4)*, 156–159.

Childers, J. M. (1991). Plateauing in law enforcement. *FBI Law Enforcement Bulletin*, June, 16–18.

Cooper, W. (1982). Police officers over career stages. *Canadian Police College Journal 6*, 93–112.

Deal, T. E., and A. A. Kennedy (1982). *Corporate Cultures: The Rites and Rituals of Corporate Life*. Reading, MA: Addison-Wesley.

Denton, D. K. (1991). *Horizontal Management: Beyond Total Customer Satisfaction*. New York: Lexington.

Enter, J. E. (1986). The rise to the top: An analysis of police chief career patterns. *Journal of Police Science and Administration 14(4)*, 334–346.

Gordon, J. (1992). Performance technology: Blueprint for the learning organization? *Training*, May, 27–36.

Kilmann, R. H., (1989). A completely integrated program for creating and maintaining organizational success. *Organizational-Dynamics, 18*, 5–19.

Kotter, J. P., and J. L. Heskett (1992). *Corporate Culture and Performance*. New York: Free Press.

Kouzes, J. M., and B. Z. Posner (1991). *The Leadership Challenge: How to Get Extraordinary Things Done in Organizations*. San Francisco: Jossey-Bass.

Lewin, K. (1951). *Field Theory in Social Science*. New York: Harper & Row.

Maddock, I. (1982). Why industry must learn to forget. *New Scientist*, February.

McGill, M. E., J. W. Slocum, and D. Lei, (1992). Management practices in learning organizations. *Organizational Dynamics, 21* 5–16.

Nadler, G., and S. Hibino (1990). *Breakthrough Thinking*. Rocklin, CA: Prima Publishing and Communications.

Naisbitt, J. (1982). *Megatrends*. New York: Warner.

National Manpower Survey of the Criminal Justice System, Volume 2: Police (1978). Washington, DC: U.S. Government Printing Office.

Perry, N. J. (1988). Here come richer, riskier pay plans. *Fortune*, December 19, 51.

Peters, T. (1987). *Thriving on Chaos*. New York: Knopf.

Peters, T. J., and R. H. Waterman, Jr. (1982). *In Search of Excellence*. New York: Harper & Row.

Rawlins, C. L., and H.-J. Daumer (1987). Police manager life style choices: A high need for security. *Journal of Police Science and Administration 15(2)*, 145–152.

Schein, E. H. (1984). Coming to a new awareness of organizational culture. *Sloan Management Review*, Winter, 3–16.

Senge, P. (1990). *The Fifth Discipline: The Art and Science of the Learning Organization*. Garden City, NY: Doubleday.

Stacy, R. D. (1992). *Managing the Unknowable: Strategic Boundaries between Order and Chaos in Organizations*. San Francisco: Jossey-Bass.

Toffler, A. (1990). Powershift: Knowledge, Wealth, and Violence at the Edge of the Twenty-first century. New York: Bantam Books.

Waller, G. L. (1991). Managing career plateauing in law enforcement through interventions. Unpublished master's thesis. Department of Management, College of St. Scholastica, Duluth, MN.

Wilson, J. A., and Elman, N. S. (1990). Organizational benefits of mentoring. *Academy of Management Executive 4(4)*, 88–94.

Index

Law-enforcement
administrators
(*cont.*)
supervisor training,
282–84
using ideas/information of
officers, 284–86
Law enforcement demands,
50–60
contradictory require-
ments of police work,
54–55
job hassles, 55–57
police personality:
haracteristics of, 51–54
effect on, 57–59
Learning organization, 304–6
Light stimulation, and shift
work, 69
Listening skills, supervisors,
125–26
Long-term stress effects,
41–43
Los Angeles Police
Department:
peer counseling program,
257–58
spousal orientation/train-
ing programs, 274
Lying, and working under-
cover, 165

M

Managing-by-walking-
around, 305
Marriage encounter pro-
grams, 274
Massage, 220, 224
Media, as source of stress,
11–12
Meditation, 217, 229,
247–49
Memory devices, use of, 156

Mental discipline, and stress,
221
Mental preparation, 5–6, 102
Mental rehearsal, for court
testimony, 157–58
Mentorship, 203
Microsleep, 64
Migraine headaches, 43
Mind and body, 34–39
Minorities, stressors, 13
Moral injunctions, incompat-
ibility of, 56
Multiple personality disorder,
164
Murder, 8
Muscular response, 44
Mutilating accidents, 7
Myers-Briggs Type Indicator,
124

N

Napping, 63–64
break, 70
National Study of the
Changing
Workforce, 265–66
Native American officers,
200
Natural deaths, 8
Negative experiences, as
source of stress, 12
Neighborhood Advisory
Groups (NAG),
144–45
Neurolinguistic programming
(NLP), 222–23, 239
New York Telephone, peer
counseling program,
256
Nutrition, 39–41
and shift work, 68–71
and stress, 221

O

Officer misconduct, as source
of stress, 9–10
Officer physical fitness,
290–91
Organizational culture,
changes in, 301–4
Orientation, 203
on effects of shift work, 68
Overreaction of stress
response, 36

P

Paradigm change, 299–301
Parasympathetic nervous
branch, 34–35
Peer counseling, 256–58, 289
Personal failure, as source of
stress, 8–9
Personal space, 76–77
Physical activity, and shift
work, 70
Physical fitness, 290–91
Physiology:
of shift work, 62–63
of stress:
general adaptation syn-
drome (GAS),
37–39
headaches, 43–44
immune response,
44–45
long-term stress effects,
41–43
mind and body, 34–39
muscular response, 44
nutrition, 39–41
*Police: Street Corner
Politicians* (Muit),
291–92
Police brutality, 9–10
Police Chief, The (journal), 5,
124

Police Executive Research Forum (PERF), 306
Police personality characteristics, 51–54
  emotional expressiveness, 52–53
  emotional restraint, 52
  group cohesiveness, 53
  independent style, 53–54
  realistic orientation, 54
Police shootings, 7, 101–15
  talking with fellow officers about, 107
  See also Postshooting trauma
Police stress scale, 25
Positive experiences, as source of stress, 13
Positive mental rehearsal, for court testimony, 157–58
Positive self-talk, 217, 224, 240–42
Postshooting trauma, 101–15
  case examples, 103–10, 112–14
  emotional reactions to, 102–10
  officer victims, 110–12
  behavioral descriptors of, 111
Posttraumatic stress reactions, 96, 102
Preferred Provider Contracts, 290
Professional development, 306–7
Profiling, 80–82
Progressive muscle relaxation (PMR), 217, 223, 231–33, 247–49
  training cautions, 233–34
Protected time, for stress-coping practice, 219, 221

Public opinion, as source of stress, 11–12
Public reaction, 133–47
  community-oriented policing, 143–45
  cooperation:
    obtaining, 143–44
    police need for, 142–43
  fears about officers, 137–38
  misperceptions of the police, 134–37
    case example, 136–37
  police hostility toward public, 139–43
  racism, 138–39
  what the public wants, 137
Public relations, 288
Pyramid structure, changes in, 297–99

Q

Quality circles, 121–22, 285–86
Quality control, 121–23
Quieting the mind, 217

R

Racism, 138–39
Reciprocal inhibition, 242
Relaxation, and stress, 220
Report writing, 155–56
Resistance stage of GAS, 38
Retreat distance, 76
Rewards, 126, 298, 302
Risk, need for, 17, 18–20
Role playing, 82–83, 242
Rotating shifts, 64
Rural/small-department law enforcement, 207–15

absence anonymity, 211
boredom, 209–10
conflict of interest, 211–12
highly armed public, 213
isolation of, 208–9
limited professional development, 212–13
limited resources, 210–11
peer support, lack of, 213
stress, coping with, 213–14

S

Scalar principle of management, 301
Schedules, 63, 64
  permanent, 67
Scripts, 82–83
Self-esteem, and stress, 221
Self-hypnosis, 221
Self-regulated stress, 46–47, 221
Self-talk, positive, 217, 240–42
Sensory mode approach to stress reduction, 222–24
Sergeant, 123–25, 284
Sexual harassment, 183–84
  stopping, 184–85
  types of, 183
Shift work, 61–73
  coping strategies, 68–71
  alertness cycles, 69
  break napping, 70
  effective sleeping, 70–71
  light stimulation, 69
  new friendships, 71
  nutrition, 68
  physical activity, 70
  psychological techniques, 69

U

Undercover work, 162–77
   coming out from, 171–72,
     174–76
   contact, maintaining, 174
   information about, 173
   and lying, 165
   physical dangers of, 164,
     168–70
   problems coordinating differ-
     ent agencies,
     170–71
   psychological dangers of,
     163, 164–68
   role development, 173–74
   selecting individuals for,
     172–73
   stress management implica-
     tions, 172–76

V

Vascular headaches, 44
Verbal skills, officers, 291–92
Visual cues, 222–24, 239

W

Wolpe, Joseph, 242
Women, stressors, 13
Women in law enforcement,
   See Female officers
Work conditions, changes in,
   as source of stress,
   12
Work-family stress connection, 263–80
   children, effects on,
     269–70
   departmental interven-
     tions, 272–75
   divorce, 267
   family meetings, 271–72
   family safety, 266
   and law enforcement,
     264–66
   marital intimacy, 267–69
   positive effects of stress,
     276–77
   professional help, 275–76

Workshops, stress-manage-
   ment techniques,
   273

Y

Yerkes-Dodson Law, 37
Yoga, 217, 220, 221, 223,
   224, 229, 247–49
You Just Don't Understand:
   Women and Men in
   Conversation (Tannen),
   253

Z

Zone of stability, 16–32, 102
   cumulative life changes,
     27
   definition of, 17–18
   influences on size of,
     26–29
     childhood traumas,
       26–27
     inner critic, 28–29